Blowing
Smoke

Blowing Smoke

WHY THE RIGHT KEEPS SERVING UP WHACK-JOB FANTASIES ABOUT THE PLOT TO EUTHANIZE GRANDMA, OUTLAW CHRISTMAS, AND TURN JUNIOR INTO A RAGING HOMOSEXUAL

Michael Wolraich

Da Capo Press
A Member of the Perseus Books Group

Copyright © 2010 by Michael Wolraich

All rights reserved. No part of this publication may be reproduced, stored in a
retrieval system, or transmitted, in any form or by any means, electronic, mechanical,
photocopying, recording, or otherwise, without the prior written permission of
the publisher. Printed in the United States of America. For information, address
Da Capo Press, 11 Cambridge Center, Cambridge, MA 02142.

Editorial production by *Marra*thon Production Services. www.marrathon.net
DESIGN BY JANE RAESE
Set in 11.5-point Apollo

Cataloging-in-Publication data for this book is available from the Library of Congress.
ISBN 978-0-306-81919-3

Published by Da Capo Press
A Member of the Perseus Books Group
www.dacapopress.com

Da Capo Press books are available at special discounts for bulk purchases in the United
States by corporations, institutions, and other organizations. For more information,
please contact the Special Markets Department at the Perseus Books Group,
2300 Chestnut Street, Suite 200, Philadelphia, PA 19103, or call (800) 810-4145,
ext. 5000, or e-mail special.markets@perseusbooks.com.

2 4 6 8 10 9 7 5 3 1

To Freedom, the Constitution, the Founding Fathers, Fox News, America except the elitist parts, Capitalism, Non-gay marriage, Being born in the U.S. instead of Kenya like some people, Guns, Mooseburgers, Freedom again, Christmas, and Glenn Beck's ferocious chalkboard.

Not necessarily in that order.

CONTENTS

PREFACE

"WHY IS IT OKAY TO DISCRIMINATE AGAINST WHITE MALES?" demanded MSNBC commentator Pat Buchanan, his voice shrill with outrage. His colleague Rachel Maddow had invited him onto her liberal news and opinion show to discuss the Supreme Court nomination of Judge Sonia Sotomayor, but the debate quickly shifted to affirmative action. Warming instantly to the topic, Buchanan indignantly denounced the tragic suffering of white males in America, rhythmically chopping his hands through the air as if he could physically whack the whole idea of affirmative action to bits. He admonished Maddow and her friends "up there and in New York," chiding, "You never look at these guys who are working class guys with their own dreams, just like Sonia Sotomayor."[1]

The much younger Rachel Maddow seemed bemused by Buchanan's tirade. She dismissed his reproaches and replied with a half smile, "You're living in the 1950s, Pat."

But Maddow was wrong. For there was no affirmative action to speak of in the 1950s, and the notion that white people suffered from reverse discrimination did not become popular until the late 1970s. Moreover, Buchanan's rhetoric about white victims has become all too common since the election of President Obama, whom right-wing stars like Rush Limbaugh and Glenn Beck have accused of racism against white people.[2]

A few days after the Maddow-Buchanan duel in July 2009, I wrote a blog post about a lawsuit over the national motto of the United States: In God We Trust. During my research for the article, I learned that the doctrine of separation of church and state is really a "liberal scam" to discriminate against Christians, who are apparently suffering from even greater oppression than America's white males. Rush Limbaugh's younger brother David explained the details in his 2004 book, *Perse-cution: How Liberals Are Waging War Against Christians.*[3] Perhaps for-mer representative John Hostettler (R-IN) read it. When Congress sought to curb abusive proselytizing in the Air Force Academy in 2005, he accused Democrats of "denigrating and demonizing Christians," and fumed on the House floor, "The long war on Christianity in America . . . continues unabated with aid and comfort to those who would erad-icate any vestige of our Christian heritage."[4]

As I read about the long war on Christianity, with Buchanan's rage against affirmative action still fresh in my mind, the parallels between accusations of white victimization and Christian persecution popped brightly out of the screen of my laptop computer. Liberal bloggers often mock conservatives' "persecution complex," but I had previously con-sidered conservative complaints about mistreatment to be a reflexive gripe—like the line from "Charlie Brown" by the Coasters: "Why's everybody always pickin' on me?" But in July 2009, it suddenly oc-curred to me that the persecution accusations amounted to more than political grumbling; they represented key tactics in a pervasive, deep-seated political strategy by the right.

I had no idea how deep it sat.

As I burrowed backward in history, persecution narratives appeared like hidden patterns in the mosaic at nearly every critical moment in the evolution of modern conservatism, from the formation of the reli-gious right to the rise of Fox News. At the same time, the present-day political scene in the fall of 2009 abruptly went mad. Tea Party protest-ers carried signs comparing Obama to Hitler as Glenn Beck warned of communist conspiracies at the highest levels of government. And everywhere that madness reigned, I found the thread of persecution paranoia winding though the mania.

I call this thread *persecution politics.* It is a rhetorical strategy to con-vince millions of white, heterosexual, Christian, conservative gun-owners that an evil conspiracy of liberal elites, black radicals, illegal immigrants, gay fascists, and other disturbing bad guys are taking away their rights, their guns, their health care, their freedom, their tradi-tions, their children, and their favorite television programs. *Blowing*

Smoke is the story of persecution politics—how it began, why it works, and what it has done to the country.

As you may have gathered from the title, this book does not attempt to present the kind of even-handed "liberals say–conservatives say" analysis so popular in the news media. While there are certainly plenty of liberal crazies running amok through the blogosphere, I do not believe that left-wing paranoia has attained anything close to the mainstream popularity of right-wing paranoia in recent history. But mindful of the dictum that you can't prove a negative, I won't attempt to defend this point. If you want to read about left-wing craziness, I'm sure that Ann Coulter will produce a penetrating treatise on the subject soon enough.

That said, while I seldom hesitate to poke right-wing leaders in the eye or other parts of the anatomy, my objective is not to attack conservative ideology. Though I disagree with many tenets of modern conservatism, I believe that most of them have rational foundations, and I believe in the value of reasonable opposition. My target is not conservative doctrine but the paranoid rhetoric that some conservatives employ. I hope that moderate conservatives who are skeptical of right-wing paranoia can appreciate this book as well as liberals.

Whether you're conservative or liberal, if you don't regularly listen to Glenn Beck and other right-wing commentators, you may be shocked by the quotes that you'll read here. My objective, however, is not to present a top-ten list of the darndest things that conservatives say. Rather, I aim to draw out a consistent narrative that right-wing leaders have been communicating to their audiences, sometimes subtly in the folds of a not-so-funny joke, sometimes explicitly in a provocative call to arms. I've tried to accurately communicate the contexts of the quotes, and whenever possible, I've included links to the original sources in the endnotes so that you can enjoy the full Fox News audio-video experience.

Due to time and space constraints, there are a couple of relevant topics that you won't find in this book. In the early days of persecution politics, right-wing leaders often warned of feminist plots to emasculate America's virile manhood. But opposition to the feminist movement is a complicated topic. These days, women's rights plays a much smaller role in right-wing paranoia than it once did, so I left it out. Sorry, feminists. I also gave short shrift to abortion, another complex issue that has played a big role in the growth of the right wing. Conservatives have often used abortion to demonize liberals as "baby killers," but otherwise the topic is tangential to the central theme of the book, so it didn't make the cut either. Sorry, baby killers.

Finally, let me state for the record that I have not received funding from radical billionaire George Soros or any other progressive benefactors. However, if Mr. Soros or other wealthy philanthropists would like to do business, I would be happy to discuss terms. My rate for character assassination depends on the prominence of the target and the degree of smearing. The arrangement would remain strictly confidential, of course. Please contact my agent for details.

JUST AS I WAS WRAPPING UP the final edits on *Blowing Smoke,* Rachel Maddow aired another show about race relations in America. After a full year of white persecution stories on Fox News, her perspective seems to have changed since she dismissed Buchanan as old-fashioned. Presenting case after case of conservatives using racist scare tactics to promote white solidarity, she explained:

> It's about making white people feel like they are victims of black people. Black people are the racists. White people need someone to stand up for them. It's good politics. It always has been in this country and it still is.[5]

Rachel Maddow clearly gets persecution politics. But there's so much more than she described on that program. This is how it goes . . .

1

HOW BILL O'REILLY SAVED CHRISTMAS

Introducing the Right Wing's Magic Formula for
Turning Everything from Health Care to Holiday Greetings
into a Secret Plot against White Christian Conservatives

The central belief of every moron is that he is the victim of a myste-
rious conspiracy against his common rights and true deserts.
—H. L. Mencken

DECEMBER 2004. *The nation was at war. As citizens blithely prepared for*
the coming holidays, sinister forces quietly chiseled away the moral foun-
dation on which the country stood. From Denver's salted avenues to New
York's urban flora, in schools and shopping malls, the hateful destroyers
methodically bled the people of their liberties. One day, the people were
forbidden to sing. The next, they were forbidden to pray. Foreign intruders
would soon steal their livelihoods, socialists would confiscate their prop-
erty, fascists would euthanize their grandparents, and perverts would cor-
rupt their children.

The wise ones saw the peril. They tried to warn the others, but the de-
stroyers silenced their voices. Grinning smugly from judges' benches and
news editors' desks, the villains bent the laws and warped the news. The
people were helpless before their awesome power.

But one man had the wisdom to see and the strength to speak. The vil-
lains tried to stop him, but his voice rang out across the land, shattering
the silence like a yapping terrier at two in the morning. The people heard
him speak the truth. They found courage and joined their voices to his,
producing a tremendous chorus of yaps across the nation. The destroyers
screeched with rage, but they could not silence the clamor. One by one, the

people threw the evildoers from their pedestals and erected giant plaster Ten Commandments monuments and hand-painted resin nativity scenes in their places.

The battle is not yet finished, but the people are rising, and Jesus stands by them. Their liberty will be secured, their property will be protected, their grandparents will expire of natural causes, and no one will pervert anyone.

And so it was that Bill O'Reilly saved Christmas.

DARK SUITED, GRAY HAIRED, AND STERN, Bill O'Reilly is the picture of a serious journalist. He rarely smiles. Indeed, his mouth hardly moves except at critical rhetorical moments. Then he leans forward, raises the sharp peaks of his eyebrows, and enunciates with exaggerated motion as if his lips have broken their restraints and aspire to escape his face. A moment later, the lips are captive again, and O'Reilly continues his stern oration, permitting movement only from shoulders and eyebrows to punctuate the disgust he feels for the events that he is obliged to report.

O'Reilly's demeanor befits a war correspondent, and indeed, he is an admirer of the late Walter Cronkite.[1]* But there are no bullets or bombs in the conflict O'Reilly describes every night. He speaks of a *culture war* in American society between a radical left and a traditional right, pitting "the secular progressives who want drastic change" against "the traditionalists who really want to keep the country pretty much the way it is."[2]

O'Reilly makes no secret of his sympathies in this struggle. He is a journalist-soldier, a self-described "T-Warrior" (traditionalist warrior), a lean, mean commentating machine. As he wrote in his bestselling book, *Culture Warrior,* "My weapons will be facts and superior analysis based on those facts."[3] He bravely wields his facts and superior analysis in defense of traditional Americans at risk of losing their freedom, their heritage, and their inalienable right to watch *The O'Reilly Factor.*

---

* "Walter Cronkite." O'Reilly qualifies his admiration to Cronkite's Vietnam War days, before he became a "real radical left guy." ("Bill O'Reilly Calls Himself 'T-Warrior,'" *ABC News,* 20 Sep. 2006, http://abcnews.go.com/2020/story?id=2465303.)

In December 2004, Bill O'Reilly launched his greatest campaign, gravely announcing to his 3 million nightly viewers that an alliance of secular progressive warmongers was poised to capture a strategic prize: Christmas. In a series of Fox News television segments entitled "Christmas Under Siege," O'Reilly alleged that parade organizers in Denver had barred a religious-themed float from the city's holiday parade, that New York City mayor Mike Bloomberg had referred to the Rockefeller Center Christmas tree as a "holiday tree," and that Federated Department Stores, which owns Macy's and Bloomingdales, had "denigrated" Christmas with marketing material that proclaimed "Happy Holidays," "Season's Greetings," and other offensive slurs.

The objective of the secular progressives, O'Reilly charged, was not simply to destroy the holiday, but to undermine Christianity itself in order to promote a depraved agenda. He explained:

> But the real reason it's happening has little to do with Christmas and everything to do with organized religion. Secular progressives realize that America as it is now will never approve of gay marriage, partial birth abortion, euthanasia, legalized drugs, income redistribution through taxation, and many other progressive visions because of religious opposition. But if the secularists can destroy religion in the public arena, the brave new progressive world is a possibility.[4]

Though the secularists were few in number, O'Reilly attributed their success to well-placed connections. "Now most people, of course, love Christmas and want to keep its traditions," he reported. "But the secular movement has influence in the media, among some judges and politicians."

As evidence of this plot, O'Reilly cited the example of the degenerate nation of Canada. According to his statistics, only 61 percent of Canadians believed that religion was important for their nation, and a frightening 16 percent did not claim affiliation with any religion. Though Canada was once a "traditional religious country," O'Reilly observed that in modern Canada, gay marriage was legal, drugs had been decriminalized, "any kind" of abortion was available, welfare benefits were double those of the United States, the military was nonexistent, and the age of consent was fourteen.[5] "Can you imagine American adults being allowed to fool around with children that age?" O'Reilly asked, aghast.*

Thus, if Federated Department Stores and the mayor of New York were permitted to continue to use generic holiday terminology, Americans would soon be able to buy drugs, marry gay people, go on welfare, and have sex with fourteen-year-olds. The only thing that they would not be able to do would be to enlist in the military because there wouldn't be a military anymore, except perhaps for a few metrosexual cavalrymen with splashy red coats and fancy hats.[†]

"A Very Secret Plan"

Who are these mysterious secular progressives who would so callously expose the nation to depravity? In 2004, O'Reilly described "committed secularists in the media, courts and education system" and "the people at *The New York Times, The L.A. Times*—the far left wing of the Democratic Party."[6] In 2005, he implicated the American Civil Liberties Union (ACLU) and billionaires George Soros and Peter Lewis:

---

* "Fool around with children." The Canadian age of consent had been set at fourteen in 1892, but in 2008 the government bucked the secular trend and raised it to sixteen. Adolescent sex remains legal in the more depraved parts of Europe. For instance, the age of consent is twelve in Vatican City. ("Canada's age of consent raised by 2 years," *CBC News* 1 May 2008, http://www.cbc.ca/canada/story/2008/05/01/crime-bill.html.) Andrew Sullivan, "Red Hot Catholic Love—At Twelve Years' Old," *The Atlantic,* 23 Feb. 2010, http://andrewsullivan.theatlantic.com/the_daily_dish/2010/02/red-hot-catholic-love.html.

† O'Reilly neglected to mention one other ominous trend that correlates even more closely with Canadian degeneracy: a rapid rise in the popularity of golf. Prior to the 1990s, golf was not even one of the top five most popular recreational activities in Canada. By 1998, it was the most popular. The correlation between golf and moral decay suggests a link between the whacking of small white balls and the war on Christmas. Some theorists have also hypothesized that the culprit is not the ball whacking itself but rather the clothing fashions associated with ball whacking. The moral of the story: Say "Merry Christmas," stay away from Canadian teenagers, and don't wear plaid. (Lance W. Roberts, Rodney A. Clifton, Barry Ferguson, *Recent Social Trends in Canada, 1960–2000* [Montreal: McGill-Queen's University Press, 2005]: 545.)

George Soros and Peter Lewis are the far-left, secular progressive billionaires who have funded—they pour money into the ACLU, they pour money into the smear websites, you know, they buy up a lot of the media time. And they basically want to change the country from a Christian-based philosophical country to a secular progressive country like they have in Western Europe. OK? Now, the ACLU is their legal arm, and the smear websites are their media arm. And they pour a lot of money into both. And the ACLU runs around the country suing everybody and intimidating people . . . And in tandem, you use your left-wing smear websites to go after anybody who stands up for Christmas. If you stand up for Christmas, they come after you. So the tandem intimidates. The tandem intimidates. Suing on one hand; smearing on the other hand. And the store CEOs, they got it. We don't want to get involved in that. We don't want to be sued. We don't want to be smeared, so we're going to say "Happy Holidays." Intimidation and lawsuits; the combo has worked . . . I mean, the ACLU and George Soros and these websites don't operate day to day without a plan. There is a plan . . . a very secret plan."[7]

Thus, the "secret plan" was revealed. According to O'Reilly, billionaires Soros and Lewis provided cash, the ACLU provided the lawsuits, and the unnamed smear sites provided the smearing. As a result, if you owned a department store and posted a sign wishing your customers a merry Christmas, you would be sued and smeared by the dark overlords of suing and smearing until you begged for mercy, which is useless because everyone knows that the godless don't do mercy, especially at Christmastime. Granted, no store has ever actually been sued or smeared for posting "Merry Christmas" signs, mainly because the practice is completely legal and commonplace, but that's the beauty of intimidation. The very thought of ACLU-affiliated smear teams sniffing around their stores was sufficient to send the CEOs of large retail chains into frantic apoplexies of nondenominational holiday cheer.

With Christmas out of the way at retail stores, there would be nothing to stand between the American people and a deluge of godless Canadian depravity except for a few demoralized Christians in tattered green and red sweaters. Say hello to drugs, socialism, gay marriage, and Jesus-free holidays: the future of secular America.

"Superior Analysis"

A more cautious journalist might have simply reported the secular holiday activities and perhaps rebuked the government officials and corporate officers for abandoning Christmas traditions. But O'Reilly is not known for caution. He is a T-Warrior, and his chief weapons are "facts and superior analysis based on those facts." For instance, it is a fact that the ACLU has filed First Amendment lawsuits against overtly religious Christmas displays on public property. It is also a fact that George Soros's charitable foundation, the Open Society Institute, has donated money to the ACLU.* Based on these facts, O'Reilly employed his superior analysis to deduce that George Soros and the ACLU have a "secret plan" to destroy Christmas. Indeed, O'Reilly's analysis is so superior that it even works with nonfacts, such as the widely circulated canard that Soros funded the liberal fact-checking website MediaMatters.org.[†] The site's editors have repeatedly debunked the claim, but that did not

---

* "Donated money to the ACLU." OSI has contributed almost $1 million per year to the ACLU, amounting to 2 percent of the ACLU's annual budget and 0.2 percent of OSI's $500 million annual budget. ("Echoing Lyndon LaRouche, Horowitz and Poe smear 14-year-old George Soros as Nazi 'collaborator'; new book features doctored quotes, factual errors," *Media Matters*, 2 Aug. 2006, http://mediamatters.org/research/200608020003; "About OSI: FAQs," *Open Society Institute & Soros Foundations Network*, 21 Jul. 2010, retrieved, http://www.soros.org/about/faq#m_expenditures>; "$8 Million Gift Will Boost ACLU Campaign to Fight Bush Administration's Assault on Civil Liberties," *ACLU*, 15 Jan. 2003, http://www.aclu.org/about/support/13308prs20030115.html.)

[†] O'Reilly bears personal animosity toward Media Matters, which frequently critiques his unsupported assertions and reported his infamous invitation to Al Qaeda: "You want to blow up the Coit Tower [in San Francisco]? Go ahead." O'Reilly has called the website "vile," "anti-American," and "the most vicious element in our society today." Most of Media Matters' content consists of transcripts of Fox News talk shows. ("O'Reilly to San Francisco: '[I]f Al Qaeda comes in here and blows you up, we're not going to do anything about it . . . You want to blow up the Coit Tower? Go ahead,'" *Media Matters*, 10 Nov. 2005, http://mediamatters.org/mmtv/200511100008.)

stop O'Reilly from insisting that "smear sites" like Media Matters had joined the alleged anti-Christmas conspiracy.[8]

Perhaps O'Reilly's suspicions were correct. Maybe George Soros and Peter Lewis hold regular brainstorming sessions with snickering ACLU lawyers and a pack of drooling webmasters where they plot the end of Christianity on a whiteboard over decaf soy lattes. But there is a point at which nimble analysis leaves behind the lumbering facts and enters the magical land of wild speculation, where paranoia and conspiracy frolic. *Merriam-Webster* defines conspiracy theory as "a theory that explains an event or set of circumstances as the result of a secret plot by usually powerful conspirators."* Sure enough, O'Reilly had it all—the circumstances, the explanation, the secret plot, and the powerful conspirators. If he had mixed in some evil priests, secret codes, and a sexy French cryptologist, he could have made another sequel to *The Da Vinci Code*. (Possible titles: *The Billionaire's Secret, The Christmas Enigma, The Protocols of the Elders of Zion*.)

Is belief in conspiracy a symptom of paranoia? Not necessarily. Conspiracies exist, and courts often convict defendants of conspiracy to commit crimes. But to build a conspiracy case, prosecutors require evidence like paper trails, phone records, and witness testimonies, and they don't usually declare themselves to be targets of the conspiracy. By contrast, Bill O'Reilly offered nothing to support his conspiracy accusation save a speculative motive and a record of charitable donations to a nonprofit organization that he fears and despises, having said of the ACLU, "They're terrorizing me and my family . . . They're putting us all in danger."[9] If baseless claims that enemies secretly conspire to persecute you and your kind constitute superior analysis, then superior analysis would seem to have much in common with paranoid delusion.

---

* "Conspiracy theory." To be fair, Bill O'Reilly might not accept dictionaries as objective sources. Fox News "media critic" Bernard Goldberg argued on *The O'Reilly Factor* that "the dictionary is written by some liberal person." O'Reilly responded by bashing the liberal media, leaving his position on dictionary bias unspecified. ("Bernard Goldberg Complains about the Liberal Bias in O'Reilly's Dictionary," *News Hounds*, 18 Mar. 2009, http://www.newshounds.us/2009/03/18/bernard_goldberg_complains_about_the_liberal_bias_in_oreillys_dictionary.php.)

Indeed, O'Reilly's brand of analysis is all too typical of paranoid conspiracy theory. The idea that influential villains secretly plot against ordinary men and women in a struggle to shape history carries innate psychological appeal that leads people to embrace conspiracy narratives with insufficient evidence and often in direct contradiction to available evidence. People want to believe in frightening conspiracies, and Bill O'Reilly is adept at giving people what they want.

Contrary to his boasts, O'Reilly's primary weapons in this endeavor are neither facts nor analyses. His weapons are *stories*. The war on Christmas has the trappings of a gripping fantasy novel. Powerful villains bent on domination prey on the innocent. The reluctant hero, an ordinary man of the people, discovers his power and rises to the nation's defense. Villains are unmasked. Epic battle between good and evil ensues. Herein lies Bill O'Reilly's genius. In the "Christmas Under Siege" television segments, he artfully reframed mundane political and cultural events as plot elements in a compelling story with powerful psychological appeal—and thereby seduced his audience and spawned a public sensation.

The Persecution Formula

The war on Christmas fantasy has three elements that make it effective. First, O'Reilly postulated a *slippery slope*. Today, it's holiday trees and municipal parades. Tomorrow, it will be legalized drugs, gay marriage, socialism, sex with fourteen-year-olds, and so on. The slippery slope magnifies small issues. Isolated instances of Christmas-spirit downers would not, on their own, catalyze the kind of passion required to dominate cable news. Mayor Bloomberg's "holiday tree" reference and the absence of a particular float in a Denver parade didn't affect many people, and even those affected did not suffer hardship serious enough to merit national news. But legalized drugs, gay marriage, socialism, and the rest affect the entire nation. By arguing that "holiday trees" contributed to such an abhorrent future, O'Reilly astronomically raised the stakes. As he explained, "The struggle today is not about Christmas, but about the spirit of our country."[10]

Nonetheless, the slippery slope argument only goes partway. A gradual drift is a tenuous and abstract threat. To make the scenario more frightening, O'Reilly offered a second element: *the secret plot*. He explained, "But if the secularists can destroy religion in the public arena, the brave new progressive world is a possibility." The addition of villainous conspirators made the slippery slope seem both plausible and frightening by suggesting that a sinister hand would guide the nation step by step from "holiday trees" to the "brave new progressive world," reframing innocent "Season's Greetings" as an ominous scheme by influential enemies. Thus, a seemingly innocuous policy was merely the first slippery step in the bad guys' "very secret plan."

The conspiracy would have been menacing enough on its own, but to instill mortal fear, O'Reilly painted the clash as an epic battle between "us" and "them," where the "us" were the traditional conservatives who made up his audience and the "them" were the radical secular progressives. For starters, he adopted martial vocabulary like "culture war" and "Christmas Under Siege." But in a move that was both significant and strategic, O'Reilly also appropriated the language of the civil rights movement to present Christians as a persecuted demographic. He told listeners:

> I am not going to let oppressive, totalitarian, anti-Christian forces in this country diminish and denigrate the holiday and the celebration. I am not going to let it happen. I'm gonna use all the power that I have on radio and television to bring horror into the world of people who are trying to do that . . . And anyone who tries to stop us from doing it is gonna face me.[11]

Meet Bill O'Reilly, fearless champion of the diminished, the denigrated, and the uncelebrated.

O'Reilly's language of *persecution* turned the conspiracy-driven slippery slope into a pitched battle between traditional Christians fighting for the survival of their religion and secular progressives seeking to destroy it. In game theory, such a conflict is called a *zero-sum game,* which means that one side's gain is the other side's loss. In O'Reilly's game, every victory by the evil secular progressives erodes the fundamental rights of the righteous Christians whom they despise. Every "Season's Greetings" becomes a form of discrimination that must be fiercely opposed by people of conscience, people like Bill O'Reilly and his fellow T-Warriors.

The Plot Heard around the World

O'Reilly's simple conspiracy formula—*slippery slope, secret plot,* and *persecution*—was extremely effective for garnering public attention, galvanizing supporters, and growing his audience. Prior to his 2004 "Christmas Under Siege" program, the idea of a concerted "war" on Christmas had been limited to a fringe website, vdare.com, favored by white supremacists. Once O'Reilly debuted his conspiracy theory on Fox, eager conservatives tripped over one other to join battle against the evil secular progressives. Heedless to the risk of being sued and smeared by Soros and company, conservative commentators fearlessly regurgitated O'Reilly's three or four examples of Christmas oppression and added their own perverse conspiracy theories.

- December 13: Pat Buchanan blamed "the gay lobby" and insisted that Macy's generic holiday messages constituted "hate crimes against Christianity."[12]
- December 13: Jerry Falwell called the ACLU's attempts to "purge God from America" a "national crime."[13]
- December 16: Rev. Franklin Graham, son of Rev. Billy Graham, told Fox News host Sean Hannity, "There are groups in this country that hate Jesus Christ. They hate God's son. And they want to do everything to discredit his name, to take his name out of our society." Hannity replied, "There's outright hatred and bigotry on a level that I don't think we have seen in our lifetime." (Liberal

beanbag Alan Colmes said nothing of consequence and was ignored as usual.)[14]

- December 16: Proving that Canada had not been completely lost to secular drug-loving pedophiles, Judi McLeod of the *Canadian Free Press* complained of secularism at Target department stores and alleged that "politically correct times have the assassination of the Christmas spirit on radar." (For the record, there are no Target stores in Canada.)[15]
- December 17: Charles Krauthammer eruditely blamed "the more deracinated members of religious minorities, brought up largely ignorant of their own traditions, whose religious identity is so tenuous that they feel the need to be constantly on guard against displays of other religions."[16]
- December 17: Paul Weyrich, cofounder of the Heritage Foundation, blamed the ACLU and the "militant secularizers" who make up 14 percent of the population.[17] (This number is somewhat at odds with O'Reilly's claim that 90 percent of the population celebrates Christmas.[18] O'Reilly not only refused to back down but responded the following year by raising the total to 95 percent.)[19]
- December 21: From the European front of the war on Christmas, Anthony Browne of the *Times,* a British daily, blamed the BBC and declared that "Christianity is being insidiously erased from the map."[20]
- December 22: Colonel Oliver North imagined the Magi walking along an American highway "accompanied by a vast army of liberal protestors chanting, 'Hey hey, ho ho, Jesus Christ has got to go.'"[21]
- December 22: William F. Buckley Jr. drew a careful distinction between the bureaucrats who "have drunk deep of ACLU doctrines" and "genuine anti-Christians: people who wince when Christianity is deferred to, people who hate Catholicism as the axis of Christianity and who will seek any opportunity to hinder or belittle it."[22]

And so on. The many blog posts and screeds from obscure fringe publications inspired by O'Reilly's program were even more hyperbolic. And that was just 2004. By the following Christmas, Fox News anchor John Gibson had written a bestseller entitled *The War on Christmas: How the Liberal Plot to Ban the Sacred Christian Holiday Is Worse Than You Thought,* and the Heritage Foundation, which calls itself a think tank, sponsored a symposium to discuss it. Anxious culture warriors founded a new organization to combat the persecution of Christians called the Christian Anti-Defamation Commission (not the most original folks). Christmas 2005 also boasted a few boycotts and more extreme outrage from the original participants and other conservative bigwigs who missed the Christmas pudding train the year before, from Rush Limbaugh to Ann Coulter to Jackie Mason.*

The fervor surrounding the "War on Christmas" eventually subsided, and O'Reilly declared in 2007 that "the forces of darkness" had lost.[23] He also reassured viewers that secular progressives had not opened up a second front on Easter:

> After the thumping that the department stores and all-over crazies took over Christmas, these people say, "You know, I don't think we want to come up against O'Reilly and these other people on Easter. Let's just let it go."[24]

So much for the all-powerful secular progressive conspiracy.

Conservatives Gone Wild!

But even as the forces of darkness capitulated to O'Reilly, various elements of the formula that O'Reilly popularized spread like a termite infestation through the woodwork of conservative ideology. For example,

* Jackie Mason, the aging Jewish comedian, is also a serious conservative ideologue. He offered *The O'Reilly Factor* his own colorful explanation for the war on Christmas: "It's in now to be . . . to hate religion. It's in now to be hip, to be a swinger because they're living a dirty, filthy, obscene, vulgar life, and they're guilt-ridden about it. So any connection with religion somehow feels like an interference to their lifestyle. So they want to eliminate religion; they shouldn't feel dirty." ("Jackie Mason on the 'UCLA types' and O'Reilly on the 'George Soros crew' said to be destroying Christmas," *Media Matters,* 5 Dec. 2005, http://mediamatters.org/research/200512050009.)

based on the *persecution* component of O'Reilly's formula, Christian victimization became a growth publishing industry with titles like *Persecution: How Liberals Are Waging War Against Christians; Speechless: Silencing the Christians: How Liberals and Homosexual Activists Are Outlawing Christianity (and Judaism) to Force Their Sexual Agenda on America;* and the winner in the Self-Important Title category, *The Criminalization of Christianity: Read This Book Before It Becomes Illegal!* (Five years after release, it's still available on Amazon.)

Christians are not the only alleged victims of liberal persecution. Other authors have translated the persecution narrative from discrimination against Christians to discrimination against white people. In a book called *Liberal Fascism, National Review* columnist Jonah Goldberg catalogs the many ways in which liberals resemble fascists, from environmentalism to vegetarianism to hip-hop (hip-hop?), and contends, "The white male is the Jew of liberal fascism."* Political commentator and one-time presidential candidate Pat Buchanan has written several scary prophesies about the death of white America. In one, he fretted that "by 2050, more than 100 million Hispanics will be in the United States, concentrated in the Southwest that borders on Mexico. As the Serbs are losing Kosovo, so we may have lost the Southwest."[25] Rush Limbaugh called white people "the new oppressed minority."[26] And Bill O'Reilly, ever the narcissist, has taken white persecution personally, complaining that the liberal critics of the *New York Times Book Review* panned his book *Culture Warrior* because "they despise the white man power structure."[27]

The election of a black president and his nomination of a Latina Supreme Court justice fit perfectly into the narrative of white victimology. Former House Speaker Newt Gingrich joined commentators Glenn Beck and Rush Limbaugh in calling Justice Sotomayor a racist. Limbaugh further suggested that her nomination reflected President

---

* *"Liberal Fascism."* My favorite quote from the book: "[Rudolf] Hess would bring his own vegetarian concoctions to meetings at the Chancellery and heat them up like the office vegan with some macrobiotic couscous." Hess is surely rolling in his grave. (Jonah Goldberg, *Liberal Fascism: The Secret History of the American Left, from Mussolini to the Politics of Change* [New York: Doubleday, 2007]: 386.)

Obama's own racial bigotry, and Glenn Beck accused Obama of harboring "a deep seeded [*sic*] hatred for white people or the white culture."*[28]

Taking it one step further, Beck also applied the white persecution theme to Obama's health care plan, claiming that it was really just a stealth policy to provide slavery reparations to African Americans by redistributing health insurance benefits from white people. He explained:

> [Obama] believes in all the "universal" programs because they "disproportionately affect" people of color. And that's the best way, he feels, to right the wrongs of the past. These massive programs are Obama brand reparations or in presidential speak: leveling the playing field.[29]

The specter of health care "redistribution" illustrates the way conservatives like Beck present liberal policies in terms of a zero-sum game. In Beck's view, guaranteeing heath care is not a way for the country as a whole to take care of its least fortunate; it is a way for the government to take benefits from the white team and give them to the black team.

Other commentators presented an alternative version of the zero-sum game that pitted American citizens against illegal immigrants. Here is Mark Steyn of the *National Review* filling in for Rush Limbaugh:

> And what's interesting is that under the whole death panel scenario, you know, you'll be an 87-year-old who's paid his taxes all his life, but they're not going to give you the procedure because they think it's more in the country's interest to give it to a 38-year-old illegal immigrant who shouldn't even be here in the first place.[30]

The idea that illegal immigrants would receive health care benefits at the expense of American citizens so captured some conservatives' imaginations that when President Obama declared in a speech to a joint ses-

---

* "Deep seeded hatred for white people." A moment later, Beck backtracked: "I'm not saying he doesn't like white people." And then forwardtracked: "I'm saying he has a problem. He has a, this guy is, I believe, a racist."

sion of Congress that the Democratic plan would not insure illegal immigrants, Rep. Joe Wilson (R-SC) interrupted him, shouting, "You lie!"

Who else wants a piece of Grandma's health care? The homosexuals, of course. A petition to "Stop Obama's Socialist Health Care Takeover" warns:

> Your tax-dollars will pay for preferential hiring of homosexual hospital administrators, who distribute $50,000 grants to gender-confused activists for unneeded elective surgery to mutilate their own genitals (and force Christian doctors to perform it).[31]

Imagine, America's seniors may soon start dying because their health care benefits have been rationed to illegal transsexual immigrants on welfare.

The redistribution of benefits is only the most obvious way in which the health care bill is said to discriminate against white people. The bill also includes a stealth tax on tanning salons. "This is a race-based tax," declaimed right-wing radio host Jim Quinn, "and it took this administration with a racial chip on its shoulder to come up with a tax that only taxes white people."[32]

In addition to persecution fantasies, the health care debate has also been burdened by an unhealthy dose of the slippery slope component of O'Reilly's formula. For instance, on *Fox News Sunday with Chris Wallace,* the former director of Faith Based Initiatives in the Bush administration, Jim Towey, denounced a Veterans Administration end-of-life guide he called a "death book," stating, "This is a slippery slope that kind of makes people . . . feel like they're a burden and that they should do the decent thing and die."[33] Glenn Beck as usual took the argument a step further. On one program he described how economic conditions led Nazi Germany to implement a eugenics program that sterilized and executed hundreds of thousands of handicapped people. The same, he darkly suggested, could happen here if economic conditions worsened. He even wept on air at the thought of what could happen to his daughter with cerebral palsy.[34] The implication: Obama's health care policy will cause us to slide down the slippery slope of devaluing human life, and then an economic crisis will lead us to begin murdering the disabled.

The Regular Schmo

Where O'Reilly the "T-Warrior" is angles and scowls and ego, Beck the "regular schmo" is doughy and goofy and self-deprecating. His head is constantly in motion, nodding and shaking like a bobblehead in an earthquake. He crinkles his forehead, stares quizzically into space, sticks out his tongue in concentration, and occasionally breaks into tears. His voice travels from grave undertone to shrill dismay to angry shout and becomes nasal and pinched when he parodies his ideological adversaries. He employs props to underscore his points—cutting a watermelon in half to criticize an environmental bill ("green on the outside, and inside it's deep, communist red")[35] or dowsing a guest with liquid from a gas can and then lighting a match ("President Obama, why don't you just set us on fire?").[36]

It's an entertaining shtick, but the physical comedy belies paranoid illusions far darker than O'Reilly's Christmas fantasy. Beck applies the *secret plot* element of O'Reilly's formula with a level of zeal and dedication unmatched on cable television. He places the masterminds of the plot in the White House, alleging that Obama has filled the executive branch with radical "czars" who are not accountable to voters: "A shadow government is giving the Obama administration unprecedented power with virtually no oversight."[37] Beck claims that the czars are deliberately wrecking the country and ballooning the national debt in order to generate a national emergency that they will exploit to justify a totalitarian revolution:

> These people are evil people that just have no respect for the republic
> in any way, shape or form and are going to fundamentally transform the
> nation . . .[38]

And later:

What they're laying the ground for, anything from the right—some awful event—I fear this government, this administration, has so much framework already prepared that they will seize power overnight before anybody even gives it a second thought.[39]

Beck has also expanded the victim role in the *persecution* element of the conspiracy. Beck's persecuted are not only Christians and white people; they include all the "regular schmos" out there who don't subscribe to radical Marxism. He explained:

This isn't about Republicans vs. Democrats. This is about Republicans and Democrats and Independents against radicals, revolutionaries and anti-capitalist nut jobs . . . I'm going to continue to expose these connections and plans that are out of step with almost everybody in this country—unless you live in the basement of Nancy Pelosi's house in the most radically progressive neighborhood in the country while eating arugula and roast beef sandwiches!*[40]

Notwithstanding the inanity of his insinuations, Beck is an even better storyteller than Bill O'Reilly, and his conspiracy fantasies are extraordinarily popular. Despite an undesirable 5:00 p.m. timeslot, Beck almost drew even in viewership with O'Reilly, and in January 2010, Americans voted him the nation's second-favorite TV personality after Oprah Winfrey.[41] *Time* magazine paid homage to his popularity by featuring his protruding tongue on its cover.[42] Conservative leaders, taking note of his success, have been singing his praises and parroting his talking points. Employing cutting-edge technology, Sarah Palin touted Beck's journalism on her Facebook page:

FOX News' Glenn Beck is doing an extraordinary job this week walking America behind the scenes of 1600 Pennsylvania Avenue and outlining

---

* "Arugula and roast beef sandwiches." Arugula, of course, has long been the leafy green of choice among basement-dwelling anticapitalist nut jobs, but the radicalization of roast beef is a frightening turn of events that should alarm beef lovers and cattle farmers across the nation. What's next? Marxist corndogs?

who is actually running the White House . . . I invite all my friends to watch.*[43]

Rush Limbaugh came on Beck's show, congratulated him on his excellent reporting, and declared:

> All of these disasters are exactly what Obama wants. The more crises, the better. The more opportunity for government to say, "Let us come in and fix the problem." . . . This is statism, totalitarianism versus freedom. And if these people are allowed to go where they want to go unchecked, then some people, a lot of people . . . will wake up one day and find, "My God, what the hell happened?"[44]

Between Beck, O'Reilly, Limbaugh, a host of commentators and politicians, and legions of angry bloggers, we are in the midst of a full-scale crazy blitz from the right. The atmosphere at Fox News has become so acrid that *Daily Show* comedian Jon Stewart called Bill O'Reilly "the most reasonable voice on FOX"—a distinction he compared to being "the thinnest kid at fat camp."†[45] It seems as if conservative commentators have been competing with one another to see who can spin the scariest conservative nightmare around every Democratic initiative: the bank and auto bailouts will lead to communism; same-sex marriage will lead to legalized polygamy, bestiality, and pedophilia; AmeriCorps is a fascist civilian force for rounding up conservatives; and on and on. But always, the people who make such arguments fall back on one or more of O'Reilly's three tactics:

- *Slippery slope:* these policies lead the nation down the road to abomination.
- *Secret plot:* these policies are part of an evil conspiracy.
- *Persecution:* these policies discriminate against "us."

---

* "I invite all my friends to watch." Facebook says: "18,639 people like this."

† "Fat camp." O'Reilly returned the backhanded compliment, noting that he has "no beef with moderate liberal Americans who hold sincere beliefs and do not traffic in hatred," unlike "George Soros and some of the loons on NBC."

Don't Tread on Me

The tactics work. In October 2009, the Democracy Corps, a nonprofit political research group founded by Democratic political strategists James Carville and Stan Greenburg, conducted a series of focus groups that revealed widespread paranoia among the Republican base, which constitutes "one-in-five voters in the electorate, and nearly two out of every three self-identified Republicans."[46] The report concluded:

> These conservative Republican voters believe Obama is deliberately and ruthlessly advancing a "secret agenda" to bankrupt our country and dramatically expand government control over all aspects of our daily lives. They view this effort in sweeping terms, and cast a successful Obama presidency as the destruction of the United States as it was conceived by our founders and developed over the past 200 years.

These voters fervently believe that they represent a persecuted minority "whose values are mocked and attacked by a liberal media and class of elites." Moreover, they are convinced that the "elites" are "actively working to advance the downfall of the things that matter most to them in their lives—their faith, their families, their country, and their freedom."

Their hero, of course, is Paranoiac-in-Chief Glenn Beck. The report continues, "They believe [Glenn Beck] embodies the best of conservative media—determination to unearth the stories the liberal media tries to bury, love of country, and refusal to be intimidated, even as the liberal media unleashes waves of attacks on his past and his credibility." A number of focus group participants, particularly women, feared that Beck's defiance of powerful liberal forces put his life in danger. The report wryly added, "Of course, his willingness to face this danger head on only adds to his legend."

Moreover, the believers have become proselytizers. According to the Carville-Greenburg report, the persecution mythology represents political gospel to its adherents, who feel "a responsibility to spread the word, to educate those who do not share their insights, and to take back the country that they love. Their faith in this country and its ideals leaves them confident that their numbers will grow, and that they will ultimately defeat Barack Obama and the shadowy forces driving his hidden agenda."

The spirit of evangelism described in the report found an outlet in the "Tea Party" protests that proliferated across the nation—aided by Fox News's frequent and favorable coverage. The protests are modeled on the 1773 Boston Tea Party that presaged the American Revolution, but while the original Boston Tea Party challenged the autocratic authority of King George III and the British parliament, today's Tea Parties remonstrate again at America's duly elected president and Congress.* The analogy underlies the protesters' paranoia, for many see Democrats as essentially foreign occupiers whose intent is not to strengthen the nation but to subjugate the inhabitants of what Sarah Palin called "the real America." Indeed, Rep. Michele Bachmann (R-MN), a prominent Tea Party promoter, calls herself "a foreign correspondent in enemy lines."[47]

Correspondingly, those who share Bachmann's point of view regard Republicans who compromise with Democrats as traitors. In the 2010 Republican primaries, Tea Party supporters have cast out a number of Republican incumbents for consorting with the enemy and supplanted them with paranoia-prone right-wing extremists. For instance, Sharon Angle, the Republican Senate nominee in Nevada, wants to abolish Social Security and has spoken of a possible need for "Second Amendment remedies"; that is, armed revolution to overthrow a tyrannical government.[48] Bill Randall, a Republican congressional nominee in North Carolina, suggested that BP and the government colluded to create the oil leak in the Gulf of Mexico for political purposes.[49] And Rand Paul, the Republican Senate nominee in Kentucky, has expressed reservations about the 1964 Civil Rights Act and concerns about a secret plot to create a "North American Union" under a single currency.[50]

---

* "Boston Tea Party." The costumes are also different. While the original tea protestors in Boston dressed as American Indians, today's Tea Party participants are more likely to don colonial garb. The gatherings sometimes resemble tours of the Liberty Bell and Constitutional Hall except that the Ben Franklin imitator carries a sign that says "NO Pubic Option [*sic*]."

If these men and women win their elections, they will join an elite group of Tea Party favorites already in Congress, people like "foreign correspondent" Rep. Michele Bachmann, who has warned of a plot to establish a "one world currency" and "the eventual unraveling of our freedom";[51] Paul Broun (R-GA), who accused Obama of preparing a Nazi-like civilian security force to round up conservatives;[52] Steve King (R-IA), who wants to abolish the IRS and attacked Obama for favoring black people;[53] and Louie Gohmert (R-TX), who is concerned about federal legislation to prosecute Christians for "thought crimes."[54]

Persecution Politics

Over the course of this book, I will argue that the extreme ideas expressed by conservative media stars, Tea Party organizers, and some Republican leaders are not random cases of paranoid insanity. They are part of a growing political movement to cast white, Christian, gun-owning conservatives as the victims of a vicious alliance between liberal elites, blacks, illegal immigrants, homosexuals, and other assorted villains. I call this movement and the tactics employed by its leaders *persecution politics.* Persecution politics did not begin with the Tea Parties. It did not even begin with Fox News or Rush Limbaugh. Its roots go back to the 1970s, when the election of a black president seemed like an impossible dream.

The realization of that dream in November 2008 did not substantially change the rhetoric or the tactics of the persecution politics movement. Obama's election simply accelerated its passage from a fringe pathology to a nationwide epidemic that has infected millions and is now tearing the country apart at its seams. Between demonizing liberals and purging conservatives who compromise with them, right-wing paranoia is ravaging what was left of reasonable discourse in the fractured world of modern American politics. The conspiracy theories may attract audiences and galvanize voters, but they spoil mutual trust, scuttle the possibility of compromise, and found ideology on fabrication. The many "town hall meetings" that politicians hosted during the health care battle—where people screamed their favorite conspiracy theories, carried assault weapons for show, and brawled like drunken soccer hooligans—are microcosms of our scarred political landscape. When Obama spoke to the nation to defend the Democrats' health care plan, he was forced to publically deny evident falsehoods that could be easily confirmed by anyone who bothered to read the plan, and this act of stating the obvious was widely applauded as a vigorous response as if obvious facts were some kind of rhetorical weapon . . . and nonetheless called a lie by those who spread the falsehood in the first place. As Yeats wrote, "The best lack all conviction, while the worst are full of passionate intensity."

The growth of persecution politics should concern Democrats of course, but it should also concern Republicans. Moderate Republicans, who once dominated the GOP, are on the verge of extinction, and Tea Party supporters are now purging conservative Republicans for not being conservative enough. Republican Party chairman Michael Steele's attempt to marginalize Rush Limbaugh as an "entertainer" was crushed by party conservatives, and he humbly apologized. In the 2008 primaries, the nation witnessed Republican candidates kowtow to immigrant bashers and declare their fidelity to creationism. The next Republican presidential nominee will likely be someone with at least one foot stuck in the mud of persecution politics.

Worrisomely, the tidal wave of paranoid hysteria shows no sign of slacking. The growth of cable news, talk radio, and blogs have produced a right-wing echo chamber in which conservative commentators shout ever louder to make themselves heard over the shrill cries of their colleagues, and television audiences measure the plausibility of each new conspiracy theory against a swiftly falling standard. We are witnessing a race to the bottom of a bottomless pit.

While the frenzied growth of right-wing paranoia has become difficult to ignore, few leaders offer any ideas for countering it. Many on the left, including President Obama, have blamed the trend on the economic recession and seem to assume that the storm of hysteria will wear itself out as the economy improves—much as a hurricane abates when it leaves the ocean. Some Democrats have even welcomed the right-wing extremism as an opportunity to score short-term political points. Meanwhile, Republican leaders have ignored, condoned, or even promoted the hatred emanating from the Tea Parties—either because they're afraid to antagonize their right-wing constituents or because they regard the paranoia as a useful tool for energizing the conservative base and recruiting supporters.

Over the course of this book, I will argue that right-wing persecution politics is not a temporary side effect of the recession; the voices of paranoia are not harmless entertainers on the fringe but participants in a pervasive movement with deep roots that is growing and evolving and inducing pernicious effects in American society. There are ways to reverse the tide and to nurture a healthier political environment, but they will require a concerted effort across the political spectrum. In order to understand what these solutions are and how they can be effective, we must first understand the persecution politics movement: where it comes from, why it is working, and where it is leading us.

To that end, we will embark on a sort of paranoia safari, touring backward and forward through history to catch glimpses of the ferocious beasts that populate the wastelands of conservative conscience. (Visitors are advised to remain within the safety of the vehicle at all times.) By the end of the tour, we will possess a richer understanding of the feeding habits and reproductive strategies of these dangerous creatures. We can then seek to understand how they escaped the preserve and form a strategy for protecting civilization from their encroachments.

2

WEEP FOR YOUR CHILDREN

How School Desegregation and
Imaginary Anti-Christian Brainwashers Gave Birth
to Right-wing Persecution Politics

*What makes them so dangerous is that Secular Humanists look just
like you and me. Some of them could be your best friends without you
knowing that they are Humanists. They could come into your house,
play with your children, eat your food and even watch football with
you on television, and you'd never know they have read* Catcher in
the Rye, Brave New World, *and* Huckleberry Finn.

—**Art Buchwald**

O N SEPTEMBER 1, 2009, the *Drudge Report,* a conservative news
site, proclaimed in a typically muscular font, several point sizes
too large for comfortable reading:

REID SHOCK: KENNEDY DEATH "GOING TO HELP US"

Directly beneath the feature story, in a more subdued type, Drudge
presented an unrelated headline:

Obama to make unprecedented address to all public school students; September 8

. . .

The announcement of a presidential "back to school" speech was
hardly breaking news. A few weeks earlier, Damon Weaver of Pahokee,
Florida, age eleven, had scooped the story in an exclusive interview
with President Barack Obama, which he published on YouTube. During
the interview, Obama told Weaver of his plans to deliver a speech about

"the importance of education, the importance of staying in school, how we want to improve our education system, and why it's so important for the country." At the end of the hard-hitting interview, Weaver invited Obama to be his homeboy; the president enthusiastically accepted. Various news outfits, including Fox News, covered the story of Weaver's interview with little fanfare on August 14.

On August 27, a blogger using the screen name Misfit4Peace posted an article titled "Obama to make unprecedented address to all public school students" on dailypaul.com, a popular Web forum for libertarians and conspiracy theorists owned by Rep. Ron Paul (R-TX). The article began:

> The long march continues apace as Great Leader drives us toward the new America with nationalized everything . . . if you have a strong stomach read the word.docs linked below with recommended classroom activities before and after the speech (be warned, if you love the Constitution you will want to barf).[1]

The document described many nauseating discussion questions like:

- What is the president trying to tell me?
- What is the president asking me to do?
- What new ideas and actions is the president challenging me to think about?
- Note: The fourth question has been redacted for liability reasons. It has been included in small print in the footnote. Pregnant women, the elderly, and readers with a history of stomach problems are advised to avert their eyes as they arrive at the bottom of the page.*

---

* DISCLAIMER. By reading THE FOURTH QUESTION, you agree that the author is not liable for any damages resulting from your reading of THE FOURTH QUESTION, either silently or aloud, including, without limitation, cleaning costs, medical expenses, and pain and suffering. THE FOURTH QUESTION: *What specific job is the president asking me to do?*

The story then floated around the conservative blogosphere for a couple of days, possibly contributing to a spike in sales of Pepto-Bismol, before the *Drudge Report* found it and pinned the headline to the middle of its news site, sparking a national conflagration of paranoid hysteria.

Jim Greer, chairman of the Republican Party of Florida, led the way with an outraged press release the same day. Calling Obama a "Pied Piper," Greer angrily denounced the president's designs on his children in a press release:

> As the father of four children, I am absolutely appalled that taxpayer dollars are being used to spread President Obama's socialist ideology . . . President Obama has turned to American's [sic] children to spread his liberal lies, indoctrinating American's [sic] youngest children before they have a chance to decide for themselves.*[2]

The next day, Fox News, smelling a ratings winner, followed suit with full-throated condemnations of the planned speech. Sean Hannity expressed concern to Michelle Malkin that the whole idea seemed "very close to indoctrination."[3] Malkin replied with a discourse on the left's exploitation of schoolchildren "as guinea pigs and as junior lobbyists for their social liberal agenda." On *The O'Reilly Factor,* commentator Monica Crowley dabbled in dystopia: "Look, just when you think that this administration can't get any more surreal and Orwellian, here he comes to indoctrinate our children."[4] Evidently, Ms. Crowley has a limited imagination when it comes to dystopian nightmares.

Glenn Beck, however, has no such limitations, and he gleefully used the opportunity to flog his own imaginative dystopian conspiracy theories:

---

* Jim Greer resigned several months later amid accusations of financial mismanagement. As he left, Greer blamed right-wing opponents for sabotaging him on account of his support for moderate governor Charlie Crist. These opponents may have been concerned that Crist would facilitate Obama's socialist indoctrination of America's children. (Jane Sutton, "Florida Republican party chairman quits amid splits," *Reuters,* 5 Jan. 2010, http://www.reuters.com/article/idUSTRE60458520100105.)

Gang, you have a system that is wildly, wildly out of control, and they are capturing your kids. As Van Jones himself has said, the earlier we get the kids, the earlier we make this adjustment with the youth, the easier this transition is going to be. Stand guard America. Your republic is under attack.[5]

Bill O'Reilly and Rush Limbaugh were both on vacation the first week of September (coincidence?), so their initial thoughts on the back-to-school threat went sadly unrecorded.

Conservative parents across the nation reacted with alarm to the news of the planned indoctrination program. Many vowed to keep their children home on the day of the speech to protect their impressionable young minds from socialist taint. A grassroots Twitter drive was originally called National Skip Day but later modified to the slightly more responsible-sounding and acronym-friendly "Parentally Approved Skip School Day."[6] Many schools allowed students to opt out of the televised speech. Others refused to show it at all.[7]

A week later, as protestors gathered outside a Virginia high school with placards that read "Mr. President, Stay Away from Our Kids," Obama delivered his "unprecedented address"* to schools across the country.[8] The speech was crammed full with socialist agitprop, like "Here in America, you write your own destiny" and "I hope you'll all wash your hands a lot, and stay home from school when you don't feel well, so we can keep people from getting the flu this fall and winter."[9] Schoolchildren across the nation were reportedly inspired to pursue their own destinies and wash their hands regularly for the rest of the day.

If the brouhaha over Obama's speech strikes you as much ado about nothing, then you are obviously not a conservative partisan in the

---

* "Unprecedented address." Actually, the address had been "precedented," once by Ronald Reagan, who educated kids about the Boston Tea Party, "America's original tax revolt," and twice by George H. W. Bush, who informed kids that saying no drugs "won't make you a nerd." (Ronald Reagan, "Remarks and a Question-and-Answer Session with Area Junior High School Students," *Ronald Reagan Presidential Library,* 14 Nov. 1988, http://www.reagan.utexas.edu/archives/speeches/1988/111488c.htm; George Bush, "Address to Students on Drug Abuse," *The American Presidency Project,* 12 Sep. 1989, http://www.presidency.ucsb.edu/ws/index.php?pid=17509.)

thrall of persecution politics. According to the paranoid right's world-view, there is a secret progressive conspiracy committed to persecuting traditional Americans and enacting a radical agenda in a series of incremental steps. One of the first steps in the conspirators' grand plan is to brainwash America's youth. As one concerned blogger wrote before Obama's speech:

> We can learn a lot from the spread of propaganda in Europe that led to Hitler's power. A key ingredient in that spread of propaganda was through the youth. And it's not just Nazi Germany. Totalitarian regimes around the world have sought to spread their propaganda and entrench their power by brainwashing the children.[10]

Another contributor enthusiastically invoked the dreaded "slippery slope":

> I remember from history class that some other very prominent figures in history started out like this, all about education and change for the better. Capture the hearts and minds and all that. You can call it what you will but Obama Youth or Hitler Youth . . . This is much too slippery a slope, this day and age with the role of government becoming more invasive the last thing I want is for "them" to get a tooth into my kids.[11]

A Very Brief History of Corrupting the Youth

The fear of juvenile indoctrination goes way back. Way, way back. In 399 BC, the city-state of Athens executed the philosopher Socrates for corrupting the youth with subversive and impious ideas. Two millennia later, in 1547, the city of London banned playhouses for "corruptions of youth and other enormities,"[12] which forced Shakespeare's playing company to build the famous Globe Theatre outside the city limits.* In

---

* Oliver Cromwell's Puritans later burned down the Globe and outlawed theater in all of England. They also banned Christmas trees (too pagan), caroling (too Catholic), and nativity scenes (too idolatrous). Now that's a war on Christmas.

1688, as a pretext for seizing the English throne, William of Orange formally protested Catholic activities in England, including the construction of "several colleges of Jesuits in diverse places for the corrupting of youth."[13]

More recently, in 1946, Rep. George Dondero (R-MI) warned that the country was being "systematically communized" by left-wing teachers at public schools, resulting in "an entire generation of voters who do not appreciate our Constitution, or our national history."[14] In 1954, psychologist Fredric Wertham published a widely publicized book, *Seduction of the Innocent,* about the corrupting influence of comic books in which he alleged that Batman and Robin were gay lovers, Wonder Woman was a "cruel, 'phallic' woman," and Superman was unrealistic:

> He gives children a completely wrong idea of other basic physical laws. Not even Superman, for example, should be able to lift up a building while not standing on the ground, or to stop an airplane in mid air while flying himself.*[15]

The Segregation Academies

In 1954, the same year that Wertham published *Seduction of the Innocent,* the U.S. Supreme Court ruled in *Brown v. Board of Education of Topeka* that segregated schools violated the Equal Protection Clause of the Fourteenth Amendment, setting in motion a chain of events that would lead to the birth of the persecution politics movement in the late 1970s.

One of the men who precipitated these events was a Baptist minister named Jerry Falwell. In 1956, at the age of twenty-three, Falwell

---

* "Not even Superman." Wertham did not present his views on the physics lesson offered by a red-suited man who rides a flying-reindeer-drawn sleigh to the home of every Christian child in the world within twenty-four hours, bearing gifts for each one. Nonetheless, Wertham's work influenced the Senate Subcommittee on Juvenile Delinquency to subpoena comic book publisher William Gaines. Though the subcommittee did not blame Gaines for any crime, the negative publicity forced his company into bankruptcy.

founded a church in Lynchburg, Virginia. In his sermons, Falwell railed against the *Brown v. Board of Education* decision, proclaiming:

> If Chief Justice Warren and his associates had known God's word and had desired to do the Lord's will, I am quite confident that the 1954 decision would never have been made . . . The facilities should be separate. When God has drawn a line of distinction, we should not attempt to cross that line.[16]

After the Supreme Court decision, white politicians and parents sought alternative means to uphold God's "line of distinction." They found it in the "seg academies"—all white private schools that blossomed like daisies across the South after public schools desegregated. Holmes County, Mississippi, was typical of "desegregated" Southern school districts. In the first year after public school desegregation, white enrollment in the county's public schools dropped from 771 to 28. In the second year, it dropped to zero.[17] Prince Edward County, Virginia, simply shut down its public schools, leaving black students without any school in the county that would take them.

Southern state governments did what they could for the cause, offering tuition grants—what Republicans now call vouchers—so that poor white students could continue to be educated in an environment free of dark pigmentation. When a federal court found such grants unconstitutional in 1969, the seg academies sought out tax-deductible donations to subsidize low-income whites. For example, one Holmes County academy sent out fundraising letters that warned:

> Unless we receive substantial contributions to our Scholarship Fund there will be many, many students, whose minds and bodies are just as pure as those of any of their classmates and playmates . . . who for financial reasons alone, will be forced into one of the intolerable and repugnant "other schools."[18]

In 1969, black parents in Holmes County filed a lawsuit demanding that the IRS deny tax exemptions to the three seg academies in the county. The courts ruled that using federal tax funds to finance private schools for purposes of segregation violated the Equal Protection Clause of the Fourteenth Amendment, and the IRS began withholding tax exemptions from openly segregated schools. Nonetheless, seg academies easily skirted the new rules by adopting officially nondiscriminatory admissions policies while still practicing de facto segregation, and private all-white schools continued to proliferate in the South.

The first seg academies were exact replicas of the secular public schools they had replaced, but over time, most of the academies adopted Christian affiliations, such as Jerry Falwell's Lynchburg Christian Academy, which the *Lynchburg News* described as "a private school for white students."[19] A 1973 *Wall Street Journal* article documented the emergence of this new variety of seg academy. "These days, Christian schools and segregation academies are almost synonymous," said a coordinator of the education task force of the Southern Regional Council.[20]

Thus, when the IRS proposed strengthening the tax exemption rules in 1978 to force the seg academies to actively recruit minority students and teachers, many Southern Christians reacted with fury and alarm at the dual threat to white privilege and Christian education. As a result, the IRS proposal played right into the hands of a young conservative strategist with big plans.

Kicking the Sleeping Dog

In 1962, nineteen-year-old Paul Weyrich, a radio journalist and devout Catholic from Racine, Wisconsin, called on the chairman of the Wisconsin Republican Party to denounce a Supreme Court ruling that banned prayer in public schools. But the chairman refused to get involved, insisting, "Our businesspeople would think it was strange that we are getting involved in a religious issue."

"That was the moment," Weyrich explained in an interview, "that I said to myself, 'By golly, this is just off the track. I'm going to see to it that one day the party will listen to these kinds of issues.' And that really became my mission in life."[21]

Soon after, Weyrich went to work for Republican politicians in Washington where he continued to struggle to persuade the party to embrace socially conservative causes like outlawing abortion, ending busing, and supporting school prayer. In 1973, Weyrich founded the Heritage Foundation, the think tank that would revolutionize conservative political scholarship by discarding the scholarship. The following year, Weyrich left Heritage Foundation because the board of directors wouldn't put enough emphasis on social issues.[22] That's like leaving the Roman Catholic Church because the pope won't put enough emphasis on religious issues (which, incidentally, Weyrich also did, joining the Eastern Orthodox Church in 1968).

After leaving Heritage, Weyrich focused on the political potential of the growing fundamentalist and evangelical churches, but he was stymied in his effort to mobilize them. The fundamentalist and evangelical communities were accustomed to keeping their distance from politics, adopting the position expressed by Jerry Falwell in 1965, "Preachers are not called upon to be politicians, but soul winners."*[23] Weyrich elaborated:

> Christian conservatives of the evangelical and fundamentalist type had been told for years—ever since the Scopes Trial—that they should not be involved in politics, that it was a sin to be involved in politics. That you would lose your soul if you were involved in politics.[24]

Years later, Falwell and others promulgated a myth that the shock of *Roe v. Wade* finally woke the slumbering religious right—enraging Christians across the country and prompting Falwell to launch his influential political organization, the Moral Majority. The chief problem with this story is that it's false. Many fundamentalist organizations, in-

---

* By 1976, Falwell had changed his point of view, declaring, "This idea of 'religion and politics don't mix' was invented by the devil to keep Christians from running their own country." I leave it as a logic exercise for the reader to deduce the inspiration behind Falwell's earlier opinion that preachers should not be politicians. (Susan Page and Cathy Lynn Grossman, "Falwell was a uniter and a divider," *USA Today*, 31 Jul. 2007, http://www.usatoday.com/news/religion/2007-05-15-falwell-obit_N.htm.)

cluding the Southern Baptist Convention to which Falwell belonged, were originally pro-choice and viewed abortion as a "Catholic issue." W. A. Criswell, former president of the SBC, declared after *Roe v. Wade:*

> I have always felt that it was only after a child was born and had a life separate from its mother that it became an individual person, and it has always, therefore, seemed to me that what is best for the mother and for the future should be allowed.[25]

And W. Barry Garrett of the *Baptist Press* wrote, "Religious liberty, human equality and justice are advanced by the Supreme Court abortion decision."[26]

Moreover, Falwell did not found the Moral Majority because of his outrage against the Supreme Court. The Moral Majority was Paul Weyrich's brainchild. Weyrich was certainly concerned about abortion, but his primary objective in founding the organization was to unite fundamentalists, evangelicals, Catholics, and even Jews in a variety of social and political causes. Weyrich believed that the new organization needed a popular Protestant figurehead. He first tried to recruit Pat Robertson, who turned him down. Falwell, his second choice, accepted—but it took some persuading. In addition, Ed Dobson, a former Falwell associate, explicitly dismissed the significance of abortion in the early planning of the Moral Majority, recalling:

> The Religious New Right did not start because of a concern about abortion. I sat in the non-smoke-filled back room with the Moral Majority, and I frankly do not remember abortion ever being mentioned as a reason why we ought to do something.[27]

According to Weyrich, even fundamentalists and evangelicals who opposed legalized abortion did not originally see the need for a political response to *Roe v. Wade* and other Supreme Court decisions:

> Their attitude was "If there are abortions and if there's no prayer in the public school and there are all these problems, we're living in our own

little communities, and there's not going to be any abortions among our kids, and we have opened Christian schools and prayer will be recited there, and we simply don't need to be involved."[28]

The issue that did finally propel the religious right into action was not abortion but the 1978 IRS proposal to crack down on segregated schools. Weyrich explained:

> What galvanized the Christian community was not abortion, school prayer, or the ERA. I am living witness to that because I was trying to get those people interested in those issues and I utterly failed. What changed their mind was Jimmy Carter's intervention against the Christian schools, trying to deny them tax-exempt status on the basis of so-called de facto segregation.[29]

Richard Viguerie, who along with Weyrich has been credited with founding what was once called the New Right, claimed that the IRS desegregation proposal "kicked the sleeping dog. It galvanized the religious right. It was the spark that ignited the religious right's involvement in real politics."[30]

Thus, in a crucible of racism and piety, baked red-hot by the fear of corrupted youth, a movement was born. The role of the IRS desegregation proposal in the birth of the religious right has been well documented. Less discussed has been the fiction—the fuel—that fired the imaginations of those who answered the call. For while the IRS proposal clearly threatened segregated education, its impact on religious education was incidental. Any school—religious or secular—that failed to meet the modest requirements could easily adjust by recruiting minorities. For people to see the IRS proposal as an attack on Christian education, they had to see the desegregation objective as a pretext, an excuse for going after the Christians. Weyrich's wording, "Carter's intervention against the Christian schools . . . on the basis of so-called de facto segregation," suggests exactly this point of view.

These days we have come to expect the right wing to represent any Democratic initiative as a pretext for Christian persecution, but it was not always so. Before the 1980s, *religious* and *right* were not fused to-gether. Fundamentalists and evangelicals hailed the election of Jimmy Carter, a former Sunday school teacher, a friend of Rev. Billy Graham, and the first evangelical president of the United States. He was not a president one would suspect of seeking to corrupt Christian youth. But with the IRS proposal, Carter seemed to mutate almost instantaneously in the minds of many evangelicals from good Christian leader to anti-Christian autocrat. What made the transformation seem plausible to them was the appearance of a new villain on the American political landscape in the late 1970s, an ideological network that had cunningly invaded Carter's government in its fiendish bid to indoctrinate Chris-tian youth with atheistic, immoral, and unpatriotic ideas. It was called *secular humanism*.

Nailing Jell-O to a Tree

Humanism is a vague term, in use since the Renaissance, denoting the study of human history and culture (hence the term *humanities*). In the twentieth century, religious reformers used the term to describe an em-phasis on human, as opposed to divine, affairs. In this vein, a number of American intellectuals signed a document called the Humanist Man-ifesto in 1933 that laid out the tenets of *religious humanism*. The loose movement would later produce a rather insignificant organization of several thousand members (about the size of a single modern mega-church) called the American Humanist Association.

Secularism is also a vague term, coined in 1851 by English atheist and convicted blasphemer George Jacob Holyoake to denote a rejection of theological answers to questions of science and ethics.

Secular humanism is a concept so nebulous that its definition defied even William Safire, who stumbled through a column that compared the exercise to "trying to nail Jell-O to a tree."[31] The term's gelatinous nature stems from its origins, or rather from its lack of origins in any genuine political movement. For secular humanism is a make-believe doctrine—invented by Christian theologians to blame an imagined enemy for the diminishing influence of religion in modern society. It was later repurposed by the American religious right as a "code word for the precepts and practices of almost anyone this side of Communism who disagrees with them, including liberals, feminists, atheists, civil libertarians, internationalists."[32]

The first historical record of secular humanism appeared in 1933, courtesy of Anglo-Catholic Rev. William George Peck, who in a series of lectures predicted the imminent collapse of the "false gospel of secular humanism."[33] Ten years later, the nonexistent Jell-O doctrine had not only avoided collapse, it now threatened Christianity "more powerfully than in any period since the end of the Dark Ages" according to the archbishop of Canterbury, William Temple.[34] And in 1949, a San Francisco conference of Episcopal bishops warned their colleagues, "We have been contaminated by the secular humanism of our time,"[35] as if it were toxic slime from the Andromeda galaxy. In 1965, at the end of the revolutionary Second Vatican Council, Pope Paul VI sounded like a beaten pontiff bowing to the new alien overlords:

> Secular humanism, revealing itself in its horrible anticlerical reality has, in a certain sense, defied the council . . . But we call upon those who term themselves modern humanists, and who have renounced the transcendent value of the highest realities, to give the council credit at least for one quality and to recognize our own new type of humanism: we, too, in fact, we more than any others, honor mankind.[36]

Back to School

But while secular humanism may have threatened England and subjugated Rome, it was no match for Max Rafferty, superintendent of Public Instruction of California and defender of youth from the onslaught of secular humanist brainwashers. Early in his career, Rafferty became a conservative darling by blaming problems in the public school system on a dull reading curriculum that included stories about "the stupid adventures of Muk-Muk, the Eskimo Boy, or Little Pedro from Argentina."[37] Then in 1969, Rafferty's emergency response team produced the groundbreaking *Guidelines for Moral Instruction in California Public Schools,* which located the true villain behind Muk-Muk and Little Pedro: *secular humanism.* In addition to accusing secular humanists of promoting boring literature, the guidelines also blamed them for teaching such evils as sex education, Marxism, and evolution.[38]

Outraged American conservatives soon answered the secular humanist infiltration of the American education system in the courts. In 1972, the religion editor of the *Washington Evening Star* sued the National Science Foundation "in the interest of 40 million evangelistic Christians" for funding a biology textbook that failed to mention the important science of creationism. The suit accused the government of "establishing as the official religion of the United States, secular humanism."[39] He lost.*

Between 1971 and 1976, a group called Parents Rights sued the state of Missouri six times. Unhappy about secular humanism in Missouri's public schools, the parents demanded their tax money back. They lost all six times.[40]

In 1976, Rep. John Conlan (R-AZ) introduced an amendment prohibiting federal funds for educational programs "involving any aspect of the religion of secular humanism," which passed in the House but failed in the Senate. In the subsequent congressional election, Conlan lost. Two years later, he published an article in the *Texas Tech Law Review* to defend his position that secular humanism was a religion. To bolster the argument, he and coauthor John Whitehead described the alleged creed's central tenets (evolution, Man-worship), listed its

---

* The case for secular humanism's religious credentials stems from a footnote to a 1961 Supreme Court case in which Justice Hugo Black suggests, "Among religions in this country which do not teach what would generally be considered a belief in the existence of God are Buddhism, Taoism, Ethical Culture, Secular Humanism, and others." (Christopher P. Toumey, "Evolution and Secular Humanism," *Journal of the American Academy of Religion,* 61:2 [Summer, 1993]: 277–278.)

† John Dewey is one of America's most important philosophers and an influential educational reformer who criticized the traditional rote learning approach to pedagogy and promoted teaching practices that emphasized children's individuality. He was a *religious*

prominent adherents (Hitler, Stalin, and John Dewey†), and capitalized its name.[41] Since Secular Humanism was a religion, they reasoned, teaching religious dogma like evolution in public schools violated the First Amendment.

The year 1978 featured a bonanza of court cases against the new religion of Secular Humanism. Creationists sued the Smithsonian when it presented an exhibit on evolution, accusing the museum of "establishing a religion of secular humanism."[42] They lost. Sixty-two fundamentalist schools in North Carolina refused to file a report required for state approval on the grounds that public schools teach a religion of secular humanism.*[43] They lost. Fundamentalist preachers and teachers in Kentucky sued for exemption from state licensing and certification requirements. They lost.

Rev. John C. Macon, head of the Eastern Association of Christian Schools, explained the rationale behind the legal battles against the "contamination" of secular humanism:

> When the public school system was founded in the 1850s, it had a strong emphasis on morals. Gradually it was torn down and replaced with John Dewey and secular humanism, and we built our own schools. This legal

---

humanist who opposed what he called *militant atheism*. Nonetheless, conservatives have caricatured Dewey as a pernicious *secular* humanist, the architect of the liberal occupation of American public schools. The conservative magazine *Human Events* ranked Dewey's *Democracy and Education* the fifth "most harmful" book of the past two hundred years after *The Communist Manifesto* and *Mein Kampf*. Right-wingers frequently represent Hitler, Stalin, and Dewey as an evil triumvirate of youth corruptors, despite the fact that Dewey was a staunch anticommunist who despised Stalin and presciently called Hitler "the greatest threat to world peace today" five years before the Nazis unleashed their *blitzkrieg* on Europe. ("Ten Most Harmful Books of the 19th and 20th Centuries," *Human Events* 31 May 2005, http://www.humanevents.com/article.php?id=7591; "Dr. John Dewey Dead at 92; Philosopher a Noted Liberal," *New York Times,* 2 Jun. 1952, http://www.nytimes.com/learning/general/onthisday/bday/1020.html.)

* The president of the Organization of Christian Schools even complained about modern math because "it teaches very strongly that all things are relative and there are no absolutes." ("Christian School Administrators Vow to Fight Judge's Decision," *Wilmington Morning Star,* 112:2 [6 Sep. 1978]: 2-A.)

fight is a way of saying "we're not abandoning this one; those who have strong religious feelings will not compromise. We will not keep abandoning the ship to the cancerous liberal element that wants to contaminate everything."[44]

So when the IRS moved against seg academies in August of 1978, the Christian soldiers were already manning the trenches and deploying advance teams. They knew exactly who was behind the proposal and what its hidden purpose was. A former Nixon staffer and up-and-coming news commentator named Pat Buchanan spelled out the coercive role of the IRS in secular humanism's stealthy slippery-slope assault:

> The so-called "segregation academies" established everywhere that some judge has handed down an integration order or busing decision have long been Public Enemy No. 1 at the IRS. But this new "procedure" is a new departure. And its implications are sweeping. If allowed to stand, every private school in the country can be threatened with loss of its tax exemption if it does not conform with the social values of the secular humanism which is the newly established religion in the United States.[45]

The response to public entreaties from Weyrich, Buchanan, and other conservative leaders was overwhelming. The IRS received 120,000 letters of protest, more than it ever collected in response to a proposed change.[46] Southern defenders of white privilege like Sen. Strom Thurmond (R-NC) joined religious right newcomers like Rep. Steven Symms (R-ID) and Sen. Orrin Hatch (R-UT) in excoriating the IRS.

Sen. Jesse Helms (R-NC), who exemplified both Southern racism and Christian evangelicalism, was a fitting leader for the legislative counterattack against the "collectivist, totalitarian . . . counterfeit religion" of secular humanism.[47] He sponsored a bill to prohibit the IRS from enforcing antidiscrimination rules. This time, the bill passed, and the IRS capitulated, leaving singed globs of secular humanist goo splattered across the steps of Capitol Hill. Paul Weyrich and Jerry Falwell launched the Moral Majority. The religious right had found its roar.

"The Most Dangerous Religion in America"

Yet for all its ferocity, the roar of the right was like that of a cornered animal. It was a roar of *fear*. True believers imagined themselves to be beset on all sides by howling humanists who threatened daily to contaminate innocent Christian children with dangerous propaganda. Perversely, the victory against the IRS did not lead the right wing to discount its estimation of secular humanist might. On the contrary, they inflated it—manufacturing a rich mythology of the secular humanist menace that included world domination and all manner of social ills.

In 1979, Duncan Homer, an evangelical preacher from Texas, published a book called *Secular Humanism: The Most Dangerous Religion in America*. Senator Jesse Helms contributed the introduction. A stream of religious right luminaries endorsed it. The book laid out the secular humanists' secret plan to destroy Christianity in order to eliminate opposition to the establishment of a "new world order" that was "Anti-God, Anti-Christ, Anti-Bible, and Anti-American." Sound familiar? Twenty-five years later, Bill O'Reilly would add "progressive," drop "humanism," and spin the exact same fantasy about "progressive secularists," still conspiring after all these years.*

Homer's book also propagated the same three tactics that O'Reilly favored. To support his belief in a conspiracy to destroy Christianity, Homer quoted at length from a newsletter by R. J. Rushdoony, a paranoid extremist theocrat who advocated the public stoning of homosexuals, among other enlightened ideas:

---

* Unlike O'Reilly, Homer saw the theory of evolution at the heart of the conspiracy. He wrote, "Every single anti-Christian 'ism' that has come down the pike in the last century or more has found as its pseudoscientific foundation in the idea of evolution. Whether we are talking about Nazism, Fascism, Communism, Secular Humanism, Freudianism, Behaviorism, or any one of a dozen other 'isms,' they all rest their case on evolution."

The extreme right seems to have a thing against *isms*. For example, in 1965, a KKK grand dragon declared his opposition to "niggerism, Catholicism, Judaism, and all the isms of the whole world." I would call the phenomenon *anti-ism-ism* were it not for the risk of a mind-blowing paradox. (Homer Duncan, *Secular Humanism: The Most Dangerous Religion in America,* [revised] tenth printing, 1984 [Lubbock, TX: MC International Publications, 1979]: 41; John Herbers, "The Klan: Its Growing Influence; Membership Placed at 10,000 in South," *New York Times,* 20 Apr. 1965: 24.)

- *Slippery slope:* "These efforts are directed at present mainly against small or independent groups, those least able to defend themselves. Meanwhile, major church groups are not disturbed or upset. Legal precedents established against these smaller groups can later be applied against all others."[48] (Rushdoony)
- *Secret plot:* "It is a well-planned war. When virtually all 50 states embark on a common program, in unison, and appear with federal directives in hand, it is no accident. Of course, they declare themselves innocent of any attempt to control a Christian School, church, missions agency, or organization."[49] (Rushdoony)
- *Persecution:* "I am now strongly convinced that the aim of Humanism is to completely destroy Biblical Christianity."[50] (Homer)

The same year, Dr. Tim LaHaye, another founder of the Moral Majority and the future creator of *Left Behind,* the bestselling apocalypse–pulp fiction series, published his own book on what he simply called "humanism." LaHaye dedicated his book, *The Battle for the Mind,* to theologian Francis Schaeffer, whom many regard as the intellectual father of the religious right. With his nape-length white hair and protuberant goatee, Schaeffer looked like a pasty version of an Indian guru; and from his retreat in the Swiss mountains, Schaeffer played the part perfectly, treating Christian evangelicals and counterculture hippies alike to his theological disquisitions on the conflict between traditional Christianity and humanist modernity. An evangelical version of C. S. Lewis, Schaeffer was erudite and cultured, as comfortable with modern art and French existentialism as he was with the Bible. He criticized the use of "humanism" as a buzzword, carefully defining the term in a way that religious humanists like John Dewey might have appreciated, even if they fiercely opposed his position.

But if Schaeffer was the intellectual father of the religious right, LaHaye is the crazy uncle who dropped out of school, joined the army, and came back from the war . . . different. He seems gentle enough at first glance. With his carefully brushed *Leave It to Beaver* hairstyle and the paternal manner of an elementary schoolteacher, LaHaye resembles Mr. Rogers in a polyester suit. So it is a bit jarring when he sweetly tells you that the Rapture is imminent, and you're going to die in agony and then burn in hell for eternity, you humanist scum.

Where Schaeffer immersed himself in Western philosophy, LaHaye simply dismissed the West's entire intellectual tradition as a Satanic plot. From Schaeffer's elaborate history of the struggle between Christian and secular ideas, LaHaye gleaned that the Greeks were evil (and gay), the Romans were corrupted by the Greeks and thus rendered evil (and gay), the Catholics were evil (but not gay . . . well . . . not most of them), the Renaissance was evil, the Enlightenment was evil, modern science was evil, and the intellectual ideas of the twentieth century were the evilest of all. (And yet, Dr. LaHaye takes tremendous pride in the ideals upon which the United States was founded.)

In his book *Battle for the Mind,* LaHaye transformed Schaeffer's humanists from ideological opponents into grotesque plotters of world domination. He wrote:

> Most people today do not realize what humanism really is and how it is destroying our culture, families, country—and one day the entire world. Most of the evils in the world today can be traced to humanism, which has taken over our government, the UN, education, TV, and most of the other influential things in life.[51]

In addition to controlling the government, LaHaye revealed that humanists had penetrated more deeply into the American media business than anyone had imagined. He wrote, "Almost every major magazine, newspaper, TV network, secular book publisher, and movie producer is a committed humanist." Calling humanism "the most serious threat to our nation in its entire history," LaHaye predicted that if Christians did not "wake up to who the enemy really is," the humanists would accomplish their goal of a "complete world takeover" by the year 2000.*

---

* The Year 2000 Humanist World Domination Project has been indefinitely delayed. For an updated schedule, please purchase the revised edition of this book, *Blowing Smoke: But Not for Much Longer (Diabolical Laughter),* scheduled for publication in 2012.

"Is Humanism Molesting Your Child?"

Discovering secret secular humanist individuals and organizations in positions of power soon became a cottage industry of the right wing. In 1979, Senator Helms opposed the creation of the Department of Education and the nomination of its first secretary, Shirley Hufstedler. Hufstedler had previously served on the board of the Aspen Institute for Humanistic Studies, so Helms concluded that she was one of the secular humanists "who are taking over our schools, our society, our businesses, our institutions at every level."[52] But the Aspen Institute is a nonpartisan leadership-training organization. Its name derives from its founder's support for the study of the humanities.

In addition to the IRS and the Department of Education, conservatives hunted down secular humanists in the courts and in nonprofit organizations like the National Education Association, the American Library Association, NOW (National Organization for Women), the NAACP (National Association for the Advancement of Colored People), the ACLU, Planned Parenthood, and People for an American Way, to name a few. They also accused secular humanists of controlling the United Nations, Hollywood, and the media. Dallas Cowboy coach Tom Landry, whose political opinions were important because of his coaching record, warned the audience of a massive prayer rally that secular humanism was "sweeping America." As an example of its influence, he cited the film *On Golden Pond,* explaining, "The language was as bad as I've ever seen in a movie."[*][53]

Citizens' protection organizations with names like "Young Parents Alert" and "We The People Concerned With Education" materialized in suburbs and small towns across the country to marshal parents against the secular humanist scourge. They distributed leaflets with frantic titles such as "Weep for Your Children," "The Hate Factory,"

---

* According to the *New York Times, On Golden Pond,* rated PG, "includes some slightly vulgar words in its dialogue." (Vincent Canby, "Fonda at His Peak in 'On Golden Pond,'" *New York Times,* 4 Dec. 1981: C10.)

and "Is Humanism Molesting Your Child?" They purchased advertisements in local newspapers with chilling warnings like

> SECULAR HUMANISM cannot survive in daylight.
> Become informed and pass the word.
> PROTECT YOUR CHILDREN! Call 799-0217 or 763-5661[54]

and

> SECULAR HUMANISM! WHAT IS IT?—
> MARION COUNTY CITIZENS FOR MORALITY WILL SHOW THE FILM
> "LET THEIR EYES BE OPENED." SEE THE FULL SCOPE OF THIS
> UNGODLY, UNAMERICAN PHILOSOPHY BEING TAUGHT IN PUBLIC
> SCHOOLS ACROSS AMERICA. PARENTS AND CONCERNED CITIZENS
> ARE URGED TO ATTEND—at QUINCY'S STEAK HOUSE, 2617 E. Silver
> Springs Blvd.[55]

Angry parents' groups agitated to remove depraved books like *Catcher in the Rye* and *Brave New World* from school libraries and classroom curricula. In Branson, Missouri, a *Sports Illustrated* swimsuit edition was returned to the publisher in a brown paper bag. According to the American Library Association, there were attempts to remove, restrict, or deny access to 148 different books in thirty-four states during the first half of 1981. Lest one conclude that such actions amounted to censorship, Terry Todd, national chairman of the Stop Textbook Censorship committee, explained that secular humanists were the true censors, since they had substituted "humanist" literature for "decent" books like *The House of Seven Gables, A Midsummer Night's Dream,* and *Huckleberry Finn.**[56]

In various brochures, films, and pamphlets, parents learned that secular humanism "'brainwashed'" students to accept suicide, abortion, and euthanasia. It encouraged children to lie, fostered "'socialistic'" thinking, and conditioned them to think that there was no such thing as right or wrong.[57] It was responsible for crime, drug abuse, pornography, masturbation, prostitution, incest, the decline of American

---

* "Decent books." Hawthorne, Twain, and Shakespeare, all of whom had been censored in their lifetimes by crusading moralists, were no doubt furiously knocking their skulls against the walls of their respective coffins.

power, and "one-world socialist government."[58] According to one pamphlet, secular humanism even caused "stomach aches, headaches, nightmares or other similar complaints and/or disorders that cannot be accounted for."[59]

"Two years ago I didn't even know what secular humanism was," said parent Joy Cook of Blunt, South Dakota. "Now I realize you can be a humanist without knowing it and that there are humanists doing everything."[60]

On the legislative front, Senator Orrin Hatch took up John Conlan's crusade and succeeded in inserting an amendment into the Education for Economic Security Act that prohibited the use of certain federal funds for "any course of instruction the substance of which is secular humanism." But Hatch neglected to define the notoriously Jell-O-like doctrine, so the sticky task trickled down to the Department of Education. But the department also dodged the Jell-O, so the requirement oozed on, still undefined, to local school boards and then quietly expired the following year without effect.[61]

Judge W. Brevard Hand, "Defender of the Constitution and Religious Liberty"

Was there no one with the will, the fortitude, and the shrewd intellect to defy the fearsome onslaught of secular humanism? There was. The Honorable William Brevard Hand, federal district judge of Mobile, Alabama, was a "pleasant, courtly member of the local gentry who runs his courtroom competently and courteously."[62] U.S. Attorney Jeff Sessions, who later became a U.S. senator (R-AL) and ranking Republican on the Senate Judiciary Committee, called Judge Hand a "superb constitutional scholar" whose "integrity is above reproach."* Another lawyer described Judge Hand as a defender of a *"Gone with the Wind*

---

* Before winning his Senate seat, Sessions failed in his own attempt to become a federal judge because senators accused him of calling the NAACP "un-American" and "Communist-inspired" and to his labeling a white civil rights lawyer "a traitor to his race." (United States Senate Committee on the Judiciary, *Nomination of Jefferson B. Sessions III, to be U.S. District Judge for the Southern District of Alabama* [Washington, DC: United States Senate, 1987]: 30, 66, 339.)

ideology, fighting for the oppressed, underdog white Southerner whose culture is being undermined by integrationists and by technocratic central government."

In a 1983 school prayer case, Judge Hand became a hero of the religious right for boldly ruling that while the Constitution prohibited the U.S. Congress from establishing a religion, it did not prohibit the state of Alabama from doing so. In his decision, Hand irrelevantly claimed that the public schools were "rife with efforts at teaching or encouraging secular humanism—all without opposition from any other ethic— to such an extent that it becomes a brainwashing effort." During a preliminary hearing, Hand also stated that the courts had ignored "the religions of atheism, materialism, agnosticism, communism and socialism" and asked, "If the state cannot teach or advance Christianity, how can it teach or advance the Antichrist?"

Hand's brazen disdain for Supreme Court precedent earned his ruling second place in the list of the "Ten Worst Non-Supreme Court Decisions"[63] by legal historian Bernard Schwartz.* It also provoked a stern smack-down by the U.S. Court of Appeals. The Supreme Court declined to review the case after the appeals ruling.

Unbowed, Hand tilted at the same windmill from the opposite direction four years later. In 1987, six hundred Alabama parents backed by Pat Robertson's 700 Club sued the Board of School Commissioners of Mobile County for violating the First Amendment by distributing forty-four textbooks that promoted "the religion of secular humanism." In order to determine the merits of the case, Judge Hand judiciously listened to a number of "expert" witnesses, such as conservative writer Russell Kirk. Kirk had written a book titled *The Assault on Religion,* which he happened to have dedicated to "Judge W. Brevard Hand, defender of the Constitution and religious liberty."[64] After the testimony,

---

* First place went to the 1859 Mississippi Supreme Court. In rejecting the cross-state inheritance claims of a freed slave in Ohio, the court determined that black people occupied an "intermediate place between the irrational animal and the white man."

The justices expressed concern that should the state of Ohio grant citizenship to "the chimpanzee or the ourang-out-ang (the most respectable of the monkey tribe)," Mississippi would be forced to honor the primates' property rights—a classic slippery-slope argument. (The court did not elucidate the reasoning behind its praise for the "ourang-out-ang.")

Judge Hand found himself to be in agreement with Mr. Kirk and with his own opinion in the 1983 school prayer case. He concluded that secular humanism was in fact a religion and banned all forty-four textbooks, though he later pardoned four home economics books on condition that the secular humanist bits be removed.

The U.S. Court of Appeals smacked Hand down once again. At that point, the plaintiffs realized that Hand's "superb constitutional scholarship" didn't stand much chance in the secular humanist-controlled Supreme Court, and they declined to appeal.

And with that victory, the once mighty religion of Secular Humanism sank into decline, gradually disappearing from church sermons, newspaper ads, court dockets, and news reports until there was nothing left but a clammy residue. Ask anyone under the age of thirty what they think about secular humanism, and you will likely get a blank look. Paradoxically, the most obvious remnant of the hysteria is a still-active organization called the Council for Secular Humanism. Humanist Paul Kurtz founded the organization in 1980 to exploit the publicity generated by the right-wing hysteria. The organization's Facebook page has 1,126 fans.

Secular Humanism's Spawn

But though the dream has faded, the war against secular humanism left a rich legacy that conservative strategists have tapped again and again. Bill O'Reilly's "progressive secularists," for example, are direct descendents of the mythical secular humanists of yore. Though the progressive secularists focused on Christmas spirit rather than textbook indoctrination, they shared the secular humanists' objective of a "brave new progressive world" and their penchant for Christian persecution. Indeed, many influential secular humanists, including the ACLU, the activist judges, and the liberal media, evidently converted to progressive secularism en masse sometime in the 1990s, joining forces with new secular schemers like George Soros, Peter Lewis, and Media Matters.org.

In 2010, Glenn Beck stripped O'Reilly's progressive secularists of their secularism, leaving them bare "progressives." He told listeners:

> What we're talking about is an ideological movement that has set its sights on the destruction of the Constitution and the fundamental transformation of our Republic. It is called the Progressive Movement.[65]

Beck's progressives, led by Obama, Pelosi, and documentary director Michael Moore, are even more vicious and ideologically amorphous than their predecessors. Combining the revolutionary ambitions of 1950s communists with the repressive tendencies of the 1970s secular humanists, the progressives don't actually stand for anything except the destruction of all that is good in America. Every cause they champion is just part of their master plan to seize power and tyrannize everyone. But that's a story for another chapter.

More broadly, conservatives found in the chimera of secular humanism and the IRS desegregation threat a new strategy for extending and mobilizing their political base: invent a liberal conspiracy that indoctrinates children with immoral, anti-Christian ideas. They have repeatedly exploited the fear of malicious brainwashing to provoke outraged hostility toward anything they oppose, including women's rights, gay rights, sex education, pornography, and the teaching of evolution, as well as to incite resentment against a certain president who "may be a Marxist."[66] In the process, they began to hew a new fissure in American society, transforming modest political divisions into a ferocious unbridled conflict between white Christian conservatives and their imaginary persecutors on the left. The fissure has grown steadily through the decades, exacerbating factionalism and undermining mutual trust until it reached a point where the president of the United States cannot speak to America's students about the value of education without provoking a nationwide paroxysm of paranoid hysteria.

3

MORE OR LESS NORMAL PEOPLE

Plumbing the Paranoia of Persecution Politics

Years ago, it meant something to be crazy. Now everyone's crazy.
—Charles Manson

A T POINTS IN THE BOOK, we'll take a break from our wildlife safari to ask what it all means and why it's happening. For instance, in this chapter, we will talk about the phenomenon of social paranoia and its relation to persecution politics. While you may be tempted to charge ahead to ogle more right-wing craziness, I urge you to be patient and consider my mostly brilliant and penetrating commentary. These chapters are the glue that binds the pages together, and they seek to provide the answers we're looking for.

The word *paranoia* was given to us by the Greeks, who gave us many other great words like *chaos, asparagus,* and *Philadelphia.* The Greeks seem to have had a particular knack for medical words, perhaps because of the influence of the famous Greek physician Hippocrates, known as the father of medicine. *Para* is Greek for "beside," and *nous* is Greek for "mind." Thus, *paranoia* literally meant "beside one's mind," i.e., nuts. Hippocrates used the term to describe the delirium associated with a high fever.

The concept disappeared during the Dark Ages, along with many other clever Greek ideas. Medieval health care providers often regarded madness as a manifestation of demonic influence and treated it with holy water, the sign of the cross, foul-smelling brews, and exuberant Latin curses; for example, "Thou lustful and stupid one . . . thou wrinkled beast, thou mangy beast, thou beast of all beasts the most beastly

. . . I cast thee down, O Tartarean boor, into the infernal kitchen! . . . Loathsome cobbler . . . dingy collier . . . perfidious boar . . . envious crocodile . . . malodorous drudge . . . wounded basilisk" and so on.[1]

The Europeans went on cursing demons for a millennium or so before finally concluding in the 1700s that Hippocrates might have been onto something after all. By the late 1800s, they had moved beyond the Greeks, establishing the field of psychiatry. The new psychiatrists reworked the old Greek concept of paranoia by narrowing its application to a specific kind of delusion in which the victim believes that he is being persecuted. They diagnosed the affliction as a symptom of psychosis, yet another Greek word. To the ancient Greeks, *psychosis* meant "animation, the spirit of life," but psychiatrists redefined it less poetically as a mental derangement characterized by loss of contact with reality.[2]

"He Hates (Persecutes) Me"

Building on the psychiatric tradition in the early 1900s, Sigmund Freud chose a psychotic German judge named Daniel Paul Schreber for the subject of his seminal analysis of paranoia, *The Schreber Case*. Among many other delusions, Daniel Schreber believed that his physician, Dr. Flechsig, was gradually transforming him into a woman in order to sexually abuse him and that God planned to inseminate him with the seeds of a new human race once the transformation was complete. Freud, being Freud, concluded that Schreber's paranoia was a manifestation of repressed homosexual lust for his father.[3]

[WARNING: THE FOLLOWING PARAGRAPH CONTAINS A HIGH CONCENTRATION OF WHAT IS POPULARLY KNOWN AS PSYCHOBABBLE.
TIMID READERS ARE ENCOURAGED TO SKIP IT. YOU MAY SAFELY READ THE FOOTNOTE, HOWEVER, AS IT IS AMUSING AND SCATOLOGICAL.]

According to Freud's interpretation, Schreber had transferred his latent homosexual longings for his father onto his physician, Dr. Flechsig. But since these desires were deeply disturbing to Schreber, he repressed them and subconsciously concluded, "I do not *love* him— Indeed I *hate* him." The feeling of hatred, however, was also disturbing to Schreber because it contradicted the love that he actually felt for Flechsig and, indirectly, his father. To compensate for the resulting anxiety, Schreber then projected his own feelings of hatred onto Flechsig. Freud wrote, "*He hates* (persecutes) *me,* which will entitle me to hate him." Finally, Schreber's sexually frustrated subconscious directed his thwarted libidinal impulse inward, resulting in narcissism (i.e., self-love) and the megalomaniacal delusion that God would impregnate him with the seeds of a new human race.*

HAVING DEMONSTRATED his irrefutable conclusion in the Schreber case, Freud acknowledged that one would need to consult a large number of cases in order to confidently apply the findings to paranoia in general. He then proceeded to confidently apply the findings to paranoia in general.

Freud's analysis was a big hit in psychoanalytic circles, and paranoid schizophrenics were diagnosed with repressed homosexuality for much of the twentieth century until the theory was eventually tossed for lack of evidence and general silliness. Modern psychiatrists now regard severe paranoia as a schizophrenic disorder and treat it with antipsychotic medication and cognitive behavioral therapy, though some psychoanalysts still follow Freud in rooting for the source of paranoia in the depths of the subconscious. In particular, they often return to the concept of *projection* that Freud described in *The Schreber Case.* Projection is a defense mechanism whereby the mind deals with an uncomfortable impulse by pretending that it belongs to someone else. The uncomfortable impulse could be homosexual lust, as Freud diagnosed in the Schreber case, or it could be physical aggression, dishonesty, hatred, etc. A paranoiac with infidelity urges, for example, might irrationally believe that her lover was cheating on her, while a paranoiac with homicidal urges might imagine that others were trying to murder him.

But whether one leans toward the psychoanalysts or the psychiatrists, the psychosis model of paranoia doesn't really explain the polit-

---

*Schreber eventually concluded that God also lusted after him and was the true culprit behind his sexual transformation. God's sexual appetites were a bit sadistic, however. For example, He would often torture poor Schreber by inducing in him an urgent need to defecate precisely the moment that someone had occupied the bathroom.

ical paranoia that has been sweeping the country. Bill O'Reilly and Glenn Beck may lose touch with reality at points, but neither they nor the majority of their viewers are clinically psychotic. Most of the men and women who believe in secret Marxist conspiracies and plots to destroy Christmas are ordinary people capable of maintaining jobs and personal relationships free from crippling psychoses. Moreover, the popular growth of persecution politics suggests that even if some people are psychologically predisposed to paranoid ideas, external factors must be exploiting those predispositions. Masses of people didn't suddenly go crazy at the same time by sheer chance.

"The Paranoid Style in American Politics"

In 1964, eminent historian Richard Hofstadter sought to distinguish the social phenomenon of mass paranoia from the individual psychoses that Freud studied. In a famous essay published in *Harper's Magazine,* Hofstadter labeled the former "the paranoid style in American politics." He explained:

> I call it the paranoid style simply because no other word adequately evokes the sense of heated exaggeration, suspiciousness, and conspiratorial fantasy that I have in mind. In using the expression "paranoid style" I am not speaking in a clinical sense, but borrowing a clinical term for other purposes.[4]

As Hofstadter observed, the paranoid style has relevance precisely because the people who practice it are not clinically insane. It influences "more or less normal people" in large numbers. Paranoid schizophrenia is a disease of the mind. What Hofstadter called the paranoid style is a disease of society.

It's not a new phenomenon. Hofstadter documented the Illuminati and Freemason conspiracy theories that raged in the early years of the republic and the anti-Catholic paranoia that exploded in the mid-1800s.

But he focused primarily on the anticommunist paranoia of his day, particularly the conspiracy theories of Joseph McCarthy in the 1950s and the John Birch Society in the 1960s. Hofstadter argued that the anticommunists' paranoid style differed from previous instances in that adherents of the earlier movements felt that though the nation was threatened by foreign powers, upstanding American citizens still possessed their own country, whereas twentieth-century anticommunists believed that America had "been largely taken away from them and their kind."[5] In their view, communists had deeply infiltrated the country, occupying "the very centers of American power" and ravaging the nation "step by step, by will and intention." Joseph McCarthy named top government officials as conspirators, including secretaries of state George Marshall and Dean Acheson; JBS founder Robert Welch implicated former presidents Truman and Eisenhower.

The secular humanism hysteria of the 1970s and 1980s completed the migration from foreign to domestic enemies that Hofstadter described in 1964. Though domestic subversives played leading roles in the communist conspiracy theories, the primary threat was still a foreign power. Anticommunists feared Moscow, much as anti-Catholics feared the pope and anti-Masons feared international societies. But the secular humanists were home grown, serving no higher power than themselves—at least no higher mortal power. They already controlled the levers of power and influence, including the media, the schools, the courts, and the White House. This perception that domestic enemies had subjugated the country persisted long after the secular humanists faded away; these days it manifests in Tea Party battle cries to "take our country back."

The similarities between the communist and humanist conspiracy theories are not coincidental. Before joining the Moral Majority, anti-humanist Tim LaHaye was active in the JBS and inherited many of the organization's conspiracist ideas.[6] Nor was LaHaye the only religious right founder who began his career as a red-baiter. Jerry Falwell claimed that Martin Luther King Jr. was a communist subversive and that the Soviets had teemed up with Satan to promote public school desegregation. He proclaimed in a sermon:

The true Negro does not want integration. He realizes his potential is far better among his own race. Who then is propagating this terrible thing? First of all, we see the hand of Moscow in the background. We see the Devil himself behind it.[7]

Thus, in the 1970s, right-wing leaders like LaHaye and Falwell simply swapped one conspiratorial enemy for another, replacing the communist menace with the secular humanist menace. Some proponents were explicit about the exchange. At a 1977 conference for charismatic Christians, one speaker warned, "Secular humanism is more of a threat than the anti-Christ or communism."[8]

Projecting Intolerance

There is one significant difference between Hofstadter's anticommunists and the antihumanists of the 1970s and 1980s. Antihumanism became popular after the civil rights movement and amid the feminist and gay rights movements. Many of its proponents had been accused of racism, sexism, prejudice against homosexuals, and fascist tendencies. They were on the losing end of an emerging national ethic that reviled discrimination and intolerance, and this dynamic informed their paranoia in the form of projection.

Alluding to Freud's theory, Hofstadter wrote, "It is hard to resist the conclusion that this enemy is on many counts the projection of the self."[9] Hofstadter's use of projection is somewhat looser than Freud's. Where Freud described projection as a defense mechanism in which the mind deals with an uncomfortable impulse by pretending that it belongs to someone else, Hofstadter argued that political paranoiacs attribute "both the ideal and the unacceptable aspects of the self" to their enemies. That is to say, they imagine that their enemies have qualities to which they secretly aspire as well as qualities that they subconsciously abhor in themselves.

Thus, Hofstadter observed that paranoid organizations often emulated their enemies' idealized qualities. The Ku Klux Klan imitated

Catholic liturgy by dressing in priestly robes and developing elaborate rituals. The JBS masked its operations using front groups and secret cells, much like the supposed communist subversives. Conversely, Hofstadter suggested that conspiracists also projected their own unwanted and repressed sexual impulses into dark fantasies about bizarre sexual and sadomasochistic practices that they attributed to Masons, Catholics, Jews, and so on.

Postcommunist conspiracy theorists also seem to project both ideal and unwanted aspects of themselves onto their enemies. For instance, religious-right leaders have imitated their visions of secular youth indoctrination by expanding Christian schools to produce what one evangelical leader bluntly called an "army that is going to take the future," and have sought to replicate secular humanists' imagined political muscle by deliberately placing Christians in "places of influence and power."[10]

Likewise, modern conservatives also project undesirable impulses onto their enemies. Much as nineteenth-century conspiracy theorists accused Masons and Catholics of deviant sexual practices, many of today's paranoid conservatives obsess over the wildly promiscuous and disturbing sexual behaviors that they attribute to gays and lesbians, which we'll discuss in the next chapter.

But what really sets the modern paranoid style apart from that of Hofstadter's anticommunists is the new right's eagerness to project offenses like bigotry and intolerance onto its perceived enemies—the very offenses of which conservatives have been accused ever since the civil rights era. The great secular humanist conspiracy offers a perfect example: right-wing leaders represented secular humanism as an intolerant state religion that abridged the constitutionally protected civil rights of Christians, reversing the accusation that opponents had been leveling at religious fundamentalists. The Christians were not intolerant of secular beliefs, they argued; it was the fanatical secularists who were intolerant of Christian beliefs. We will see this pattern again and again as we continue our tour of right-wing persecution politics: affirmative action is "reverse racism;" secular Christmas greetings constitute "hate crimes;" gay rights "discriminates" against Christians; political correctness is "fascist;" and so on.

Conservatives have even translated their projections of liberal bigotry into another form of imitation by establishing their own institutions to protect the rights of the underprivileged and oppressed; that is to say, white Christian conservatives. These include the Christian Anti-Defamation Commission and the Christian Defense League (which mimic the Jewish Anti-Defamation League);* the American Civil Rights Union and the American Civil Rights Institute (which mimic the ACLU), the National Association for the Advancement of White People (an NAACP imitator founded by ex-Klansman David Duke); and a couple of amalgamations, the Christian Civil Liberties Union and the Catholic League for Religious and Civil Rights.†

Indeed, the modern promoters of the paranoid style surpassed their predecessors by inventing enemies who consist almost entirely of projected attributes. Previous conspiracy theories were at least founded on real organizations. An international society of Masons existed, and its members conducted politics and business in their lodges. The Roman Catholic Church is a powerful global institution that has historically sought to suppress Protestantism. Communism is a well-defined ideology, and many of its adherents, including Stalin, sought to export the revolution to the United States. But secular humanism had no lodges, no popes, no doctrines, and no members. It was a blank canvas on which conservatives could paint whatever they pleased. And so they painted a distorted replica of the ugly picture that modern society had so recently painted of them. They painted *intolerance*. What bound secular humanists together—atheists, socialists, feminists, homosexuals, civil rights activists, environmentalists, internationalists, and so on—

---

* The Christian Defense League was the brainchild of a former Klansman who implored in a form letter, "The NAACP represents the negro; the ADL [Anti-Defamation League] represents the Jews; who represents YOU—the white Christian?" (D. Boylan, "A League of Their Own: A Look Inside the Christian Defense League," *Cuban Information Archives*, 1 Jan. 2004, http://cuban-exile.com/doc_026-050/doc0046.html.)

† Jon Stewart on Christian persecution: "Does the Christian persecution complex have an expiration date? Because . . . uh . . . you've all been in charge pretty much since . . . uh . . . what was that guy's name . . . Constantine. He converted in, what was it, 312 A.D. I'm just saying, enjoy your success. (Jon Stewart, "Headlines: Hot Docket," *The Daily Show*, 28 Jun. 2005, http://www.thedailyshow.com/watch/tue-june-28-2005/headlines---hot-docket.)

was alleged hatred and intolerance for Christianity. Secular humanism's so-called tenets, from evolution to moral relativism, were simply the means by which they persecuted the Christians they despised. Secular humanism was not an institution upon which Christian intolerance was projected; it was the very projection of Christian intolerance.

This counterattack demarcates the new paranoid style of modern conservatism from the old paranoid style that Hofstadter described. Of Bill O'Reilly's three tactics, the slippery slope and the conspiracy theory were inherited from the previous generation of anticommunist conspiracists; but the third tactic, persecution, is new. It was born of and in reaction to the civil rights movement. Over the past forty years, right-wing conservatives have applied the new persecution rhetoric in every conceivable context, from gun rights to gay marriage to health care. This frequent, repetitive projection of intolerance constitutes what I call persecution politics.

This new paranoid style has been a resounding success. The last time political paranoia reached so deeply into American mass consciousness was at the height of McCarthy's Red Scare. The John Birch Society, which Hofstadter focused on, never really escaped the fringe. It had from 60,000 to 100,000 members at its peak.[11] Other right-wing publications of the day had a combined circulation of about a million.[12] By contrast, Bill O'Reilly and Glenn Beck have nightly audiences in the millions, and their books are always number one nonfiction best sellers. Beck has estimated his combined media footprint from television, radio, Web, and publishing to be 30 million per month.[13] Though he's prone to exaggeration, there is no question that he is a media powerhouse who would incite the envy of the old JBS leaders whose ideas he inherited.

But what we have yet to understand is the appeal of the paranoid style that has made it so popular. Hofstadter told us what it was, but he didn't explain *why* it was. To reach that understanding, we'll first need to plunge back into history for a richer appreciation of the phenomenon of projection in right-wing politics.

4

ATTACK OF THE GAY FASCISTS

The Religious Right Battles Homosexual Plots to Abolish Marriage, Corrupt Children, and Discriminate against Straight People

> *I just think people should be very free with sex—they should draw the line at goats.*
>
> —Elton John

Q: What do ducks, goats, donkeys, turtles, dogs, and dolphins have in common?

A: They'll be legally allowed to marry people unless same-sex marriage is stopped.

SO SAID JAMES DOBSON, founder of the religious right juggernaut, Focus on the Family: "It is certain that some self-possessed judge somewhere will soon rule that three men, or three women, can marry. Or five men and two women . . . Or marriage between daddies and little girls? Or marriage between a man and his donkey?"[1]

So said Bill O'Reilly: "Laws that you think are in stone—they're gonna evaporate, man. You'll be able to marry a goat—you mark my words!"[2] And later, "You can marry 18 people, you can marry a duck."[3]

So said Sen. Rick Santorum (R-PA), more or less: "Every society in the history of man has upheld the institution of marriage as a bond between a man and a woman . . . It's not, you know, man on child, man on dog, or whatever the case may be."[*4]

---

* "Man on dog." Santorum's remark prompted his flustered Associated Press interviewer to blurt out, "I'm sorry, I didn't think I was going to talk about 'man on dog' with a United States senator, it's sort of freaking me out."

So said Sen. John Cornyn (R-TX): "It does not affect your daily life very much if your neighbor marries a box turtle. But that does not mean it is right . . . Now you must raise your children up in a world where that union of man and box turtle is on the same legal footing as man and wife."*[5]

O'Reilly and friends have concluded that people may soon be able to legally wed donkeys and dolphins because they fail to distinguish between some change and *any* change. If you allow men to marry men and women to marry women, they reason, then you must drop all restrictions—you must allow anyone to marry anything. The question, given this line of reasoning, is why did they stop at goats and box turtles? Among my childhood friends, if one of us were to say something like, "I love this cinnamon roll," another would inevitably and hilariously rejoin, "Well, why don't you marry it then?" And indeed, if same-sex marriage becomes legal, why not? If a child of eight wants to walk down the aisle with his frosted pastry, who is to say no? The Supreme Court upheld corporations' First Amendment rights. Why should they not have the right to marry as well? (It would give a whole new meaning to the phrase "married to the company.") Soon enough, people will be able to marry Beethoven's Ninth Symphony, the Empire State Building, the theory of evolution, and the word *lugubrious*. Mark my words, you'll one day be able to marry your own left butt cheek.

All hail the mighty logic of the slippery-slope argument. There is nothing that you cannot link down some twisty trail of hypothetical reasoning. Right-wing slippery-slopists have predicted that gay marriage will lead to crime, poverty, drug abuse, teen pregnancy, school failure, and health problems.[6] They've warned that it will result in the legalization of child molestation, the collapse of Social Security and the health care system, the end of religious freedom, the destruction of democracy, and assorted wrathful-God catastrophes.[7]

Same-sex marriage opponents are particularly obsessed with slippery-slope arguments because an increasing number of Americans

---

* The box turtle was written into a speech that Cornyn's office provided to the *Washington Post*. He claims that he did not use it in the actual speech. The turtle was not available for comment.

don't view homosexuality as morally abhorrent, and it's difficult to come up with other reasons why homosexual men and women shouldn't be allowed to marry one another. According to an October 2009 poll, 39 percent of Americans support same-sex marriage and 57 percent support civil unions.[8] Even those who disapprove of homosexuality may not be sufficiently motivated to combat a practice that does not directly affect their lives. For instance, 92 percent of Iowans polled six months after the Iowa Supreme Court legalized same-sex marriage concluded that the ruling had brought no real change to their lives.[9] In the face of such apathy, right-wing leaders commonly promote frightening visions of social disaster, not to mention bizarre human-animal pairings, in order to scare their constituents into action.

This approach is not entirely new. In 1872, the Supreme Court of Tennessee refused to recognize an interracial marriage performed in Mississippi out of concern that "we might have in Tennessee the father living with his daughter, the son with the mother, the brother with his sister, in lawful wedlock, because they had formed such relations in a state or country where they were not prohibited. The Turk or the Mohammedan, with his numerous wives, may establish his harem at the doors of the capitol, and we are without remedy."[10] Tennessee's anti-miscegenation laws were finally overturned in 1967. So far, the state has managed to avoid recognizing incestuous and polygamous marriages.

In Jerry Falwell's critique of *Brown v. Board of Education,* he fretted that school desegregation would lead to interracial marriage. In this prediction, he was correct. But Falwell also predicted that interracial marriage would mean the destruction of the white race.[11] According to reports, the white race is still hanging in there.

The Gay Agenda

But the white race and Tennessee's marriage laws never had to contend with the fearsome power of the Gay Agenda. As with secular humanism, the gay agenda is an empty nondoctrine invented by right-wing

Christians. In 1992, a small fundamentalist church produced a graphic video called *The Gay Agenda* about the deviant sexual practices of homosexuals. In the video, a white-haired and distinguished Dr. Stanley Monteith informed viewers that average homosexuals had between three hundred and five hundred sexual partners in a lifetime and regularly ingested fecal material.[12] He enlightened them concerning the exotic arts of "rimming," "fisting," and "golden showers." The video, which should perhaps have been titled *Gays Gone Wild,* featured explicit scenes from a gay pride parade as well as a march by the infamous North American Man/Boy Love Association, with a voiceover that announced, "Homosexuals have a long history of focusing on youth."[13] The lurid footage and gross-out descriptions of disturbing sexual practices offer a textbook example of Richard Hofstadter's description of conspiracists' preoccupation with illicit sex.

James Dobson's Focus on the Family and Pat Robertson's 700 Club distributed the video to evangelicals eager to witness homosexuality in the flesh. Pentagon officials and congressional leaders reviewed it while evaluating Bill Clinton's "Don't Ask, Don't Tell" policy. They might have been surprised to learn that Dr. Monteith was a former member of the John Birch Society.[14] Monteith would later declare that AIDS was a "genocidal program" developed by the New World Order to kill blacks and Latinos in order to fulfill the prophesies of Revelation. But lest anyone doubt Monteith's credibility, before he retired to pursue the New World Order full time, he was a real medical doctor.[15]

The Gay Agenda has been menacing America ever since. There are videos like *Gay Agenda in Schools.* ("You may be asking yourself, how will same-sex marriage affect my family? Well, based on the evidence, everything changes when same-sex marriage becomes legal.")[16] There are books like *The Gay Agenda: It's Dividing the Family, the Church, and a Nation.* ("Beware, administrators, teachers, students, and parents! The gay lifestyle is being actively promoted in books, by speakers, in seminar themes . . . in fact, it's everywhere.")[17] And *The Homosexual Agenda: Exposing the Principal Threat to Religious Freedom Today.* ("Whether SpongeBob is actually homosexual or not is irrelevant.")[18] And of course there are speeches and sermons and blogs and many,

many letters to editors. ("The 'Gay Agenda' is far reaching and encompasses every other liberal agenda there is.")[19] Justice Antonin Scalia even alluded to the gay agenda in a brooding Supreme Court dissent in which he grumbled that the Court had "signed on to the so-called homosexual agenda."*[20]

Of course, the gay agenda is not just about rimming and fisting and frolicking in fountains of urine. These folks mean business. According to James Dobson, the primary objective of the homosexual activists' "master plan" is "the utter destruction of the family." Subsidiary goals include "muzzling of the clergy and Christian media," "granting of special privileges and rights in the law," "overturning laws prohibiting pedophilia," and "indoctrination of children."[21] What about legal recognition of monogamous love between two members of the same sex? Don't be naïve. According to Dobson, who as a psychologist knows a lot about homosexuality, "most gays and lesbians do not want to marry each other." Same-sex marriage, he explained, is a ruse. The gay agenda's true intention is to destroy marriage altogether. That way, everyone could enjoy the benefits of marriage "without limiting the number of partners or their gender."[22]

Dobson's description of the future of marriage sounds like some sort of depraved communal living arrangement, as if the casts of *Queer Eye,* *The L-Word,* and *Big Love* were to move in with *The Brady Bunch,* resulting in a new swimming pool and a radical redesign of Mr. Brady's den. Of course, we all know what communal living will do to the nation's capitalist economy. Rep. Steve King (R-IA) certainly knows:

> If there's a push for a socialist society where the foundations of individual rights and liberties are undermined and everybody is thrown together living collectively off one pot of resources earned by everyone, this is

---

* The gay agenda according to Jon Stewart: "Gay marriage, civil rights protection, Fleet Week expanded to Fleet Year, Federal Emergency Management Agency (FEMA) assistance for when it's raining men, Kathy Griffin to host everything and a nationwide ban on pleated pants." (Jon Stewart, "The Most Immature Montage Ever," *The Daily Show,* 14 Aug. 2007, http://www.thedailyshow.com/watch/tue-august-14-2007/the-most-immature-montage-ever?videoId=91535.)

one of the goals they have to go to, same sex marriage, because it has to plow through marriage in order to get to their goal . . . Not only is it a radical social idea, it is a purely socialist concept in the final analysis.[23]

So basically, the gay agenda is about establishing a new social order in which the once proud United States collapses into a degenerate pile of socialistic communes-from-hell in which men, women, children, and promiscuous ducks spend their days eating one another's feces. Giddy up.

Save Our Children

So we've got the slippery slope to bestiality and polyandrous communes. We've got the secret plot, commonly known as the gay agenda, that guides the nation down the incremental steps to *Sodom and Gomorrah II: Stalin's Revenge*. What about persecution? Obviously, the gay agenda is hostile to Christianity, but to fully appreciate the suffering of traditional Americans who have been victimized by the gay agenda, we will need to step back in time. It begins, as usual, with the children.

In chapter 2, we heard conservatives complain that secular humanists had indoctrinated their children with anti-Christian propaganda, and we noted that the right has continued to cry "Pied Piper" in a variety of contexts. The most fearsome Pied Piper in right-wing imagination is the Militant Homosexual. The Militant Homosexual has been corrupting American children for almost as long as the Secular Humanist, and he has maintained his potency long after the Secular Humanist's prominence receded.

Unlike the secular humanists, militant homosexuals were not invented by theologians. In 1969, a police raid on a Greenwich Village gay bar called the Stonewall Inn sparked a series of riots that mixed violent resistance with flamboyant kick lines. One participant later published a firsthand account of the Stonewall Riots in a book called *The Gay Militants*. The riots catalyzed the formation of confrontational gay rights organizations, such as the Gay Liberation Front and the Gay Activists Alliance, which newspapers described as militant homosexual groups.

The right wing did not seem overly concerned about homosexuals throwing bricks at New York cops, perhaps because they had already given up on New York City as brimstone fodder, but when Miami introduced an ordinance in 1977 to guarantee equal employment and housing rights for homosexuals, the nascent right-wing myth machine roared into action. It began with a beauty queen.

Anita Bryant, former Miss Oklahoma, former mediocre pop singer, spokesperson for the Florida Citrus Commission, *Good Housekeeping* magazine's "Most Admired Woman in America," was very concerned about discrimination, so she sent a letter to the Dade County commissioners who were to vote on the proposed ordinance. The letter stated:

> I have never condoned nor teach my children discrimination against anyone because of their race or religion, but if this ordinance amendment is allowed to become law, you will in fact be infringing upon my right or rather DISCRIMINATING against me as a citizen and mother to teach my children and set examples or point to others as examples of God's moral code as stated in the Holy Scriptures.*[24]

Bryant's rhetorical judo move to represent herself as the aggrieved victim of discrimination was one of the earliest instances of the Freudian projection that would become a staple of persecution politics. It was not Bryant who was discriminating against homosexuals; it was the militant homosexuals who were discriminating against her. You can

---

* The Catholic archdiocese of Miami also opposed the ordinance. Speaking at the hearing, a representative of the archdiocese argued that allowing homosexuals to be hired as teachers was like letting "a fox in the chicken coop." The archdiocese would later admit to having allowed priests accused of child abuse to continue to work with children. ("Days without Sunshine: Anita Bryant's Anti-Gay Crusade," *Stonewall Library and Archives Exhibition,* 6 Jun. 2007, http://www.stonewall-library.org/anita/; Daniel de Vise and Jay Weaver, "Church Kept Accused Priest on Job," *Miami Herald,* 23 Oct. 2003: 1A; Fred Grimm, "Priest was protected, not the children," *Miami Herald,* 4 Apr. 2010: 1B.)

almost hear Freud murmuring from his funeral urn, *"They hate* (perse-cute) *me,* which will entitle me to hate them."

Bryant's suffering, however, did not impress the Dade County com-missioners, who voted 5-3 in favor of the ordinance. But Bryant was not ready to give up her right as a mother to discriminate against the homosexuals who were discriminating against her. She campaigned for a referendum to challenge the ordinance, declaring:

> No one has a human right to corrupt our children . . . Before I yield to this insidious attack on God and his laws, and on parents and their rights to protect children, I will lead a crusade to stop it as this country has never seen before.[25]

Naturally, Bryant called her crusade Save Our Children.

Over the course of the campaign, Bryant reinvented the Militant Ho-mosexual as a devious and deviant conspirator:

> What we are standing up against is militant homosexuals who are highly financed, highly organized, and who were able to ramrod the amend-ment through in our city.[26]

The true objective of the militant homosexuals, according to Bryant, was not the right to hold jobs and buy houses. Since they were unable to reproduce biologically, their only hope of survival was "to recruit your children and teach them the virtue of becoming a homosexual."[27]

In addition to pioneering the projection strategy, Bryant also wrote the script for the slippery slope to bestiality, fretting that if the gays were granted rights, "Next we'll have to give rights to prostitutes and to people who sleep with St. Bernards and to nail-biters." The prospect of militant nailbiters and St. Bernardophiles unleashed on the streets of Miami was evidently even scarier than that of militant homosexuals. Thankfully, it has yet to occur, even though Miami homosexuals did eventually get their rights.

The Save Our Children campaign was an instant media hit. Bryant easily collected 64,000 signatures. Smelling an opportunity, Jerry

Falwell, Pat Robertson, Senator Jesse Helms, and other distinguished gentlemen of the right soon joined the fray. Falwell added his own insight into the character of militant homosexuals, who he claimed would "just as soon kill you as look at you."[28] Falwell shared the stage with Jack Wyrtzen, head of Word of Life International, who declared to a chorus of amens that if the ordinance were upheld, it could mean "the end of the United States of America."

The militant homosexuals fought back by militantly boycotting orange juice and sending Anita Bryant militant postcards that read "We are switching to prune juice, and we will send you the results."[29] They wore T-shirts with militant messages like "Squeeze a fruit for Anita."[30] Though Florida Citrus stood by her, Bryant felt the squeeze when the Singer Sewing Machine Company cancelled a syndicated television show that she was to host. In a press conference, she declared, "The blacklisting of Anita Bryant has begun,"[31] seemingly oblivious to the fact that she had championed the "blacklisting" of homosexuals. She would later declare herself to be the victim of "a national conspiracy to do away with Anita Bryant,"[32] seemingly oblivious to the fact that she had once again referred to herself in the third person.

Nonetheless, despite the "highly financed, highly organized" efforts of the militant homosexual conspiracy, Bryant's referendum succeeded in a landslide vote, winning by 69 percent. As with the campaign against the IRS desegregation effort, success did not cause the right wing to lower its opinion of the power of the conspirators. After the success of Save Our Children, the Militant Homosexual became more powerful than ever.

The Homosexual Explosion

Tim LaHaye, the humanist avenger and Moral Majority founder discussed in chapter 2, has a knack for writing conspiratorial screeds when the moment is ripe. His 1978 book, *The Unhappy Gays: What Everyone Should Know About Homosexuality,* documented "the homosexual explosion" taking place in America:

At the instigation of the pro-homosexual media, public schools, politi-cians in high places, and gay militants, the tidal wave of homosexuality that has reached enormous proportions today threatens the very exis-tence of a moral America."[33]

According to LaHaye, as soon as the "organized, militant" homosexual community achieved its goal of equal employment, homosexuals would infiltrate the nation's schools to prepare the nation's ripe young minds for gay brainwashing. He wrote:

> When all job discrimination for homosexuality is removed (and it will be if the silent majority remains silent), teachers can be expected to brainwash our children with the "blessings" of the unhappy gay life. Misery loves company, and you can expect homosexual teachers single-handedly to double the homosexual community within 10 years . . . Per-mitting homosexuals to orient young, impressionable minds toward homosexuality will be the bottom line in our culture. When we cross that line, I believe we will have descended to the ultimate in abomina-tions.*[34]

The Militant Homosexual and his ward, the Gay Agenda, have been oppressing American children ever since. In 1981, Jerry Falwell echoed Anita Bryant and Tim LaHaye in saying, "Please remember, homosex-uals do not reproduce! They recruit! And, many of them are after my children and your children."[35] Years later, Falwell became the object of international ridicule after outing Tinky Winky, the purple Teletubby:

> The character, whose voice is obviously that of a boy, has been found carrying a red purse in many episodes . . . He is purple—the gay-pride color; and his antenna is shaped like a triangle—the gay-pride symbol.[36]

---

* "Abominations." In addition to predicting the destruction of America and speculating about the sexual orientation of the Antichrist, LaHaye also offered helpful parenting tips, such as "Whenever a mother makes her son number one in her life, she begins to raise a pervert." (Tim LaHaye, *The Unhappy Gays: What Everyone Should Know About Homosexu-ality*, paperback [Wheaton, IL: Tyndale House, 1978]: 72.)

But to believers in the gay conspiracy, Falwell's accusation did not seem absurd. If the homosexuals control the media, and if they aim to recruit children, then they would naturally create gay characters to seduce America's toddlers. Indeed, Tinky Winky is only one of many children's characters that the religious right has accused of homosexual tendencies. *Sesame Street*'s Ernie and Bert, the *Lion King*'s Timon the meerkat and Pumbaa the warthog, and SpongeBob SquarePants are all suspect, not to mention the original tights-wearing dynamic duo, Batman and Robin. A 2005 video about tolerance that featured children's characters from Dora the Explorer to Clifford the Big Red Dog singing "We Are Family" sent the right wing into apoplexy. James Dobson called the video "pro-homosexual" and criticized it for "manipulating and potentially brainwashing kids."[37]

When the Militant Homosexual retired in the 1990s, the Gay Agenda took over his responsibilities and introduced devious new recruiting tactics. Among other conquests, the Gay Agenda infiltrated the American Library Association and contaminated school libraries with "pro-homosexual books" like *King and King,* a children's story about two princes who fall in love. One Wisconsin couple, upset by "the overt indoctrination of the gay agenda into our community youth," petitioned their local library to balance its gay propaganda with books that affirm "traditional heterosexual perspectives."[*][38] Rush Limbaugh's worst fears were confirmed when he discovered a "radical leftist marriage book" for children titled *How to Get Married . . . by Me, the Bride,* in which the narrator of the story declares, "You can marry your best friend or your teacher or your pet or your daddy, and sometimes you can marry a flower."[39] (Had Limbaugh read the book, he would have learned that the narrator is a know-it-all six-year-old with a number of comically confused ideas about marriage. Had he visited Amazon.com, he would have discovered that the "radical leftist" author has a history of brainwashing susceptible children. Her other children's books include *The*

---

[*] "Traditional heterosexual perspectives." Apparently, stories like "Snow White," "Sleeping Beauty," and "Cinderella" did not sufficiently affirm traditional heterosexual perspectives. Perhaps they wanted a story in which two princes fall in love and then die of AIDS as their kingdoms perish in a hail of brimstone. It could be called "Burn in Hell, Gay Kings!"

Jesus Storybook Bible, Baby's Hug-a-Bible, and *Old MacNoah Had an Ark.*)[40]

Gay Fascists

But the Militant Homosexual and the Gay Agenda are after more than America's children, who are only a means to an end. Like the Secular Humanist, their ultimate goal is the eradication of Christianity and the creation of a brave new progressive world. Terry Randall, founder of the antiabortion group Operation Rescue, warned his members:

> If the militant homosexuals succeed in their accursed agenda, God will curse and judge our nation . . . Their cries for tolerance are really a demand for our surrender. They want us to surrender our values, our love for God's law, our faith, our families, the entire nation to their abhorrent agenda.[41]

In their ruthless pursuit of Christians, the dynamic duo often join forces with various incarnations of the shape-shifting Secular Humanist. For instance, James Dobson wrote to members of Focus on the Family:

> I really believe that the level of anger arising out of the homosexual community primarily, but the whole humanistic movement that's out there . . . as they gain political power—and they got it now—they're going to continue to oppress us.[42]

Similarly, former House Speaker Newt Gingrich told Bill O'Reilly of "a gay and secular fascism in this country that wants to impose its will on the rest of us, is prepared to use violence, to use harassment. I think it is prepared to use the government if it can get control of it."[43]

The specter of gay fascism is perhaps the most twisted example of projection in the right-wing arsenal. Thousands of homosexuals died in the Holocaust, and the Nazis imprisoned some 50,000 others.[44] Yet, in 1994, two conservative writers sought to prove that Nazis were not intolerant of homosexuals; the Nazis *were* homosexuals. *The Pink Swastika* scrapes together a mound of alleged homosexual influences on Nazi doctrine, from Plato's *Republic* to Gnosticism to paganism; for example, "In pagan cultures, homosexuals often hold an elevated position in religion and society."*[45]

This rambling collection of syllogistic fallacies is the likely inspiration behind Pat Robertson's claim that "many of those people involved with Adolf Hitler were Satanists; many of them were homosexuals. The two things seem to go together."[46] (It doesn't get any eviler than Homosexual Nazi Satanists.)

Bryan Fischer of the American Family Association even used the gay Nazi theory to protest a proposal to repeal the military's "Don't Ask, Don't Tell" policy, arguing that gay soldiers would be too mean. He explained:

> Hitler recruited around him homosexuals to make up his Stormtroopers, they were his enforcers, they were his thugs. And Hitler discovered that he could not get straight soldiers to be savage and brutal and vicious enough to carry out his orders, but that homosexual solders [*sic*] basically had no limits and the savagery and brutality they were willing to inflict on whomever Hitler sent them after. So he surrounded himself, virtually all of the Stormtroopers, the Brownshirts, were male homosexuals.[47]

Thought Crimes

But what, exactly, you may be wondering, are the mean homosexuals doing to the Christians? With all the talk of "harassment" and "vio-

---

* "*The Pink Swastika*." In 2009, one of the authors, Scott Lively, participated in a conference in Uganda to warn its citizens of the threat from the gay agenda. In addition to the Nazis, Lively added Rwandan extremists to the list of genocidal homosexual movements. After the conference, he boasted that he had delivered "a nuclear bomb against the gay agenda in Uganda." His boast proved apt, if somewhat anachronistic, when the Ugandan parliament subsequently increased the penalty for sodomy to death by stoning. That should stop those murdering homosexuals. (Scott Lively, "Report from Uganda," *The Pro-Family Resource Center,* 17 Mar. 2009, http://www.defendthefamily.com/pfrc/archives.php?id=2345952.)

lence" and "discrimination" and "oppression," you'd think that legions of demonic jackbooted gay thugs in leather chaps were rounding
the poor Christians into concentration camps and peeing on them. Fortunately, the Christians have so far been allowed to roam free, but they
are at dire risk from hate crime. Not hate *crimes*. No one is beating up
Christians yet. The Christians are at risk from hate crime *legislation*,
specifically the Hate Crimes Prevention Act, also known as the
Matthew Shepard Act.

On October 7, 1998, two young men, Aaron McKinney and Russell
Henderson, of Laramie, Wyoming, lured a third young man, Matthew
Shepard, into their truck by posing as homosexuals. They robbed him
of $30, smashed his face and skull with a huge .357 Magnum, and left
him tied to a split-rail fence in the frigid Wyoming countryside. The
bicyclist who found Shepard unconscious 18 hours later at first mistook
him for a scarecrow. Shepard died five days later from severe brainstem
damage without ever regaining consciousness.[48] Members of the West-
boro Baptist Church of Topeka, Kansas, traveled to Casper, Wyoming,
to picket Shepard's funeral. They carried signs that read "Fag Matt in
Hell" and "No tears for queers."[49]

At the murder trial, McKinney's lawyers presented the "gay panic"
defense, arguing that Shepard's sexual advances drove their client to
temporary insanity. A former bartender helpfully testified that he too
had knocked Shepard unconscious after being propositioned by him.
The judge rejected the defense, and McKinney received two life
sentences.

After the trial, President Clinton urged Congress to extend federal
hate crime legislation to homosexuals, women, and people with dis-
abilities, but the measure failed. Democrats continued to push for the
extension but did not succeed until they captured control of the legislature. The House finally passed the Matthew Shepard Act in 2007.

The religious right responded as if the government had started
rounding up Christians and burning down the churches. James Dobson
explained that the "true intent" of the Matthew Shepard Act was to
"muzzle people of faith" and warned, "If you read the Bible a certain
way with regard to morality—you may be guilty of committing a
'thought crime.'"[50] Pat Robertson agreed that "if anybody speaks out

about homosexuality, says it's a sin, says it's wrong, says it's against the Bible, that individual would be charged with a quote, hate crime."[51] Rep. Louie Gohmert (R-TX) clambered onto the "thought crime" bandwagon as well,[52] but he couldn't resist a rambling digression into a bestiality-necrophilia-pedophilia-fascism slippery-slope bonanza from the House floor, proclaiming:

> You'd have to strike any laws against bestiality, if you're oriented toward corpses, toward children, you know, there are all kinds of perversions, what most of us would call perversions. Some would say it sounds like fun, but most of us would say were perversions. . . . When you lose morality in a nation, you create economic instability leading to economic chaos. And when you have economic chaos, it is tragic, but people have always been willing to give up their liberties, their freedoms in order to gain economic stability. It happened in 1920's and 1930's Germany. They gave up their liberties to gain economic stability, and they got a little guy with a mustache who was the ultimate hate monger.*[53]

The list of outraged Christian conservatives goes on and on, but let's stop with Andrea Laffery, the director of the Traditional Values Coalition, who put the matter quite plainly: "The goal is to undermine the First Amendment and persecute Christians who oppose homosexuality."[54]

Despite the secret having been discovered, Democrats proceeded with their plan to undermine the First Amendment and persecute Christians. When George W. Bush threatened to veto the Matthew Shepard Act, Democrats bided their time until Obama was elected and brought it back. Safely attached to a large defense bill, the act finally became law eleven years after Matthew Shepard's tragic death.

---

* An example of hatemongering by the little guy with a mustache in 1942: "We want to fill our culture again with the Christian spirit. We want to burn out all the recent immoral developments in literature, in the theatre, and in the press—in short, we want to burn out the poison of immorality which has entered into our whole life and culture as a result of liberal excess during the past years." (Norman Hepburn Baynes, *The Speeches of Adolf Hitler, 1922–1939, Vol. 1* [New York: Oxford University Press, 1942]: 871–872.)

The Thomas More Law Center, a conservative "civil liberties" group, has challenged the law on the grounds that it curtails free speech, infringes upon religious liberty, creates "thought crimes," and violates some 30 percent of the Bill of Rights. But unless the plaintiffs can find a new hero with the stature of Judge William Brevard Hand, humanist-avenger, the suit is unlikely to succeed. Most religious right leaders have already moved on to the same-sex marriage wars, which still burn fierce and hot in ballot initiatives and court cases across the country, leaving behind only the smoldering ashes of their once blazing outrage.

5

MAD AS HELL?

Why Politicians and Journalists Are Wrong about the Source of "Populist Rage"

Fear is the path to the dark side. Fear leads to anger. Anger leads to hate. Hate leads to suffering.

—Yoda

IT IS DIFFICULT TO IMAGINE a more perfect example of right-wing persecution politics than the opposition to the Matthew Shepard Act. A bill designed to discourage hate-fueled violence against homosexuals is represented as a malicious, discriminatory assault on Christians masterminded by the people that it was designed to protect. Those who subscribe to this point of view categorically reject the possibility of discrimination against homosexuals in general and Matthew Shepard in particular. Rep. Virginia Foxx (R-NC), for example, insisted that Shepard's murder was a simple burglary gone awry. (No homophobia here, folks, just the bloody pulp of a dying gay man tied to a fence, move along.)[1] They then project the hatred and discrimination onto supporters of the Matthew Shepard Act, complaining that the Christians, not the homosexuals, are the victims of persecution.

In the face of this point of view, one may wonder, "Who do they think they're fooling?" If that's what you're thinking, the answer is—not you. The persecution politics narrative is not designed for anyone who might be tempted to question it. There is a rational case to be made for opposing the Matthew Shepard Act, but the fantasy of a plot to persecute Christians by prosecuting "thought crimes" is not it. Notwithstanding the occasional William Brevard Hand, this story won't persuade the courts, it won't persuade liberals, it won't persuade moderate conservatives, it won't persuade anyone who applies the slightest bit of critical analysis. It wasn't even embraced by Fox News.

Instead, promoters dispersed the narrative through the right wing's internal recirculation system—Christian television, talk radio, church sermons, mailing lists, blogs, books, and dinner conversations. It's like an airplane full of swine flu victims. The Inspiration Network, for example, treated viewers to a seven-part documentary series, *Speechless: Silencing the Christians,* about hate crimes, the gay agenda, and the war on Christmas. Rev. Donald Wildmon* complemented the documentary with a book by the same name that asks, "Why has a coalition of liberal secularists, homosexual activists, and Fortune 500 companies united to wage war on Christianity?"[2] Ann Coulter contributed the foreword, writing, "[Liberals are] like roaches. They operate in the dark. Shine a light on them and they scatter."[3]

Don't Blame the Stupids

In the face of such insights from luminaries like Coulter and Wildmon, one might be forgiven for concluding that the combined brainpower of the people who did tune in to *Speechless: Silencing the Christians* was roughly equivalent to the average intelligence of a flaccid carrot. But while it might be comforting for liberals to imagine that right-wing voters have the mental capacity of a limp root vegetable, there is no reliable evidence to make the case and some evidence suggesting the contrary. For instance, a *New York Times*–CBS poll indicated that Tea Party supporters tend to be better educated than the average American.

---

* Rev. Wildmon founded the American Family Association, which owns and operates two hundred radio stations across the country. He gained notoriety for organizing nationwide opposition to Martin Scorsese's *The Last Temptation of Christ*. The AFA mailed 500,000 flyers warning that Universal Studios was "a company whose decision-making body is dominated by non-Christians"—in other words, Jewish money. (Aljean Harmetz, "Film on Christ Brings Out Pickets, and Archbishop Predicts Censure," *New York Times,* 21 Jul. 1988, http://www.nytimes.com/1988/07/21/movies/film-on-christ-brings-out-pickets-and-archbishop-predicts-censure.html.)

Thirty-seven percent are college graduates, as opposed to the national average of 25 percent.*[4]

Moreover, you don't have to be stupid to be paranoid. It's fun to point out that neither Glenn Beck nor Rush Limbaugh graduated from college, but Pat Robertson, who is a zanier conspiracist than either one of them, has a law degree from Yale. One of America's most influential conspiracists was Samuel Morse, coinventor of the telegraph and author of *Conspiracy Against the Liberties of the United States,* which detailed the secret Jesuit plot to hand the country over to the Austrian empire. Henry Ford, the brilliant industrial innovator, blamed World War I on a conspiracy of Jewish bankers. And Kurt Gödel, perhaps the greatest logician in history, became convinced that secret enemies intended to poison him. He eventually stopped eating and died of starvation. So much for logic.

Most important for our purposes, calling conservatives stupid does no more to explain the success of right-wing persecution politics than calling conservatives crazy. On the contrary, such accusations shrug off the possibility of explanation. The primary benefit of calling one's political opponents stupid and/or crazy is the pleasant feeling of smugness that it accords the accuser, which probably explains the popularity of the charges in the liberal blogosphere.

The Angry Right

If paranoid conservatives aren't universally stupid or clinically insane, how do we explain their affinity for ideas that are both stupid and insane? Let's now consider one of the most popular explanations for the current rash of right-wing paranoia: rage. According to the rage hy-

---

* "Better educated." After the poll results came out, I overheard a group of liberal New Yorkers at a bar trying to make sense of the fact that so many Tea Party supporters were well educated. One concluded that they were lying. Another argued that the modern American education system had become inadequate. A third propounded his theory that schools these days focused too much on test scores. Apparently, they didn't read the bit about how 75 percent of Tea Party supporters are older than forty-five and thus received their educations long ago.

pothesis, paranoid conservatives are extraordinarily angry, and they embrace crazy conspiracy ideas in order to discharge their fury onto convenient targets; for example, health care reform, illegal immigrants, or Barack Hussein Obama.

The rage hypothesis seems to be the media's default explanation for the recent growth of right-wing paranoia. The headlines of 2009 and 2010 have been full of references to "populist rage" and "the angry right." A *Newsweek* cover depicted a mob of mustachioed fedora-clad men bearing pitchforks and looking slightly constipated—headline, "Populist Rage."[5] *Time* magazine edified the nation with Glenn Beck's protruding tongue on its cover—headline, "Mad Man."[6] Former Labor secretary Robert Reich evoked lurid horror-film imagery in an article for Salon.com:

> Angry right-wing populism lurks just below the surface of the terrible American economy, ready to be launched not only at Obama but also at liberals, intellectuals, gays, blacks, Jews, the mainstream media, coastal elites, crypto socialists, and any other potential target of paranoid opportunity.[7]

(*Angry Populists II:* Just when you thought it was safe to go back into the country . . .)

The rage thesis seems to get recycled every decade or two. Richard Hofstadter opened his essay "The Paranoid Style of American Politics" with the statement, "American politics has often been an arena for angry minds." In the 1990s, the "angry white male" was a popular character in the narratives of Clinton-era political pundits. According to the media, packs of angry white males roamed the countryside, terrorizing liberal politicians and local school boards until a cavalry of minivan-driving soccer moms subdued them a couple of years later.

In 2004, Thomas Frank documented the emergence and eventual triumph of the paranoid right on the Kansas political scene in his powerful and influential book, *What's the Matter with Kansas?: How Conservatives Won the Heart of America*. Frank blamed conservative demagogues for fomenting class resentment among working-class

Kansans. According to his well-developed version of the rage thesis, the discontented populace of the Great Plains sought liberal culprits to blame for their bleak economic conditions and feelings of cultural alienation. Frank argued that right-wing leaders had cribbed the class war rhetoric of nineteenth-century left-wing populism almost verbatim, replacing yesterday's robber barons with today's "liberal elites" to provide an appealing target for working-class anger.

The rage explanation is attractive because the paranoid rhetoric of the right wing obviously expresses anger. Frank deftly describes what he calls the *plen-T-plaint*, "a curious amassing of petty, unrelated beefs with the world . . . The plen-T-plaint is the rhetorical device that makes Bill O'Reilly's TV show a hit, as he gets indignant one day about the Insane Clown Posse and gets indignant the next about the Man-Boy Love Association [NAMBLA]."[8]

If O'Reilly is a master of staged indignation, Glenn Beck, who was still confined to radio when *What's the Matter with Kansas?* came out, is a virtuoso of dramatized rage. He shouts, sobs, and thunders at the progressive vampires who are "sucking the blood out of the Republic."[9] In one made-for-YouTube moment, he literally shrieked at a caller, his voice breaking into a nearly unintelligible squeal, "GET OFF MY PHONE, YOU LITTLE PINHEAD!"[10]

Tea Party participants also make a big show of how angry they are—shouting epithets at Washington and carrying signs with gratuitous exclamation points. In the *New York Times*–CBS poll, 53 percent of Tea Party supporters described themselves as "angry" about the way things are going in Washington, as opposed to 19 percent of the general public. A prominent Tea Party organization in Nevada even named itself Anger Is Brewing.

It's the Economy, Stupid (Or Is It?)

But what is the source of this frothing river of rage? What has made conservatives so angry that they have lost their wits and begun imagining terrible liberal plots to persecute them? Here, the rage explanation becomes speculative. A poll can question people about what they feel angry about. When asked, Tea Party supporters cite a hodgepodge of injustices including health care reform, government spending, socialism, and lack of representative government.[11] But such answers beg the question by invoking the very paranoia that we are trying to explain. To fill in the details of the rage hypothesis, we would need to locate the true source of the anger for which the paranoid right has substituted its convenient fictions. We would need a poll to somehow probe, "Come on, what are you *really* angry about?"

When reading *What's the Matter with Kansas?* it can be difficult to keep track of what exactly Thomas Frank believes that Kansans are really angry about. At times, he cites a backlash against the cultural shifts of the 1960s. Later, he roots the anger in traditional populist resentment against elites. And, sometimes, the bitterness just seems endemic, an unpleasant personality trait of a certain type of irascible Kansan.* But most often, Frank blames economic changes. Specifically, he argues that Kansas's tumbling manufacturing base and growing income disparities produced an underground reservoir of working-class resentment that conservative demagogues channeled into hostility toward liberal "elites."

Economic frustration also seems to be the consensus choice for explaining the growth of the Tea Parties and the popularity of Glenn Beck. *Newsweek* provided readers with "a historical tour of populism" that cited past examples of economic turmoil coinciding with populist politics.[12] *Time* magazine argued that Glenn Beck exploited conservatives' "economic uncertainty."[13] Robert Reich cited "the terrible American economy."[14] President Obama blamed the "vitriol" on "an economy that is making people more anxious."[15] His advisor David Axelrod likewise attributed the right wing's "disaffection" to "severe economic conditions."[16]

---

* "Irascible Kansan." Frank calls them "bitter self-made men." They seem to be some kind of elite unit of angry white males, like navy SEALS. (Thomas Frank, *What's the Matter with Kansas?: How Conservatives Won the Heart of America,* paperback ed., 2005 [New York: Henry Holt and Company, 2004]: 141–148.)

Many of those who blame the paranoia on economic conditions are unaware of the psychological underpinnings of their argument. The commonsense idea is based on what social psychologists call the *frustration-aggression theory*. According to the theory, when people are blocked from achieving a desired goal (frustration), they become angry (aggression). But instead of directing their anger toward the source of the frustration, they displace it onto vulnerable targets such as minorities.[17] The theory is sometimes called the *scapegoat theory* of prejudice, but it differs from classic scapegoating in that the frustrated individuals are redirecting their emotions, not transferring blame. For instance, one famous study found that in the old South, lynchings became more frequent whenever the price of cotton fell. The authors concluded that while Southern whites did not hold blacks responsible the price drops, the economic consequences produced frustration, leading Southern whites to wrathfully vent their anger at black victims.[18]

So, in the context of today's persecution politics, a proponent of the frustration-aggression theory would argue that economic deprivation has produced widespread frustration, resulting in a surge of anger and aggression. But instead of directing their aggression at the source of the hardship—financial deregulation and high-risk investments—many people have displaced their aggression onto conveniently accessible villains to whom they ascribe incredible powers for evil—liberal elites, militant homosexuals, etc.

If the theory is correct, one could address the growth of persecution politics either by fixing the underlying economic conditions that created the frustration or by redirecting the aggression toward the true source of the hardship. Thus, Thomas Frank suggested that Democrats dropped the ball by allowing Republicans to redirect working-class anger from corporate fat cats to "liberal elites" and should recover their traditional working-class constituency by aggressively taking on the corporate interests that have exacerbated the economic decline of the lower middle class. President Obama, on the other hand, complacently predicted that the surge of anger that followed his election will dissipate once the country emerges from recession.

But there are reasons to suspect that the frustration-aggression theory

is at best an incomplete explanation for the growth of right-wing paranoia. When psychologists originally applied the theory to group scapegoating in 1940, it seemed like a plausible explanation for the fascist
anti-Semitism that arose during Germany's economic depression. Subsequent psychological studies, however, failed to confirm the phenomenon in the context of large social groups, and some earlier
corroborating studies, such as the one that correlated cotton prices and
lynchings, have been heavily criticized as flawed.[19]

Moreover, today's Tea Party demographics don't support the hypothesis. If Tea Parties appealed to victims of the recession, you would expect them to attract the poor and unemployed, but according to the
New York Times–CBS poll, 56 percent of Tea Party supporters earn over
$50,000 a year, including 20 percent who earn over $100,000—in contrast to 44 and 14 percent of all poll respondents. Only 6 percent of Tea
Party supporters are unemployed and looking for work—as opposed
to 15 percent of all respondents.[20] Thus, most Tea Party supporters do
not seem to fit the model of the bitter working-class stiff staggering
under the weight of economic hardship.

Finally, while economic changes may contribute to the growth of political paranoia, historical data suggest that the relationship is far from
simple. One recent statistical study found a correlation between political extremism and economic decline, but the effect was modest, and
the authors concluded, "The empirical results in this paper instead
show that it is unlikely that even strong recessions can change political
outcomes."[21] And while some paranoid movements in American history
have coincided with economic recessions, there are also counterexam-
ples that challenge the hypothesis that such movements are primarily
driven by economic decline. For instance, the worst period of mass
paranoia in recent U.S. history was the Red Scare, which took place
amid the tremendous postwar economic boom of the 1940s and 1950s.

I don't mean to suggest that rage plays no part in persecution politics. There is no denying the angry tone of right-wing paranoid rhetoric, and Thomas Frank is entirely correct in his description of Bill
O'Reilly's plen-T-plainting exploitation of conservative ire. Economic
anxieties may also play a contributing role. But we should question the

received wisdom that persecution paranoia is founded on the misdirected resentments of the economically deprived—especially when there is a much more straightforward explanation at hand.

Fear Leads to Anger, Anger Leads to Hate

To see the alternative, let's briefly return to the Red Scare. The most obvious contributing factor to the paranoia of the day was not an economic downturn but the very real threat from the newly powerful Soviet Union and its communist allies. The Soviets developed the nuclear bomb in 1949, the same year that Mao proclaimed the People's Republic of China. North Korea invaded South Korea the following year with assistance from China and the Soviets, and the United States intervened to counter the spread of communism. Meanwhile, back home, the country reeled from a series of high-profile spy cases including those of Alger Hiss and the Rosenbergs. These events catalyzed the Red Scare, which exploded in 1950 for the obvious reason that communist aggression scared the heck out of Americans.

It's worth noting that what we often call *the* Red Scare was actually the Second Red Scare. The First Red Scare, from 1917 to 1920, also occurred during a period of economic growth. It was provoked by the Russian Revolution and a series of bombings and attempted bombings by anarchists in the United States—anarchists being a subspecies of communists in the eyes of old-school commie-haters.

In each case, conservatives soon whipped reasonable fears into a hysterical hateful frenzy, but the fear preceded the hate. Indeed, it is natural to suppose that the fear *produced* the hate. If you believed that your fellow Americans were conspiring to incite a violent revolution or provide nuclear weapons to a ruthless enemy, you'd probably hate them too. Similarly, given the fear of many conservatives that "gay and secular fascists" sought to indoctrinate their children and outlaw their religious beliefs, is it any wonder that they got angry? Perhaps Frank and others have got it backward. The rage hasn't caused the paranoia; the paranoia has caused the rage.

This order of precedence jives with the rhetoric of persecution politics. While conservative voices often express indignation and sometimes fury, the most evident emotion associated with persecution narratives is not anger but *fear*. Except at the extreme fringe, right-wing leaders do not call for the imprisonment of secular humanists or the stoning of homosexuals; they call for protection. They paint pictures of enemies that are as powerful as they are evil, and they raise the possibility of imminent defeat, perhaps even the extinction of their race, religion, or culture. As I mentioned before, the roar of the paranoid right resembles that of a cornered animal.

Paranoia for Fun and Profit

But there is something funny about the fear. The people who promote persecution politics tend to behave in the exact opposite manner from what one would expect from folks who were genuinely afraid. The defeat of the IRS desegregation proposal did not give conservatives confidence that the secular humanists were less powerful than they had feared. On the contrary, the proposal's defeat preceded most of the secular humanist hysteria. It was afterward that conspiracists like Tim LaHaye magnified the power of the mythical secular humanists, imagining that they now controlled the government, the media, the courts, and the schools, and predicting that they would soon achieve complete victory. Before long, people were blaming secular humanists for everything from drug abuse to stomachaches.

Likewise, before Anita Bryant's 1977 Save Our Children campaign in Miami, the right wing barely reacted as cities across the country enacted antidiscrimination protections for homosexuals. Conservatives didn't begin to accuse militant homosexuals of conspiring to take over the nation until after Bryant's successful campaign. At that point, they mobilized in cities like Wichita and St. Paul that had previously enacted gay rights laws and got the laws repealed by frightening locals with warnings that homosexuals were recruiting schoolchildren.

Conversely, when the right wing loses, the paranoia fears recede.

Jittery conspiracists should have seen the U.S. Court of Appeal's repudiation of Judge Hand's ruling, which effectively extinguished the dream that courts would end secular humanist education, as a fearsome sign of secular humanist power. Instead, they shrugged their shoulders and moved on to other villains.

Controversial gay rights issues like same-sex marriage still elicit right-wing vitriol, but the guarantees of equal employment and housing that once drew fearful opposition have quietly become commonplace. Miami finally extended equal rights to homosexuals in 1998 with scarcely a whimper from the right.

In short, the right wing's successes seemed to inflame its fears; its failures seemed to dampen them. This upside-down behavior suggests that the fear of political conspiracies is different from the fear of other dangers, like terrorists or man-eating sharks. Normally, fear is something imposed on us from without. We read about a bombing or a shark attack, and we worry that we could be next. But there were no secular humanists out there, nor militant homosexuals recruiting children in the schools—no external threat to ignite the fears of nervous Christians.

A cynical analyst might conclude that right-wing leaders have been manipulating their credulous Christian supporters for political gain. Such an analyst might observe with raised eyebrow that paranoid hysteria tends to explode just before controversial bills and ballot measures come up for a vote and then immediately dissipate. But former governor Mike Huckabee praised *Speechless: Silencing the Christians,* the scourge of liberal cockroaches, calling its author, Rev. Wildmon, "one of the national leaders who is driven by principles and not by politics." So surely the good reverend would never stoop to manipulative fearmongering.[22] Likewise, James Dobson is much too principled to fabricate a threat in order to expand his sprawling operation in Colorado Springs, Bill O'Reilly is too honest to exaggerate for the sake of his media ratings, and the various Republican legislators care too much for the truth to scare the bejeezus out of their constituents for the sake of a few campaign contributions.

Unfortunately for the curious cynic, unless these leaders have been secretly recording their machinations like Richard Nixon, there is no way to know what they truly believe. We can raise our eyebrows until our foreheads ache but, without evidence, such speculation resembles Bill O'Reilly's "superior analysis." Moreover, it's not implausible to imagine that many right-wing paranoia proponents believe in their own wacky ideas. Complicity in promulgating a convenient fiction does not prevent one from believing the fiction oneself.

More important, it would be a mistake to treat the rank and file as passive victims of exploitation. To learn about the secular humanist menace, people had to buy books, tune to radio stations, listen to sermons, and attend meetings. There is a psychological phenomenon, *selective exposure,* according to which people tend to seek out information that coheres with their existing beliefs and avoid information that contradicts their beliefs. Conservatives who limit themselves to Glenn Beck, Rush Limbaugh, Tea Party newsletters, and other right-wing media sources selectively expose themselves to paranoid conspiracism. Thus, if they're being manipulated, they are at least complicit in their own manipulation.

In addition, most right-wing conspiracy theories, such as the great secular humanism plot, are such obvious piles of political flimflam that people who believe in them have to really *want* to believe in them. Contrary to appearance, paranoid conservatives do not lack critical faculties. They apply their critical skills with great zeal whenever President Obama opens his mouth. But when Glenn Beck promotes a juicy conspiracy theory about bloodsucking progressives, those same critical skills go into cold storage.

The selective criticism is an example of another psychological phenomenon called *confirmation bias,* according to which people tend to sympathetically interpret evidence that supports their beliefs and find fault with contrary evidence. In one famous study, participants were shown fictional studies about the deterrent effect of the death penalty. Those who supported the death penalty were far more skeptical of studies that challenged the deterrent effect. Those who opposed it were far more skeptical of studies that supported the deterrent effect. The investigators concluded:

> When provided with a more detailed description of the procedures and data, together with relevant critiques and authors' rebuttals, subjects seemed to ignore the stated results of the study . . . Both proponents and opponents interpreted the additional information, relative to the results alone, as supporting their own initial attitudes.[23]

Paranoid conservatives make a religion of confirmation bias. They swallow the most ludicrous conspiracy theories like buttered popcorn while subjecting alternative ideas to withering criticism. Thus, they not only open themselves up to manipulation by right-wing leaders, they plunge headfirst into it, frolicking almost joyfully among the conspiratorial ideas that their leaders manufacture. Such behavior suggests that the disciples of persecution politics receive some positive psychological value from the feeling of paranoia. On some level, they must want to be paranoid.

But why would anyone want to be paranoid?

6

OBAMA'S AMERICA

How Old-fashioned Southern Racism
Became Civil Rights for White People

*The white people of the South are the greatest minority in this nation.
They deserve consideration and understanding instead of the persecution of twisted propaganda.*

—Strom Thurmond

WHITE STUDENT BEATEN ON SCHOOL BUS; CROWD CHEERS
—Drudge Report, September 15, 2009

THE MAGIC WORD in this *Drudge* headline, the one that earned it a
gargantuan font, is "white." The conservative editors of the
Drudge Report are not particularly interested in school bus beatings.
They're not even particularly interested in racially motivated school
bus beatings. But if the victim is white, the assailants are black, and a
busload of black students calls out, "Beat his ass!" and "Boom, boom,
boom!" then *Drudge* throws a fat-font fit.

And not just *Drudge*. Fox News aired footage from the school bus
surveillance camera. The anchorman grimly warned viewers that the
video was "disturbing," perhaps because it had been edited with a
slow-motion replay of flailing punches as a voiceover intoned, "The
two suspects are fourteen and fifteen. They are African American. The
victim is white."[1] On the Fox News show *Kelly's Court*, host Megyn
Kelly indignantly demanded punishment for the assailants, for the
cheering children, for the parents of the cheering children, and for the
hapless bus driver. She declared, "The scars this kid is going to suffer

for the rest of his life thanks to those hooligans on that bus can't be
. . . can't be overstated." Though the fact that the victim did not require
hospital care suggests that the scars could in fact be overstated[2]—unless
perhaps Kelly was referring to the emotional scars inflicted by public
humiliation on national television.

At the front of the persecution parade, twirling his big black-bigotry
baton like an enraged, overweight drum major, marched Rush Limbaugh, fulminating about the hellish state of "Obama's America."

> Greetings, my friends. It's Obama's America, is it not? Obama's Amer-
> ica—white kids getting beat up on school buses now. I mean, you put
> your kids on a school bus, you expect safety, but in Obama's America,
> the white kids now get beat up with the black kids cheering, "Yeah,
> right on, right on, right on!"[3]

The black-on-white school bus assault must have seemed like a god-
send to Limbaugh, timed as it was with a *Newsweek* article titled "See
Baby Discriminate" about a scientific study that suggested a biological
predisposition for racism—which Limbaugh interpreted as a liberal
broadside against white people. He continued:

> And of course, everybody says, "Oh, the white kid deserved it, he was
> born a racist, he's white." *Newsweek* magazine told us this. We know
> that white students are destroying civility on buses, white students de-
> stroying civility in classrooms all over America, white congressmen de-
> stroying civility in the House of Representatives.

By that point, Limbaugh had become so excited by his own oratory
that he surrendered any remaining shred of coherence and attempted
to connect Obama's "socialist" economic polities to segregated buses:

> We can redistribute students while we redistribute their parents' wealth.
> I mean, we can just redistribute everything, just return the white stu-
> dents to their rightful place—their own bus, with bars on the windows
> and armed guards. They're racists, they get what they deserve.

Make that segregated *prison* buses for white schoolchildren.

The hyperbole is vintage Limbaugh. His rhetorical strategy is to raise his pitch a couple of notes higher than what he really means to convey—singing a piercing F-sharp to communicate a shrill E. The exaggeration entertains his audience and infuriates liberals, which suits Limbaugh just fine. And when those high notes cross the line of acceptable public discourse, Limbaugh just shrugs and passes the offense off as "satire." Indeed, it's not always easy to distinguish Limbaugh's hyperbole from parodies on *The Daily Show*. For instance, here is Jon Stewart's take on the school bus assault: "Because Barack Obama is president it is now open season on white children . . . and black people are now allowed to hit them."[4]

But there are two important differences between Limbaugh's hyperbole and Stewart's parody. One, Stewart is funny. Two, Stewart exaggerates to highlight absurdity, whereas Limbaugh exaggerates for rhetorical emphasis, like calling someone the worst person in the world when you really mean that he's just a big fat liar.

So what did Limbaugh really mean when he suggested that Obama wanted to pack white children into "their own bus with bars on the windows?" He meant that the Obama administration discriminates against whites the way racist state governments used to discriminate against blacks. When he said, "We can redistribute their parents' wealth," he meant that Obama wants to take money from middle-class white people and give it to poor black people. Finally, when Limbaugh said, "They're racists, they get what they deserve," he meant that Obama hates whites. The message, in short: *He will call you names, he will take your money, and he will persecute your children because he hates you and everything you stand for.* "Boom, boom, boom!" went the persecution drums as Limbaugh hurled his baton into the air, and the crowd went wild.

Unfortunately for Limbaugh, reality sometimes interferes with exploiting someone's personal misfortune to make a political point. Though the police captain who investigated the school bus assault initially described the attack as racially motivated, he later retracted that assessment, explaining, "It was premature on my part . . . The incident appears now to be more about a couple of bullies on a bus dictating where people sit."[5] Limbaugh, *Drudge,* and Fox News soon dropped the story, leaving it to the white supremacists that showed up in Belleville, Illinois, the following week, dressed in black and carrying bullhorns and Nazi flags. At a rally near the city hall, they demanded that the assailants be prosecuted for hate crimes, shouting, "Double standard!" and "White power!"[6] Yes, the Nazis were concerned about hate crimes. Welcome to Obama's America.

The Good Ol' Days

It wasn't always this way. Once upon a time, white supremacists wore white, black people were colored, yellow buses were segregated, and coloreds who assaulted whites met swift justice. Bigots wore hostility across their chests like the emblem of a team uniform. They preached about God's "line of distinction" in their churches and enforced it in their schools, on their buses, and at their lunch counters, not to mention on their toilet seats. When civil rights activists and the National Guard finally came to erase the lines of distinction that fissured across the American countryside, the bigots responded with venom and violence.

But slowly, year by year, the nation matured. The lines of distinction began to wash away, and racial intolerance became a shameful offense. It's not easy to be a racist in the twenty-first century. In 2009, a Louisiana justice of the peace who refused to grant marriage licenses to interracial couples insisted, "I'm not a racist. I just don't believe in mixing the races that way."* He explained his nonracism in detail: "I have piles and piles of black friends. They come to my home, I marry them, they use my bathroom."[7] (In that order?)

Even white supremacists feel obliged to mask their white supremacism. David Duke, former Klan leader and founder of the NAAWP (Na-

---

* "Mixing the races that way." Which raises the question, in what way does he believe in mixing the races? American Indian–Tibetan? They both have a brownish hue and wear colorful traditional costumes, so maybe that's okay. Or perhaps he means that the races can mix in other ways. They can be bridge partners, for instance.

tional Association for the Advancement of White People), energetically condemns "any effort of any race to be supreme over or control other races," which is quite open-minded of him, though it isn't what most people mean by "white supremacy." Duke also insists that he is not "anti-black" but rather "pro-European American," which he believes to be a genuine distinction. Duke writes, "I love my people and I am not willing for my people to face discrimination or the ethnic cleansing, dissolution and genocide of massive immigration."[8] (While white genocide has not historically been a significant problem in the United States, one can never be too cautious with all these brownish-hued supremacists coming over our borders.)

Anxious racists aside, the nation has progressed far in a relatively short period of time. Reading old news articles from the 1960s and 1970s, the transformation in the way Americans treat racial distinctions is striking. For instance, a 1961 *Time* magazine article titled "Nigger, Go Home" described a mob of several hundred white people howling curses at "Negroes" who had been offered temporary refuge by a church in a white Chicago neighborhood after their residential hotel burned down.

> Down in the basement, the Negroes could hear every bitter shout: "Nigger, nigger, go home," and "Nigger lovers never go to heaven," and "We'll rock you out," and "Get the niggers out of there."

Fearing damage to his church, the pastor expelled the refugees. Racists pelted them with oranges, apples, and eggs as they walked to Red Cross station wagons that took them to black churches several miles away.[9]

Six weeks after the incident, Barack Hussein Obama II was born in Honolulu, Hawaii. His birth certificate lists his mother's race, "Caucasian," and his father's race, "African."* Forty-eight and a half years later, President-elect Barack Hussein Obama II and his family moved

---

* "His birth certificate." It should be noted that according to a *New York Times*–CBS poll, 20 percent of Americans don't believe that Obama was born in the United States, and 22 percent aren't sure. If Obama's birth certificate is a forgery, we don't really know what race he is . . . or if his parents were even human.

into the most exclusive address in the nation. The Secret Service protects them from any would-be egg throwers. *Time* magazine's editors wouldn't think of publishing "the N-word" on *Time's* inoffensive pages, and the mob scene from 1961 is almost inconceivable.

A New Breed of Racism

That does not mean, however, that racism is dead. It has simply mutated. Amy Ansell, a professor of sociology at Bard College, writes of "a new breed of racism" that has been carefully sanitized. The new breed avoids overt hostility and notions of racial superiority, focusing instead on "the alleged threat blacks pose—either because of their mere presence or because of their demand for 'special privileges'—to the economic, sociopolitical, and cultural vitality of the dominant (white) society." Ansell observes that the new breed of racism has adopted "the vocabulary of equal opportunity, color blindness, race neutrality, and, above all, individualism and individual rights."[10]

Of course the individual rights that concern the new racists are those of white people. They argue that affirmative action policies discriminate against whites, especially white men. They complain that federal social programs like welfare and health care "redistribute" resources to noncitizens (read, Latinos) and the undeserving poor (read, African Americans). They fret that "American" culture is being diluted and that white populations are being overwhelmed by minority population growth and waves of immigration. The new breed of racism has retained the "us versus them" mythology of the old breed, but it has transformed "them" from inferior brutes to privileged cheaters and trespassers who have been taking advantage of and oppressing "us." In other words, the new breed of racists practices persecution politics.

To be clear, not every objection to affirmative action, welfare, immigration, and so on is founded on persecution paranoia. There are reasonable cases to be made against any of these policies. Affirmative action is particularly troublesome because it is by nature discriminatory. Over the years, the courts have carved a torturous legal path that rejects numerical race quotas but permits consideration of race for the sake of promoting diversity. The dissenting Supreme Court justices and many of their supporters who call for complete race neutrality are not paranoid racists.

But it's usually quite easy to distinguish reasonable opposition from fear-mongering persecution politics. Just look for us-versus-them rhetoric and self-righteous squawking about civil liberties from people who show little enthusiasm for racial equality except when they believe that their dear "European Americans" are threatened. Code words like *special privileges* and *reverse racism* are dead giveaways. The new racism is not a principled objection to excesses of the civil rights movement but a distorted imitation of it, a dark two-dimensional shadow that mimics the movement's profile and gestures.

The Fightin' Little Judge

The founding father of the new racism was not a Republican but a Southern Democrat named George Wallace. Alabamans called him the Fightin' Little Judge because of his prowess as a bantamweight boxer in his youth. He looked the part. With heavy eyebrows made for glowering, a robust jaw made for jutting, and thick, dark hair made for Brylcreeming, Wallace could easily have starred in an old Hollywood boxing flick. As a federal judge in the 1950s, Wallace developed a reputation for fairness and tolerance—relative to the norms of Alabama at the time—and the NAACP endorsed his first gubernatorial campaign in 1958. But after his KKK-backed opponent trounced him in the race, Wallace confided to an aide, "I was outniggered by John Patterson. And I'll tell you here and now, I will never be outniggered again."[11]

Wallace kept his word. In his second campaign for governor in 1962, he made "segregation forever" the centerpiece of his political strategy. When a dismayed supporter asked him why, Wallace explained, "You know, I tried to talk about good roads and good schools and all these things that have been part of my career, and nobody listened. And then I began talking about niggers, and they stomped the floor."[12] Sure enough, white Alabamans adored the new George Wallace and elected him governor with the largest popular vote in the state's history.

For all his racist appeal, Wallace seldom denigrated blacks directly. Even in Alabama in the early 1960s, overt racism was becoming taboo, so Wallace played semantic games to pretend that he and his supporters were big fans of their black compatriots—as long as they didn't have to be in the same room with them. According to Wallace's curious lexicon, "a racist is one who despises someone because of his color, and an Alabama segregationist is one who conscientiously believes that it is in the best interest of Negro and white to have a separate education and social order."[13]

In place of black people, Wallace targeted their patrons, the "integratin', scalawaggin', carpetbaggin' liars" from Washington, DC, who were oppressing the good (white) folks of Alabama. In his inaugural address, Wallace, with no sense of irony, summoned his fellow citizens to "rise to the call for freedom-loving blood that is in us and send our answer to the tyranny that clanks its chains upon the South . . . I say segregation now, segregation tomorrow, segregation forever."[14] When JFK sent the Alabama National Guard to forcibly integrate the University of Alabama, Wallace stood defiantly at the entrance and decried "the oppression of the rights, privileges and sovereignty of this state by officers of the federal government."[15]

As Wallace himself insisted shortly before his death in 1998, "My vehemence was against the federal government folks. I didn't make people get mad against black people. I made 'em get mad against the courts."[16] In other words, Wallace didn't attack black people; he defended white people.

Wallace's new racism sounded the perfect note for a white culture that was still deeply racist but no longer willing to admit it. The victim rhetoric particularly appealed to Southerners still nursing wounds from the Civil War, but Wallace also attracted nationwide support from white voters who wanted to join the hate parade, particularly after the nation convulsed with assassinations and race riots. While Southern racism had always been more virulent than elsewhere, racism was once more American than apple pie, and nothing brings out one's inner bigot like rampaging black youths.

In 1968, Wallace ran for president as the American Independent Party candidate on a strident "law and order" platform that he assured reporters had nothing to do with race, innocently asking, "When does it come to have racial overtones in this country to stand for law and order?"[17] His not-racially-overtoned message was clearly effective. At his peak, Wallace had support from 23 percent of the electorate, and he ultimately won five Southern states in the election. No third-party presidential candidate since Wallace has won a single electoral vote.

In the late 1970s, after an assassination attempt derailed his presidential aspirations and left him paralyzed, Wallace experienced a rebirth of sorts. Repenting his prior political tactics, Wallace personally apologized to many of the people that he had attacked throughout his career. Running for governor in 1982, he sought the forgiveness of the black community and won again, this time with 90 percent of the black vote. As governor, he appointed a record number of blacks to state government positions.

The Southern Strategy

By the time Wallace repented, the "new breed of racism" genie had long since left its bottle and adopted new masters who were subtler and less fickle. Richard Nixon, for instance, was aware of Wallace's remarkable third-party run. He was also aware that Republican presidential candidate Barry Goldwater's opposition to the 1964 Civil Rights Act had enabled him to make unprecedented inroads into the Democratic South. Nixon put two and two together. But there was a catch. To win the South, he had to oppose civil rights; but if he opposed civil rights, he would lose the North. What was a crafty conservative politician to do?

Enter the Southern Strategy stage right [cue "Sweet Home, Alabama"]. The key to Nixon's Southern strategy was not simply to court white Southerners by exploiting racist sentiments but to do so while appearing to support civil rights. So Tricky Dick threaded the needle, declaring, "There are those who want instant integration and those who want segregation forever. I believe we need to have a middle course."[18] He articulated his profound support for *Brown v. Board of Education* and the Civil Rights Act. At the same time, he decried the use of federal power "to force a local community to carry out what a Federal administrator or bureaucrat may think is best for that local community," and he commanded Justice Department civil rights officials to "do what the law requires and not one bit more."[19]

Nixon also sought to steal George Wallace's thunder by appropriating his law and order race codes. In his 1968 campaign, Nixon selected Governor Spiro Agnew of Maryland as his running mate. Agnew was a surprise pick whose chief qualification was his notorious accusation that black leaders in Baltimore had been complicit in the city's devastating race riots.[20] With Agnew by his side, Nixon reinvented himself as a gunslinging lawman who would save America from dangerous criminals with harsh prison sentences and pithy slogans like "Nixon's the One." Of course, the dangerous criminals were implicitly black, and their victims implicitly white. Richard Rovere, a political journalist at the *New Yorker,* wrote of the Nixon-Agnew law and order campaign:

> It is becoming clearer with each passing day that the principal issue this year will be, in a word, race. Nixon and Agnew may insist that they are not using a "code" term for race when they speak of "law and order," but race is what voters, Negro and white, understand it to mean, just as they did in 1965.[21]

Law and order was only one element of Nixon's evolving race strategy. Welfare reform was the second. In 1969, journalist Pete Hamill captured the growing sense of resentment among working-class whites in an article titled "The Revolt of the White Lower Middle Class." The men that Hamill interviewed were fed up with hearing that "400-years-of-slavery bit." One disgruntled white ironworker seethed:

None of them politicians gives a good goddam. All they worry about is the niggers. And everything is for the niggers. The niggers get the schools. The niggers go to summer camp. The niggers get the new play-grounds. The niggers get nursery schools. And they get it all without workin'. . . . They take the welfare and sit out on the stoop drinkin' cheap wine and throwin' the bottles on the street. They never gotta walk outta the house. They take the money outta my paycheck and they just turn it over to some lazy son of a bitch who won't work. I gotta carry him on my back. You know what I am? I'm a sucker. I really am. You shouldn't have to put up with this. And I'll tell ya somethin'. There's a lotta people who just ain't gonna put up with it much longer.[22]

A White House advisor forwarded the article to Nixon with the observation that "the bitterness of the urban white worker . . . is a social and political fact of first-rate importance." Nixon agreed and ordered his speechwriters to craft a welfare reform speech that would appeal to "working poor and tax payers" as opposed to "welfare recipients, unemployed, blacks."[23] Later, Nixon would tell his chief of staff, "The whole problem is really the blacks . . . The key is to devise a system that recognizes this while not appearing to." In case his race prejudice wasn't obvious enough, Nixon gratuitously added, "There has never in history been an adequate black nation . . . they are the only race of which this is true."[24]

One of the people who crafted Nixon's white persecution narrative was an advisor and speechwriter named Pat Buchanan. Buchanan had been a journalist before joining Nixon's administration, and he would later become a famous political pundit and third-party presidential candidate. Paunchy, jowly, and a little bit goofy on the surface with an egotistical, amoral, mean-as-hell core, Buchanan has always reminded me of Gene Hackman's portrayal of Lex Luthor in the old Superman films. During his exasperated squabbles on *The McLaughlin Group*, I half expect him to blurt out, "Why is the greatest criminal mind of our time surrounding himself with total nincompoops?"

In a confidential 1971 White House memo titled "Dividing the Democrats," Buchanan recommended strategies for luring blue collar and Southern whites from the Democratic Party. With frequent references to George Wallace, Buchanan proposed a series of manipulations to pit South against North, white against black, and blue collar against white collar. He suggested wooing Poles, Irish, Slovaks, and Italians and spurning blacks, Puerto Ricans, Mexican Americans, and American Indians, "the darlings of the mass media" who just happened to be dark-skinned. He recommended attacking the "loafing classes" and the "welfare mommas" and urged Nixon to "tear up the pea patch" by seeking "a constitutional end to the national pressure to integrate races in housing and schooling." Years later, Nixon described Buchanan as "a decent, patriotic American . . . but he has some strong beliefs that I believe are wrong."[25] Of course, Nixon had a low bar for "decent."

"Discrimination in Reverse"

After Nixon resigned in disgrace, Buchanan returned to journalism. In one of his early columns, titled "Discrimination in Reverse," he launched what would become a lifetime campaign against affirmative action, complaining that the government had become "the paramount practitioner of racism."

> To many, what the government is doing today, in its conscious favoritism toward blacks, feminists, Indians, and the Spanish-speaking, is no more defensible than what the segregationists of another era used to do, for just us white folks.[26]

Indeed, Buchanan might have had a point—if the government had barred whites from skilled jobs, good schools, lunch counters, voting booths, swimming pools, and public bathrooms. Or if government thugs beat up white men who had the audacity to speak to black women or hanged them for the slightest offenses.

But conservative persecution politics requires a distorted sense of perspective that minimizes discrimination against minorities and magnifies any imposition on the majority, so that the two seem more or less equivalent. At the time that the first affirmative action policies were initiated in the early 1960s, blacks were effectively shut out from skilled jobs and management positions. Even in progressive towns like New York City, job placement agencies illegally used notations like "POK" (person of color) and "NFU" (not for us) to distinguish black job candidates.[27]

Yet in 1963, white plumbers in Cleveland complained that "special privilege" was involved in the hiring of black plumbers. A clerical employee from Western Electric Co. reported, "Some of the girls who have been with the company a long time think they're being passed over in favor of less qualified colored girls." And a construction company lawyer in Philadelphia complained that pressure from the NAACP to employ more blacks in skilled jobs would mean "discrimination against whites."[28] (Six years later, less than one percent of Philadelphia's 10,000 skilled ironworkers, steamworkers, sheet metal workers, electricians, elevator workers, plumbers, and pipefitters were black. Philadelphia's overall population at the time was 35 percent black.)[29]

The first Supreme Court test of affirmative action occurred in 1978, the same pivotal year that the IRS proposed to strengthen desegregation requirements and the year after Anita Bryant's Save Our Children campaign. In the mid-seventies, the UC Davis School of Medicine had twice rejected Allan Bakke, a white male applicant, even though it had accepted minority applicants with lower academic scores. Bakke sued the university for violating his rights under the Equal Protection Clause of the Fourteenth Amendment. The Supreme Court, led by Justice Lewis Powell, ruled in Bakke's favor and ordered UC Davis to enroll him. In his decision, Powell rejected admission quotas as unconstitutional, but his ruling also legitimated the use of race in admissions decisions, as long as it was only one of multiple factors.

The new breed of racists, however, refused to countenance this distinction. In subsequent years, they would continue to misrepresent any affirmative action policy as a "race quota." The specter of race quotas is a powerful tool of persecution politics. At one time, universities used quotas to keep out undesirable minorities like Jews. By labeling any affirmative action policy a race quota, conservative leaders imply that such policies are designed to limit the number of undesirable white students.

Pat Buchanan was certainly dissatisfied by the 1978 *Bakke* decision. He attacked both Democrats and Republicans for practicing "preferential treatment" for minorities and called for a savior to come to the rescue of the white victims of reverse discrimination:

> What the victims need is a voice, a presidential candidate unafraid of confronting the "constituency of consciences" and its echo chamber, the national press. Anybody want to bell the cat?[30]

The Great Communicator

Ronald Reagan swatted constituencies of consciences as if they were vaguely annoying liberal gnats. Reagan was no bigot. Growing up in Illinois, his family was uncommonly tolerant. In his youth, Reagan fetched black visitors who had been barred from the town's hotel to stay in his parents' home. Yet Reagan also resisted federal action against entrenched racism. He opposed the Civil Rights Act of 1964 and the Voting Rights Act of 1965, calling the latter "humiliating to the South," by which he presumably meant the part of the South that was permitted to vote.[31]

Reagan backed up his "principled" stands against federal civil rights policies by demonizing minorities and dismissing the very idea that white Americans might discriminate against them. For example, in 1964, white Californians were suffering from a new state law that prohibited landlords from denying people housing because of ethnicity, religion, sex, marital status, physical handicap, or familial status. So they did what Californians do best: they launched a ballot initiative. Proposition 14 prohibited the state from interfering with landlords' "absolute discretion" to rent or refuse to rent to whomever they saw fit, i.e., blacks and Latinos. The president of the influential California Republican Assembly explained that denying people their inalienable right to discriminate against minorities was the first step on the slippery slope to socialist revolution, explaining:

> The essence of freedom is the right to discriminate. Discrimination means free choice. In socialist countries, they always take away this right in order to complete their takeover.[32]

Reagan called the California Republican Assembly the "conscience of the Republican Party" (which is exactly right in my opinion).[33] As for Proposition 14, Reagan didn't see any victims worthy of legal protection. Black complaints of real-estate discrimination were simply "staged attempts to rent homes, when in truth there was no real intention of renting, only causing trouble."[34] The proposition passed, but the California Supreme Court tossed it out due to unconstitutionality in 1966. Later that year, Californians elected Reagan their governor.

Attacking downtrodden minorities soon became Reagan's standard operating procedure. In his 1976 presidential campaign, the former Hollywood actor assembled a rollicking cast of colorful villains to graphically illustrate the scheming beneficiaries of government largess. The Welfare Queen with eighty names, thirty addresses, and twelve Social Security cards earned $150,000 and drove a Cadillac to pick up her welfare checks.*[35] The Strapping Young Buck purchased T-bone steaks with food stamps while outraged working people clutched their sad packages of ground beef.[36] The Witch Girl lived off food stamps while studying for a degree in witchcraft.[37] Perhaps the three amigos threw wild parties in one of the plush housing projects that Reagan denounced, where the apartments had "11-foot ceilings, with a 20-foot balcony, a swimming pool and a gymnasium."[38] They might even have invited the Militant Homosexual, who would have brought the farm animals.

---

* Reagan's "welfare queen" was an exaggerated caricature of Linda Taylor, a Chicago woman who was arrested for having used four aliases to defraud the government of $8,000. Taylor was clearly one of the great scam artists of our time, like Bernie Madoff and Enron's Jeffrey Skilling. ("'Welfare Queen' Becomes Issue in Reagan Campaign," *New York Times*, 15 Feb. 1976: 51.)

They don't call Reagan "the Great Communicator" for nothing. His welfare stories were much more effective at catalyzing working-class resentment than Nixon's wonkish reform proposals. Reagan gave the pampered schemers faces—black faces. Of course, he didn't say they were black. He didn't have to. He played on stereotypes of welfare recipients and their tastes in automobiles, and he used loaded language like "strapping young buck."

In theory, a "young buck" may refer to any energetic young man, but in certain parts of the United States—the parts where Reagan just happened to use the term—it had acquired a particular connotation due to its use at slave auctions. One former slave described his memory of a slave auction as follows:

> They have white gloves there, and one of the bidders takes a pair of gloves and rubs his fingers over a man's teeth, and he says to the overseer, "You call this buck twenty years old? Why there's cut worms in his teeth. He's forty years old, if he's a day." So they knock this buck down for a thousand dollars. They calls the men "bucks" and the women "wenches."[39]

"Buck" continued to be used as a racial slur well into the twentieth century. As late as 1965, the imperial wizard of the KKK justified the murder of civil rights activist Viola Liuzzo on the grounds that she shouldn't have been "sitting on the front seat with a young buck nigra."[40]

At the same time that Reagan was demonizing black welfare recipients, he also attacked the affirmative action programs. In his stump presidential campaign speeches, Reagan denounced "special privileges" and labeled affirmative action policies "racial quotas," saying, "You do not alter the evil character of racial quotas simply by changing the color of the beneficiary."[41] Calling affirmative action "evil" was too subtle for Senator Orrin Hatch's tastes. He presented it as an "an assault upon America, conceived in lies and fostered with an irresponsibility so extreme as to verge upon the malign. If the government officials and politicians who presided over its genesis had injected heroin into the bloodstream of the nation, they could not have done more potential damage to our children and our children's children."[42]

If you were a hard-working white American who resented having to pay taxes, the prospect of your hard-earned money going to T-bone-eating young bucks and Cadillac-driving welfare queens might make you angry. The prospect of lazy blacks getting special treatment that gave them unfair advantages might make you even angrier. You'd have nothing against black people, of course, but you might feel that you and your fellow white people were getting a raw deal from the government, that you were "suckers." It might make you vote for the man who promised to help you.

Reagan won in a landslide, sweeping the still-Democratic South despite Carter's Southern roots. (Against Ford, Carter had won every Southern state except Virginia. Against Reagan, he won only his native Georgia.) After that, the South never looked back. With only a couple of exceptions during the Clinton and Obama elections, the Southern states have voted Republican in every presidential election since 1980.

In 1981, Bob Jones University, a fundamentalist Christian college, sought Reagan's help with the IRS. Despite Jesse Helm's successful crusade against secular humanism, the IRS still prohibited tax exemptions to institutions with openly discriminatory language on their books. Bob Jones University had begun admitting married blacks in 1971, but it still officially prohibited interracial dating on the grounds that "God intended segregation of the races and that the Scriptures forbid interracial marriage," so the IRS continued to deny tax exemption.[43] Answering the call of the university's president, Bob Jones III, Reagan ordered the IRS to reestablish its tax exemption. A media uproar ensued; Reagan retracted his order. Then Reagan sought congressional legislation to block the IRS policy. More uproar ensued; Reagan backed off again. Finally, everyone moved on except for Bob Jones III, who grumpily called Reagan "a traitor to God's people."[44]

In other instances, Reagan stood firm. In a 1984 case concerning another Christian college, the Supreme Court limited the Civil Rights Act's effectiveness by ruling that its antidiscrimination provisions applied only to discriminatory programs. Therefore, whole institutions could not be penalized for violations by specific departments. In response, Congress amended the Civil Rights Act to override the ruling and restore the previous enforcement capabilities. Reagan vetoed the amendment on the grounds that it would "vastly and unjustifiably expand the power of the Federal Government" and threaten "cherished values as religious liberty"—once again representing (white, Christian) Americans as threatened by civil rights policy.[45] But Congress overrode Reagan's veto.

Reagan didn't achieve his welfare reform objectives either. While the Democrats did pass a welfare reform bill at Reagan's urging in 1988, it fell well short of the radical reductions he had championed.

But Reagan's domestic legacy was not policy. It was *mythology*. There were two elements to the myth. First, the black beneficiaries of welfare and affirmative action weren't victims—hence the duplicitous Welfare Queen, the indolent Strapping Young Buck, and the "special privileges" for minorities. Second, the white wage-earners were victims—hence the hamburger meat–eating taxpayers and the "reverse discrimination" against white people.

In chapter 1, we discussed the idea of the zero-sum game, which means that one side's gain is the other side's loss. If you view race relations through the prism of a zero-sum game between two teams, then anything that the government does to benefit the black team necessarily damages the white team. Reagan's mythology framed welfare and affirmative action programs as elements in a zero-sum game between whites and blacks. Welfare for the shiftless blacks robs the industrious whites of their hard-earned incomes. Affirmative action for unqualified blacks discriminates against deserving whites. Thus, those who subscribe to the mythology regard such programs as essentially persecuting white people.

Many of Reagan's supporters internalized this conflict. Democratic pollster Stanley Greenberg coined the term *Reagan Democrat* in a classic 1984 study that documented the political evolution of Macomb County, Michigan, which had voted overwhelmingly for JFK in 1960 and even more overwhelmingly for Reagan in 1980. According to Greenberg:

These white Democratic defectors express a profound distaste for blacks, a sentiment that pervades almost everything they think about government and politics. Blacks constitute the explanation for their vulnerability and for almost everything that has gone wrong in their lives . . . The special status of blacks is perceived by almost all of these individuals as a serious obstacle to their personal advancement. Indeed, discrimination against whites has become a well-assimilated and ready explanation for their status, vulnerability and failures.[46]

These attitudes survived long after Reagan left office. A 1993 poll showed that 35 percent of whites believed that blacks "generally preferred to accept welfare than work for a living" and 20 percent believed that blacks "were not as hard-working as everyone else," but 33 percent believed that a black candidate was more likely to be hired than an equally qualified white candidate. Such opinions were not reserved to recalcitrant old grandparents. While a third of those over the age of fifty held prejudiced views, they were nearly matched by people under thirty.[47] Similarly, a 1994 poll found that 55 percent of Americans wrongly believed that most welfare beneficiaries were black. Among these, 69 percent assumed that most welfare recipients didn't want to work, and 64 percent believed that most of them didn't really need welfare.[48]

The Exeter-Yale GOP

Reagan's successor, George H. W. Bush, was the reluctant heir of the Republican Party's proud new role as the defender of white people. Bush knew how to talk the talk, but one had the sense that his heart wasn't in it. As a student at Yale, Bush had headed the United Negro College Fund, but when he ran for the U.S. Senate in Texas, he opposed the 1964 Civil Rights Act. He lost the race but became a congressman in 1966 and established a strong civil rights record, bucking his Southern constituency in the process.

Back on the campaign trail for president in 1988, Bush started toss-
ing race cards again. He relentlessly hammered opponent George
Dukakis for a policy that enabled William Horton, a black convict, to
rape a white woman while on weekend furlough from prison; the campaign's Willie Horton ad is infamous for coded "law and order" racism.
As president, Bush appointed Clarence Thomas, an African American
but also a fierce critic of affirmative action, to the Supreme Court. Finally, Bush vetoed the Civil Rights Act of 1990 on the grounds that it
"introduces the destructive force of quotas."[49] But the act addressed
compensation for employment discrimination and had nothing to do
with affirmative action. It introduced "quotas" only insofar as *quota*
had become the new code for "pampering black people."

The following year, Congress passed the Civil Rights Act of 1991,
which one pundit described as "the Civil Rights Act of 1990 with one
more year of political maneuver and acrimony thrown in. The basic issues haven't changed, only the tactics of supporters and opponents."[50]
But this time, Bush assured the nation, "Unlike last year's bill, a bill I
was forced to veto, this bill will not encourage quotas or racial prefer-
ences."[51] Quotas, it seems, are in the eye of the beholder. Pat Buchanan,
for one, still beheld lots and lots of quotas. He attacked Bush for caving
to Democrats and charged, "It's a quota bill and it's horrible for business: Every minority malcontent is going to be suing . . . The whole
idea of merit is going out the window."[52]

Buchanan was so incensed by Bush's callous disregard for white
Americans suffering from lawsuits by minority malcontents that he ran
for president. "If you belong to the Exeter-Yale GOP club, that's not
going to bother you greatly because, as we know, it is not their children
who get bused out of South Boston into Roxbury," Buchanan charged,
"It is the sons and daughters of Middle America who pay the price of
reverse discrimination advanced by the Walker's Point GOP* to salve
their social consciences at other people's expense."[53]

Meanwhile, David Duke evidently concluded that Pat Buchanan was
too soft on reverse discrimination, because he ran in the Republican

---

* "Walker's Point GOP." Walker's Point is the former name of the Bush compound in Kenne-
bunkport, Maine.

e Nazi uniform that he once
ed the phrase *growing under-*
ters' concerns about welfare,
ately for Duke, Buchanan co-
y and wrapped up the racist
donors, and media attention.
k Pat Buchanan sounds more
o differ, countering, "David
ind to go down there and sue
that dude for intellectual property theft."*[56]

Buchanan didn't win the nomination, but he snagged a fat consolation prize—the keynote address at the Republican convention. He defiantly delivered what has become known as the Culture War speech, in which he introduced America to the full force of persecution politics, proclaiming, "There is a religious war going on in our country for the soul of America. It is a cultural war, as critical to the kind of nation we will one day be as was the Cold War itself."[57] In the mode of the Nixon-Agnew law and order campaign, Buchanan concluded his fiery speech with a martial allusion to the race riots that had recently shaken Los Angeles:

[The 18th Cavalry] had come into L.A. late on the 2nd day, and they walked up a dark street, where the mob had looted and burned every building but one, a convalescent home for the aged. The mob was heading in, to ransack and loot the apartments of the terrified old men and women. When the troopers arrived, M-16s at the ready, the mob threatened and cursed, but the mob retreated. It had met the one thing that could stop it: force, rooted in justice, backed by courage . . . Here were 19-year-old boys ready to lay down their lives to stop a mob from molesting old people they did not even know. And as they took back the streets of L.A., block by block, so we must take back our cities, and take back our culture, and take back our country. God bless you, and God bless America.

---

* "Intellectual property theft." Buchanan's legal threat against Duke was empty. According to intellectual property experts, you can't trademark racism.

Let's unravel Buchanan's little parable. The dark-skinned mob represents rampaging liberals seeking to force "radical feminism," "abortion on demand," "homosexual rights," and "discrimination against religious schools" on the American people, who cower helplessly in their nursing home. But, hark, here comes the Eighteenth Cavalry, a.k.a. the Republican Party, brave Christian solders [sic] who would sacrifice their lives to stop dangerous liberals from molesting traditional American citizens. That's persecution politics.

Needless to say, Buchanan's story is a pile of hooey. The residents of the Vermont Knoll Retirement Center defended the center from rioters by forming a human shield around the building. By the time the cavalry arrived hours later, all was quiet. According to the center's director, "There were no guns drawn. No mob attacking . . . I don't know where he got those facts, but they were not correct."[58]

Brown Becomes the New Black

Speaking of the LA riots, most analysts believed that they had been sparked by police brutality against an African American named Rodney King, a logical conclusion because the riots began in a black neighborhood the day after the highly publicized acquittal of the cops who beat up King. But Pat Buchanan never lets logic stand in the way of political opportunity. Always a forward thinker, Buchanan had moved beyond the black-white conflicts of the Wallace era. Black race riots were so 1968. In 1992, brown was the new black. Mexican brown. Observing that many of the rioters were Hispanic, Buchanan concluded, "Foreigners are coming into this country illegally and helping to burn down one of the greatest cities in America."[59]

Illegal Latino immigrants offer a number of advantages over blacks as a target for persecution politics. First, whites didn't enslave Latinos for two hundred years and then repress them for another hundred, so the media is less sensitive to verbal attacks on them. Second, illegal immigrants have no claim to taxpayer support, since they're not officially American. Even the most hardened welfare opponent might acknowledge some moral imperative to assist American families that have nothing to eat and nowhere to live. But many Americans don't believe that "illegals" deserve anything from us and, besides, if we gave them benefits, it would just encourage more welfare parasites to come over the border. It was in this spirit that the citizens of California once more took government into their own hands in 1994 and passed Proposition 187, a.k.a. Save Our State, to deny social services, health care, and public education to illegal immigrants. Californians, incidentally, also went after affirmative action two years later with Proposition 209, a.k.a. the California Civil Rights Initiative.* Both propositions were supported by civil rights heroes Pat Buchanan and David Duke.

The trouble with contemporary racism, however, is that society's taboos are too constraining for effective fearmongering. A conservative pundit who wants to keep his syndicated column and his regular slot on *The McLaughlin Group* can't disseminate theories about militant black conspiracies to kill whitey. While quotas and welfare might be oppressive,† they won't lead to concentration camps for white people. If you really want to scare the bejeezus out of white America, you need a credible threat to the white race that won't get you fired. You need more dark people.

Fortunately for practitioners of race-based persecution politics like Pat Buchanan, demographic changes are working in their favor. In

---

* California's government-by-proposition, which has rendered the California state government virtually impotent to deal with financial crises or much of anything else, demonstrates that the nation's founders knew what they were doing when they set up a representative democracy. It seems that the only people less competent to govern than elected officials are the people that elected them.

† "Quotas and welfare might be oppressive." Tim Fay, a reverse discrimination survivor, has founded a website, Adversity.nct, dedicated to the victims of reverse discrimination. According to Fay, quota victims may suffer from posttraumatic stress disorder: "Feelings of depression, apathy, or sadness may develop within hours, weeks, or a few months of the incident . . . Victims of Post Traumatic Stress Disorder induced by reverse discrimination often experience gastrointestinal disorders, substance abuse problems . . . Victims' marriages and friendships are frequently shattered in the aftermath of reverse discrimination incidents. One insightful victim to whom I spoke last week candidly attributed his advanced colon cancer and the dissolution of his marriage to his repeated experiences with reverse discrimination." (Tim Fay, "Post Traumatic Stress Disorder among Victims of Reverse Discrimination," *Adversity.Net*, 17 Mar. 2000, http://www.adversity.net/post_traumatic_0.htm.)

November 1993, the face of a young woman graced the cover of *Time* magazine. She was dark haired and dark eyed. Her nose was slightly broad, and her lips were slightly thick. Her skin had an olive complexion. She was not real. A computer had generated her face from a mix of several races. She was, according to *Time*'s editors, "The New Face of America." The lead article quoted a policy analyst who proclaimed, "We have left the time when the nonwhite, non-Western part of our population could be expected to assimilate to the dominant majority. In the future, the white, Western majority will have to do some assimilation of its own."[60]

Pat Buchanan made the same point more pejoratively:

> Mexicans not only come from another culture, but millions are of another race. History and experience teach us that different races are far more difficult to assimilate. The sixty million Americans who claim German ancestry are fully assimilated, while millions from Africa and Asia are still not full participants in American society.

Millions of African and Asian Americans might beg to differ. Buchanan is correct, of course, that it took African Americans a couple of centuries to become full participants in American society, but the reason for that should be rather obvious, even to a man like Pat Buchanan.

The irony is that Mexicans and other Latin Americans are not all that different from America's "white, Western majority," racially or culturally. Most speak a European language, belong to a European church, and carry a solid chunk of European DNA in their chromosomes. While Latin America is less developed than the United States, the immigrants aren't exactly Stone Age tribespeople who have never used telephones, and their culture is no more alien to our own than that of the Eastern European immigrants who have been assimilating quite nicely for a century.*

---

* "Never used telephones." Michael Savage, a conservative talk radio expert on the true nature of the immigrant, disputes that. "We're getting refugees now who have never used a telephone, a toothbrush, or toilet paper. You're telling me they're going to assimilate? They will never assimilate. They come here and they bring their destitute ways to this

But the Eastern Europeans have one thing that most Latin Americans lack—pale white skin. Pat Buchanan himself laid out the pigment problem back in 1984:

> The burning issue here has almost nothing to do with economics, almost everything to do with race and ethnicity. If British subjects, fleeing a depression, were pouring into this country through Canada, there would be few alarms. The central objection to the present flood of illegals is they are not English-speaking white people from Western Europe; they are Spanish-speaking brown and black people from Mexico, Latin America and the Caribbean.[61]

Forget about the "Spanish-speaking" bit. Americans are accustomed to non-English-speaking immigrants, and Spanish-speaking immigrants from Spain do not disturb us. Forget about the "Mexico, Latin America and the Caribbean" bit as well. White English-speakers from Jamaica or South Africa would not bother us either. That leaves only "brown and black people." That's the *real* burning issue here.

To Buchanan, the color of your skin says something important about you—about your cultural traits and possibly your genetic aptitudes. Moreover, the difference between "your" cultural traits and aptitudes and "our" cultural traits and aptitudes constitutes a terrible threat to "us." In a 1990 column, Buchanan predicted that the United States would become a third world country "if we do not build a sea wall against the waves of immigration rolling over our shores."[62] He then connected this invasion of brown people to the demands of black people already in our midst as if the black and the brown teams were joining forces to defeat the white team:

> The Negroes of the '50's became the blacks of the '60's; now, the "African-Americans" of the '90's demand racial quotas and set-asides, as the

---

country, and they never assimilate. And then their children become gang-bangers." ("Savage: 'We're getting refugees now who have never used a telephone, a toothbrush, or toilet paper. . . . . [T]hey never assimilate. And then their children become gang-bangers,'" *Media Matters*, 25 Jun. 2008, http://mediamatters.org/mmtv/200806250001.)

Democrats eagerly assent and a pandering G.O.P. prepares to go along. Who speaks for the Euro-Americans, who founded the United States?

Here you have persecution politics in a nutshell. In 1990, blacks held 5 percent of U.S. congressional seats and Latinos held 3 percent. There was not a single black or Latino senator.[63] And yet Buchanan concluded that there was no one to speak for the "Euro-Americans."

National Suicide

As the new millennia dawned, Buchanan grew increasingly fatalistic about the future of the white race. His 2002 book, *The Death of the West: How Dying Populations and Immigrant Invasions Imperil Our Country and Civilization,* begins with a quote from T. S. Eliot: "This is the way the world ends, not with a bang but a whimper."* In his 2007 book, *Day of Reckoning: How Hubris, Ideology, and Greed Are Tearing America Apart,* Buchanan argued that America is literally self-destructing:

> America is indeed coming apart, decomposing, and . . . the likelihood of her survival as one nation through mid-century is improbable—and impossible if America continues on her current course. For we are on a path to national suicide.[64]

For Buchanan, "national suicide" is synonymous with racial heterogeneity. He argued that "the American majority," by which he meant America's white population, is simply not procreating quickly enough to keep ahead of the tsunami of dark-skinned immigrants and fast-breeding minorities.

---

* "Not with a bang but a whimper." T. S. Eliot was a fitting choice. In 1933, Eliot declared, "The population should be homogeneous; where two or more cultures exist in the same place they are likely either to be fiercely self-conscious or both to become adulterate. What is still more important is unity of religious background; and reasons of race and religion combine to make any large number of free-thinking Jews undesirable." (T. S. Eliot, *After Strange Gods: A Primer of Modern Heresy* [London: Faber and Faber, 1934]: 20.)

The American majority is not reproducing itself. Its birthrate has been below replacement level for decades. Forty-five million of its young have been destroyed in the womb since *Roe v. Wade* as Asian, African, and Latin American children come to inherit the state the lost generation of American children never got to see."[65]

Right-wing radio host Michael Savage also saw a connection between the great white depopulation and the Gay Agenda. "With the [Latino] population that has emerged, since they breed like rabbits, in many cases the whites will become a minority in their own nation," he told listeners. "The white people don't breed as often for whatever reason. I guess many homosexuals are involved. That is also part of the grand plan, to push homosexuality to cut down on the white race."[66]

Without a single dominant (white) culture, Buchanan predicted that the nation would "Balkanize," becoming culturally, geographically, and racially divided. The black and brown folks don't melt nicely into the pot the way the white immigrants of old did. They don't share the culture of "the American majority," and they lack Euro-Americans' moral and intellectual fiber. "Almost as many African-American males are in jail or prison as are in colleges or universities," Buchanan charged. "Half of all African-American and Hispanic students drop out of high school. The other half graduates with the math and reading skills of seventh-, eighth- and ninth graders. Yet by 2050 the number of African-Americans and Hispanics will have almost doubled from today's 85 million, to 160 million."*[67]

Buchanan even found a way to fit the Culture War into his grand epic of national collapse. He warned readers that America's "ethnocul-

---

* Buchanan's arguments resembled those of another book that warned of the "immigrant flood" threatening America's infertile founding race with extinction. The author described the newcomers as immoral, lazy, ignorant, disloyal, unpatriotic, drunk, unskilled, criminal, unsanitary, and unattractive—but extremely fertile. The book, titled *The Old World in the New: The Significance of Past and Present Immigration,* was published in 1913. The problematic immigrants were Greek, Polish, Italian, Irish, Jewish, Lithuanian, Bulgarian, Romanian, and Portuguese. (Edward Alsworth Ross, *The Old World in the New: The Significance of Past and Present Immigration* [New York: The Century Co., 1914]: 300.)

tural core has begun to dissolve."[68] (*Scotty to bridge, she cannae take much more of this, captain!*) America's ethnocultural core apparently consists in our shared faith in Christ, heterosexual marriage, and the late Terri Schiavo's vegetative brain. It is the glue that preserves a multiethnic nation likes ours from disintegration in ethnic conflict. In other words, Christian faith is what prevents one ethnic group from hating another ethnic group. Ponder that one for a while.

La Reconquista

Buchanan's Balkanization theory is not just figurative. In his 2006 book, *State of Emergency: The Third World Invasion and Conquest of America,* Buchanan introduced nervous white readers to the Reconquista. The original Reconquista refers to the Christian recapture of Spain from the Moors, led by Charlemagne and others. Back in the 1980s, Mexicans referred jokingly to U.S. real estate acquisitions by affluent Mexicans as a *reconquista* of the territories that Mexico lost to the United States during the Mexican-American War in the late 1840s.[69]

But the new Reconquista movement is much scarier—a nefarious strategy to take back the Southwest by immigration blitzkrieg. The movement appears to have been first discovered in the late 1990s by a white nationalist border vigilante named Glenn Spencer. Spencer revealed an international plot by the Mexican government, the Democratic Party, the liberal press, multinational corporations, organized labor, the Roman Catholic Church, and the Ford Foundation to establish a "fifth column" of Mexican subversives to recolonize the Southwest, which they refer to by its Aztec name, Aztlán.[70]

Spencer toured the white supremacist lecture circuit for years, but his discovery remained on the fringe until Pat Buchanan publicized it in 2006. Buchanan, being a good Catholic, dropped the church from the conspiracy, but he kept the Ford Foundation, the corporations, and the Mexican government. He even used Spencer's "fifth column" language, writing:

Regimes like Mexico's now look on citizens who leave to work or study in the United States as agents of influence, a fifth column inside the belly of the beast . . . Stated bluntly, the Aztlan Strategy entails the end of a sovereign, self-sufficient, independent republic, the passing away of the American nation. They are coming to conquer us.[71]

Once Buchanan officially approved the Reconquista conspiracy theory, the rest of the right wing quickly jumped on board, and it has become a staple of anti-immigrant persecution politics, promoted by conservative media stars like Michelle Malkin, Glenn Beck, and Lou Dobbs.

Bill O'Reilly, on the other hand, doesn't believe that Mexican immigration is a plot to recapture the Southwest. In his opinion, it's just an "economic scam" by Mexico to export its "poverty and education problem" to the United States.[72] That said, he also claimed that the U.S. government permits illegal immigration because politicians are intimidated by minorities who are plotting to destroy "the white power structure" through population growth, explaining:

There's no reason on earth the federal government doesn't secure the border. No reason on this earth. But they're afraid to be demonized as racist because the real racists who want a color-based country attack them vehemently if they put up a wall or put the military on the border.[73]

See, it's not the immigration opponents who are racists. According to O'Reilly's projection of intolerance, the "real racists" are the secret proponents of illegal immigration who want a "color-based country."

The fearmongering over illegal immigration eventually found its way into state law in 2010 with Arizona SB 1070. The law requires aliens to carry registration documents at all times and empowers police to demand documents from those whom they suspect of being in the country illegally. In the article "Whose Country Is This?" Pat Buchanan argued that Arizona acted because the U.S. government "refuses to enforce America's immigration laws."[74]

A second lesser-known Arizona law that followed on the heels of SB 1070 invoked persecution politics even more explicitly. The law prohibits ethnic studies classes that "promote resentment toward a race or class of people" (i.e., whites), "are designed primarily for pupils of a particular ethnic group" (i.e., Latinos), or "advocate ethnic solidarity instead of the treatment of pupils as individuals." With a hat tip to the Reconquista conspiracy, it also prohibits classes that "promote the overthrow of the United States government."[75]

"Governor Brewer signed the bill because she believes, and the legislation states, that public school students should be taught to treat and value each other as individuals and not be taught to resent or hate other races or classes of people," said the governor's spokesperson—three weeks after the governor gave the police authority to arrest Latinos who don't carry immigration documents.

Tom Horne, the Republican state superintendent of public instruction who had fought for years to end Tucson's ethnic studies programs, explained the true rationale behind the bill. "They are teaching a radical ideology," he said of the ethnic studies courses, "including that Arizona and other states were stolen from Mexico and should be given back."[76]

A Brief Interlude

The timing of the Reconquista outbreak, starting in 2006, is notable. Immigration had been all over the news in the 1990s, but on September 11, 2001, the nation's gaze jerked suddenly from the south to the east. The attack on the World Trade Center, followed by wars in Afghanistan and Iraq, pushed fears of the Latino invasion from the front of most Americans' minds. People became concerned about securing the nation's borders not from illegal immigrants but from bombs and terrorists.

The terrorism fears that the right wing bathed in for the next five years had a substantial racist element for sure, but the "war on terror" is not a good example of persecution politics. First, the primary threat is external, not internal. The villainous masterminds embodied by Osama bin Laden and Saddam Hussein were foreigners. Local terrorist cells were represented as extensions of Al Qaeda's power, just as Japanese Americans were seen as agents of the Japanese empire in the 1940s, and suspected communists were seen as Soviet tools in the 1950s. Second, there is actually a terrorism threat. Unlike secular humanists, gay recruiters, welfare queens, and reconquistadors, Islamic terrorists exist, and they conspire to attack the United States. While the threat has been repeatedly overblown, liberals have been accused of weakness, innocent Muslims have been demonized, and President Obama's middle name has been repeated ad nauseam, there is no mainstream narrative of powerful American elites conspiring with radical Muslims to persecute white Christian conservatives through terrorism.

Even if George W. Bush had not been obsessed with Islamic terrorism, it is unlikely that he would have pushed a race-based persecution politics strategy. The nation's obsession with welfare went into decline after the Clinton-Gingrich reforms in the 1990s. Bush and his political strategist, Karl Rove, saw Latinos as fertile recruiting targets, so they avoided anything that might antagonize them. Bush often emphasized his Spanish-language skills and his personal relationship with the Mexican president, Vicente Fox.

Pat Buchanan, meanwhile, shuffled about in the political wilderness, a lonely conservative voice muttering about Jewish neocons who colluded with Israel to ensnare the United States in a war that was not in the nation's interest.[77] By 2006, however, the U.S. had begun to shake itself loose from 9/11 fever. Color-coded threat levels had become background noise, the wars in Iraq and Afghanistan had become page six stories, Bush's favorability ratings had swooned, and Democrats swept into Congress. From the right-wing fringes, persecution politics began to snarl and bay.

The Change We've Been Waiting For

The 2008 Republican primary was a study in immigration demagoguery. Just as George Wallace once vowed that he would not be "out-niggered," so did the eleven white men running for the Republican

nomination compete to out-"illegal" each other.* They accused one another of giving scholarships and driver's licenses to illegal immigrants,
of failing to secure America's borders, of supporting amnesty for illegal
immigrants, of employing Guatemalan gardeners, and of running sanc-
tuary cities for illegal aliens (which sounds like the plot of sci-fi thriller
District 9). After one immigrant bash during a Republican debate, the
anti-immigration crusader Tom Tancredo declared, "All I've heard is
people trying to out-Tancredo Tancredo."[†78]

And then there was Barack Obama. When Obama launched his campaign in 2007, the racist fringe went nuts of course, but the big conservative media stars approached with caution. Bill O'Reilly reported
that white Americans were "terrified" that anything they said about
Obama might be interpreted as racist condescension. Glenn Beck said
that he didn't have many African American friends because he was
afraid of saying "something that somebody would take wrong, and
then it would be a nightmare."[79] (Beck must not have many socialist or
fascist friends either.)

Limbaugh, bolder than the rest, took the lead by openly taunting
the media and daring them to call him a racist. On one show, he discussed a *Los Angeles Times* opinion piece titled "Obama the 'Magic
Negro.'" Limbaugh then proceeded to repeat the phrase "Barack the

---

* Illegal is such a perfect slur for illegal immigrants. Dropping the word *immigrant* renders
them stateless and homeless, neither here nor there, and reduces their essence to one of
pure violation, unlawfulness in the flesh.

† Tom Tancredo likes to conflate terrorism with immigration to maximize the scary factor.
In campaign appearances, he warned people that illegal immigrants were "coming here to
kill you, and you, and me, and my grandchildren." He did not explain why the immigrants
hate his grandchildren so much. In a similar vein, Rep. Sue Myrick (R-NC) warned that
Arab terrorists are learning Spanish in Venezuela and sneaking across the border disguised
as illegal Mexican immigrants. Rep. Louie Gohmert (R-TX) claimed that terrorists are sending women to give birth on U.S. soil so that their terrorist babies have American citizenship—"And then one day, twenty . . . thirty years down the road, they can be sent in to
help destroy our way of life."
(Ed Quillen, "Preventing Wars, the Tancredo Way," *Denver Post*, 26 Jul. 2005: B7; Sue
Myrick, "Myrick Calls for Taskforce to Investigate Presence of Hezbollah on the US Southern Border," *U.S. House of Representatives*, 25 Jun. 2010, http://myrick.house.gov/index.
cfm?sectionid=22&itemid=558; Walid Zafar, "Rep. Gohmert Warns of Baby Terrorists,"
Media Matters, 25 Jun. 2010, http://politicalcorrection.org/blog/201006250005.)

Magic Negro" twenty-seven times over the course of the show, eventually singing the words to the tune of "Puff the Magic Dragon," and predicted that the media would skewer him.[80] He must not have received the reaction that he'd hoped for because he then had a conservative comedian record a full version of the song in the impersonated voice of Al Sharpton, which Limbaugh played repeatedly throughout the campaign.*[81]

Ultimately, the right-wing media settled on two persecution politics tactics to challenge Obama's candidacy. The first was to present Obama as an "affirmative action candidate," to use Limbaugh's words.[82] Limbaugh found Obama's candidacy so astounding that he surmised it had been arranged by a Soros-run anti-Clinton conspiracy to front a black candidate:

> We know that George Soros is involved with Obama, but there's somebody that's putting the words in his mouth . . . There must be real animosity toward the Clintons at high levels of this party. To go with a veritable rookie whose only chance of winning is that he's black.[83]

Glenn Beck, who eventually found the courage to express his inner racist, suggested that Hillary Clinton give Obama "an additional 5 percentage points just for the years of oppression."[84] Ann Coulter followed up by suggesting that "B. Hussein Obama's" first big accomplishment was to be born "half-black."†[85]

Curiously, conservatives like Coulter make a big deal of the fact that Obama's mother was white, as if to prove that Obama didn't deserve the affirmative action from which he allegedly benefitted. Limbaugh called Obama a "half-minority" and a "Halfrican-American."[86] (Conservatives must have loved the "Halfrican" knee-slapper because various right-wing talk show hosts used it repeatedly.) Fox's Monica

---

* "Barack the Magic Negro." Limbaugh is the right-wing media celebrity version of a five-year-old boy who shouts naughty words so that his parents notice him.

† "Half-black." Coulter is the right-wing media celebrity version of a ten-year-old girl who tries to get kids to like her by saying the meanest things she can think of.

Crowley even denied Obama his half-blackness. She promoted a fiction that "Barack Obama is not black African, he is Arab African." (Does Crowley know what Arabs look like?) She continued, "And yet, this guy is campaigning as black and painting anybody who dares to criticize him as a racist. I mean, that is—it is the biggest con I think I've ever seen."[87] (Does Crowley know what a con is?)

The second strategy, which soon became the primary one, was to project racial hatred onto Obama by turning him into an "angry black man." This was a difficult trick to pull off because "angry" is not an adjective that comes to mind when describing Obama. The first attempts relied on guilt-by-association to tie Obama to people who were much more obviously "angry blacks." Fox News's Sean Hannity led the charge. First, he invited a guest onto *Hannity & Colmes* who asserted that Obama's church was "more like a cult or an Aryan Brethren Church . . . They refer to themselves as an African people, and that somewhat disturbs me from the viewpoint of, well, do they consider themselves Americans? Do they consider themselves Christians? Are they worshipping Christ? Are they worshipping African things black?"*[88] Another guest compared the church to the Ku Klux Klan.[89]

Next Hannity reported that Obama's pastor, Rev. Jeremiah Wright Jr., had praised Louis Farrakhan, the paranoid anti-Semitic leader of the Nation of Islam, which led him to conclude that Obama "associated" with Farrakhan.[90] This logic relies on the transitive property of association—if A associates with B, and B associates with C, then A associates with C. If you then apply the associative property of belief—if A associates with B, and B believes X, then A believes X—you'll see that Obama is in fact the paranoid anti-Semitic leader of the Nation of Islam.

But combining the transitive property of association with the associative property of belief is somewhat contentious, so Hannity decided to cut out the middle man and go straight for the spouse. He revealed that Michelle Obama's senior thesis included the words "Blacks must join in solidarity to combat a White oppressor." According to the principle of contextual irrelevancy, the fact that she was referring to some-

---

* As far as I can tell, the "Aryan Brethren Church" appears to be entirely made up.

one else's beliefs was immaterial. Finally, Hannity synthesized Rev. Wright's Farrakhan association, the African fetish of his cultlike church, Michelle Obama's senior thesis, and her infamous comment that for the first time in her life she was proud to be American. Unifying these four elements in accordance with the Grand Theory of Bovine Fecal Obfuscation, Hannity concluded, "A pattern begins to emerge. It's only fair to ask: Do the Obamas have a race problem of their own?"[91] And that was all *before* Rev. Wright's "god damn America" comment came out.

The mainstream media lapped up Obama's "race problem" like chocolate milk, evenhandedly presenting both sides of the issue as if there were actually two sides to the issue. Obama eventually concluded that he would have to address the matter directly. He delivered a powerful speech about American race relations that former Republican secretary of state Colin Powell called "a very, very thoughtful, direct speech"[92] and MSNBC's Chris Matthews praised as "the best speech ever given on race in this country."[93]

But people like Sean Hannity only heard one sentence, "[My grandmother] uttered racial or ethnic stereotypes that made me cringe." That's all that they had to hear to confirm what they already believed: Obama hates white people. When Obama tried to clarify the comment a few days later, he further confirmed their dark suspicions by calling his grandmother a "typical white person," which caused them to repeat the phrase "threw his grandmother under the bus" in every other sentence for the next twelve months. According to Limbaugh, Obama's comment revealed that he had officially converted from Halfrican to all-black: "Obama has disowned his white half . . . he's decided he's got to go all in on the black side."[94]

The Maverick

Two factors kept the general election from becoming an all-out race fest. First, Obama eventually denounced Rev. Wright and studiously avoided giving the right any ammunition that it could twist into a persecution narrative. Second, Senator John McCain chose not to play the race game. McCain had vowed early on to run a respectful campaign. He soon proved that *respectful* is a relative term. He ran ads that compared Obama to celebrity Paris Hilton and a false messiah called "the One." He sought to associate him with bad guys like Bill Ayers the Weatherman, Tony Rezko the slumlord, Mahmoud Ahmadinejad the Islamic despot, and Hamas the terrorist organization. But McCain did not do the one thing that his advisors and his vice presidential candidate urged him to do.

"Wright is off the table," said one top campaign official. "It's all McCain. He won't go there. His advisers would have gone there." Early in his campaign, McCain promised not to talk about Rev. Wright, and except for a brief reference in April of 2008, he remained true to his word. A Republican official explained, "There's a slippery slope in politics on the racial divide, and Senator McCain made it very clear early on that he did not want to get into that area . . . McCain doesn't want to be known as a racist candidate."[95] And so, when John McCain conceded the election on November 4, he was able to praise in good faith the "special significance" of Obama's historic election.

If Nixon's old strategist, Pat Buchanan, can be believed, McCain's restraint may have cost him the presidency. The day after the election, Buchanan wrote an article called "An Unnecessary Defeat?" in which he argued that McCain had screwed up:

> While Barack was locking up black America, McCain failed to hold on to Bush's share of the white working class . . . Perhaps fearful his "good guy" reputation with his old buddies in his media "base" would be imperiled, McCain ruled Wright off limits and seemed hesitant even to go after the Ayers connections. Lee Atwater would not have been so ambivalent. Leo Durocher put it succinctly: "Nice guys finish last."[96]

McCain, needless to say, is no fan of Pat Buchanan. Back in 1999, he observed, "It is evident to me by Pat Buchanan's own rhetoric that he has left the Republican Party."[97] Unfortunately, it seems that the Republican Party has left the Republican Party. In 2010, Republicans have nominated a number of candidates whose sensibilities are much closer to Buchanan's than to McCain's. McCain himself is running hard against a strong primary challenge from a man who believes that same-sex marriage would lead to man-horse unions.[98]

"Forced Reparations"

John McCain's gracious concession speech may have been the last generous word Obama heard from Republicans on the subject of race. In winning the presidency, Obama fulfilled the fears of white racists across the country—and thus fulfilled the dreams of those who prey on such fears. Before Obama became president, the new breed of racists had to distinguish between the perpetrators of reverse discrimination—predominantly white judges and politicians—and the beneficiaries—blacks and Latinos. With a black man in the White House, the perpetrators and beneficiaries of the persecution narrative merged. Where the right used to explain that Democrats favored minorities because the party was beholden to "special interests," they now assume that Democrats favor minorities simply because the leader of the party is a minority.

Thus, Rush Limbaugh argued in 2009 that Obama's policies are designed to benefit black people in order to compensate them for centuries of slavery:

> The objective is unemployment. The objective is more food stamp benefits. The objective is more unemployment benefits. The objective is an expanding welfare state. And the objective is to take the nation's wealth and return to it to the nation's quote, "rightful owners." Think reparations. Think forced reparations here if you want to understand what actually is going on.[99]

Two months later, Glenn Beck seconded Limbaugh's reparations theory:

> Everything getting pushed through Congress—including this health care bill—is transforming America. And it's all driven by President

Obama's thinking on one idea: reparations . . . He believes in all the "universal" programs because they "disproportionately affect" people of color. And that's the best way, he feels, to right the wrongs of the past. These massive programs are Obama brand reparations or in presidential speak: leveling the playing field.[100]

The reparations theory presents the zero-sum game in stark relief: There is a white team and a black team. Obama plays for the black team. He hates the white team. He wants to take resources from the white team and give them to the black team. "Us" versus "them." Persecution politics.

A Wise Latina

But let's not forget the brown team. The pinnacle of race-driven persecution politics was the right-wing response to Obama's nomination of Judge Sonia Sotomayor for the Supreme Court. It is the nature of modern American politics for the opposition party to challenge Supreme Court nominees any way that they can. And when a black president nominates a Latina judge, the obvious route for a Republican challenge is *race*. But they can't mention race, not in 2010. Instead, they took the exact same tact that they took against Obama. They called Sotomayor an unqualified affirmative action nominee and an angry Latina.

Pat Buchanan, for example, called Sotomayor "an affirmative action pick" who was chosen because she was Hispanic. He attacked her support for "reverse discrimination against white males" and declared, "Her entire career is based on advancing people of color, which happens at the expense of white folks."[101] Rush Limbaugh said, "She's not the brain that they're portraying her to be. She's not a constitutional jurist. She is an affirmative action case extraordinaire," and compared her to David Duke, claiming, "She brings a form of bigotry or racism to the court."[102] Glenn Beck was more concise: "I think the woman is a racist . . . I think the woman is not so bright."[103] Tom Tancredo condemned Sotomayor's membership in the National Council of La Raza, a Latino civil rights organization much like the NAACP, describing it as "a Latino KKK without the hoods or the nooses."[104] Even Newt Gingrich chimed in, calling Sotomayor a "Latina woman racist."[105]

By that point, the Republican establishment evidently concluded that the right wing had crossed the line between racism and racism, and they moved to quell the eruption, sort of. Sen. John Cornyn (R-TX) found Sotomayor's "wise Latina" speech "troubling" but said that Limbaugh and Gingrich were not setting "the kind of tone that any of us want to set."[106] Sen. Jeff Sessions (R-AL) was also "troubled" by Sotomayor's speech, but after dogged questioning on *Meet the Press* finally admitted that he would prefer that Limbaugh and Gingrich not use the word *racist,* though he quickly added, "But people have a free right to speak and say what they want and make the analogies that they want."[107] Republican National Committee chairman Michael Steele was one of the only prominent Republicans to express any enthusiasm for the nomination of a Hispanic judge. He urged his party to stop "slammin' and rammin'" Sotomayor.*[108]

In any case, the criticism had an effect, sort of. Newt Gingrich more or less apologized, and everyone else shut up—except for Rush Limbaugh, who because of a psychological condition is incapable of shutting up. Limbaugh took the opportunity to ramp up his "angry black man" attack on Obama by arguing that the nomination of a white-hating Latina was a "reflection of Barack Obama's own racial identity, his own bigotry." He then proceeded to tell a lurid white persecution story in which the archvillain, Obama, seeks to oppress white people, especially white Republicans:

> How do you get promoted in a Barack Obama administration? By hating white people—or even saying you do, or that they're not good or put

---

* "Slammin' and rammin.'" Michael Steele, an African American, is also one of the only prominent Republicans to support affirmative action, not to mention the use of the words *slammin'* and *rammin'*. David Duke has called him a "radical Black racist."

(David Duke, "GOP traitors appoint Black racist as Chairman of the Republican Party," *DavidDuke.com,* 2 Feb. 2009, http://www.davidduke.com/general/gop-traitors-appoint-black-racist-as-chairman-of-the-republican-party_7443.html.)

'em down, whatever. Make white people the new oppressed minority, and they're going right along about it 'cause they're shutting up. They're moving to the back of the bus. They're saying, "I can't use that drinking fountain? Okay! I can't use that restroom? Okay!" That's the modern day Republican Party, the equivalent of the Old South: the new oppressed minority.[109]

The Racist Regime

A couple of months later, Limbaugh took another dip in the cesspool after Obama criticized the arrest of black Harvard professor Henry Louis Gates in Gates's own home. Limbaugh claimed that the comment revealed Obama's dirty secret:

I think Obama is largely misunderstood by a lot of people. . . . Let's face it, President Obama's black, and I think he's got a chip on his shoulder. I think there are elements in this country he doesn't like and he never has liked. And he's using the power of the presidency to remake the country.[110]

This time, Limbaugh didn't divulge which "elements" Obama didn't like. But Glenn Beck did:

This president I think has exposed himself as a guy, over and over and over again, who has a deep seeded [sic] hatred for white people or the white culture . . . He has a—this guy is, I believe, a racist.[111]

This last comment earned Beck an advertising boycott; sixty-two companies signed on in the first month.[112] Beck seemed to get the message, and he has avoided direct racism accusations against Obama ever since, dwelling instead on Obama's marxist-fascist-potential-mass-murderer qualities.

But, for the most part, the limited reticence and self-criticism that the right has exhibited regarding race relations has only addressed the explicitness of the message, not the message itself. Rush Limbaugh touched on the crux of the matter when he said of Judge Sotomayor, "So here you have a racist. You might want to soften that, and you might want to say a reverse racist."[113] Somehow, adding the prefix "reverse" sanitizes the word "racism" to the point that mainstream Republicans feel comfortable using it. But Limbaugh's bemusement over the "softening" is justified. For if you label a policy "reverse racism," then you imply that its supporters are "reverse racists," and what is a reverse racist but a person who is prejudiced against white people?

Thus, the message that many constituents hear when Republican politicians claim to be "troubled" by Sotomayor's "wise Latina" comment or by Obama's associations with a fiery black minister or by policies that give "special privileges" to minorities is the same as Limbaugh's less guarded rhetoric. It is the message of persecution politics, the message that those constituents seem to want to hear—"They hate us because we're white."

So it should not have been terribly surprising when on the eve of the final health care vote in the House of Representatives, angry protesters spat on Rep. Emanuel Cleaver (D-MO) and screamed, "Nigger!" at Rep. John Lewis (D-GA), both African American congressmen. In response, Rep. Steve King (R-IA) dismissed the behavior—"I don't think it's anything," while Rep. Devin Nunes (R-CA) blamed it on the Democrats—"When you use totalitarian tactics, people, you know, begin to act crazy."[114] But these are cynical and disingenuous evasions. Conservatives have been exploiting racial animosity for political gain since 1964. They have been softly whispering that blacks and Latinos are taking advantage of white people and that liberal policies are designed to help the black and brown teams at the expense of the white team. So there is little wonder that some of their fervent supporters savagely shout what these leaders have been tenderly crooning.

As usual, Rush Limbaugh sings it best. After President Obama criticized Arizona's harsh immigration law in 2010, Limbaugh defiantly delivered one of the finest examples of racist projection in recent memory—proudly ringing the bell of persecution politics for all to hear. In a radio segment called "A Message to the President: Freedom Knows

No Race, Sir," Limbaugh once again accused Obama of racism. This time, he explicitly warned of an Obama-led alliance between blacks and Latinos to fight against white Americans:

> Obama says he's going to reconnect via the immigration bill, young people, African-Americans, Latinos, and women for 2010 to help stem the tide of Democrat losses in November. He did not say he was going to reach out to white people . . . This is the regime at its racist best. What's the regime doing? Asking blacks and Latinos to join him in a fight. What is a campaign if not a fight? He's asking young people, African-Americans, Latinos, and women to reconnect, to fight who? Who's this fight against?[115]

A black man comes to power in America. He hates white people. He gives their jobs to unqualified minorities. He redistributes their income to lazy, scheming minorities. He gives their health care to illegal immigrants. He lets their children get assaulted on buses. He is one of *them,* and he hates *you*. Welcome to Obama's America.

7

THE SWEETEST OF DRUGS

Deep Thoughts about Cognitive Dissonance and the Appeal of Persecution Fantasies

Opposition may become sweet to a man when he has christened it persecution.

—George Elliot

IN 1954, a team of undercover psychologists infiltrated a UFO cult led by a Dorothy Martin, a Michigan housewife who claimed to be able to communicate with aliens from the planet Clarion.* The aliens warned her that a massive flood would submerge much of the continental United States on December 21, 1954. One of the psychologists, Leon Festinger, had a theory about what would happen to that cult if the prophesied flood failed to materialize. You might expect disappointed disciples to face the fact that their mistaken prophet was a charlatan, but Festinger had observed that when the doomsday predictions of historical religious cults proved mistaken, the opposite often occurred. The fervor of the members dramatically increased, and they began proselytizing aggressively, leading to rapid growth of the move-

---

* "UFO cult." The word *cult* conveys the image of charismatic megalomaniac leaders like David Koresh or Jim Jones, but Dorothy Martin's cult was a gang of misfits so desperate for orders from the aliens that they fell for every hoax that various juvenile pranksters played on them. The group also included two competing channelers. Dorothy Martin scribbled messages from an alien named Sananda, who was also Jesus Christ. A second participant channeled the voice of the Creator. Sometimes the Sananda and the Creator engaged in petty squabbles. For instance, while Sananda directed the group to avoid meat, the Creator encouraged them to "have some protein." (Leon Festinger, Henry W. Riecken, Stanley Schachter, *When Prophecy Fails,* Kindle ed. [London: Pinter & Martin Ltd., 1956]: 1884.)

ment. "The individual will frequently emerge, not only unshaken, but even more convinced of the truth of his beliefs than ever before," Festinger wrote. "Indeed, he may even show a new fervor about convincing and converting other people to his view."[1]

There was no apocalyptic flood in 1954, of course, and the UFO cult behaved exactly as Festinger had predicted. While Dorothy Martin had previously shunned journalists and welcomed new members with caution, she suddenly went on a public relations blitz, inviting anyone who inquired into her home to be proselytized. While a few cult members dropped out, most became more fervent than ever and joined Martin in proselytizing.

Festinger called the psychological condition that led to the escalated passion *cognitive dissonance*. Cognitive dissonance occurs when a person holds two inconsistent opinions or beliefs at the same time. For example, a smoker's knowledge that smoking is unhealthy conflicts with his awareness that he keeps on smoking anyway. Similarly, the UFO cultists' belief that their leader communicated with an advanced alien race from Clarion conflicted with the undeniable fact that the United States did not suffer from the massive flood that the aliens had predicted.

According to Festinger, the condition of cognitive dissonance produces significant psychological discomfort, and the mind generally feels pressure to reduce or eliminate the contradiction. One obvious way to do that is to reject one element of the dissonance. A smoker, for example, could quit smoking. But as millions of smokers can attest, that's not always easy to do. Likewise, most of the UFO cultists had profoundly committed themselves to the alien prophecy. They had quit their jobs, exhausted their savings, and repeatedly warned their skeptical families and friends of the impending disaster. Shrugging their shoulders and admitting their error would not have been easy. One cultist disconsolately stated in the despairing hours after midnight on the day of the prophecy, "I've given up just about everything. I've cut every tie: I've burned every bridge. I've turned my back on the world. I can't afford to doubt. I have to believe."[2]

An alternative mechanism for relieving the psychological pressure is to rationalize some resolution to the dissonance. Millions of smokers, for example, say they plan to quit in the near future. Many also underestimate the number of cigarettes they smoke, and some even find reasons to doubt the well-established health risks. Similarly, at 4:45 a.m. on December 22, 1954, Dorothy Martin received a message from God that in light of the righteousness of her little Michigan crew, He had decided to spare the earth from the massive flood. Martin's jubilant followers enthusiastically embraced the explanation, and the next day, they alerted the press that the country had been saved.

Festinger theorized that rationalization can somewhat reduce cognitive dissonance but that for it to be fully effective, people need others to ratify the rationalization. Thus, members of the UFO cult relied on each other to bolster their confidence in the new explanation for the nation's miraculous salvation. But in the case of severe dissonance, even the affirmation of a few peers may not be sufficient to relieve the psychological pressure. To truly assure themselves of the validity of their rationalization, people may feel the need to persuade a wider audience. As Festinger explained:

> If more and more people can be persuaded that the system of belief is correct, then clearly it must, after all, be correct. Consider the extreme case: if everyone in the whole world believed something there would be no question at all as to the validity of this belief. It is for this reason that we observe the increase in proselyting following disconfirmation. If the proselyting proves successful, then by gathering more adherents and effectively surrounding himself with supporters, the believer reduces dissonance to the point where he can live with it.[3]

The Inequality Taboo

Festinger's simple yet powerful theory of cognitive dissonance was an instant sensation in psychology circles, and it has often been applied to diverse contexts by serious academic psychologists and . . . *ahem* . . . pop-psychology writers. One such application occurred in a controversial book called *The Bell Curve*. In the book, psychologist Richard

Herrnstein and political scientist Charles Murray argued that human intelligence is hereditary, that poor people are dumber than rich people, and that average intelligence varies significantly among races. Though Murray worked for a conservative think tank, the authors maintained a detached scientific objectivity in their statistical analysis. For example, the statistics proved that affirmative action was "leaking a poison into the American soul" and that welfare encouraged "the wrong women" to inject their low-IQ, prison-bound babies into the nation's deteriorating gene pool.[4]

A discussion of *The Bell Curve* and its critical reception is beyond the scope of this book, but there is one relevant conclusion that Herrnstein and Murray tossed out almost as an aside. They suggested that members of the "white elite" live in denial of the obviously inferior minds of certain minorities and that the denial has produced mass cognitive dissonance that may one day explode with fearsome consequences:

> Racism will emerge in a new and more virulent form. The tension between what the white elite is supposed to think and what it is actually thinking about race will reach something close to breaking point. This pessimistic prognosis must be contemplated: When the break comes, the result, as so often happens when cognitive dissonance is resolved, will be an overreaction in the other direction. Instead of the candor and realism about race that is so urgently needed, the nation will be faced with racial divisiveness and hostility that is as great as, or greater, than America experienced before the civil rights movement.[5]

The authors speculate that this overreaction could lead to a "custodial state" in which the nation's cognitively inferior minorities would be moved to "a high-tech and more lavish version of the Indian reservation." In other words, the only way to save the black and brown people from being stuck in moron-reservations is to be honest about how stupid they are and discourage them from having babies.

Only that's not the way cognitive dissonance works. The UFO cultists didn't respond to their rude reality check by overreacting in the opposite direction. They didn't become fanatical anticultists—they became more fanatical cultists. Festinger's idea is striking because it explains why cognitive dissonance produces a reaction so contrary to logical explanation. If denying race-specific intelligence variations leads to cognitive dissonance, then people should produce elaborate rationalizations to defend the idea that the races are intellectually equivalent.

But let's draw this line out further. There is no doubt that many Americans, including the "white elite," harbor racial prejudices, but not because of genetic intelligence differences among races. The *Newsweek* article "See Baby Discriminate" that so infuriated Rush Limbaugh in 2009 argued that humans are biologically predisposed to racial prejudice.[6] And even without such a predisposition, the fact that certain minorities have disproportionately high dropout and crime rates would lead many people to make negative inferences about their intelligence and ethics. This is what Obama meant by his "typical white person" comment about his grandmother—"If she sees somebody on the street that she doesn't know, well there's a reaction that's in our experiences that won't go away and can sometimes come out in the wrong way. And that's just the nature of race in our society."[7]

So maybe you see a black man on the street, and you hug your purse a little closer. If you think of yourself as a tolerant person, that nervous feeling may be uncomfortable to you. You may even scold yourself. That's cognitive dissonance. You harbor two inconsistent beliefs—that the black man is dangerous and that it's wrong to judge someone by the color of his skin. Most of the time, it's no big deal. Cognitive dissonance happens; you deal with it. If you're really uncomfortable with the idea that you harbor any trace of racism in your soul, you may deny those feelings.

Or . . . you may deny the opposing belief that it's wrong to judge someone by the color of his skin. That is the approach that Herrnstein and Murray took in *The Bell Curve*. They embraced racial generalizations and rejected the idea that racial generalizations are wrong. Judging by the book's popularity, their strategy for dealing with the cognitive dissonance of racial prejudice is a common one.

But rejecting what Murray called the "Inequality Taboo"[8] wasn't easy, for aversion to negative racial generalizations is now deeply ingrained in the American conscience. To avert the psychological stress of championing such generalizations, you might need to find some way to rationalize your conclusions. You might, for example, try to prove that your prejudicial ideas are actually good for ethnic minorities by inventing a bizarre dystopia involving reservations for dull-witted black and brown people. You might further imagine yourself to be a courageous defender of freedom of thought who stands tall against the roar of the "white elite's" dangerous dogma. And if Festinger's theory was right, then you might also seek out social affirmation for your rationalizations. You might, for example, publish a book that goes well beyond statistical analysis to make a passionate case for and win converts to your bold racial generalizations.

The Intolerance Taboo

Now let's suppose that your prejudice goes beyond purse hugging in the presence of a strange black man. Let's suppose that deep down, you really hate those black people . . . or those brown people or those homosexuals or those Jews or those women or whomever it is that you've been taught that it's wrong to hate. You've got some serious cognitive dissonance on your hands. You might be able to shrug off the Inequality Taboo that Murray mentioned, but there's another weightier taboo that's tougher to repudiate: the Intolerance Taboo. The Inequality Taboo is just a foothill in the Intolerance Taboo Mountains. In twenty-first-century America, no one wants to be a bigot. Bigots are mean and angry. They scream epithets and abuse minorities. They lynch black people and slaughter Jews. Bigots are bad.

So how does your conflicted mind untie the knot of contradiction? How do you admit your hate without admitting your bigotry?

One tactic is to reverse the equation. You project your hateful feelings onto the people you hate and those who aid them. You convince yourself that they hate you. Now you have justification for your hatred.

You don't hate them because they're black or homosexual or Jewish, you hate them because they and their liberal allies hated you first. You hate them because they persecute you and your kind. You are not the bigot; you are the victim of bigotry. As Sigmund Freud wrote of Daniel Schreber, "*He hates* (persecutes) *me,* which will entitle me to hate him."

This hypothesis presents an answer to the question we asked at the end of chapter 5: "Why would anyone want to be paranoid?" Developing a fear of persecution by minorities, and also by liberals on behalf of minorities, is a way of expunging the sin of bigotry. Paranoia allows people to hate with a clear conscience—it lets them convince themselves that their enemy *deserves* to be hated. And by providing a reason to hate, paranoia reduces the painful cognitive dissonance between feeling intolerant and believing intolerance is wrong. Reducing the pressure of cognitive dissonance feels good. It feels so good that people *selectively expose* themselves to right-wing fearmongers; they watch and read and listen to the men and women who make them feel so pleasantly afraid. Moreover, like the UFO cultists, they don't challenge the ideas that make them feel good. Their confirmation biases lead them to embrace absurd theories without question. And the more severe the cognitive dissonance (that is, the bigger the gap between intolerant beliefs and aversion to those beliefs), the more pressure a person will feel to reduce the dissonance, and the more exaggerated his persecution paranoia is likely to become.

If this explanation is correct, would it mean that all conservatives are closet racists? Not at all. Most conservatives aren't paranoid, and not all paranoia is driven by repressed feelings of intolerance, let alone racial intolerance. Persecution politics is a particular kind of social paranoia and the proposed explanation applies only to this specific case. That is, when someone espouses preposterous theories that a minority group is ruthlessly oppressing his own dominant group, it may be an attempt to rationalize his animosity toward the minority.

Of course, one need not be a member of a dominant social or ethnic group to play persecution games. In one sad twist of right-wing persecution politics, Georgia Right to Life posted billboard ads in 2010 that declared, "Black children are an endangered species." You can also go to their website, toomanyaborted.com, to find out how in the 1960s "the open racists went underground, joining forces with the eugenicists. Abortion is the tool they use to stealthily target blacks for extermination."[9] Georgia Right to Life calls such tactics "minority outreach."* Just as in the case of white persecution politics, these tactics exploit racial animosity, but in this instance, the animus belongs to the minority rather than the majority.

"Sweet Crack-Pipe of Moral Indignation"

The myth of persecution also offers psychological benefits beyond rationalizing away cognitive dissonance. Victim status confers a certain moral legitimacy. The victim attracts sympathy, his offenses are downplayed, and his grievances are elevated. A comedian named John Rogers eloquently described this phenomenon in a blog about evangelical attempts to remove Christian children from public schools:

> One of the great secrets of human nature is that the one thing people want more than love, security, sex, chocolate or big-screen TVs is to feel hard done by. Because being hard done by is the shit. Feeling hard done by is the sweetest of drugs. If you're being persecuted—it must mean you're doing the right thing, right? You get the mellow buzz of the moral high ground, but without arrogantly claiming it as your own. You get an instant, supportive community in a big dark scary world of such scope it may well literally be beyond rational human processing. When you are hard done by, you get purpose in a life where otherwise, you'd

---

* Right-wing minority outreach still has some kinks to work out. For starters, white Republicans need to shake the habit of belittling the historical oppression of African Americans. Rep. Trent Franks (R-AZ), for example, said, "Far more black children, far more of the African-American community is being devastated by the [abortion] policies of today, than were being devastated by the policies of slavery." (Eric Kleefeld, "GOP Rep. Franks: African-Americans 'Devastated' More by Abortion Today Than under Slavery," *Talking Points Memo,* 26 Feb. 2010, http://tpmlivewire.talkingpointsmemo.com/2010/02/gop-rep-franks-african-americans-devastated-more-by-abortion-today-than-under-slavery-video.php.)

have to find your own. And when you ride that high, then no amount of logic, no pointing out that in actuality you and your beliefs are at a high point of popularity and influence for the last hundred years—is going to pry that sweet crack-pipe of moral indignation from your hands.[10]

Of course, long before the blogosphere came into being, long before the printing press was invented, sages used to deliver their wisdom personally from elevated positions in public spaces. One such sage reportedly proclaimed to a large crowd that had gathered on a hillside to hear him speak:

> Blessed are those who are persecuted for righteousness' sake, for theirs is the kingdom of heaven. (Matt. 5:10, English Standard Version Bible)

Presumably, the blessing of the sage has added to his followers' pleasure in imagining that they are being hard done by.

A Society of Archie Bunkers

Yet there are pieces missing from the simple proposition that being hard done by is the shit. It tells us why the feeling of persecution is intrinsically appealing to people, but it does not tell us how persecution politics became a national movement or why it bloomed in the second half of the twentieth century.

According to the conventional story, as told by Jerry Falwell and other culture warriors and accepted without challenge by the media and even by most liberal analysts, cultural conservatism emerged in the 1970s as a backlash against liberal reforms like the legalization of abortion, the prohibition against school prayer, and the Equal Rights Amendment.

But Paul Weyrich and other architects of the Moral Majority played down the significance of these issues in the founding of the religious right. As we noted previously, Christian persecution politics bloomed with the IRS action against the seg academies. White persecution politics began even earlier with George Wallace's stand against desegregation. In both cases, as discussed in chapter 5, the distinguishing emotion that the paranoid leaders expressed was not anger but fear: fear of powerful enemies who sought to oppress white Christians. So when we ask why right-wing persecution politics bloomed in the late twentieth century, we won't find the answer by listing the issues that made conservatives angry.

Yet we've also seen that the fear was self-generated, based on obviously fabricated or exaggerated threats. People sought out and opened themselves to scary stories because the fear felt so good; it absolved their guilt, resolved their cognitive dissonance, and produced that "mellow buzz of the moral high ground." So we won't find the answer by listing the threats that made conservatives scared either.

Once again, Festinger's hypothesis can help. He and his colleagues infiltrated the UFO cult to prove the hypothesis that cognitive dissonance would produce a frenzy of proselytizing as cult members sought to affirm their rationalizations for the failed prophecy. He even hinted that the world's great religions might have been spawned by just such bursts of evangelism (precipitated, for example, by the untimely execution of a promised messiah and his failure to bring about the prophesied end of the world).

But Festinger laid out fairly stringent conditions for cognitive-dissonance-induced proselytizing. Some of these do not apply to the type of social phenomena we've been discussing. For instance, he stipulated that the believers must take some important action that is difficult to undo, such as quitting their jobs or exhausting their savings, and that there must be some real world event that produces undeniable evidence to contradict their beliefs.

While it would be impossible to set up, in a political context, the kind of eloquent, well-defined demonstration that Festinger captured in the UFO scenario, there might be enough parallels to draw valid comparisons and present a sufficiently plausible explanation. For example, prior to the civil rights movement, the nation's commitment to racial inequality and intolerance was certainly substantial. Discriminatory segregation was a way of life in the South that pervaded every element of society. In 1928, the famous historian Ulrich Bonnell Phillips called Southerners' commitment to preserving white dominion "the cardinal test of a Southerner and the central theme of Southern history."[11] And even in other parts of the country, segregation was common in schools, workplaces, and communities.

Yet in little more than a decade, racial intolerance evolved from an accepted and officially sanctioned practice to a shameful and officially forbidden activity. The new racism taboos must have shocked and over-whelmed people who grew up knowing no other way. Another distin-guished historian, C. Vann Woodward, observed in 1968:

> Since the last World War, old racial attitudes that appeared more vener-able and immovable than any other have exhibited a flexibility that no one would have predicted. One by one, in astonishingly rapid succes-sion, many landmarks of racial discrimination and segregation have dis-appeared, and old barriers have been breached . . . Increasingly the South is aware of its isolation in these attitudes, however, and is in de-fense of the institutions that embody them. They have fallen rapidly into discredit and under condemnation from the rest of the country and the rest of the world. Once more the South finds itself with a morally dis-credited Peculiar Institution on its hands.[12]

Similarly, George Wallace's biographer described how the world looked to white Southerners in the early 1960s and why Wallace's per-secution rhetoric appealed to them:

> Day after day, white Southerners looked at the television and what did they see? They saw a kind of morality play in which there were the heroic, the civil rights activists, and these horrific bestial, violent white Southerners. And now you have George Wallace, standing up, standing up for America, he says, but really standing up for white Southerners.[13]

But Wallace did more than stand up for white Southerners. He gave them a new mythology that would enable them to deny their bigotry and assume the mantle of the aggrieved victim. As they absorbed America's evolving values of tolerance, Wallace's rationalization gave them the key to escape the cognitive dissonance between racist beliefs and the ideals of tolerance and equality.

This pattern repeated itself in less severe ways across the cultural spectrum. Feminists challenged male chauvinism. Gay rights activists challenged homophobia. Religious reformers, including religious humanists, challenged dogmatism. In every case, cultural conservatives were cast as intransigents, bigots, chauvinists, and prudes. They became a society of Archie Bunkers, scorned and ridiculed. In *What's the Matter with Kansas?* Thomas Frank neatly described modern culture's contempt for what O'Reilly would call traditionalists:

> The "Middle Americans," after all, are the people the ads and the sitcoms and the movies warn us against. They are the prudish preacher who forbids dancing, the dullard husband who foolishly consumes Brand X, the racist dad who beats his kids, the square cowboy who is gunned down by the alternative cowboy, the stifling family life we are supposed to want to escape, the hardhat who just doesn't get it.[14]

In Frank's view, the media's scorn provoked working-class resentment, which fed the backlash against "liberal elites." But this suggestion buys into the persecution myth that Hollywood is culturally distinct from Kansas. Middle Americans don't live in a foreign country. They are capable of enjoying *Seinfeld* and *Frasier,* just as those elitists on the coasts are capable of appreciating *Married with Children* and *Roseanne*. Notwithstanding Pat Buchanan's fear that the nation's "ethnocultural core" has begun to dissolve, we can rest assured that American culture still drives through Kansas en route from California to New York. If anything, the growth of media and rapid transit has made American culture more cohesive than it was in the 1950s.

Similarly, the social upheavals of the 1960s were not confined to the coasts, leaving the rest of the country in some kind of permanent stasis. If a New Yorker and a Birminghamian had been simultaneously cryogenically frozen in 1959 and thawed out in 2010, I'd wager that the

Birminghamian would be more shocked by the transformation of his hometown. The biggest cultural shift of the 1960s was not the length of men's hair or the availability of cannabis. It was the nationwide embrace of two ideals that had been present since America's founding but long diminished and constrained: *tolerance* and *equality*. These two ideals drove the civil rights movement, feminism, gay rights, religious pluralism, and nearly everything that the nation has fought over since 1964.

While today's conservatives may reject what they view as the excesses of the 1960s and 1970s, few would reject the ideals of tolerance and equality that underlie them. These ideals have become fully embedded in America's "ethnocultural core," and conservatives, like virtually every other American, have fully internalized them. For bigots like Jerry Falwell and George Wallace, the process of assimilation must have been wrenching. Within the span of a few years, American society had come to revile racists' deeply held beliefs. More important, insofar as the racists internalized the new ideals, they likely began to revile their own beliefs, producing cognitive dissonance.

The rationalizations of persecution paranoia reduced that dissonance and thus gave the bigots back their virtue. As imaginary victims of intolerance, they could assimilate the new cultural ideals while hanging on to their comfortable animosities. At the same time, they could repudiate their new status as national pariahs. It was a perfect solution.

Spreading the Word

Almost perfect, anyway. There was one problem: the rationalizations were lies. In their more extreme forms, they were ridiculously obvious lies. Those who claimed to be persecuted must have realized that on some level, just as Festinger's UFO cultists must have recognized that their prophet was a fraud. Thus, if Festinger's theory holds, we should be able to find examples of proselytizing among believers in persecution politics as they seek to bolster their confidence in flimsy rationalizations by winning converts who affirm the lies.

And, indeed, the insecurity of persecution theorists is palpable. Paranoid conservatives incessantly reassure themselves and the world of their tolerance and open-mindedness. George Wallace, for instance, drew a fine distinction between a racist "who despises someone because of his color" and a segregationist "who conscientiously believes that it is in the best interest of Negro and white to have a separate education and social order." Pat Buchanan defended Wallace by saying, "I don't think the Governor owes anyone an apology. How do you blame Governor Wallace who stands with his traditions and customs and state, and defies an entire national establishment?"[15] Richard Nixon assured his constituents that their feelings of resentment against blacks were not racist:

> When a mother sees her child taken away from a neighborhood school and transported miles away, and she objects to that, I don't think it is right to charge her with bigotry. When young people apply for jobs—in politics or in industry—and find the door closed because they don't fit into some numerical quota, despite their ability, and they object, I do not think it is right to condemn those young people as insensitive or racist.[16]

Anita Bryant promised, "I never condoned nor teach my children discrimination against anyone because of their race or religion." Sean Hannity challenged Obama to point to "a single instance in which President Bush or McCain or Karl Rove or Sean Hannity or talk radio or any other major Republican has made an issue of Obama's race."[17] Tea Party leader Mark Williams, whose race baiting is so inflammatory that the National Tea Party Federation eventually ejected his Tea Party Express organization, insisted, "It's impossible for there to be a racist element in the tea party."[18] The Louisiana justice of the peace who refused to perform interracial marriages assured journalists, "I have piles and piles of black friends." And David Duke repeats in almost every article he writes that he's not antiblack; he's pro–European American.

But even more than professing their tolerance, leaders of the paranoid right endlessly rehearse accusations of intolerance against their liberal and minority opponents. George Wallace raged, "You know who the biggest bigots in the world are—they're the ones who call others bigots."[19] Pat Buchanan complained, "What the government is doing today, in its conscious favoritism toward blacks, feminists, Indians, and the Spanish-speaking, is no more defensible than what the segregationists of another era used to do."[20] Anita Bryant insisted that homosexuals were "infringing upon my right or rather DISCRIMINATING against me as a citizen and mother."[21] Rush Limbaugh rhetorically asked, "How do you get promoted in a Barack Obama administration? By hating white people."[22] Tom Tancredo called one civil rights organization "a Latino KKK."[23] Tea Party leader Mark Williams called Obama a "half-white racist president" and told CNN, "The racists have their own movement. It's called the NAACP."[24] Bill O'Reilly described Latino civil rights supporters as "the real racists" and secular Christmas messages as "bigotry."[25] But leave it to Pat Robertson to deliver a persecution politics tour de force on behalf of oppressed Christians:

> Just like what Nazi Germany did to the Jews, so liberal America is now doing to the evangelical Christians! It's no different! It is the same thing! It is happening all over again! It is the Democratic Congress, the liberal-biased media and the homosexuals who want to destroy all Christians! Wholesale abuse and discrimination and the worst bigotry directed toward any group in America today! More terrible than anything suffered by any minority in our history![26]

To what extent do these pundits and politicians really believe the ideas they promote? Are they motivated by discomfort with their own intolerance, or is it all just rhetorical strategy? There is no way to know and, ultimately, it doesn't matter. What matters is that their rhetoric appeals to people who *are* uncomfortable with their own intolerance; the constant repetition of assurances and accusations soothes their doubts.

But how can we demonstrate the insecurities of the rank and file? Festinger insisted that it was important to observe the proselytizing activity of a group's ordinary members, since the leaders may have motives other than their personal convictions. Rush Limbaugh and Glenn

Beck, for instance, earn more money when they grow their audiences, so of course they proselytize. Likewise, politicians like George Wallace gain more votes and donors when they win converts, so they have strong independent reasons to proselytize as well.

Sure enough, it is easy to find a steady stream of passionate grassroots proselytizers of persecution politics. In the days of the secular humanist scourge, citizens' protection groups and concerned parents' organizations distributed warning pamphlets and screened informational movies to warn their fellow citizens of the danger to children's tender minds (and stomachs). Local anti–gay rights groups popped up around the country in the wake of Anita Bryant's Save Our Children campaign. The religious right is famous for its powerful grassroots machinery. And, in 2010, the mantle of persecution politics is worn by the Tea Parties, a disorganized and leaderless collection of enthusiastic proselytizers. In short, grassroots evangelism runs through the heart of persecution politics.

The insecurity of persecution theorists offers an explanation for the curious phenomenon whereby the right wing's successes seem to inflame its fears, while its failures seem to dampen them. When Jesse Helms led the successful congressional charge against the secular humanists at the IRS, he validated the right's persecution theories, giving them confidence in their paranoid ideas. Conversely, when the Supreme Court threw out Judge William Brevard Hand's ruling, it undercut the right's shaky conviction that secular humanism was in fact a religion. Similarly, Anita Bryant's success showed paranoid conservatives that the majority of people in Miami agreed with them, bolstering their confidence, whereas the nation's growing acceptance of homosexuality undermined their certainty that protecting homosexuals from job discrimination would enable gay recruiters to turn the United States into the next Sodom and Gomorrah.

The intellectual insecurity of political paranoiacs is the Achilles heel of right-wing persecution politics. True victims of psychotic paranoia are virtually immune to external challenges: they can absorb any criticism into their paranoid worldviews. Their minds simply don't work right. In contrast, political paranoiacs may put up a good fight against their critics, but the fact that they are, in Richard Hofstadter's words, "more or less normal" means they are capable of seeing through their own delusions and thus susceptible to external stimuli. Indeed, whereas the true victim of paranoia lives in a solipsistic world of his own making, the political paranoiac depends on a constant stream of affirmation from the world outside. Without it, the paranoia withers and droops.

But we're not quite ready to investigate solutions yet. There are more pieces to this puzzle.

8

RETURN OF THE INTERNATIONAL JEW

The Making of George Soros,
Global Supervillain of Right-wing Persecution Mythology

You're not quite evil enough. You're semi-evil. You're quasi-evil. You're the margarine of evil. You're the Diet Coke of evil, just one calorie, not evil enough.

—Dr. Evil

D ESPITE THE INTRINSIC psychological appeal of the right wing's tales of oppression and calamity, one glaring defect strains the creditability of such stories, a defect so defective that even most steadfast culture warriors cannot ignore it: *Democrats*. A party that is so bumbling and fractious that it can barely pass a watered-down health care bill—even with a large legislative majority, a popular president, and that ineffable force of political energy known as a mandate—can scarcely be expected to pull off the eradication of Christianity or the subjugation of the white race. Think of what it would do to Democrats' approval ratings.

Moreover, when Bill O'Reilly first led the Fox News posse into the lawless land of persecution politics, the Democrats were not only bumbling but powerless. Republicans controlled the White House and both chambers of Congress, and the Supreme Court was tilting right. There was no one remaining in the federal government for a nervous conservative to fear.

But Bill O'Reilly is a resourceful man, and he wielded a formidable weapon. His *superior analysis* cuts through political spin like a Ginsu knife through an overripe tomato. Beneath all that pulpy red mush, virtually unseen among the namby-pamby red splotches that passed for liberal leadership, O'Reilly found a bona fide villain—rich, powerful, cunning, and unscrupulous, with the will and the means to aggressively pursue his radical agenda unhindered by public opinion, moral constraints, parliamentary protocols, or the U.S. Constitution.

In the game of persecution politics, one of the right's chief tactics is to select a vulnerable representative of the left, present that person as the de facto leader of the Democratic Party, and then caricature him or her as the epitome of savagery and evil in order to scare the crap out of Americans. You could call it the bogeyman formula. O'Reilly didn't invent the bogeyman formula. Conservatives have been using it since the Red Scare, if not before, and they aggressively pursued a bogeyman strategy (or rather, bogeywoman strategy) against Hillary Clinton in the 1990s. But O'Reilly innovated by linking the bogeyman formula to the persecution formula, preparing a blueprint for the deluge of persecution paranoia that was to follow. O'Reilly's bogeyman-in-chief was a billionaire investor named George Soros.

"The Jewish Problem"

O'Reilly's selection of Soros as evil incarnate was no accident. To see what made the man such an attractive target, we need to travel back to his roots. Soros was born in Budapest in 1930 with the name György Schwartz. His father changed the family's last name to the less Jewish-sounding "Soros" when George was six years old because Hungarian Jews suffered from a degree of persecution that American Christians can only dream of. As an ally of Nazi Germany, Hungary instituted a number of anti-Jewish laws starting in the late 1930s that restricted where Jews could work and whom they could marry. Young György's school had segregated classrooms.[1]

Fortunately for the Soros family, Hungarian premier Miklós Horthy, a.k.a. His Serene Highness the Regent of the Kingdom of Hungary, was only moderately anti-Semitic compared to other Hungarian politicians and their Nazi allies. In one letter, he urged his prime minister to move slowly on solving Hungary's "Jewish problem." The letter offers a sample of what counted as moderation in 1940 Hungary:

> As regards the Jewish problem, I have been an anti-Semite throughout my life. I have never had contact with Jews. I have considered it intolerable that here in Hungary everything, every factory, bank, large fortune, business, theater, press, commerce, etc. should be in Jewish hands, and that the Jew should be the image reflected of Hungary, especially abroad. Since, however, one of the most important tasks of the government is to raise the standard of living, i.e., we have to acquire wealth, it is impossible, in a year or two, to eliminate the Jews.[2]

Due to Horthy's caution, the Hungarian Jews were relatively safe for a while. As the Nazis exterminated Jews in German-occupied territories, the Hungarian government dithered. But in 1944, Hitler concluded that his "moderate" ally wasn't working hard enough to solve the Jewish problem. The Germans invaded Hungary and swiftly annihilated 450,000 Hungarian Jews, almost 70 percent of the Jewish population.[3] George Soros and his immediate family survived because of the resourcefulness of his father, who arranged for George to assume a false identity and sent him to live with a Hungarian official.

The Conspiracy Theory of Society

After the war, George Soros finished high school and moved on his own to London, where he survived by working menial jobs while attending the London School of Economics. There he studied with the famous philosopher Karl Popper. Popper had written a book called *The Open Society and Its Enemies* that extolled freedom and democracy and attacked totalitarianism and Marxism. His work deeply influenced the young Soros. Years later, after moving to New York and amassing a fortune as a currency trader, Soros founded a charitable organization called the Open Society Institute to put Popper's ideas into effect in Hungary and other former Eastern Block nations.

Incidentally, Karl Popper also coined the term *conspiracy theory*. He did not use the term to describe specific paranoid beliefs, as we do today, but as a general way of understanding the world. He defined the conspiracy theory of society as "the view that an explanation of a social phenomenon consists in the discovery of the men or groups who are interested in the occurrence of this phenomenon (sometimes it is a hidden interest which has first to be revealed), and who have planned and conspired to bring it about."[4]

According to believers in the conspiracy theory of society, "whatever happens in society—especially happenings such as war, unemployment, poverty, shortages, which people as a rule dislike—is the result of direct design by some powerful individuals and groups." Popper claimed that widespread conspiracy beliefs would lead to "heresy hunts, national, social, and class hostility."[5] Sound familiar?

It is certainly familiar enough to George Soros. After the Iron Curtain collapsed, Soros donated generously to Hungary and other Eastern Block countries, funding scholarships, university endowments, and science grants. In return for his generosity, anti-Semites in the new Hungarian parliament accused him of participating in an international Jewish conspiracy to bankrupt Hungary in order to restore communist rule— despite the fact that Soros had been an ardent opponent of Hungary's communist regime.[6]

There is one difference, at least, between Hungarian anti-Semitism in the 1990s and the discrimination that Soros grew up with. In contrast to Hungary's Nazi-era leaders, the new breed of anti-Semite denies any hostility toward Jews. For instance, Istvan Csurka, one of the most prominent leaders of the new breed, rarely says the word *Jew*. Instead he uses code words like *non-Hungarian elements* and *cosmopolitan*. He also insisted, "I am not anti-Semitic and never have been, and all my writings prove that." Then he added, "But it cannot be excluded that some of those who won't stand up for Hungarian renewal are Jews."[7]

The International Jew

Anti-Sorosism first arrived in the United States in 1996, courtesy of an American expatriate in Germany named F. William Engdahl.* In an article titled "The Secret Financial Network Behind 'Wizard' George Soros," Engdahl connected Soros to the evilest Jews ever to roam the earth, the dreaded *Rothschilds*. He wrote:

> Soros is one of what in medieval days were called Hofjuden, the "Court Jews," who were deployed by the aristocratic families. The most important of such "Jews who are not Jews," are the Rothschilds, who launched Soros's career.[8]

The Rothschild family is the gold standard of global bogeymen, and the conspiracy theories surrounding it provide a model for the tactics that O'Reilly would later employ against Soros. The Rothschilds were a family of moneylenders from the Jewish ghetto of Frankfurt, Germany. In the early 1800s, the family patriarch, Mayer Amschel Rothschild, dispatched his five sons to the financial capitals of Europe—Frankfurt, Vienna, London, Paris, and Naples—where they proceeded to amass an immense fortune and enter conspiracy lore for centuries to come.

First and foremost, according to the conspiracy theories, the Rothschilds *love* war. If it were legal (and if present trends continue, it may be soon) the Rothschilds would marry war. They started the French Revolution, the American Revolution, the Russian Revolution, the Na-

---

* Engdahl calls himself an "economic researcher, historian, and freelance journalist," which sounds much better than "crackpot conspiracy theorist." He covers diverse topics ranging from global warming (conspiracy to cover up "global freezing") to the Gates Foundation (toxic vaccines to reduce third world population) to the Dalai Lama (brainwashed by Nazis). (F. William Engdahl, "Global Warming or Global Freezing: Is the Ice Really Melting?" *FinancialSense.com*, 24 Sep. 2009, http://www.financialsense.com/editorials/engdahl/2009/0924.html; F. William Engdahl, "Bill Gates talks about 'vaccines to reduce population,'" *FinancialSense.com*, 4 Mar. 2010, http://www.financialsense.com/editorials/engdahl/2010/0304.html; F. William Engdahl, "Why Washington Plays 'Tibet Roulette' with China," *CCTV.com*, 25 Apr. 2008, http://www.cctv.com/english/20080425/111113.shtml.)

poleonic Wars, the War of 1812, the American Civil War, the Boer War, World War I, World War II, the Cold War, the Korean War, the Vietnam War, the Iraq War, the Afghanistan War, and World War III (pending).

The Rothschilds also love assassinating people. They killed Abraham Lincoln, JFK, RFK, MLK, Czar Nicholas II, Princess Diana, Yitzhak Rabin, and Michael Jackson. Yes, some say the rich Jews killed the King of Pop.[9] Moreover, every important person from Winston Churchill to Warren Buffett to George W. Bush has been a Rothschild stooge. Hitler was actually one-fourth Rothschild. Ergo, the Rothschilds planned the Holocaust (or fabricated the Holocaust hoax, depending on whom you ask). They also sank the *Titanic,* bombed Hiroshima, and planned 9/11, to name a few of their dastardly crimes.

In the old days, when hating Jews was still hip, Rothschild conspiracists were more openly anti-Semitic. For example, one prominent American conspiracy theorist from the early twentieth century published an article called "The High and Low of Jewish Money Power," which explained that the Rothschilds were the progenitors of a new breed of "international Jewish financier" whose "absence from national or patriotic illusions" freed them to wreak havoc and war in the interest of profit.[10] The name of the conspiracy theorist was Henry Ford, founder of the Ford Motor Company. After his success with the Model T, Ford bought up a Michigan newspaper in order to pursue his passion: anti-Semitism. (Everyone needs a hobby.) Ford's *Dearborn Independent* published weekly screeds about the power and malevolence of the Jews. It also reprinted an infamous anti-Semitic forgery, *The Protocols of the Learned Elders of Zion,* which "documented" the secret Jewish plot to take over the world.

But even in Ford's day, most Americans disapproved of excessively vitriolic anti-Semitism, so the *Dearborn Independent* pioneered the tactics that would later characterize twenty-first-century persecution politics: pooh-poohing discrimination against Jews and projecting bigotry onto them. One article, "'Jewish Rights' Clash with American Rights," attempted to deny the existence of anti-Semitism on the grounds that Arabs were Semitic people, and Jew-haters had no problem with Arabs. The article concluded, "There is no such thing as anti-Semitism. There is only a very little and a very mild anti-Jewism."[11] In other words, the problem of anti-Semitism was simply a case of semantic confusion. (Hitler must have missed that memo.)

While there was apparently no anti-Semitism to be found in 1920, there was by contrast "a tremendous amount of anti-Goyism, or anti-Gentilism," according to the *Dearborn Independent*.[12] Jews demanded a "specially privileged system" while seeking to obliterate all traces of Christianity—Christian prayers in public schools, Christian references in state constitutions, and their old nemesis, Christmas trees.

> The non-Jew is the "persecuted one." He must do everything the way the Jew wants it done; if not he is infringing on Jewish "rights." . . . Jews' determination to wipe out of public life every sign of the predominant Christian character of the United States, is the only active form of religious intolerance in the country today.[13]

The *Dearborn Independent*'s arguments were deeply persuasive to anti-Semites of the era. Adolf Hitler kept a life-sized portrait of Henry Ford on his wall, and in 1938, the Nazis awarded Ford the Grand Cross of the German Eagle, a sort of Nobel Prize in anti-Semitism.[14]

Father Charles Coughlin, known as the grandfather of hate radio for his anti-Semitic radio show, lunched with Ford once a month and later called him "a sincere man who knew the truth when he saw it."[15] On his radio show, Coughlin railed against the "international conspiracy of Jewish bankers," whom he blamed for the Great Depression. After Hitler's massive pogrom against the Jews in 1938—called *Kristallnacht* ("Crystal Night") because of the shattered glass from the windows of Jewish shops, synagogues, and homes—Coughlin accused the Jews of asking for it, claiming, "Jewish persecution only followed after Christians first were persecuted."[16]

But the Nazis didn't stop at broken windows, and the horrors of the Holocaust ruined the good name of anti-Semitism forever after. After Coughlin's speech, some radio stations canceled his programs. In 1939, the Roosevelt administration took regulatory action to force Coughlin off the air; in 1942, the Catholic Church eventually shut him down completely by threatening to defrock him. These days, you can't even spin a conspiracy theory about evil Jewish financiers without being accused of anti-Semitic bigotry. As William Engdahl complained:

> Anyone who dares to criticize Soros or any of his associates is immediately hit with the charge of being "anti-Semitic"—a criticism which often silences or intimidates genuine critics of Soros's unscrupulous operations. The Anti-Defamation League of B'nai B'rith considers it a top priority to "protect" Soros from the charges of "anti-Semites" in Hungary and elsewhere in Central Europe.[17]

But it's hard to avoid charges of anti-Semitism when you criticize a wealthy investor as a "Court Jew," especially when the investor in question was a victim of the Nazis, having lost most of his friends and extended family in the Holocaust. Unless he wasn't a victim . . . unless he was actually a Nazi himself . . . yeah, that's the ticket. Engdahl wrote:

> Soros admitted in a radio interview that his father gave him Nazi credentials in Hungary during the war, and he looted wealthy Jewish estates. Further research showed that this operation was probably run by the SS.[18]

Apparently, the Hungarian official who took the fourteen-year-old Soros in during the war was called upon to inventory a large estate that the Nazis had confiscated from a wealthy Jew. He took Soros along with him, and the adolescent Nazi collaborator spent his time wandering the grounds and trying to find a place to urinate where no one would notice his circumcised penis.[19]

In addition to fabricating Rothschildian plots and treating "anti-Semitism" with scare quotes, Engdahl employed one other trick from the *Dearborn Independent*. Like Ford's "international Jewish financiers," Engdahl represented Soros as a man whose lack of national identification freed him from the moral constraints of mere mortals:

Soros is American only in his passport. He is a global financial operator, who happens to be in New York simply because "that's where the money is."[20]

And so, Soros joined his Rothschild predecessors as a global supervillain willing to sow worldwide chaos and destruction in order to enrich himself and his crew. Engdahl continued:

The political agenda of Soros and this group of financial "globalists" will create the conditions for a new outbreak of war, even world war, if it continues to be tolerated.[21]

Engdahl published his article in the *Executive Intelligence Review,* the comically misnamed journal of archcrackpot Lyndon LaRouche. LaRouche soon adopted Soros as his favorite new evil mastermind. Taking Engdahl's "Court Jew" slur literally, LaRouche dedicated a 1997 issue of the *Executive Intelligence Review* to documenting the Soros–Queen Elizabeth II drug cartel. The lead article was titled "George Soros: Drug Pusher for the Queen."[22] Subsequent issues also emphasized Engdahl's Nazi-collaboration slur, calling Soros "a small cog in Adolf Eichmann's killing machine" and "a Nazi beast-man seizing Jewish properties."[23]

A few months after LaRouche's exposé, Prime Minister Mahathir Mohamad of Malaysia blamed Soros for deliberately creating the Asian financial crisis of 1997. Like the new Hungarian anti-Semites, Mahathir was careful to avoid alleging any Jewish conspiracy: "We do not want to say that this is a plot by the Jews." Then he added, "But in reality, it is a Jew who triggered the currency plunge, and coincidentally Soros is a Jew."[24] Even more coincidentally, Mahathir's party handed out translated compilations of Henry Ford's *Dearborn Independent* at a political conference a few years later.[25]

Meanwhile, back in the U.S.A., anti-Sorosism occupied itself quietly on the fringe for the next few years. Other than Soros's progressive position on drug policy—he supports needle exchanges, methadone treatment, and medical marijuana—most people did not associate his politics with liberalism, and Soros described himself as a moderate Republican.[26] Engdahl even accused Soros of aligning himself with former president George Bush Sr. and former conservative British prime minister Margaret Thatcher.

Right-wing Journalism

In 2003, everything changed. Infuriated by the policies of George W. Bush, Soros decided to send his political philanthropy homeward, telling the *Washington Post,* "America, under Bush, is a danger to the world. And I'm willing to put my money where my mouth is."[27] He gave $23 million to political action groups during the 2004 election, including the brash liberal grassroots organization MoveOn.org.[28]

But Republicans have their own rich guy—Richard Scaife, heir to the Mellon fortune and owner of the *Pittsburgh Tribune-Review,* whom the *Washington Post* has called the "Funding Father of the Right."[29]* Having sponsored efforts to impeach Bill Clinton in the 1990s, Scaife knows a thing or two about taking down presidents. But his tactics differ from those of Soros-supported organizations. While MoveOn.org's antagonistic political ads have invited criticism, the organization's approach of buying ads and fundraising for liberal candidates is fairly conventional. Scaife, by contrast, uses his media holdings to back scurrilous investigations of his political opponents. For instance, in 1994 Scaife's *Pittsburgh Tribune-Review* hired reporter Christopher Ruddy to investigate the suicide of Deputy White House Counsel Vince Foster. Ruddy's ill-founded conclusion that Foster might have been murdered nurtured a torrent of right-wing paranoia about homicidal White House conspiracies.[30]

After his success in smearing the Clintons, Ruddy founded the magazine *NewsMax* in 1998. Richard Scaife soon bought out the original investors; he and Ruddy now own 100 percent of the company.[31] *Forbes* magazine has called *NewsMax* "a news powerhouse and a must-read

---

* "Funding Father of the Right." There is some irony in the contrast between the Republican big donor's inherited wealth and the Democratic big donor's rise from penniless student to global capitalist. Okay, maybe not that much irony.

on the conservative media circuit."[32] Sarah Palin has called it "very valuable, very helpful," adding, "I appreciate all that you guys are doing to get a good message out there."[33] (I wonder why Palin didn't mention *NewsMax* when Katie Couric asked her what newspapers and magazines she read.)

NewsMax has been a frequent source of bogeyman stories and other speculative attacks on liberals. It often repackages conspiracy theories from the paranoid fringe and presents them to right-wing politicians and commentators, who in turn circulate sanitized versions of them to the general public. So when George Soros announced his opposition to President Bush in 2003, *NewsMax* used its standard bogeyman method to go after him. Only this time, the strategy carried the distinctive odor of persecution politics. The successful demonization of George Soros would provide a model for subsequent witch hunts of Jewish, Latino, black, and homosexual bogeymen in the years to come.

This is how it worked. One of *NewsMax*'s contributors is a self-described "award winning journalist" named Richard Poe.* In 2004, Poe applied his outstanding investigative talents to exposing George Soros's dark secrets. In a penetrating *NewsMax* article, he revealed that Soros had spent twenty-five years "recruiting, training, indoctrinating and installing a network of loyal operatives in fifty countries, placing them in positions of influence and power in media, government, finance and academia." These "foot soldiers" were awaiting Soros's command to "metaphorically skewer their respective Caesars."[34] Soros's latest, greatest target was the United States, for which he planned a "regime change."

And once again, the "international Jewish financier" raised his ugly schnoz. According to Poe:

[George Soros] seems to operate today as something of a lone wolf, answering to no particular master and loyal to no one—but still willing to

---

* "Award winning journalist." According to Poe's *LinkedIn* profile, the Syracuse Press Club awarded him "Best Newspaper Column" when he served as the Events editor at the *Syracuse New Times* for less than a year in 1984. ("Richard Poe," *LinkedIn,* retrieved 1 Apr. 2010, http://www.linkedin.com/pub/richard-poe/10/755/495.)

lend a hand in geopolitical intrigues by this or that government, provided there is money to be made.[35]

Only this time, the "Jewish" bit was left out. Indeed, Poe presented Soros as a self-hating Jew and an atheist whose animosity toward President Bush was driven by a profound hatred for religion. In other words, Soros was one of those "Jews who are not Jews."*

"The Guy That James Bond Goes After"

Bill O'Reilly must have read Richard Poe's article with deep skepticism. He invited the award-winning journalist into the no-spin zone for a hard-hitting interview in which he pummeled Poe with tough questions like, "If Soros is what you say he is, and I have no reason to doubt it. I mean, what I know about the man pretty much matches up to what you found out."[36] (With the right inflection, that statement could be construed as a tough question.)

Of course, O'Reilly is a very fair, very balanced journalist. He has repeatedly voiced his opposition to liberal "smear tactics" and "character assassination." And so it was with great fairness and consideration of the facts that Bill O'Reilly presented his opinion of George Soros—over and over and over again. In O'Reilly's words, George Soros is a big left-wing loon, a total radical, Mr. Socialism, as far left as you can get without moving to Havana, definitely anti-Israel, a crusading atheist, a dogmatic globalist, an incredible imbecile, the most powerful

---

* "Jews who are not Jews." In a subsequent book, *The Shadow Party: How George Soros, Hillary Clinton, and Sixties Radicals Seized Control of the Democratic Party,* Poe regurgitated Richard Engdahl's Nazi accusation, calling Soros a "collaborator in fascist Hungary" who survived by "assimilating to Nazism." In his defense, Poe's coauthor David Horowitz insisted that they never actually said Soros was a Nazi. That is true. They did not actually say Soros was a Nazi. ("Echoing Lyndon LaRouche, Horowitz and Poe smear 14-year-old George Soros as Nazi 'collaborator'; new book features doctored quotes, factual errors," *Media Matters,* 2 Aug. 2006, http://mediamatters.org/research/200608020003; David Horowitz, "Soros' Team Steps Up to the Plate," *FrontPageMagazine.com,* 4 Aug. 2006, http://www.frontpagemag.com/Articles/ReadArticle.asp?ID=23696.)

Democrat in the country, the Godfather, the single most dangerous individual in the United States of America, a real sleazoid, the guy that
James Bond goes after—"They ought to hang this Soros guy."[37] (Had
O'Reilly lived in the Middle Ages, he might have had a respectable career as a Latin demon-cursor.)

Not that O'Reilly would ever malign Soros's character. He explained,
"I don't go after him. I tell you what exactly George Soros is doing. All
right? And then I back it up with facts. But I don't say George Soros is
evil or he's a terrible guy."[38] Unlike, say, the guy that James Bond goes
after.*

The thing about the guy that James Bond goes after is not just that
he's an evil guy. Evil intentions alone would not prompt MI6 to send
its most debonair spy to infiltrate some sleazoid's secret lair underneath
a volcano. The ideal James Bond villain has four essential elements:

1. A cunning plot to destroy the world
2. Immense financial resources for building sadistic weaponry of
   massive proportions
3. A crew of villainous collaborators
4. A fluffy cat

George Soros has llamas, but other than that, he'd make a perfect
Bond villain.[39] Let's break down points one to three.

1. A cunning plot to destroy the world
Here is O'Reilly's full James Bond villain quote:

---

* "The guy that James Bond goes after." Ernst Stavro Blofeld? Auric Goldfinger? Octo-
pussy? And who exactly is James Bond in this analogy?

  Phil Kent, author of *Foundations of Betrayal: How the Liberal Super Rich Undermine
America,* evidently found that serious Bond villains weren't evil enough. As a guest on
the *O'Reilly Factor,* he called Soros the name of the evilest spy movie mastermind ever: *Dr.
Evil.* Indeed, if Soros were to shave his head and acquire a grotesque facial scar, the resem-
blance would be uncanny. Then Dr. Evil would have a Mini-Me and an International-
Jewish-Financier-Me. ("'Factor Investigation': George Soros," *Fox News,* 24 Apr. 2007,
http://www.foxnews.com/story/0,2933,268045,00.html.)

I think he's got some crazy vision of some one-world insanity. He's like the guy that James Bond goes after and slides down the volcano and blows up. That's who he is . . . There's more to it than money for him. He doesn't like our country and our system.[40]

Okay, so Soros doesn't want to destroy the world exactly; he just wants to transform it according to his crazy vision. As we saw in chapter 1, he has a "secret plan" to destroy Christmas in order to replace the current system with a "brave new progressive world." That was 2005. In 2006, O'Reilly claimed that Soros's secular progressives were plotting to capture the courts and were "brainwashing young, idealistic, and easily led Americans,"[41] much like their ancestors, the diabolical secular humanists. By 2007, Soros had concocted a more brazen Dr. Evil–like stratagem. According to O'Reilly, Soros and other "radical financiers" like insurance tycoon Peter Lewis were plotting to "buy a presidential election"; that is to say, "find and fund a candidate who will tacitly do what he or she is told to do."[42]

2. Immense financial resources for building sadistic weaponry of massive proportions

In addition to his devious plans, Soros has plenty of money to fund smear sites, political action committees, and other sadistic political weaponry. Bill O'Reilly is obsessed with the idea that certain "secular progressive" organizations are Soros tools. There is the ACLU, "the most dangerous organization in the United States of America right now . . . second next to Al Qaeda."[43] There is MoveOn.org, "the new Klan."[44] And there is Media Matters, the "most vicious element in our society today."[45]

Media Matters is a not-for-profit research organization dedicated to "monitoring, analyzing, and correcting conservative misinformation in the U.S. media."[46] It was founded in 2004 by David Brock, a former right-wing journalist like Christopher Ruddy who earned renown for smearing Justice Clarence Thomas's accuser, Anita Hill, and for breaking the Troopergate story that accused Bill Clinton of engaging in an affair with Paula Jones.

But in the late 1990s, Brock had a change of heart.* Concluding that his work had been dirty politics, not good journalism, he apologized to the Clintons and to Anita Hill. In two books, *Blinded by the Right: The Conscience of an Ex-Conservative* and *The Republican Noise Machine: Right-Wing Media and How It Corrupts Democracy,* Brock publically repudiated the tactics of the right and his own contributions to them. Media Matters is his project to expose and undermine those tactics.[47]

Some have criticized Media Matters for engaging in a "gotcha" style of politics similar to what Brock once did for the right. But Media Matters isn't in the business of sinking Republican politicians or even conservative media stars—contrary to Bill O'Reilly's megalomaniacal fantasies that the organization is the smearing arm of George Soros's personal vendetta against him. Media Matters' target is not the man himself but the words he speaks. The majority of its content consists of direct quotes from Bill O'Reilly, Rush Limbaugh, Glenn Beck, and their colleagues. Its raison d'être is not to trumpet occasional verbal gaffes or "gotchas" for political gain. It is to call attention to the frequent and widespread use of misleading, paranoid, bigoted rhetoric that right-wing commentators and politicians have been pouring into the hearts and minds of millions of Americans. In essence, Media Matters' work amounts to a transcript of right-wing persecution politics. It has been an invaluable resource to me and to others who had been trying to raise the nation's awareness of fear and loathing in America long before the Tea Parties raised their furious cacophony.

But to Bill O'Reilly, Media Matters is just a smear machine. And he knows that there is only one man with the cunning and the resources to manufacture such a fiendish weapon of crass destruction—the man sliding down the volcano: George Soros.

The only trouble is that George Soros didn't fund Media Matters. Soros's Open Society Institute is unusually transparent for a secretive

---

* "Change of heart." Freudians would love Brock, a gay man who once channeled his self-loathing into right-wing politics. He said of his fellow closeted gay Republicans, "Perhaps because they were trying too hard to fit into GOP ranks, they often embodied the worst attributes of the extreme right—racism, sexism, anti-Semitism." (David Brock, *Blinded by the Right: The Conscience of an Ex-Conservative* [New York: Three Rivers Press, 2002]: 43.)

criminal operation, and there is no record of any donation to Media Matters for America. But as we've seen, Bill O'Reilly does not let mere facts stand in the way of the truth. Employing his amazing powers of superior analysis, O'Reilly followed the money and discovered that he was right all along. While OSI did not donate directly to Media Matters, it did donate to an organization called the Tides Foundation. The Tides Foundation then "funnels the money to a variety of radical hatchet men." O'Reilly explained the funneling process as follows:

> After our report on Monday, the vile Media Matters outfit is denying receiving funding from any of George Soros' outfits. Well, that is a total lie. As we laid out for you, the smear website received more than a million dollars from the Tides Foundation alone in 2005, and just by coincidence, Soros' Open Society Institute donated more than a million dollars to Tides in 2005. Figure it out.[48]

In case his audience had trouble figuring it out, O'Reilly also offered the following helpful diagram. It demonstrates the diverse ways in which Soros covertly funded Media Matters through the Tides Foundation and other front organizations:

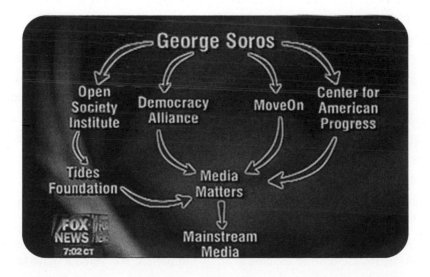

O'Reilly's diagram pioneered the development of the Fox News conspiracy chart, a formidable weapon that overwhelms secular progressives and other hostiles with a massive onslaught of arrows—like the Desert Storm shock-and-awe campaign, only with prettier graphics and fewer explosions. Overcome by this new form of superior analysis, Media Matters could only sputter that Soros's donations to the Tides Foundation had been earmarked for other programs, not Media Matters. One staff writer grumbled that if Soros wanted to fund Media Matters, he could simply write them a check.[49] But that would have been far too obvious a ploy for Soros's cunning mind.

3. A Crew of Villainous Collaborators

Having irrefutably established that Media Matters is a team of "paid assassins by George Soros,"[50] O'Reilly could focus on the next element of James Bond villainy—Soros's crew of evil collaborators. The last arrow on the conspiracy chart points to Mainstream Media. This is a very important arrow because MediaMatters.org only gets a few hundred thousand visitors per month. That's not too shabby for a website, but compared to NewsMax.com's 3 million viewers or FoxNews.com's 10 million viewers, it's not particularly scary.[51] So O'Reilly demonstrated how MediaMatters.org feeds its propaganda to the big guns:

> Media Matters is an Internet site, but directly feeds its propaganda to some mainstream media people, including elements at NBC News, columnist Frank Rich and Paul Krugman at *The New York Times,* columnist Jonathan Alter at *Newsweek,* and Bill Moyers at PBS.[52]

That said, O'Reilly does not believe that the entire mainstream media supports Soros's secular-progressive agenda—only 75 percent of them:

> The online character assassins also make good use of the mainstream print media, which are about three-quarters progressive, by my estimation. The level of ideological commitment of the leftist media varies. Leading the way, you have the most enthusiastic secular-progressives, the *New York Times* and other committed left-wing papers, but you also have le-

gions of quieter S-P [secular-progressive] sympathizers. These mainstream media enablers provide aid and comfort for the frontline troops and are invaluable in getting their message out to an even wider audience.[53]

These mainstream media enablers are part of Soros's nefarious network. Unlike the ACLU and Media Matters, he doesn't control them directly, but he's able to coordinate with them through his paid assassins. The media enablers broadcast Soros's message to a wider audience. They also shield him from scrutiny. On the *O'Reilly Factor,* Fox News commentator Monica Crowley said to O'Reilly, "This is an incredibly well-oiled, brilliantly orchestrated machine . . . This guy has been able to fly under the radar for a long time before you just exposed him because the mainstream media protects him, because they're on the same ideological page."[54]

Finally, in addition to the mainstream media enablers, O'Reilly has also implicated a few other rich secular progressives to round out Soros's crew of villainous collaborators, such as insurance mogul Peter Lewis and Esprit founder Susie Tompkins Buell, who have also donated to liberal causes. If Soros is the secular-progressive equivalent of James Bond's nemesis, Ernst Stavro Blofeld, then Lewis and Buell are the subordinate members of SPECTRE, a fictional global terrorist consortium made up of the world's great criminal organizations.

And, thus, the allegory is complete. George Soros *is* the guy that James Bond goes after. These parallels between cinematic fantasy and O'Reilly's caricature of George Soros aren't accidental. O'Reilly's version of the bogeyman formula has obvious narrative elements that enhance its appeal to his audience. But please put this idea in your pocket for now; we'll explore its full implications in a later chapter.

"The Shadow of the Court Jew"

In the meantime, O'Reilly's inclusion of Peter Lewis and Susie Tompkins Buell in Soros's intrigues raises an important question: why does Soros get to be the boss? Peter Lewis gave just as much money to

MoveOn.org and, unlike Soros, Lewis actually donated to Media Matters.[55] Moreover, Lewis, whom friends describe as "weird," "eccentric," and "a functioning pothead," has more radical drug positions than Soros.[56] He has donated to an organization that seeks to legalize and tax marijuana, in contrast to Soros's donations to medical marijuana advocates. In many ways, Lewis seems like the perfect bogeyman. And yet, O'Reilly always headlines Soros, adding Lewis as an afterthought, and few other right-wing leaders even mention Lewis, let alone Buell.

There are some obvious differences that make Soros a more attractive villain to O'Reilly and other conservatives. Soros is considerably richer than Lewis, and he was something of a celebrity even before he got behind MoveOn.org. Both men are Jewish, but Peter Lewis is from Cleveland and his money comes from insurance. George Soros is a Hungarian-born investor.[57] He has a strong Eastern European accent, he made billions speculating on financial markets—most famously during the 1992 currency crisis in the UK—and he openly uses his wealth to influence global political affairs. As a *Jerusalem Post* writer critically observed, Soros is the epitome of Henry Ford's International Jew.

> Soros unwittingly parades the shadow of the Court Jew, the Wandering Jew, and the medieval money lender who for centuries fed anti-Semitism's sick imagination.[58]

Thus, Soros's wealth, nationality, politics, and religion fit perfectly into the anti-Semitic conspiracy fantasies of men like Lyndon LaRouche and F. William Engdahl. And these same qualities also make him a clear choice for archvillain in O'Reilly's own conspiracy theories.

Does that make O'Reilly an anti-Semite? No, it does not. O'Reilly has never publicly denigrated Jews, either explicitly or using coded language, and he does not mention Soros's religion in his diatribes. But while O'Reilly never entered Father Coughlin–Henry Ford territory, he nonetheless drew from the ideas that Coughlin and Ford popularized. That is to say, O'Reilly's caricature of Soros exploited a villainous archetype with deep anti-Semitic roots. American culture offers a number of bad-guy archetypes frequently dished up in Hollywood thrillers. There is the Brutal Russian Spymaster, the Bloodthirsty Arab Terrorist, the Psychotic Evil Genius, and the Amoral Criminal Mastermind with a Somewhat British Accent. The International Jewish Financier is older than any of these. You won't see him in the movies, but his enduring appeal is demonstrated by his popularity in explicitly anti-Semitic conspiracy theories.

O'Reilly tapped into that appeal. Like Ford, Coughlin, and LaRouche, he placed the rich Jew at the center of his conspiracy theories. His caricature of Soros emphasizes precisely those traits long associated with the Rothschilds: lack of national identity, violent hostility to Christianity, support for world government, and control of the media. There are some differences. Bill O'Reilly substituted secularism for Judaism to make his caricature of Soros more acceptable to modern Americans. And he replaced the prototypical Jewish profit motive with the pursuit of a radical agenda more commonly associated with the communist revolutionaries of American conspiracy lore. But there is more than enough International Jewish Financier in O'Reilly's version of Soros for his audience to easily recognize a familiar villain, especially when the villain's secret objective is to sabotage Christianity. As Henry Ford's *Dearborn Independent* explained:

> Not only do the Jews disagree with Christian teaching . . . but they seek to interfere with it. It is not religious tolerance in the midst of religious difference, but religious attack that they preach and practice. The whole record of the Jewish opposition to Christmas, Easter and other Christian festivals, and their opposition to certain patriotic songs, shows the venom and directness of that attack.[59]

"Lord of the Democrats"

Bill O'Reilly wasn't the only one to vilify George Soros. When *News-Max*'s Richard Poe published his Soros conspiracy article in 2004, Republicans immediately realized the political potential of hanging a rich, secular Hungarian Jew with unconventional drug policy ideas around the neck of Democratic presidential candidate John Kerry. Poe's article came out on May 1, 2004. One month later, the Republican National Committee circulated an internal memo that described Soros's radical positions, calling him "Lord of the Democrats" and the "Daddy Warbucks" of drug legalization. The memo urged Republican politicians to use floor speeches and other opportunities to pillory Soros.

Republican politicians enthusiastically obliged, rushing to dig up whatever dirt they could find on this new threat to America. What they found were the penetrating investigations of Lyndon LaRouche's *Executive Intelligence Review*. Appearing on *Hannity & Colmes,* Newt Gingrich claimed that Soros only attacked Bush because he wanted to legalize heroin.[60] And Republican Speaker of the House Dennis Hastert insinuated to an incredulous Chris Wallace on *Fox News Sunday* that Soros got his money from drug operations:

HASTERT: You know, I don't know where George Soros gets his money. I don't know where—if it comes overseas or from drug groups or where it comes from. And I—

WALLACE (interrupting): Excuse me?

HASTERT: Well, that's what he's been for a number years—George Soros has been for legalizing drugs in this country. So, I mean, he's got a lot of ancillary interests out there. I don't know where George Soros gets his money.

WALLACE: You think he may be getting money from the drug cartel?

HASTERT: I'm saying I don't know where groups—could be people who support this type of thing. I'm saying we don't know. The fact is we don't know where this money comes from.[61]

Following the lead of O'Reilly and the Republican leadership, right-wing commentators joined the fun with their own LaRouche-Engdahl-derived Soros smears. Echoing Engdahl's "Jews who are not Jews" line, Tony Blankley, editor of the conservative *Washington Times,* said to Sean Hannity, apropos of nothing, "This is a man who has blamed the Jews for anti-Semitism."[62] And Ann Coulter later said to Hannity's sidekick, Alan Colmes, apropos of nothing, "George Soros, who's always going around prattling about the perfidy of the Jews . . . says the reason for anti-Semitism is the Jews."[63] This self-hating Jew attack was the perfect vehicle for highlighting Soros's Judaism without crossing into explicit anti-Semitism. Blankley and Coulter got to mention that Soros was a Jew while pretending to be standing up for the real Jews whom Soros allegedly hated so much.

Incidentally, both Blankley and Coulter also echoed Endgahl's Nazi-collaborator slur. On Hannity's show, Blankley subtly pointed out that Soros "was a Jew who figured out a way to survive the Holocaust." When an inquiring listener emailed Blankly to ask for a clarification, he spelled out the subtext: "Soros and his family converted from their Jewish faith and survived the Holocaust (there was speculation that they may have collaborated with the Nazi's [*sic*])."[64] And in a later appearance on *Hannity*, Ann Coulter called Soros "an admitted Nazi collaborator."[65]

The Republicans were so pleased by the success of their Soros bashing during the 2004 election that they followed up again the next year. When House majority leader Tom DeLay ran into trouble for ethics violations, he blamed "a Democratic conspiracy led by liberal billionaire George Soros and the grass-roots organization MoveOn.org" for smearing him.[66] He soon widened the conspiracy from Soros's henchmen to the media enablers, stating in an interview:

> Somebody ought to look at the organizations and ask the *New York Times,* the *Washington Post,* the *L.A. Times, Time, Newsweek,* AP why they're spending all these resources they are, who they talked to . . . are they collaborating with all these organizations that are funded by George Soros and his heavy hitters, and do these organizations ever talk to each other? Of course they do, they have people that are on the same boards.[67]*

---

* DeLay also tried blaming another bad guy for his ethical woes, insisting, "Satan is behind them. And Satan is behind the left. Satan is behind my prosecution." (Max Blumenthal, "Republicans Slouching Toward Gomorrah: A BuzzFlash Interview with Max Blumenthal," *BuzzFlash.com,* 9 Dec. 2009, http://blog.buzzflash.com/interviews/164.)

The Republican Party backed up DeLay by distributing to the press "detailed research" showing links between Democrats and Soros. Rep. Joe Wilson (R-SC), the man who shouted, "You lie!" during Obama's State of the Union address, charged "radical liberals, such as George Soros" with mounting a "desperate smear campaign" against DeLay.[68] Award-winning journalist Richard Poe jumped at the opportunity for yet another Soros conspiracy:

> The pattern of the attack suggests that DeLay may be confronting a political machine far wealthier, more ruthless and better skilled at media manipulation than the Democratic Party itself. When the hysteria subsides and the facts are examined, we may learn that DeLay's foe all along has been the Shadow Party—a murky and inscrutable entity controlled by leftwing billionaire George Soros.[69]

But fanning Soros paranoia didn't protect DeLay from ethics indictments, and he ultimately resigned to pursue his dream of competitive ballroom dancing.* Since then, anti-Sorosism has gone into decline. When the Democrats returned to power, right-wing leaders were finally able to look for conspirators inside the government, an opportunity that they have pursued with great relish. The anti-Semitic diehards on the fringe are still obsessed with Soros, of course, and they theorize that Obama is a Soros puppet. Lyndon LaRouche, for example, calls Soros "Obama's Godfather." (LaRouche also conjectured that the two conspired with the British to exploit the conflict between Russia and Georgia in order to launch World War III—still pending.)[70] Rush Limbaugh half-heartedly explored the Obama-Soros connection on a couple of occasions, but he also speculated that Obama's puppet master might be John Podesta or even King Abdullah of Saudi Arabia.[71] Richard Poe also continues to try to milk his Soros routine. The day after Obama's election, he wrote: "[Soros] created Obama. An Obama presidency will be a Soros presidency."[72]

---

* "Competitive ballroom dancing." Between DeLay's cha-cha on *Dancing with the Stars* and former Illinois governor Rod Blagojevich's ineptitude on *Celebrity Apprentice,* reality television has become the standard career path for disgraced politicians.

But this time, Bill O'Reilly did not invite Poe into the no-spin zone. In general, O'Reilly has treated Obama in a manner that could almost be called respectful, and he has left the president out of any more grand conspiracy narratives. Is O'Reilly trying to rebrand himself as a journalist? Does he feel that the Fox-brand paranoia that he pioneered has gone too far? Does he secretly approve of Obama? Or did Dr. Evil steal his mojo? It's not clear.

But where O'Reilly hesitated, others have charged ahead, most notably a man named Glenn Beck.

9

A GOAT FOR AZAZEL

How Good Ol' Anti-Semitism and Witch Burnings
Evolved into the Grand Conspiracy Theories
of Persecution Politics

The search for a scapegoat is the easiest of all hunting expeditions.
—Dwight D. Eisenhower

BEFORE TURNING TO MR. BECK, we have another analytical question
to answer. We've seen that George Soros is a convenient bad guy
because he resembles the archetype of the International Jew, but what
is it about the International Jew that presents such an appealing villain
in the first place? Is it another example of intolerance and cognitive
dissonance?

The tendency of Henry Ford and other American anti-Semites to
project their obvious feelings of intolerance onto Jews suggests that
cognitive dissonance may well have played a role in their paranoia. But
anti-Semitism is much less prevalent in contemporary American culture, especially when compared to racism and homophobia. It would
be implausible to suggest that everyone who fears a Soros-led conspiracy is motivated by repressed hatred of Jews. Moreover, the International Jew is one of several common conspiratorial archetypes. Others
include secret societies like the Illuminati and industrialist dynasties
like the Rockefellers, neither of which can be explained by racial or religious bigotry. Thus, even if anti-Semitism contributes to fear of the
International Jew, it does not fully explain it.

Spanking the Scapegoat

Nonetheless, we can gain insight into the appeal of the International Jew by investigating the archetype's anti-Semitic roots. Fear of Jews preceded anti-Semitic global conspiracy theories by many centuries. During the Middle Ages, superstitious Europeans often blamed Jews for various calamities. For example, when the Black Death spread through Europe in the 1300s, Christians accused Jews of poisoning drinking wells, and slaughtered their Jewish neighbors by the tens of thousands. (Between the plague and the pogroms, the fourteenth century was not a good time to be a Jew in Europe, not that the rest of the millennium was particularly rosy.)

While Jews seem to have a particular knack for collecting blame, the tendency to hold innocent scapegoats responsible for unexplained misfortune is one of those universal and horrible aspects of human nature that we seem unable to evolve out of—like kidney stones. The origin of the term *scapegoat* is biblical, more or less. The Old Testament book of Leviticus commanded Moses's brother Aaron to select two goats, one for God and the other for Azazel. After sacrificing God's goat, Aaron was supposed to confess all of the Israelites' sins while holding the head of the second goat and then send it out into the wilderness to find Azazel.* Biblical scholars are not sure who or what Azazel is. Some say it's the Devil. Some say it's a mountain. Some say it's some kind of magic goat genie. But everyone agrees that the folks who brought us the King James Bible got it completely wrong when they translated the Hebrew word *Azazel* as "scapegoat"; that is, a goat that has escaped. Nonetheless, the name stuck.[1]

Scapegoating occurs in communities as small as a group of friends and as large as a global religion. The victims are usually marginal members of the community. In small groups, scapegoats might be unpopular or eccentric individuals. In large communities, scapegoats tend to be

---

* "The other for Azazel." I think Azazel's goat got the better end of the deal, but I suppose it depends on what Azazel did with the goat once it found him. If I were the goat, I'd say the hell with it and just find some nice oasis with tasty grass.

members of cultural, religious, or ethnic minorities. For example, the first three women accused during the Salem witch trials in 1692 included a homeless beggar, a widow who did not attend church and was suspected of promiscuity, and a Caribbean Indian.

Part of scapegoating's enduring appeal is its fusion of two rather important human sentiments—suspicion and curiosity. Suspicion of strangers was an important survival trait back in the days when marauding tribes would routinely rampage through the countryside. Primitive humans who ran off when the club-wielding ruffians showed up probably survived a bit better than those who greeted them with pretty garlands.[2] Attesting to the primal source of xenophobia, primatologist Jane Goodall observed that even chimpanzees exhibit "inherent dislike or 'hatred' of strangers."[3]

On the other hand, curiosity underlies the human desire for knowledge. When something happens, particularly when something bad happens, we want to know why. By working out the causal connections that determine our environment, we can establish some sort of control over that environment. We can build fires to cook our meat, make clothing to warm our bodies, and develop drugs to fix our erectile dysfunction.

But, unfortunately, we humans are not nearly so smart as we think we are, and we often discover causal connections that don't actually exist. We're particularly prone to embrace the wrong answer when it provides some psychological benefit. For instance, a Puritan in colonial Salem could satisfy his dark suspicions of a strange Caribbean woman by blaming a teenager's psychological problems on witchcraft. Likewise, blaming an outbreak of the plague on poisoned water might offer a medieval German peasant an excuse to work out his internal aggression on those creepy Jews.

Not surprisingly, scapegoating often involves the kind of Freudian projection that we have repeatedly discussed, where people project their own hateful feelings onto the scapegoats. For instance, medieval anti-Semites projected their murderous impulses onto the Jews whom they accused of poisoning wells and subsequently murdered. Thus, the well-poisoning theory was perfectly designed to lodge itself in the

brainstem of the German peasantry: it exploited their instinctual suspicions of insular and exotic Jewish communities, it explained the devastating epidemic that was ravaging the land, and it rationalized their
violent urges.

Dawn of the Supervillain

According to historian Norman Cohn, such ancient superstitions led
directly to the "the modern myth of the Jewish world-conspiracy."[4]
What began as localized rumors about poisoned wells and sacrifices of
Christian babies eventually evolved into beliefs in a global plot by
wealthy Jewish powerbrokers to destroy Christianity. The conspiracism
satisfied the same basic urges as the scapegoating—converting suspicion of strangers into explanations of misfortunes. How do you account
for World War I, a senseless, catastrophic war that killed tens of millions? You blame the international Rothschilds who are not part of any
nation but exist somehow above and outside European society, just as
the European peasantry once blamed local Jews—isolated in their traditions and their ghettos—for the Black Death.

And if you're a Bill O'Reilly fan, how do you explain the secularization of Christmas or the liberal media that challenges your ideas? You
blame the international George Soros—a "lone wolf," a "state-less
statesman," a rich Old World Jew with a Hungarian accent. One need
not hate Jews to scapegoat George Soros, but Soros's marginal status as
an American is part of what makes him an appealing target. There have
been other less exotic scapegoats in the history of American political
paranoia, including the Rockefellers, the Illuminati, the communists,
and the Jesuits, but they have all in some way been represented as anti-
Christian (or at least anti-Protestant) and un-American. They are radicals, globalists, profiteers, or elites. They answer to Stalin, the pope, or
the Devil. They are not from what Glenn Beck and Sarah Palin have
called "the real America."

These global supervillains, the modern version of the Salem witches
and the well-poisoning Jews, had been largely absent from mainstream

American politics for decades. Even in the heydays of the Secular Humanist and the Gay Agenda, the conspiratorial bad guys seldom had names and addresses. They were amorphous atheists and homosexuals, perhaps with a Welfare Queen thrown into the mix. When a real villain was wanted, Americans looked outside the nation's borders to Leonid Brezhnev, Fidel Castro, Saddam Hussein, and Osama bin Laden. The United States had not seen genuine domestic supervillains since communist spies like Alger Hiss and the Rosenbergs were prosecuted during the Red Scare.

That all changed with George Soros and the war on Christmas. After Saddam Hussein was executed and the Bush administration seemed to give up on capturing the elusive bin Laden, Fox News and the Republican Party turned the spotlight on Soros and his gang of paid assassins. But Soros was only the first and most prominent in a new line of domestic supervillains. Like baseball pitching machines, today's right-wing media outlets regularly serve up fresh bogeymen to conservative commentators and politicians who joyfully slug at them with all their might. Most of these bogeymen differ from most of the people who watch Fox News. They might be Jewish like George Soros. They might be black like Van Jones, a former White House environmental advisor whom Beck has suspected of plotting a communist revolution.[5] Or they might be gay like Kevin Jennings, a Department of Education official whom Rush Limbaugh and Sean Hannity have accused of promoting homosexuality in the schools.[6] People like Soros, Jones, and Jennings represent the new supervillains of right-wing mythology who use their awesome powers to remake the country and persecute white Christian conservatives. Much of what the right wing calls journalism consists of "discovering" and "exposing" these secret villains. Welcome to the twenty-first-century witch hunt.

10

THE PROGRESSIVE HUNTER

Glenn Beck and His Chalkboard Save Real America
from Murderous Czars, Black Radicals, and
Other People Who Aren't from Iowa

*The whole aim of practical politics is to keep the populace alarmed
(and hence clamorous to be led to safety) by menacing it with an end-
less series of hobgoblins, all of them imaginary.*
—H. L. Mencken

IN DECEMBER 2004, when Bill O'Reilly was warning the nation that
dark forces were threatening to destroy Christmas, Glenn Beck was
touring local performance venues across the country on a "politically
incorrect comedic romp" called the Real American Christmas Tour. His
show satirized the secularization of Christmas with songs like "Happy
RamaHanuKwanzMas."[1]

As Beck's popularity grew, his routine became darker. Or perhaps,
as his routine became darker, his popularity grew. In 2006, he joined
CNN Headline News with a one-hour program offering "an unconventional look at the news of the day featuring Beck's often amusing perspective." Beck promised to present "a different take" to viewers who
were "tired of the predictable left-versus-right debates."[2] His show did
prove unconventional and unpredictable, and it was often amusing,
though perhaps not in the way that CNN intended.

Glenn Beck made his first foray into primetime paranoia during the
summer of 2006. In a series of broadcasts, Beck predicted that Iran
and/or Russia would soon invade Israel, most likely on August 22,
which would precipitate World War III. He told viewers:

We are in the early stages of World War III—it's the linchpin of World War III—the possible apocalypse in 13 days. Do you believe we're in the end times? All out Armageddon. World War III is dangerously close.[3]

When Beck spoke of Armageddon, he was not speaking figuratively. "End times" refers to the period of tribulation that precedes Christ's return.* In another broadcast, Beck asked his audience:

> Do you believe that Iran and Russia will come together to invade Israel, resulting in a world war of biblical proportions, an eventual peace treaty, and the beginning of the seven-year tribulation period, and the eventual revoking of the peace treaty by a leader who turns out to be the Antichrist, and a campaign of Armageddon, and the second coming of Christ?[4]

But August 22 passed without Armageddon, and Beck must have figured that he couldn't wait for Iran and Russia to get their acts together. Clearly, his first foray into fearmongering was a dud.

A Legendary Crank

Unbowed, Beck hit the books to learn how to construct a proper paranoia narrative. He found his muse and mentor in the late Willard Cleon Skousen. Former Bush speechwriter David Frum has described Skousen as "one of the legendary cranks of the conservative world, a John Bircher, a grand fantasist of theories about secret conspiracies between capitalists and communists to impose a one-world government under the control of David Rockefeller."[5] This was exactly the kind of man Beck needed.

One of Skousen's books is called *The Naked Capitalist*. It is ostensibly a commentary on the work of a Georgetown University historian

---

* "Christ's return." Apocalyptic predictions are popular among Christian conspiracy theorists, and they always present the hastening of the end times as a catastrophe. But according to the prophecy, good Christians get to go directly to Heaven before the end times. If I were a Christian, I'd be pretty excited about the whole thing.

named Carroll Quigley, whom Bill Clinton has cited as a major personal influence. Quigley has occasionally written about secret societies, so his work has also been popular among right-wing conspiracists like Skousen. In *The Naked Capitalist,* Skousen transformed Quigley's secret societies into an evil global conspiracy of "socialistic" bankers who were plotting to take over the world. He wrote:

> There is a growing volume of evidence that the highest centers of political and economic power have been forcing the entire human race toward a global, socialist, dictatorial-oriented society . . . The world hierarchy of the dynastic super-rich is out to take over the entire planet, doing it with Socialistic legislation where possible, but having no reluctance to use Communist revolution where necessary.[6]

According to Skousen, a religious Mormon, the global takeover by the conspiracy of the super-rich had in fact been prophesied two thousand years ago in the Bible:

> Anyone familiar with the writings of John's Apocalypse might have suspected that modern history would eventually contain the account of a gigantic complex of political and economic power which would cover the whole earth. John predicted that before the great epic of Messianic or Millennial peace, the human race would be subjected to a ruthless, world-wide conglomerate of dictatorial authority which would attempt to make all men subservient to it or be killed.[7]

Skousen's "world-wide conglomerate" formed the basis of the popular new world order conspiracy theories, according to which a "shadow government" made up of Rothschilds, Rockefellers, the Illuminati, the Learned Elders of Zion, the Council on Foreign Relations, and assorted bad guys like George Soros's plot to create a tyrannical one-world government and amass a very large fleet of black helicopters. Pat Robertson's 1992 bestseller, *The New World Order,* is one of the most popular books of the genre. In 1994, a year before the Oklahoma City bombing, Oklahoma state legislators passed a resolution calling on the U.S. Congress "to cease any support for the establishment of 'a new world order' or any form of global government."[8] The concept also inspired the Syndicate, the secretive alien-collaborators of *The X-Files* series. Skousen's role in germinating such conspiracy ideas is what David Frum meant when he called him a "legendary crank."[*]

"The Goal Is Globalization"

And so Glenn Beck set about becoming a legendary crank himself. On his September 6, 2006, radio show, Beck favorably discussed Quigley's book and Skousen's *The Naked Capitalist*: "It's the only explanation that I have heard of why our government isn't doing—why they didn't put more boots on the ground [in Iraq and Afghanistan], why we don't protect our own borders here."[9] A few weeks later, he continued the theme in an interview with CNN colleague Lou Dobbs. Beck asked:

> Was Carroll Quigley right on the shadow government, on the companies taking over and really controlling everything? Because it's really the only thing that I can put my finger on to say, "Why aren't we doing anything about illegal immigration?" We're run by companies now, aren't we?[10]

But Quigley never discussed a "shadow government." The term comes from the Skousen-derived new world order conspiracy theories. Lou Dobbs was either unfamiliar with Quigley or chose to avoid the question, so Beck pressed on: "It's not just corporate America. I mean, it's global corporations. I think we're being turned into MexAmeriCanada."

MexAmeriCanada is Beck's awkward name for the imminent union between Mexico, Canada, and the United States. Lou Dobbs, Rep. Ron

---

* "Legendary crank." Carroll Quigley was not impressed by Skousen's "commentary." He wrote, "Skousen's personal position seems to me perilously close to the 'exclusive uniformity' which I see in Nazism and in the Radical Right in this country. In fact, his position has echoes of the original Nazi 25-point plan." (Joe Conason, "Should Fox fire Glenn Beck? Or should he resign?" *Salon.com,* 16 Jul. 2010, http://www.salon.com/news/opinion/joe_conason/2010/07/16/beck.)

Paul (R-TX), and his son Rand, the Republican Senate nominee from Kentucky, call it the North American Union.*[11] There are many variations of the North American Union conspiracy theory, but the experts agree on two points.

First, the conspirators plan to deliberately devalue the dollar in order to force Americans to accept a new common currency, called the Amero. (Like the euro, get it?) The conspirators include the Federal Reserve and numerous foreign entities. Ron Paul speaks vaguely of "an unholy alliance of foreign consortiums and officials from several governments."[12] Others name the Rothschilds. Many also suspect King Juan Carlos of Spain for no obvious reason.

Second, the powers that be are constructing a massive "NAFTA Superhighway" to ship goods from Mexico to Canada.[13] According to Ron Paul's congressional website, "Proponents envision a ten-lane colossus the width of several football fields, with freight and rail lines, fiber-optic cable lines, and oil and natural gas pipelines running alongside."[14] Why such a wide road is so critical for the formation of the North American Union is unclear, but it has forced the Federal Highway Administration to deal with some unusual complaints.[15]

To further investigate the conspiracy, Beck later invited renowned MexAmeriCanada scholar Jerome Corsi onto his show. Corsi became famous in 2004 for his powerful biography of Senator John Kerry, *Unfit for Command: Swift Boat Veterans Speak Out Against John Kerry*. In 2008, Corsi would also become a staunch defender of the Obama birther theory. But in 2007, he was peddling his book *The Late Great U.S.A.: The Coming Merger with Mexico and Canada*. During the interview, Beck peppered the distinguished author with challenging questions:

> You've got the trans—the NAFTA superhighway that, again, everybody denies, but you've got it broken up in chunks being built right now. It will deliver goods from China right to Mexico through America into Canada. You say this stuff is going to eliminate the middle class. How?[16]

---

* "North American Union." When unification happens, I hope that we get to vote on the name; my personal favorite is Camerico.

The MexAmeriCanada conspiracy worked better for Beck than the Iran–Russia–World War III bit, but it wasn't quite evil enough. For one thing, there is no good way to draw an analogy between excessively wide highways and Nazi Germany. So Beck moved on to Al Gore's campaign against global warming, which has more obvious parallels to the Third Reich. In April 2007, he did a radio show about a book that he was reading on the Nazis. Then he whipped in a bit of Al Gore's *Inconvenient Truth*. Then he whipped in a bit of Skousen's world-government conspiracy theory. And voilà, instant fascist world-government conspiracy:

> I understand World War II much, much better because we're here again, gang. We are here again. And I read this one part on global warming about how they got—what was the first thing they did to get people to exterminate the Jews. Now, I'm not saying that anybody's going to—you know Al Gore's not going to be rounding up Jews and exterminating them. It is the same tactic, however. The goal is different. The goal is globalization. The goal is global carbon tax. The goal is the United Nations running the world. That is the goal. Back in the 1930s, the goal was get rid of all of the Jews and have one global government. You got to have an enemy to fight. And when you have an enemy to fight, then you can unite the entire world behind you, and you seize power. That was Hitler's plan. His enemy: the Jew. Al Gore's enemy, the U.N.'s enemy: global warming.[17]

In presenting Al Gore as a cunning Hitler-like supervillain, Beck was warming up for his future role as chief witch hunter for the right wing. Comparisons between progressive bogeymen and murderous dictators would soon become a standard part of his repertoire.* The accusation

---

* Beck's Nazi comparisons are so frequent that *The Daily Show* has accused him of "Nazi Tourette's." But when some compared Arizona's law requiring people to carry citizenship papers to Nazi Germany, Beck was aghast. "You're out of your mind?" he howled, "Are you comparing the systematic cold-blooded extermination of millions of Jews, to America making sure people are here legally. The parallels are non-existent." As opposed to Al Gore's environmentalism. (Lewis Black, "Back in Black: Glenn Beck's Nazi Tourette's," *The Daily Show,* 12 May 2010, http://www.thedailyshow.com/watch/wed-may-12-2010/back-in-black---glenn-beck-s-nazi-tourette-s.)

against Gore was also an impressive feat of Freudian projection. Glenn Beck, America's preeminent fearmonger, stoked the fear that Al Gore was employing scare tactics—by gratuitously comparing him to history's scariest fearmonger, Adolf Hitler. It's so twisted that it's genius.

Czar Wars

But Beck was just getting warmed up. He began broadcasting at Fox News on January 19, the eve of President Obama's inauguration. By March, he had tripled his CNN primetime viewership and was rivaling O'Reilly and Hannity with 2.3 million viewers per show, an incredible feat for a program with a 5:00 p.m. timeslot.[18] The *New York Times* called him "Fox News's mad, apocalyptic, tearful rising star."

> With a mix of moral lessons, outrage and an apocalyptic view of the future, Mr. Beck, a longtime radio host who jumped to Fox from CNN's Headline News channel this year, is capturing the feelings of an alienated class of Americans.*[19]

At Fox News, Beck was ready to take his conspiracism to the next level. The one element that his CNN conspiracy theories lacked was bogeymen. For some reason, he didn't play up foreigners like Ahmadinejad or Putin during the near-apocalypse of August 2006. Global corporations are too nonspecific. Al Gore is not marginal enough and a bit too nerdy to be really scary. George Soros is a good standby, and Beck has used him on occasion, but he's really O'Reilly's bogeyman. Using someone else's bogeyman is the right-wing conspiracist version of going out with your friend's girlfriend. You can hang with her in a public place, but no groping. It might have been different if O'Reilly and Soros had an open relationship, but O'Reilly is a one-bogeyman kind of guy. Everything he hates is somehow funded and controlled

---

* "Capturing the feelings of an alienated class of Americans." That makes Beck sound like some kind of sci-fi neuroterrorist. We need to call out the Starfleet Cortex Defense Squadron to liberate the feelings of innocent alienated Americans.

by Soros. Beck, by contrast, is into free-hate; the more, the hatier. *The Glenn Beck Program* is essentially a nonstop hate orgy.

Where O'Reilly favored international financiers, Beck developed a passion for government bureaucrats. Specifically, Beck is into czars. *Czar* is not an official title. It's media shorthand for an appointed official in the executive branch with a specific purview of responsibility. Unlike cabinet positions, Congressional approval is not generally required for such appointments. Woodrow Wilson had an "industry czar." FDR had a "food czar," a "manpower czar," a "synthetic rubber czar," and several others. Richard Nixon had a "drug czar" and an "energy czar." George W. Bush, who was slightly czar-struck, had about thirty-six czars depending on how you count, including a "faith-based czar," a "bioethics czar," and a pair of "AIDS czars." (One was a "global AIDS czar"; the other was just a regular "AIDS czar.") Bush also appointed an "abstinence czar" and a "birth control czar," which might have led to a drunken czar-fight in the State Dining Room were it not for the birth control czar's opposition to contraceptives.[20]

Barack Obama retained many of Bush's czar positions (not the abstinence czar) and appointed a few of his own. Glenn Beck at one point counted thirty-two czars in the Obama administration.[21] Republicans, who had voiced no opposition to Bush's czars, complained bitterly about Obama's, perhaps because they had no opportunity to filibuster them as they have done to almost every nominee who requires congressional approval. Sen. Lamar Alexander (R-TN) called the appointments "antidemocratic." Sen. Bob Bennett (R-UT) and Sen. Kay Bailey Hutchison (R-TX) said that they "undermine the constitution."*[22] Former Rep. Ernest Istook (R-OK) objected to the term czar because it's too Russian and helpfully suggested alternatives: "big boss, el jefe, head honcho, the big cheese . . . chief cook and bottle washer."[23]

The chief cook and bottle washer of the czar scare was Glenn Beck. Beck did not like those czars, not one bit. "This collection of these czars, these are evil people. These are wicked," he said. Exploiting concerns that the appointment of czars sidestepped constitutional checks

---

* To be fair to the Republicans, Sen. Robert Byrd (D-WV) also criticized Obama's czars.

and balances, Beck contrived an elaborate conspiracy theory that placed the czars at the center of the "shadow government," imbuing them with amazing powers of bureaucratic administration:

> A shadow government is giving the Obama administration unprecedented power with virtually no oversight . . . They don't need to be confirmed by the Senate; they rarely go before committees; they can claim "executive privilege" when asked to testify, and they're accountable to no one but the president himself.[24]

But who are these wicked czars? In a short series called "Know! Your! Czars!" Beck introduced them one by one:

- John Holdren, science "czar"—proposed "compulsory sterilization" and forced abortions to control population
- Cass Sunstein, regulatory "czar"—proposed bans on hunting and eating meat and proposed that your dog to be allowed to have an attorney in court.
- Carol Browner, global warming "czar"—was part of Socialist International, a group for "global governance."
- Ezekiel Emmanuel, health care adviser—proponent of the Complete Lives System, which puts values on lives based mostly by age.[25]

Angry Black Men

But the most wicked czar of them all, the czariest czar in the history of czars, was a man named Anthony "Van" Jones. If there were a czar magazine, Van Jones would be the centerfold. His official title was Special Advisor for Green Jobs, Enterprise and Innovation at the White House Council on Environmental Quality, but the folks at Fox News called him the "green jobs czar." *Time* magazine named Jones one of its "Heroes of the Environment 2008."[26] *Fast Company* named him one of "The 12 Most Creative Minds Of 2008."[27] Glenn Beck named him "Marxist anarchist," "revolutionary communist," "black nationalist," "convicted felon," and all-around "wicked dude."[28]

Jones had been radical in his youth, though not quite the way Beck described. He showed up at Yale Law School with a Black Panther book bag, hence the "black nationalist" charge. During a 1992 job internship, his boss sent him to monitor a San Francisco protest of the Rodney King verdict. He was arrested along with the protesters and released the next day when the charges were dropped; hence the "convicted felon" misrepresentation. The experience did lead Jones to embrace communism for a time, but by the year 2000 he had soured on the whole idea and embraced eco-capitalism, which is like capitalism but with less pollution.[29]

But that was more than enough for Glenn Beck, who assured his viewers, "He was a radical communist. He hasn't shed that. He's still a radical. He is still a black nationalist."[30] To prove the point, Beck played a brief audio clip from one of Van Jones's speeches, ostensibly about ecocapitalism, in which Jones said, "This movement is deeper than a solar panel . . . We're going to change the whole system."[31] Obviously, he wasn't talking about environmental policy. He was talking about the *whole* system.

"When will America wake up?" Beck then asked rhetorically with a dramatic pause. "The left has started a revolution. No different than Hugo Chavez. When Hugo Chavez was elected, he was elected by Democratic process. But he did not tell the people when he was running that he was a communist. Can we stop claiming that this man, Van Jones, is an average everyday capitalist America, an American? Is that I mean, did that sound like you, Iowa? Did that sound like you, Nebraska? Did it sound like you, Texas? Did it sound like you, Florida, Georgia, Maryland? Did it sound like you, New Hampshire? It sure sounds like Berkeley, California, San Francisco, California, and now Washington, D.C."*

And it wasn't just Van Jones who didn't sound like an American to Iowa, Nebraska, and so on. Next, Beck played a clip from a campaign speech that Barack Obama delivered the week before the election in

---

* "Did that sound like you, Iowa?" This list of states is reminiscent of Sarah Palin's infamous campaign line about "the real America." Coincidentally, or perhaps not so coincidentally, Beck's first book from 2005 is titled *The Real America: Messages from the Heart and Heartland*.

which Obama said, "We are five days away from fundamentally transforming the United States of America." He wasn't talking about solar
panels either.

"You know," said Glenn Beck, "I don't want to believe these things
about our president . . . If our founding principles are somehow or another no longer relevant, if the system in which this country was
founded is somehow unjust or unworkable now and communism,
Marxism, socialism is the right and relevant path, then that is the discussion in a republic we have. But to subversively bring in a new system through the back door in the middle of the night and build it piece
by piece by overwhelming the system, that is not acceptable."

But why, why does Obama want a revolution? To answer this question, Beck played yet another audio clip of Jones saying, "And our Native American sisters and brothers who were pushed and bullied and
mistreated and shoved into all the land we didn't want, where it was
all hot and windy, well, guess what, renewable energy . . . They now
own and control 80 percent of the renewable energy resources . . . We
owe them a debt."

Then Beck added a third black orator to the medley, playing an excerpt from a sermon in which Rev. Jeremiah Wright railed, "We believe
God sanctioned the rape and robbery of an entire continent. We believe
God ordained African slavery." Then Beck played yet another clip from
Van Jones' speech—"What about our immigrant sisters and brothers?
What about people who come here from all around the world, who
we're willing to have out in the fields with poison being sprayed on
them?" Van Jones again: "The white polluters and the white environ-
mentals are essentially steering poison into the people of colored communities." And back to Rev. Wright's sermon: "The government lied
about the Tuskegee experiment. They purposely infected African
American men with syphilis."

Beck then appealed to his audience, his voice quiet and heavy with
anguish, gradually increasing in volume, swelling with anger, "How?
How, America? I ask this sincerely. Show me where I have it wrong. I
want to be wrong, but I can't find any other way to explain this. The
president is wearing a mask. He has surrounded himself with radicals

and revolutionaries." By then Beck had reached a full shout, "He has surrounded himself his whole life with radicals and revolutionaries!"

In this powerful jeremiad, Glenn Beck went well beyond the guilt-by-association tactics that Sean Hannity employed before Obama's election. Beck's point was not simply that Obama "pals around" with black nationalists and communist revolutionaries. His point was that Obama *is* a black nationalist and a communist revolutionary. By juxtaposing their speeches in quick succession, Beck blurs these three men together. They are all angry black men who hate white people; they are all secretly building a communist revolution to redistribute the wealth and privileges of the whites they despise to the American Indians, the immigrants, and the people of color. Thus, Beck deftly combined conspiratorial villainy with the white persecution narrative.*

Like O'Reilly's caricature of George Soros, Beck's amalgamation of Obama, Jones, and Wright plays off a popular archetype from American culture—the Black Radical. The Black Radical archetype may be less familiar to younger readers, but Glenn Beck, who grew up in the 1970s, surely knows it well. Black radicals were African American civil rights activists who advocated a socialist or communist revolution. Many black radicals sanctioned violence, such as H. Rap Brown, who was imprisoned for armed robbery after a police shootout; Robert F. Williams, who fled to Cuba after trumped-up kidnapping charges were lodged against him; and Donald DeFreeze, leader of the Symbionese Liberation Army that kidnapped Patty Hearst.

The Black Radical archetype also showed up in Hollywood, taking the form of villains and sidekicks who were portrayed as violent and dogmatic. For example, the 1976 movie *Network,* which features the "mad as hell" Howard Beale character that Glenn Beck so admires, included two black radicals: a dogmatic communist organizer named Laureen Hobbs ("I'm Laureen Hobbs, a badass commie nigger") and a

---

* "Beck deftly combined." If you want to understand persecution politics, if you want to know why so many millions of Americans tune to Glenn Beck every day, listen to this radio program. I recommend playing the audio, not just reading the transcript. The URL is http://www.glennbeck.com/content/articles/article/198/29967/. Or you can google "Van Jones unhinged."

domestic terrorist called the Great Ahmed Kahn. Thus, Beck told his audience, not in so many words, that our president is a "badass commie nigger" who is preparing to realize the Black Radical dream of redistributing income to his nonwhite "brothers."

The Revolution

Phase I: Nationalize Private Industries

Unlike the archetypal Black Radical, however, Obama's revolution would not be violent, at least not at first. According to Beck, Obama's tactics are modeled after those of Venezuela's Hugo Chavez. Chavez was democratically elected, but he has used his power to nationalize private industries, take control of the media, and incarcerate critics. One of Beck's Fox News programs is titled "Is Obama Taking Pointers from Hugo Chavez?" During the show, Beck represented the federal bank and auto industry bailouts as a stealth nationalization plan equivalent to Chavez's takeover of the Venezuelan oil industry.

Phase II: Control the Media

Then to prove that Obama planned to control the media as Chavez has done, Beck introduced yet another African American czar: Mark Lloyd, chief diversity officer of the Federal Communications Commission, a.k.a. FCC diversity czar. According to Beck, Lloyd is a "Marxist, communist, fascist" who idolizes Hugo Chavez and plans to use his awesome powers as chief diversity officer to reinstate and expand the fairness doctrine. The fairness doctrine is a defunct FCC mandate that required broadcast license holders to present controversial issues of public importance in a manner that was, ahem, fair and balanced. Beck has also argued that Lloyd wants to tax conservative media outlets like Fox News into bankruptcy and then redistribute their licenses to minority-operated stations.[32]

In a rare response from the Obama administration to Fox News attacks, Mark Lloyd addressed the criticism expressed by Beck and other members of the right-wing media. He said:

I am not a Czar appointed by President Obama. I am not at the FCC to re-store the Fairness Doctrine through the front door or the back door, or to carry out a secret plot funded by George Soros to get rid of Rush Lim-baugh, Glenn Beck or any other conservative talk show host. I am not at the FCC to remove anybody, whatever their color, from power. I am not a supporter of Hugo Chavez. The right wing smear campaign has been, in a word—incredible, generating hate mail and death threats. It is the price we pay for freedom of speech. And I do support free speech.[33]

The *Washington Post* also contributed its own analysis of the diversity threat: "Lloyd occupies a midlevel position at the FCC, with responsi-bilities including increasing broadband adoption in minority commu-nities. He has no power to set policy."[34]

Nonetheless, the Great FCC Diversity War still rages at the time of the writing of this book. If you're reading it, chances are that Fox News has not yet succumbed to the totalitarian rampages of Czar Mark Lloyd the Diversifier.

Phase III: Round Up the Dissidents

Once Obama and his czars finally succeed in dispatching *The Glenn Beck Program,* they will be ready to proceed to the third phase of the Chavezian revolution: rounding up the dissidents. When incarcerating political enemies, it's usually helpful to have some kind of secret police force like the Gestapo or the KGB. Obama could use the FBI or the CIA for this task, but that would be too obvious. Alternatively, he could set up an entirely new force made up of . . . civilian volunteers.

It was a brilliant plan, but one of Obama's weaknesses as a covert revolutionary is his tendency to reveal his strategies in public forums—like a vainglorious Bond villain who reckons that, this time, there's no way for Agent 007 to escape the shark pool. Thus, Obama made the mistake of disclosing his dissident-repression strategy during a 2008 campaign speech, thinking that his opponents wouldn't notice:

We cannot continue to rely on our military in order to achieve the na-tional security objectives we've set. We've got to have a civilian national security force that's just as powerful, just as strong, just as well-funded.

The speech was not discovered by Glenn Beck, but by the distinguished Nazi-Marxist counterintelligence specialist, Rep. Paul Broun (R-GA). He told reporters:

> It may sound a bit crazy and off base, but the thing is, [Obama's] the one who proposed this national security force . . . That's exactly what Hitler did in Nazi Germany and it's exactly what the Soviet Union did. When he's proposing to have a national security force that's answering to him, that is as strong as the U.S. military, he's showing me signs of being Marxist.[35]

Glenn Beck didn't think that Representative Broun sounded crazy and off base. He played the clip from Obama's speech during his Fox News show on July 28, 2009. And on his July 28 radio show. Twice. He played it on August 7. He played it on August 28. He played it on September 2 and on September 8. He played it in an interview with Ann Coulter. He played it in an interview with Michelle Malkin.[36] (Would he play it on a boat? Would he play it with a goat?)

Beck also invited Representative Broun onto a program that he titled "A Politician Who Gets It." During the show, Broun described the steps "that someone who wants to establish an authoritarian type of government needs to do"— establish a national security force, institute gun control, and control the media, all of which, he helpfully pointed out, Obama was secretly planning to do. Broun also mentioned a recent report from the Department of Homeland Security that warned of security threats from right-wing domestic terrorists.* He warned Beck:

> We saw the Homeland Security department say that people like you and me need to be put on a terrorist watch list. They say that Christian conservatives, pro life people, pro Second Amendment people, veterans even need to be put on a terrorist watch list.[37]

---

* Subsequent to the DHS report about right-wing terrorism, a tax-dissident kamikazied his plane into an IRS office, a libertarian tried to go postal on the Pentagon, a Christian militia group calling themselves the Hutaree plotted to blow up police officers, and there were numerous death threats against Democratic legislators, some delivered via bricks through windows.

Finally, Broun complimented Beck, "I really appreciate what you do in bringing forth all this information about the czars, about what's going on in the federal government, and I just praise God for you and what you've been doing on your radio and TV programs."

In Representative Broun, Beck had clearly found a kindred spirit. As he put it, "I can't make this piece of the puzzle fit, unless this piece is about building some kind of thug-ocracy."* Then he posed one of his trademark challenging questions to President Obama:

> Mr. President, is your civilian national security force to protect us from things the Missouri State Police, your own Homeland Security and the liberal Southern Law Poverty Center have come out and said were a threat: militia groups; tea party goers; folks with "Don't Tread on Me" flags; me; Sarah Palin?[38]

But President Obama did not respond, thereby confirming Beck's suspicions.

Neither Broun nor Beck, however, described the context of the speech in which Obama unloaded his bombshell. He was discussing his plan to expand the Peace Corps and AmeriCorps—the Federal volunteer program created by Bill Clinton and enlarged by George W. Bush. Here is the next sentence after the bit that Beck quoted so abundantly:

> We need to use technology to connect people to service. We'll expand USA Freedom Corps to create online networks where Americans can browse opportunities to volunteer. You'll be able to search by category, time commitment and skill sets. You'll be able to rate service opportunities, build service networks, and create your own service pages to track your hours and activities.[39]

---

* *Thug* is a derivation of the Hindi *thag,* which means "swindler" or "thief." The *thuggee* was an Indian religious cult of murderous bandits who used to rob and ritually strangle unfortunate travelers. The Greek-derived *-cracy* is a suffix denoting a type of government. A *thugocracy* would thus be "rule by murderous Hindu bandit cult."

We can only speculate about what opportunities Obama planned to include in the volunteer database. Storm trooper? Grand inquisitor? Jackbooted thug? Obama also envisioned a social network in which volunteers would create their own "service pages" to track their activities. What might a typical "service page" look like?

Screen name	hot_4_mao
Interests	repression, torture, cooking
Favorite quote	"God damn America!"

My Revolutionary Service History	Hours	Rating
Waterboarded Rush Limbaugh	4.5	gratifying
Made Glenn Beck crouch naked for six hours	6	foul
Sent 5,000 "Happy Holidays" cards to Bill O'Reilly	15	tedious
Urinated on Christians	85	stimulating

A Reichstag Moment

But how could Obama possibly expect to get away with such an outrageous scheme? Is this not America, land of the free, home of the brave? Surely, Americans will not sit still once Obama finally unleashes his brutal volunteers, and they howl forth from their hellholes in Berkeley and Washington, DC, into the pristine heartland of the Real America.

This is where we get to the really scary stuff. Remember Al Gore's Nazi-derived fear tactics? In an interview with Christopher Ruddy, the founder of *NewsMax* magazine, Glenn explained that what he truly feared was a "Reichstag moment." The Reichstag building in Berlin is the home of the German parliament. In 1933, weeks after Hitler became chancellor of Germany, the building caught fire in a suspected arson attack. Hitler used the fire to justify mass arrests and media crackdowns, enabling him to consolidate power. Thus, Beck feared that some disaster would give the Obama administration an excuse to seize totalitarian powers. He explained, "I fear an event. I fear a Reichstag moment. God forbid, another 9/11. Something that will turn this machine on, and power will be seized, and voices will be silenced."[40]

Christopher Ruddy neglected to press Beck on the unintended irony of the Reichstag reference—Hitler had blamed the Reichstag fire on a fabricated communist conspiracy, alleging that the fire was meant to initiate the Marxist revolution. Instead, Ruddy asked, "If it happens, what should Americans do to fight it?" to which Beck responded with a grim flourish of sheer nonsense, "Read the Constitution. Act Constitutionally. Protect and defend the Constitution against all enemies, foreign and domestic."*[41]

"Everything Is Connected"

The conspiracy of bogeymen extends beyond Obama and his band of merry czars. According to Beck, "This is much bigger than Barack Obama. Powerful special interest groups began to lay this framework over the last few years."[42] "Special interest groups" is an interesting choice of words; *special interest* was Reagan-era code for minority constituencies. And sure enough, the most powerful villains of Beck's universe are minorities. We've already seen Obama, Van Jones, Rev. Wright, and Mark Lloyd, not to mention the "racist" Justice Sotomayor. Beck also fears international Jew George Soros. And Andy Stern, former president of the Service Employees International Union (SEIU). He's Jewish too. Noting that Stern had logged a lot of White House visits, Beck claimed that Stern is the guy "who's really controlling our country."[43] Then there's Bertha Lewis, the former CEO of the now defunct Association of Community Organizations for Reform Now (ACORN). She's African American. According to Beck, ACORN "has laid eggs inside of our government, not just in the White House and

---

* "Read the Constitution. Act Constitutionally." I picture colonially dressed Tea Party patriots reenacting the Great Compromise of 1787 while earnest AmeriCorps volunteers bang down the door shouting, "We are the change we've been waiting for." (For some reason, *NewsMax* chose to exclude Beck's profound answer from the official interview transcript, but it's on the video.)

through the czars and everything else but it is laying those eggs, deep and powerful eggs in something called AmeriCorps."*[44]

Of course, as Glenn Beck likes to say, "Everything is connected."[45]

[WARNING: THE FOLLOWING PARAGRAPH CONTAINS A TEDIOUS AND SOMEWHAT BEWILDERING DISCUSSION OF RELATIONSHIPS BETWEEN VARIOUS PUBLIC FIGURES. READERS WITH SHORT ATTENTION SPANS AND/OR GOOD SENSE ARE ENCOURAGED TO SKIP STRAIGHT TO THE HELPFUL DIAGRAM BELOW.]

For example, one of ACORN's founders is also on the board of directors of the Tides Foundation, which has received donations from the Open Society Institute, which is funded by George Soros. According to *NewsMax,* Soros also donated $5 million to an organization called Health Care for America Now (HCAN). Andy Stern's SEIU has also contributed to HCAN, and Beck said that ACORN has too, though I can't confirm that. Meanwhile, Beck claimed that Stern's wife (actually his ex-wife) founded the "Blue-Green Group," which "turned into" the Apollo Alliance.† Van Jones is on the board of directors of the Apollo Alliance, which is a project of the Tides Center, which is administratively linked to the Tides Foundation, which as we have seen is connected to ACORN and Soros. Thus, as Glenn Beck summarized in a falsetto tone of mock incredulity, "It's almost like these three are all connected."‡[46]

Baffled? Bored? Nauseated? Don't worry, Beck provided a helpful diagram on his trusty chalkboard:

---

* "Deep and powerful eggs." Beck often describes progressives as parasites who are using the republic as a host, so the metaphor is consistent with his Sci-Fi Channel meets Animal Planet approach to political analysis. He has also described progressives as viruses, vampires, and lizard people.

† There is no Blue-Green Group. Beck may have meant the Blue-Green Alliance but confused it with the theatrical troupe, the Blue Man Group, which would have been no less relevant.

‡ In a separate program, Beck alleged that Van Jones, ACORN, and SEIU had also conspired to block improvements to levees in New Orleans so that the paper trail of ACORN's criminal misconduct would be destroyed in a hurricane. He did not explain why ACORN didn't use arson or a paper shredder like normal criminals. ("Glenn Beck Blames Van Jones and ACORN for the Levees Failing in New Orleans," *Politicususa,* 11 Sep. 2009, http://www.politicususa.com/en/Beck-Levees.)

While Beck's chalkboard technology may be more primitive than O'Reilly's fancy computer charts, Beck has compensated with innovative tactical maneuvers, such as diversionary hand-waving techniques; he has frequently surprised enemies by spontaneously adding even more arrows to existing charts. Overall, Beck's arrow production has outpaced O'Reilly's by a factor of ten, and his flexible smart darts can literally point circles around O'Reilly's conventional arrows.

Beck also revolutionized chalkboard warfare in 2009 with the introduction of "sticky pictures" that he can attach directly to the chalkboard. Beck's sticky picture formula is top secret. Some experts speculate that it uses magnetism; others hypothesize static electricity. According to one unconventional theory, Fox News has developed a whole new technology by reverse engineering geckos. Alternatively, it could just be double-sided Scotch tape.

Finally, in yet another brilliant innovation from 2009, Beck dropped the chalkboard altogether and replaced it with what appears to be an elegant watercolor.

But it's not all about fabulous graphics. Beck's elaborate charts are simply tools of his trade—a bunch of lines and arrows that make tenuous relationships seem like cohesive conspiracies. Beck's true skill lies in his ability to produce and promulgate the conspiracy narratives that these pictures support. He is extraordinarily effective at turning ordinary men and women into vicious, powerful, revolutionary arugula-munching enemies of all that is good and pure in America; that is, white, Christian, politically conservative citizens of the heartland.

The Progressives

Beck labels these villains "progressives." Progressivism is another one of those nail-Jell-O-to-a-tree words. In the late nineteenth and early twentieth centuries, political reformists championing a diverse range of policies began calling themselves progressives. According to historians, "Progressivism was not a single movement but an aggregate of them, aiming at widely divergent goals. To one progressive, regulation of trusts might be the great end; to another, clean municipal government; to a third, equal rights for women."[47]

In 1912, Teddy Roosevelt split with the Republicans to found the Progressive Party, colloquially known as the Bull Moose Party, and ran as its presidential nominee. Aptly demonstrating the ambiguity of the term *progressive,* Roosevelt lost to Democrat Woodrow Wilson, who was also regarded as a progressive. The whole idea of progressivism eventually drowned in its own nebulousness, and the term has become little more than a synonym for *liberalism* that many on the left adopted after Reagan succeeded in stigmatizing *liberal.*

But the ambiguity suits the right wing just fine. Like secular humanism, they have turned progressivism into a waste receptacle for every person and idea they despise. Thus, Bill O'Reilly's "secular progressives" encompass George Soros, the ACLU, the *New York Times,* legalized drugs, same-sex marriage, underage sex, and Canada. Glenn Beck's "progressive" tent is even bigger. He lumps together everyone from Hitler to FDR to Che Guevara to Nancy Pelosi. Dropping the *secular* adjective has also enabled him to attack progressive churches that emphasize social and economic justice, language that he calls "Marxist code words for the new global order."[48]

In one profound *O'Reilly Factor* episode, O'Reilly and Beck engaged in a spirited debate about the essence of progressivism:

> O'REILLY: "Progressivism wants to take your stuff. That's it. That's what it is. It wants to take your stuff."
>
> BECK: "I will go a step farther. They just don't want to take your stuff. They want to control every aspect of your life."
>
> O'REILLY: "You and I agree . . . but you take it five steps further than I do."[49]

For once, O'Reilly was exactly right.

Among the many things that Beck takes five steps further than O'Reilly is the three-part persecution formula. For instance, O'Reilly presented the *secret plot* to destroy Christmas in a scattering of Fox News programs over a period of several years. By contrast, Beck presents secret plots almost every night with a torrent of zeal and fury that makes Bill O'Reilly's Christmas tale seem like a sweet bedtime story.

And while O'Reilly fears a slippery slope to a "brave new progressive world" of legalized drugs and same-sex marriage, Beck envisions nothing less than the savage despotic dystopia of George Orwell's *1984*.* "Progressives—the root of the word is 'progress,'" he explains. "You're progressing to what? Progress implies steps forward, movement, right? What are you moving toward? . . . You're moving step-by-step towards total government. And it depends on who gets you there. Is it going to be the fascists, the Nazis, or the communists?"[50]

Finally, Beck's *persecution* narrative is far more developed than O'Reilly's. O'Reilly puffs up political differences to make them seem like persecution—"Happy Holidays" messages constitute anti-Christian bigotry, and pejorative criticism of his show violates his First Amendment rights. By contrast, Beck warns that conservatives will literally be incarcerated or murdered by evil progressives. By associating the progressive revolution with the specter of black radicalism, he transformed the old communist versus capitalist narrative of Willard Cleon Skousen into a zero-sum conflict between "real America" and a progressive alliance of coastal elites and minorities. Once the progressives take control and eviscerate the Constitution, the story goes, they will establish a Marxist system that redistributes property to blacks, American Indians, and illegal immigrants, reserves health care for elites and minorities, eliminates freedom of religion, outlaws free speech, and incarcerates or executes dissidents.

Progressive Hunter

The first against the wall, Beck often warns his audience, will be one Glenn Beck. He gravely prophesied, "We're coming to a time when

---

* "*1984*." The difference between O'Reilly's and Beck's worldviews is reflected in their choice of science-fiction dystopias. O'Reilly's "brave new progressive world" is a reference to Aldous Huxley's *Brave New World,* which resembles a hippie commune gone corporate—a nonreligious, antifamily, drugged-up, sexually liberated collective of mass-produced blandness. By contrast, Beck frequently references Orwell's *1984,* a frightening vision of tyranny in which individuals are crushed beneath the mind control techniques of an omnipotent oligarchy.

voices like mine will disappear . . . There is Soros money now being funneled to stop me."[51] Sometimes, he even compares himself to great civil rights leaders: "While Martin Luther King had to face German shepherds, we have to face SEIU and leftist thugs."[52] Beck did not explain how he has managed to evade Soros and friends thus far, especially since he works in Manhattan, the heart of enemy territory. He once even dined in the same restaurant as Soros.[53] Miraculously, Soros did not attempt to eat him. Perhaps the prayers of Beck's devotees, whom he regularly asks to pray for his protection, have been effective.

Of course, Beck's frequent alarm sirens about threats to his career constitute one more act of projection. While the progressives may not be hunting him, he is surely hunting them. He boasted to his radio listeners:

> I am going to be like the Israeli Nazi hunters. I'm telling you, I'm going to find these big progressives, and to the day I die, I'm going to be a progressive hunter. I'm going to find these people who have done this to our country and expose them. I don't care if they're in nursing homes. I'm going to expose what they have done and make sure that the people understand because our Constitution, our Republic, if it survives, it will only survive because the people are waking and through the grace of God because we are that close to losing our Republic.[54]

But Nazi hunting is a poor analogy. Most Nazi hunters discreetly track war criminals and then deliver the information to national governments for extradition and prosecution. Beck, in contrast, aims to publicly shame innocent men and women whose politics he finds suspect, most of them minorities. He is no Nazi hunter. Glenn Beck is a witch hunter.

And he is very good at his job. Van Jones resigned from the White House Council on Environmental Quality after Beck revealed that he had endorsed the conspiracy theory that the Bush administration had deliberately allowed the World Trade Center attacks. That prompted Beck to say with a straight face, "I am the guy who debunked conspiracy theory."[55] Next, after a long siege by Beck and Fox News, ACORN finally disbanded when a right-wing journalist posing as a pimp video-

taped an ACORN employee advising him on the sex trade business.*
And in 2010, Andy Stern, having transformed SEIU into the fastest-
growing union in the country, decided that it was a good time to
retire.

You would think that the exodus of progressivism's most prominent
leaders would be a major triumph for Beck, but as we have repeatedly
seen, success only makes the right wing more paranoid. Within days
of Van Jones's resignation, Beck argued that in leaving the administration, Jones had become even more powerful: "He's no longer restricted
in what he can say or do, and this man is a dangerous man."[56] After
ACORN disbanded, Beck warned, "Don't fall for the silly ruse that
ACORN, by the way, is out of business."[57] When Andy Stern resigned,
Beck speculated, "There's something wrong with this Andy Stern resignation . . . Something is up there."[58]

As we observed previously, political victory affirms the shaky
psychological rationalizations upon which the conspiracy theories are
precariously perched. When Beck says, "Wake up, America!" he is
proselytizing. When he says, "America is waking up!" it means that
his proselytizing has been effective. That is to say, Beck has concluded
that the country is coming around to his point of view, which confirms
that he must be on to something. Van Jones's resignation did not prove
to Beck that the green jobs czar was harmless after all; it proved that
Americans had come to realize just how dangerous he was.

Storyteller

But Beck has a second reason for clinging to his bad guys, less psychological and more cynical. The media portrayed Jones's resignation and

---

* "ACORN employee." As it turned out, the pimp impersonator had misleadingly edited
the video to make it more sensational. In addition, the ACORN employee he had taped actually reported the "pimp" to the police after he left. But by the time this information came
out, it was too late to save ACORN or its do-gooding employee. (Rachel Maddow, "Raw
ACORN tapes tell very different story," *MSNBC,* 6 Apr. 2009, http://www.msnbc.msn.com/
id/26315908/vp/36204129.)

ACORN's collapse as Beck victories, comparing the fall of his enemies to captured scalps.[59] But for all his Nazi-hunter bluster, Beck isn't actually interested in collecting scalps. There's no money in scalps. Beck earns his living not by forcing progressives to resign but by spinning tales about them. As he himself likes to say, "I'm a storyteller."[60]

Ever since Obama's election, Beck has been composing an epic saga for national television. There are good guys—the freedom-loving Americans. There are bad guys—the Constitution-hating progressives. There are heroes—Sarah Palin and Glenn Beck, "progressive hunter." There are villains—Van Jones, Andy Stern, and ACORN. And there is a grand battle for the fate of the nation, of which the health care debate has been one skirmish. Each night, Beck presents the next installment in this riveting made-for-television docudrama. He has literally built a media empire around his conspiracy saga. According to *Forbes* magazine, Beck "has managed to monetize virtually everything that comes out of his mouth"—$13 million a year from print, $10 million from radio, $4 million on the web, $3 million from speaking events, and $2 million from television.[61]

If all the bad guys in Beck's blockbuster saga walked off the scene before the final battle, it would ruin the story. He needs his villains. Thus, he soon resurrected Van Jones as a Soros-backed progressive strategist in a program that he titled, "The Resurrection of Van Jones."[62] He reconstituted ACORN as a network of covert cells: "While ACORN is going underground with yet another name change, their words are becoming much more dangerous and meaningful."[63] When discussing the SEIU, Beck still plays ominous video clips of Andy Stern's speeches as if the guy had never left.[64]

Nonetheless, the departure of Beck's bogeymen has taken some of the wind from his sails. His ratings plummeted in April and May to 1.8 million viewers, which is still exceptional for a 5:00 p.m. timeslot but only 50 percent of his peak in late 2009.[65]* Beck being Beck, he

---

* "His ratings plummeted." To be fair to Beck, April is not a peak month for political shows, and other commentators also saw declines. (Glynnis MacNicol, "Is Glenn Beck Losing His

blamed his troubles on a progressive conspiracy. First he practiced denial, accusing Media Matters of fabricating the rating decline.[66] Then he told viewers of an "unholy alliance" seeking to shut him down. With his handy blackboard and sticky pictures, Beck connected the dots from Media Matters to Rep. Anthony Weiner (D-NY)—who raised questions about a company that hocks gold on Beck's shows—to his old friends Van Jones and Andy Stern. "Now it's official," Beck stated. "McCarthy has appeared."[67] That would be Joseph McCarthy, the senator who hunted down the secret communist conspiracy controlling the government.

Beck being Beck, he also claimed that the conspirators were pursuing the old slippery slope sneak attack in order to achieve total suppression of the media. He described his enemy's strategy as follows:

> Do it small. Take them out one at a time. I'm just the first. And if you take me out, then what happens? Does O'Reilly go? Does Sean [Hannity] go? Do you go? Once they clean this place out, then who goes? Is it Diane Sawyer, is it Stephanopoulos? Who is it? Who is next? I've never seen anything like it before. This—the Nixon enemy list? Please. This is nothing like that. This is targeting and destroying.[68]

But don't worry; all is not yet lost. Beck is still hanging in there, and he has courageously sworn that he will not be stopped. The evil progressives will have to tear the microphone from his cold, dead hands. He vowed:

> Let me tell you this: They shut me down on radio, that's fine, I'll do TV. They shut me down on TV, that's fine, I'll do Internet. They shut me down on the Internet, that's fine, I'll do stage shows. They shut me down on stage shows, that's fine, I'll go door to door. You will have to shoot me in the head. We are not stopping.[69]

Audience? (Or Merely His Mojo)," *Mediaite,* 29 Apr. 2010, http://www.mediaite.com/tv/is-glenn-beck-losing-his-audience-or-merely-his-mojo/.)

So if Glenn Beck comes knocking on your door with a stack of pamphlets about Van Jones's latest conspiracy, be kind. He's just a maligned victim of the terrible progressive conspiracy to destroy America and distribute the spoils to blacks, illegal immigrants, and American Indians.

11

AN APPEALING WONDROUS STORY

The Secret of Beck's Success

You'll notice a pattern in all stories: There are three kinds of charac-
ters: heroes, villains and there but for the grace of God go I.
—**Glenn Beck**

G LENN BECK IS no ordinary storyteller. There are many great American storytellers on television and radio, but very few run $32
million media empires and have had their tongues immortalized by
Time magazine. Beck is entertaining for sure, but his true genius is his
ability to spin stories that people believe.

Why do so many people believe Beck's stories? We've already seen
a few reasons. As we discussed in chapter 7, many people want to believe that they're being persecuted because it enables them to rationalize their own feelings of intolerance. Thus, they employ confirmation
bias and selective exposure to avoid challenging the plausibility of persecution narratives. In addition, we observed that people tend to seek
explanations for incomprehensible and troubling phenomena, and they
have a natural propensity to embrace ideas that appeal to their innate
suspicions of marginal members of the community: scapegoats.

But just because people want to believe that they're being persecuted, and just because they're looking for answers that confirm their
xenophobic suspicions, that does not mean they'll believe any demagogue with a radio show. America's airwaves host plenty of hate-radio
shock jocks peddling all manner of conspiracy theories; most have only
captured local or fringe audiences. That's because most people are put

off by raging crackpots. Confirmation bias only goes so far in facilitating outlandish beliefs. When the messenger lacks credibility, listeners reject the message. Persecution paranoia may be "the sweetest of drugs," but without an efficient delivery mechanism, consumers will cough it up.

Rodeo Clown

Part of Beck's potency is the packaging. He is the Joe Camel of right-wing paranoia, the goofy cartoon character who genially entertains while hawking addictive cancer sticks. He mocks himself relentlessly, calling himself a "rodeo clown" and his audience "sick twisted freaks."*[1] The self-deprecation routine facilitates his conspiracism. Unlike other doomsday prophets, Beck never expresses dogmatic certainty about his predictions. Instead, he hesitantly speculates about "crazy" possibilities. When he first introduced Willard Cleon Skousen's ideas to his audience, he warned, "I am absolutely about three days away from the loony bin. I'm practically damn near nuts."[2]

But Beck isn't damn near nuts at all, at least not in a clinical sense. The loony-bin routine is just part of his shtick. It's a disarming tactic that gives him the latitude to promote conspiracy theories that O'Reilly would never touch. Nonetheless, the Beck-driven paranoia that has swept the country demonstrates that Beck's audience gets the message all the same. Willard Cleon Skousen and Glenn Beck are both legendary cranks, but where Skousen was a fringe figure, Beck is America's favorite television personality after Oprah Winfrey.

---

* "Rodeo clown." As Beck gleefully professes his own imperfection, it's sometimes apparent that the rodeo clown doth protest too much. When Jon Stewart parodied him on *The Daily Show,* Beck responded, "It was hilarious. But even Jon Stewart can't make fun of me as well as I can make fun of me." A self-refuting comment if there ever was one. (Annie Barrett, "Glenn Beck reacts to Jon Stewart impersonation," *Entertainment Weekly,* 19 Mar. 2010, http://news-briefs.ew.com/2010/03/19/glenn-beck-reacts-to-jon-stewart-impersonation/.)

Frame Confusion

The Joe Camel analogy goes deeper than the pretty packaging. Like the big tobacco companies, Beck has also perfected his product with just the right combination of ingredients to facilitate delivery of the drug. To see how this process works, we'll need to examine the way people interpret the world around them. Suppose that you observe some event out of context. For example, imagine that you've just watched a YouTube clip of someone getting hit in the face by a hurtling cream pie. You might ask yourself, "What is it that's going on here?" The way you answer that question depends on how you contextualize it. You could interpret it as a practical joke, a comedy routine, or an act of political protest. It could even be some kind of physics experiment.

Each of these interpretations represents what sociologist Erving Goffman called a *frame*. Frames are the principles of organization according to which people make sense of particular experiences.[3] They offer the backstories that make those experiences meaningful. Applying different frames to the same experience can result in drastically different interpretations of the same event. For example, applying a comedy-routine frame to the cream pie video would suggest that the target was an actor who had consented to the pieing. Applying a political-protest frame to the same video would suggest that the target was a politician or celebrity unhappily surprised by receiving a cream pie in such a manner.

Often, people make mistakes by applying the wrong frame to a situation. Take the example of the New Mexico woman who discovered the image of Jesus in her breakfast tortilla in 1977 or any of the other people who subsequently found Jesus's likeness in pancakes, toast, grilled cheese sandwiches, fish sticks, Cheetos, and a Kit Kat bar.[4] The appropriate frame for making sense of Tortilla Jesus is basic chemistry. Frying a tortilla in hot oil produces chemical reactions that cause its surface to blacken, forming a random pattern. But the New Mexico woman and many of the 35,000 people who have visited her backyard Tortilla Jesus shrine applied a supernatural frame according to which the son of God prefers to reveal his presence in Americans' breakfasts.

The scapegoating examples discussed in chapter 10 demonstrate more frame confusions. Medieval Europeans looked for a deliberate man-made source of the plague and found their answer in a fabricated Jewish plot. The correct frame for explaining the epidemic is biological science, of which the medieval Europeans knew little. Similarly, seventeenth-century American Puritans looked for a supernatural explanation for the disturbing behavior of some teenage girls and thus blamed witchcraft, whereas a more appropriate frame would have been human psychology.

Glenn Beck, the modern incarnation of yesteryear's witch hunter, bases his rhetorical strategy on a related type of frame confusion. He is America's most prominent advocate of what George Soros's favorite philosopher, Karl Popper, called the *conspiracy theory of society*—the view that the explanation of a social phenomenon consists in the discovery of the men or groups who have planned and conspired to bring it about. Whenever Beck examines a political situation and inquires, "What is it that's going on here?" the only explanations he entertains are secret plots by interested parties. In other words, he always employs a conspiracy frame to make sense of political events.

For example, he asked Lou Dobbs, "Why aren't we doing anything about illegal immigration?" In his phrasing of the question, Beck had already set up the conspiracy frame. He did not consider the possibility that the U.S. government was unable to stop illegal immigration or even that it was trying to stop it. His question presumed that America's leaders were deliberately allowing illegal immigration. As such, the only way to answer the question was to speculate about why the government had chosen to allow it and who was behind the decision. Given this frame, Beck's theory of a corporate conspiracy to establish MexAmeri-Canada was a fitting answer. Beck's colleagues on the right also applied conspiracy frames to explain illegal immigration but came up with different answers. Pat Buchanan accused Mexico and the Ford Foundation of attempting to reconquer the Southwest. Bill O'Reilly accused racist minorities of trying to destroy the "white power structure" through population growth.

While O'Reilly and Buchanan apply the conspiracy frame on occasion when it suits their needs, Beck seems to be completely blinded by it. In virtually every program, he tries to solve some "puzzle" and always finds the answer in the conspiracy theory of society. From environmental policy to health care to volunteer programs, Beck invariably relates the topic back to some secret plot. For instance, when Obama initiated the "cash for clunkers" program to encourage Americans to trade in old gas-guzzling cars, Beck unearthed an automated message on the program's Web console for auto dealers that warned, "All files on this system may be intercepted, monitored, recorded, copied, audited, inspected, and disclosed to authorized CARS [Car Allowance Rebate System], DOT [Department of Transportation], law enforcement personnel."[5] He concluded that the whole program was a Big Brother plot to infiltrate Americans' personal computers.*

A Narrative Helps Make Sense of Chaos

But to represent Beck's programs as simply a series of conspiracy theories is to sell him short. Beck is a storyteller. If he were to analyze a pie-throwing video for his audience, he wouldn't just frame it as a political protest. He would first provide a history of tyrannical pie throwing by Adolf Hitler, Woodrow Wilson, and Che Guevara. Next he would play a clip of Van Jones promoting Native American "green pies." Finally, he would show a video of Obama eating cream pie and warn, "I'm not saying that our president throws pies, but this is a man who has eaten cream pie his *entire* life. When will the country wake up and start asking, Why does he eat so much pie?"

For instance, on one program, Beck puzzled over the gushing oil leak in the Gulf of Mexico. As usual, he employed a conspiracy frame to explain the failure to plug the leak, concluding that BP and the U.S.

---

* "plot to infiltrate American's personal computers" Note to the Obama administration: If you want to spy on Americans' Web-surfing habits, do not advertise your intentions in a confirmation box.

government were deliberately allowing the oil to flow so that they could use the "emergency" as an excuse to pass a "cap-and-trade" environmental bill.[6] But that's not even close to the end of the story. For the environmental bill is itself just a pretense for an even more devious agenda. "In the cap-and-trade legislation that is being proposed," Beck warned on another program, "the president has new emergency powers . . . and it allows the president to take over industries."[7] Once that happened, Beck revealed, "wicked" and "treasonous" progressives would finally complete the terrible tyrannical scheme that Woodrow Wilson planned and FDR set in motion. "This is the only power that FDR really wanted," Beck explained. "Once they have cap and trade and God forbid they have healthcare it's done."[8]

Beck's rich stories bring the conspiracy frame to life. His narratives capture his listeners' attention and stir their imagination to make the explanations more compelling. Some psychologists theorize that the narrative is a basic organizing principle of the human mind. That is, we naturally try to make sense of the world by organizing our experiences into stories.[9] This hypothesis has led to substantial research into the art of *narrative persuasion,* a technique for persuading people through storytelling. The concept has been applied to diverse fields ranging from legal argumentation to corporate sales pitches. One study found that hate groups used narrative persuasion as a kind of "sugar coating" to recruit new members, since "narratives elicit fewer counter arguments and less resistance to persuasion."[10]

In addition to its propaganda role, storytelling may play an even more important function in persecution politics. If the narrative is indeed a basic organizing principle of the human mind, then the central character of the mind's stories is the self. That is to say, each of us is the protagonist in his or her own life story, striving against adversity to achieve a happily-ever-after. Of course, some people take greater artistic license than others, which produces self-deception. Some psychologists argue that paranoid individuals have, like Don Quixote, been so seduced by fantasies of their lives that they become victims of delusion.[11] For example, psychologist Michael Bader explained the paranoia of Tea Party activists in terms of such narratives, writing:

The paranoid strategy is to generate a narrative that finally "explains it all." A narrative . . . helps make sense of chaos. It reduces guilt and self-blame by projecting it onto someone else. And it restores a sense of agency by offering up an enemy to fight.[12]

In other words, Glenn Beck's stories are the perfect vehicles for delivering the persecution politics fix. Beck makes sense of mysterious events by framing them with riveting melodramas of villainous intrigue. Those melodramas are particularly compelling to people who harbor feelings of intolerance: the portrayal of minorities and "elites" as storybook villains alleviates their cognitive dissonance by rationalizing their intolerance.

Metanarratives and the Persecution Frame

There's still one piece missing from this picture, however. Clinical psychologists tend to approach mass paranoia as a collection of individual neuroses. Thus, psychologist Michael Bader discusses Tea Party activists as if they were his patients, each struggling with his or her own paranoid fantasy. But as we discussed early in the book, the paranoid style is not a disease of the mind, it's a disease of society. Beck's stories are not the individual fantasies of millions of Don Quixotes whacking away at their own private windmills. Rather, his stories collectively make up a single epic saga shared by many of his admirers. Beck's Don Quixotes don't see themselves as solitary knights on their own quests. They are an army of Don Quixotes who have joined forces to battle the Great Progressive Windmill Menace.

Furthermore, we've seen that what Beck calls the progressive movement is just another name for the fictional conspiracy of minorities and liberal elites that has haunted right-wing persecution tales for decades. The Don Quixotes crusading against secular humanists, militant homosexuals, black radicals, illegal immigrants, and secular progressives have been fighting variants of the same great imaginary Culture War since the 1970s.

In other words, persecution politics is more than a collection of appealing stories told by various raconteurs. Such stories are simply episodes in a single communal narrative that has been seducing Americans for years. This narrative provides conservatives a *persecution frame* rich enough to make sense of almost any significant social phenomenon or political issue in the country—from gay marriage to health care policy to the secularization of Christmas. When Glenn Beck and Bill O'Reilly present political events as steps on a slippery slope concocted by malicious conspirators, they don't arbitrarily choose any old conspiracy theory to frame these events. They present them in the context of the epic battle between liberal conspirators and their white, Christian conservative victims.

Postmodernist social theorists call such grand explanatory stories *metanarratives*. A metanarrative is essentially a big myth that binds a community's values and stories into a meaningful whole. Just as an individual might make sense of his or her own life by creating a personal story, metanarratives make sense of life, the universe, and everything by turning a whole society's culture and history into a communal story. For instance, medieval Europeans made sense of their world using the metanarrative of Christian theology, which relates an epic conflict between good and evil, God and Satan. Later, Enlightenment thinkers sought to replace the religious story with a new metanarrative that pitted science and reason against ignorance and irrationality.*

During the Cold War, the conflict between the United States and the Soviet Union provided a popular American metanarrative. There were good guys—the freedom loving, God fearing capitalists of the USofA—and bad guys—the despotic atheist communists of the Evil Empire. Every political event, from antiwar protests to the United Nations to national health care, could be understood within the frame of this epic

---

* "Metanarrative." Postmodernism being postmodernism, the term *metanarrative* is ill-defined, and there is plenty of debate about what exactly counts as a metanarrative as opposed to a not-so-meta narrative. If you disagree with my examples of metanarrative, I encourage you to think *really big* whenever you read *meta*. Feel free to cross out the letters if that helps. Unless the book doesn't belong to you. In that case, you could cover the letters with a scrap of paper that says *really big*.

conflict. Even seemingly unrelated events were often subsumed under it. Thus, Jerry Falwell saw the "hand of Moscow" in the Supreme Court's *Brown v. Board of Education* decision.

While the Cold War raged, another metanarrative began to take root across the country. This story recounted the long road from America's dark ages—persecution of American Indians, enslavement of Africans, repression of women, etc.—through a period of enduring bigotry and discrimination, particularly in the South, and finally ascending to an enlightened future in which all people would live in harmony as equals. The new metanarrative celebrated civil rights leaders, feminists, and other progressive activists battling the racists, misogynists, and religious fundamentalists who resisted social change. The inequality and intolerance taboos that we discussed in chapter 7 are elements of this new metanarrative of progressive enlightenment.

Obviously, the progressive metanarrative did not appeal to those who were depicted as the racists, misogynists, and religious fundamentalists, even as they internalized its celebration of tolerance and equality. The Cold War metanarrative was much more their style. So when the great conflict between communism and capitalism began to slip into irrelevance, and the progressive enlightenment metanarrative continued to spread, Paul Weyrich, Jerry Falwell, and other leaders of the Christian right sought to supplant it with a new metanarrative that was tailored to their own political interests. The new story portrayed a domestic conflict that pitted secular humanists and gay militants against traditional Christians.

Soon enough, right-wing racists and xenophobes like Pat Buchanan adapted the religious right's new metanarrative to their own needs by adding reverse discrimination and illegal immigration to the story. It was Buchanan who named the metanarrative "Culture War" in his 1992 convention speech. He explicitly compared the Culture War to the Cold War, the right wing's previous metanarrative of choice.

The Culture War metanarrative continued to quietly blossom through the 1990s, but its progress slowed after 9/11 when President Bush ushered in a competing metanarrative: the War on Terror. Bush's story about Islamic terrorists and the Axis of Evil versus freedom-loving America was popular for a time, but without a constant supply of fresh terror, it began to falter.

Thus, the Culture War came roaring back in 2004 with Bill O'Reilly leading the charge. O'Reilly embellished the story by anointing George Soros the undeclared premier of the secular-progressive conspiracy. With an audience of millions, O'Reilly helped transform the metanarrative from a fringe gospel to a staple of the right—just in time for the election of the nation's first black president and the Fox News debut of Glenn Beck.

Following Obama's election, Beck deftly combined the new story of white Christian persecution with scary elements of the old Cold War metanarrative, including secret revolutionary cells and the slippery slope to totalitarianism. In the process, he stripped the progressive enemy of any actual political agenda. Health care, fiscal stimulus, and environmentalism became mere fronts for the conspiracy's true objective—unfettered power. Thus, Al Gore's *Inconvenient Truth* is just a scare tactic to enable the UN to seize control. Thus, Van Jones isn't interested in environmental policy; he wants to change the *whole* system. Thus, communism and fascism become interchangeable. The doctrine is irrelevant; the progressives' true objective is simply power. As Beck told O'Reilly, "They want to control every aspect of your life."[13]

Without any ideology or policy agenda, the bad guys of Beck's stories aren't really political figures at all. They resemble the villains of fantasy fiction: epitomes of evil like Sauron from *Lord of the Rings,* Emperor Palpatine from *Star Wars,* Lord Voldemort from *Harry Potter,* and the original bad guy of the Western world, Satan. These bogeymen seek power for power's sake and evil for evil's sake. In Beck's hands, the Culture War metanarrative has become more of an epic fantasy than ever before. As anthropologist George Marcus wrote:

> The plausibility of the paranoid style is not so much in its reasonableness, but rather in its revitalization of the romantic, the ability to tell an appealing wondrous story found in the real.[14]

12

SECOND AMENDMENT REMEDIES

Persecuted Gun Owners Team Up with White Christian Conservatives; Violence and Mayhem Ensue

The tree of liberty must be refreshed from time to time with the blood of patriots and tyrants. It is its natural manure.
—Thomas Jefferson

WHEN GLENN BECK PLAYED a clip from a Van Jones speech and asked his audience, "Did that sound like you, Iowa?" I chuckled a bit. Beck's story depicts a vast blanket of Real America spreading smoothly across the continent, lacerated in places by jagged holes of progressive degeneracy in and around San Francisco, Washington, DC, and other cities of ill repute. But I grew up in Iowa, a state that votes Democratic almost as often as Beck's native Washington State. Beck might be alarmed to learn that Tom Harkin, Iowa's popular and long-serving Democratic senator, once wrote an article called "Why I Am a Progressive Populist" in which he stated, "The Democratic agenda remains rooted in the progressive-populist tradition that has made the party strong and the country even stronger."[1] One of the city councilwomen in my hometown of Iowa City was an abortion rights activist and a member of the Socialist Party. She broke a record for the most votes in a reelection campaign.[2] Yet despite all the Constitution-devouring progressives running amok through the prairie, the citizens of Iowa City all turn out patriotically for the city's annual Fourth of July celebration.

Like other kids in Iowa City, I learned about the Constitution in my high school government class. Our assistant teacher for the class was a staunch libertarian. I distinctly remember a discussion with him about gun rights. He was a pudgy man with glasses, bookish and intelligent, not the kind of person I associated with gun enthusiasts. Iowa is a hunting state, full of pickup trucks with mounted gun racks and living rooms with antlers on the walls, so government protection of hunting privileges made sense to me. Gun violence was uncommon in Iowa's mostly peaceful cities and towns, but I could also understand how people from violence-wracked big cities might want to carry a pistol for self-defense. Government protection for assault weapons, however, was incomprehensible to me. You don't shoot deer with an AK-47, and it won't fit in your purse. I assumed that the NRA's opposition to assault weapons bans was based on the slippery slope argument that outlawing assault weapons would lead to a total ban on guns.

When I asked my libertarian student teacher about it after class, he presented a different argument. He believed that it was important for the citizenry to be armed in order to protect itself against government totalitarianism. This argument was novel and astounding to me. According to my Reagan-era understanding of American politics, it was the flag-burning, bleeding-heart liberals who were supposed to fear and hate the U.S. government, not the militaristic star-spangled conservatives. More than anything else I learned from that government class, this conversation stands out in my memory. To this day, when I hear people like Glenn Beck warn of totalitarianism, I imagine my nerdy, overweight student teacher valiantly fending off a fleet of black helicopters with his semiautomatic AK-47, a weathered copy of the Constitution protruding from his back pocket. *Vive la résistance!*

This vision is no joke to millions of NRA members. Recall that Rep. Paul Broun (R-GA) told Glenn Beck that one of the things "that someone who wants to establish an authoritarian type of government needs to do" is to institute gun control. Though he is surely a clever man, Broun did not invent this notion himself. It has long been an element of NRA gospel. According to Harlon Carter, executive vice-president* of the NRA from 1977 to 1985:

---

* "Executive vice-president." As in some national governments, the president of the NRA is a figurehead. The executive vice president runs the show.

Gun prohibition is the inevitable harbinger of oppression. It can only be pursued by "no-knock" laws under which jack-booted minions of government invade the homes of citizens; by "stop-and-frisk" laws under which the person of citizens can be searched on the streets at the whim and suspicion of authority.*[3]

With his polished bald head, barrel chest, "piercing ice-blue eyes," and marksmanship trophies, Harlon Carter was the sort of man you'd expect to fend off black helicopters with an AK-47 and a copy of the Constitution. At the 1977 NRA National Convention, Carter orchestrated a parliamentary coup known as the Cincinnati Revolt against the old guard leadership of the NRA—a namby-pamby collection of sportsmen and hunters who wouldn't have recognized a jackbooted minion of government if one had leapt from a black helicopter screaming, "Happy Kwanzaa, Motherfucker!"

Carter transformed the NRA from a low-key advocacy group for hunting, gun safety, and marksmanship into a lobbying juggernaut that bitterly attacked every gun control proposal before Congress as if it were America's death warrant. Testifying before Congress to oppose a fourteen-day waiting period on gun sales, Carter explained the complex theoretical underpinnings of the slippery slope principle to America's leadership:

> It is kind of like the old Bert Lahr commercial that used to be on television. He used to eat a potato chip and say "I'll bet you can't eat just one." . . . It is a little nibble first, and I'll bet you can't eat just one.[4]

Thanks to NRA lobbying, the government not only refrained from eating the whole bag, it even regurgitated some previously ingested potato chips in 1986 when Congress watered down the Gun Control Act of 1968.†

---

* "Searched on the streets." Like in Arizona?

† "Watered down the Gun Control Act." The potato chip theory doesn't seem to work in reverse. No one expressed concern that loosening gun restrictions would lead to the legalization of civilian rocket-propelled grenades or intercontinental ballistic missiles in the backyard.

Jackbooted Thugs

But for all its explanatory power, the potato chip analogy is not very scary. For effective fearmongering, you need a secret plot to drive the slippery slope. When Wayne LaPierre took over as executive vice president in 1991, he warned NRA members of just such a plot, writing:

> A document secretly delivered to me reveals frightening evidence that the full-scale war to crush your gun rights has not only begun, but is well under way . . . not just to ban all handguns or all semi-automatics, but to eliminate private firearms ownership completely and forever.[5]

Neal Knox, who directed the NRA's lobbying wing, had an even more elaborate theory. He suggested that the assassinations of JFK, RFK, and MLK, as well as various infamous murder sprees, had been planned by antigun conspirators. "Is it possible that some of those incidents could have been created for the purpose of disarming the people of the free world?" he wrote. "With drugs and evil intent, it's possible. Rampant paranoia on my part? Maybe. But there have been far too many coincidences to ignore."[*][6]

So we've got the slippery slope and the secret plot. What about the persecution? That's where Harlon Carter's "jack-booted minions of government" come in. Jackboots are knee-length leather combat boots. Though worn by soldiers and police in many nations since the days of Napoleon, they acquired special significance when the Nazis issued them to soldiers and SS officers. American gun rights activists are terrified of jackboots, which they associate with scary agents from the Bureau of Alcohol, Tobacco, Firearms, and Explosives—known as the ATF. (According to the U.S. General Accounting Office, the ATF does not issue footwear to its agents, so either the agents have been purchasing their own jackboots, or the gun rights activists are slightly confused on this point.[7])

---

* "Too many coincidences." Indeed, it is uncanny the way the public reacts to shocking gun violence by pressing for more gun control.

One of Wayne LaPierre's accomplishments at the NRA has been to expand the organization's focus from ATF footwear to the entire ensemble. For example, in a 1995 fundraising letter, he warned of bucket helmets and black uniforms, not to mention copious bloodshed and the obliteration of every right in the Constitution:

Not too long ago it was unthinkable for Federal agents wearing Nazi bucket helmets and black storm trooper uniforms to attack law-abiding citizens. Not today . . . You can see it when jack-booted government thugs, wearing black, armed to the teeth, break down a door, open fire with an automatic weapon and kill or maim law-abiding citizens . . . And if we lose the right to keep and bear arms, then the right to free speech, free practice of religion and every other freedom in the Bill of Rights are soon to follow.[8]

For the record, Nazi storm troopers wore brown, not black, which is why they were called brownshirts. Jeff Cooper, a member of the NRA board of directors, may have been trying to address this misconception when he argued that ATF agents were not in fact Nazi storm troopers. They were ninjas. He explained:

It is popular at this time to compare the behavior of our uncontrolled Federal agents to that of the Nazis in the Third Reich. It may be that this is a valid comparison, but the Nazis are long ago and far away, whereas the ninja in the U.S. are right now in full-cry and apparently without fear of any sort of control. They move mainly at night. They conceal their faces. They use overwhelming firepower and they make almost no effort to identify their targets. They are scarier than the Nazis—who at least never concealed their faces.[9]

There are a few problems with the ninja theory, however. Being stealth assassins, ninjas generally avoid cumbersome accessories like helmets and jackboots, and they are not known to attack unidentified targets with overwhelming firepower. Moreover, historians of feudal Japan even dispute the idea that traditional ninjas wore black. This concern is somewhat academic, however, since ATF agents don't wear black either. Their jackets are navy blue with yellow letters that say "ATF."[10]

"The Slickest, Most Aggressive Anti-Gun White House in History"

While the threat from ninja storm troopers was probably beneficial to the NRA's fundraising efforts, it did create a bit of challenge. When you build your donor base around defending the nation from jackbooted ninjas, you can't go back to raising money for Boy Scout gun safety programs. You need a continual supply of ninjas, or at least liberal gun eradication conspiracies, to keep the money flowing. But there has been no new federal gun control legislation since Clinton's 1994 assault weapons ban—which expired in 2004—and no high-profile ATF operations since agents stormed David Koresh's fortress in Waco, Texas, in 1993. The risk of jackbooted ninja attacks or gun control bills under Bush's watch was considered negligible.

Perhaps that is why the NRA produced a short graphic novel in 2006 called *Freedom in Peril: Guarding the 2nd Amendment in the 21st Century.** The book included cartoon pictures of all the heinous villains who sought to disarm and abuse beleaguered American gun owners, including:

- *Gun-ban bankrollers* depicting a liver-spotted George Soros with decidedly olive-toned skin
- *Disaster apologists* depicting jackbooted ninja-thugs with their knees on the neck of a prostrate old woman
- *Illegal alien gangs* depicting badass African Americans, Latinos, and Asians making gang signals

---

* *"Freedom in Peril."* The blogger known as Wonkette obtained a leaked pre-production draft. The NRA confirmed that the draft was genuine, but it's not clear whether the book was eventually published. The draft includes a letter signed by Wayne LaPierre that cheerfully states, "Only the NRA energizes the powerful pro-freedom voting bloc, resulting in election outcomes good for both American gun rights and for American business." (Ken Layne, "NRA's Secret Graphic Novel Revealed!" *Wonkette,* 22 Dec. 2006, http://wonkette.com/223889/nras-secret-graphic-novel-revealed.)

- *One-world extremists* depicting the UN and a revolver tied in a knot
- *Animal rights terrorists* depicting a tattooed woman with unshaven legs, an owl carrying TNT, an angry pig, and a lobster, which also looks angry. But it's hard to tell with lobsters.

By 2008, a new threat arose to menace America's gun owners, a threat even more menacing than illegal immigrant gangs and enraged lobsters—Barack Hussein Obama. During his election campaign, Obama promised to reenact the assault weapons ban that expired in 1994 and to close the loophole that allows gun shows to sell weapons without background checks. These proposals may not seem very menacing. That's because they're not very menacing. Even Wayne LaPierre knows that they're not very menacing. That's why the NRA invented Obama's Ten Point Plan to "Change" the Second Amendment. According to NRA flyers, Obama planned to outlaw the use of firearms for home defense, eliminate the "Right-to-Carry," shut down 90 percent of gun shops, and ban hunting rifle ammunition. According to another mailing, "Never in NRA's history have we faced a presidential candidate . . . with such a deep-rooted hatred of firearm freedoms."[11]

But Obama's election did not prove particularly devastating to the Second Amendment. Not only did he fail to enact the Ten Point Plan to "Change" the Second Amendment, he did not even implement the modest gun control initiatives that he had championed during the campaign. "We do not debate guns around here much anymore," grumbled Senate majority whip Dick Durbin (D-IL) two months after Obama took office. "We reached a point where there are not many people who will stick their political necks out to vote for sensible gun control—too big a hassle."[12] A number of prominent Democrats have even supported antigun control measures, including Senate majority leader Harry Reid (D-NV), Sen. Jim Webb (D-VA), and Rep. John Dingell (D-MI)—who once said, "If I were to select a jackbooted group of fascists who are perhaps as large a danger to American society as I could pick today, I would pick ATF."[13] Nor does the Supreme Court show any sign of diluting gun rights, having upheld individuals' constitutional right to possess firearms and struck down gun laws in Chicago and Washington, DC.

But even as the Supreme Court accommodated and the White House capitulated, Wayne LaPierre, the swaggering, gun-toting captain of one of the most formidable lobbying organizations in the country, quivered anxiously in his power tie. "The bomb is armed and the fuse is lit," he warned in 2009. "They are going to come at us with everything they've got." The Obama administration, he insisted, is "the slickest, most aggressive anti-gun White House in history."[14] A year later, still with no gun control in sight, LaPierre continued his dire prophesies, "The fact is his administration is stacked full of people that have spent a lifetime attacking the Second Amendment, and I believe there are storm clouds on the horizon, and 'stay ready' is the word."[15] (It's two words, but that's okay.)

Josh Sugarmann, founder of the Violence Policy Center in Washington, observed, "Despite the fact that they won their Supreme Court case, they act as if they lost."[16] Richard Feldman, a former NRA lobbyist, made much the same point in 2007: "I think in large measure the war has been won, but the NRA refused to accept congratulations. They would much prefer to fight pitched battles."[17]

But LaPierre's reaction to the NRA's political victories should come as no surprise. As with the secular humanists, the militant homosexuals, and the subversive czars, right-wing conspiracists have consistently responded to success by amplifying the scare tactics. That's because the paranoia has little to do with reality and everything to do with psychology. Like Glenn Beck, Wayne LaPierre is a proselytizer. Success affirms the rationalizations underlying his paranoid ideas. The Supreme Court endorsed his view of the Second Amendment, and the unpopularity of gun control demonstrated that Americans found his tale of government tyranny persuasive.

In addition to the psychological affirmation, LaPierre also receives material benefits from keeping his mythical villains at large. Like Beck, he collects a lot of money—for the NRA, the gun industry, and himself—by telling an appealing story about a tyrannical government that preys on innocent Americans. After Obama's election, anxious gun enthusiasts rushed to buy firearms before the Democrats destroyed the Second Amendment, producing a bonanza for gun dealers and causing nationwide ammunition shortages.[18] NRA membership rose 30 percent, and donations flowed. According to Richard Feldman, "You could almost sense the NRA fundraisers licking their chops because for the first time in eight years they had an identifiable bogeyman."[19]

"What Color Star Will They Pin on Our Coats?"

What's particularly interesting about LaPierre's narrative of government repression is that it's not inherently conservative. During the days of J. Edgar Hoover's anticommunist FBI, it was the left wing that feared despotic government agents. Then in the 1970s, would-be revolutionaries like the members of the Weather Underground romanticized armed struggle against fascist U.S. imperialists. Meanwhile, black radicals like Robert Williams promoted "armed self-reliance" against white lynch mobs. Williams sounded much like an NRA lobbyist when he alluded to the American Revolution and spoke of fighting against tyranny and defending families.*[20]

But the NRA would never in its wildest dreams have taken up the black radical cause. NRA leaders bound the organization to the right from the very beginning. William Conant Church, who founded the organization in 1871, was a sworn enemy of "Communists, Socialists and other outlaws" long before red-baiting came into vogue.[21] Throughout much of the twentieth century, the NRA has closely associated with the U.S. military, and it established headquarters in Washington, DC, to be near the Pentagon.

When the right wing veered into persecution politics in the late 1970s, the NRA turned in parallel. Harlon Carter staged the Cincinnati coup against the NRA old guard and transformed the organization "from a hunter-rifleman service organization to one of Washington's

---

* "White terrorists." Robert Williams had a somewhat better claim to government oppression than LaPierre, however, since blacks suffered genuine persecution from the authorities and were long prohibited from owning guns in many states.

most committed conservative lobbies" in 1977, the same year that Anita Bryant fought off the militant homosexuals in Miami and one year before the religious right defeated the secular humanists in the IRS.[22]

The alliance between gun rights activists and other paranoid conservative movements has been a fertile one, characterized by a cross-pollination of heroes and villains. Thus, Glenn Beck's fear of fascism and Representative Paul Broun's warning that Obama would confiscate guns and lock up dissidents originated in the NRA's jack-booted thug obsession, while the NRA's paranoia about George Soros and immigrant gangs came straight from Fox News and Pat Buchanan. One of LaPierre's fundraising letters even criticizes Obama for his association with Rev. Wright.[23]

Likewise, the NRA champions conservative heroes like Ronald Reagan, Newt Gingrich, Sarah Palin, and Glenn Beck. At the NRA's annual meeting in 2010, Palin warned, "Don't doubt for a minute that, if they thought they could get away with it, they would ban guns and ban ammunition and gut the Second Amendment."[24] Beck spoke about "a well-regulated militia and why you might need one because the government's not doing its job."[25]

But no one has done more to interweave the NRA's jackbooted thug narrative with the metanarrative of persecution politics than Charlton Heston. In his younger days, Heston had been a Democrat who supported the liberal Adlai Stevenson for president. Following the assassinations of Robert Kennedy and Martin Luther King Jr., Heston publically campaigned for passage of the Gun Control Act of 1968.[26] But in the 1970s, he fell under the sway of the new persecution narratives of the right and became a strong opponent of affirmative action and gun control. He worked for the Reagan administration and appeared several times on Pat Robertson's *700 Club* television program.[27] In 1997, Wayne LaPierre recruited Heston to become president of the NRA, and Heston joined the NRA's board of directors in preparation for the role.

In this capacity, Heston delivered a forceful speech on gun rights and the culture war to the Free Congress Foundation, a right-wing think tank founded by Paul Weyrich. The speech stands out as one of the most explicit and comprehensive presentations of right-wing persecution politics in recent history. Beginning with an invocation of

Abraham Lincoln, Heston told his conservative audience, "You are a victim of the cultural war. You are a casualty of the cultural warfare being waged against traditional American freedom of beliefs and ideas . . . Your pride in who you are, and what you believe, has been ridiculed, ransacked, plundered."[28]

"I remember when European Jews feared to admit their faith," warned the man who had once played Moses, "The Nazis forced them to wear six-pointed yellow stars sewn on their chests as identity badges. It worked. So what color star will they pin on our coats?"*

Then Heston began to list all the suffering "lesser citizens" of modern America:

> Rank-and-file Americans wake up every morning, increasingly bewildered and confused at why their views make them lesser citizens . . . Heaven help the God-fearing, law-abiding, Caucasian, middle class, Protestant, or—even worse—Evangelical Christian, Midwest, or Southern, or—even worse—rural, apparently straight, or—even worse—admittedly heterosexual, gun-owning or—even worse—NRA-card-carrying, average working stiff, or—even worse—male working stiff, because not only don't you count, you're a downright obstacle to social progress.

Finally, Heston issued a call to arms to the conservative heroes of the Free Congress Foundation, imploring, "Mainstream America is depending on you—counting on you—to draw your sword and fight for them." And whom should these white knights fight against? Heston counted off the bad guys—"The fringe propaganda of the homosexual coalition, the feminists who preach that it's a divine duty for women to hate men, blacks who raise a militant fist with one hand while they seek preference with the other, and all the New-Age apologists for juvenile crime, who see roving gangs as a means of youthful expression, sex as a means of adolescent merchandising, violence as a form of entertainment for impressionable minds, and gun bans as a means to lord-knows-what."

---

* "What color star will they pin on our coats?" I suggest a flag pin.

And that's persecution politics at its finest, an "appealing wondrous story" of an epic battle between the new oppressed class—straight white Christian gun-owning conservatives—and their new overlords—militant homosexuals, angry blacks, man-hating feminists, and Hollywood elites.

Refreshing the Tree of Liberty

Combining the NRA's gun rights rhetoric with the right wing's racial and religious persecution narratives, as Heston did, is like spanking a tiger with a chain saw. It joins the potent moral force of ethnic grievances with the stirring call to arms of militarists. Bearing arms to defend the Constitution from tyrants has its appeal, but bearing arms to defend one's culture, creed, and race from malevolent enemies is one of those core human imperatives that can drive people insane with fury. And sure enough, the kind of rhetoric espoused by Heston has been driving people insane with fury.

Right-wing militias have been experimenting with volatile compounds of persecution and violence for decades. The first modern militias sprouted in the 1960s and 1970s from a fecund stew of racism, religious fanaticism, and antigovernment paranoia. For example, members of the Posse Comitatus, founded in 1969, believed that white Christian Americans are the Chosen People, anointed by God to fight a religious war against the Satan-backed Jews, blacks, communists, homosexuals, and race traitors who had seized control of the federal government.[29]

In the early 1990s, militia membership exploded, and a motley collection of white supremacists, gun rights militants, antitaxers, religious zealots, and new world order conspiracists coalesced into what became known as the Patriot movement. The Patriot groups acted out the stories that leaders like Wayne LaPierre had been spinning. They stockpiled weapons and practiced military drills to prepare for the defense of white Christian Americans from the jackbooted thugs, liberal despots, international Jews, militant blacks, immigrant gangs, and other assorted villains who threatened their survival.

Some militiamen, intoxicated by paranoia, went beyond preparation. In 1984, Gordon Kahl of the Posse Comitatus was killed in a shootout when police sought to arrest him for the murder of two U.S. Marshalls. In 1994, two members of the Minnesota Patriots Council were arrested for plotting to poison federal agents with the deadly toxin ricin. In 1995, militia sympathizers Timothy McVeigh and Terry Nichols defended America from jackbooted thugs by blowing up a federal office building in Oklahoma City, killing 149 adults and 19 children. A few months later, the leader of the Oklahoma Constitutional Militia and two accomplices were arrested as they prepared explosives to bomb gay bars and abortion clinics. The following year, twelve members of the Arizona Viper Team were arrested on conspiracy and explosives charges after they were caught videotaping government buildings as potential targets. The same year, seven members of the Mountaineer Militia were arrested in a plot to blow up the FBI's national fingerprint records center in West Virginia.[30]

The Patriot movement peaked in 1996 with 370 militia groups across the nation. From there it went into a gradual decline, dropping to 42 by 2008. But after the election of the "the slickest, most aggressive anti-gun White House in history," the militias have returned with a vengeance, literally. The Southern Poverty Law Center recorded 127 Patriot militia groups in 2009, a 300 percent increase from the previous year.[31]

With the surge in militias has come a surge in violent threats. Obama received more death threats during the week after his election than any president-elect on record.[32] Outside one of Obama's "town hall" meetings on health care, a protester carried a loaded gun (legally) and a sign that read IT IS TIME TO WATER THE TREE OF LIBERTY! a reference to a Thomas Jefferson quote from 1787: "The tree of liberty must be refreshed from time to time with the blood of patriots and tyrants."*[33]

---

* "Tree of liberty." The Jefferson quote comes from a 1787 letter in which he pooh-poohed Shays' Rebellion, an armed insurrection in Massachusetts during which four rebels were killed. Jefferson regarded the insurrection as wrongheaded but no big deal. Other founding fathers, including George Washington, disagreed, and the incident encouraged many to take James Madison's view that "liberty may be endangered by the abuses of liberty as well as by the abuses of power." (Thomas Jefferson, "The 'Tree of Liberty' letter," *Atlantic*, October 1996, http://www.theatlantic.com/past/issues/96oct/obrien/blood.htm.)

Another protester, Chris Broughton, brought an AR-15 assault rifle to an Obama event in Phoenix, Arizona, and promised to "forcefully resist people imposing their will on us through the strength of the majority with a vote." When someone asked him if he was "gonna water the tree of liberty?" he replied, "I hope not."[34] The day before, Broughton had attended a sermon in which the pastor called Obama a "socialist devil, murderer" and railed, "I'm going to pray that he dies and goes to hell."[35]

After the health care bill passed, a former leader of the Alabama Constitutional Militia called for Americans to throw bricks through the windows of Democratic offices; four offices suffered shattered windows and glass doors. Ten Democratic congresspeople received death threats.[36] Protesters heckled black and gay legislators with derogatory slurs, and one congressman was spat on (which is one way to water the tree of liberty).[37]

Some have gone beyond bricks and spittle. The first year and a half of Obama's term featured an assortment of violent attacks from right-wing extremists: an antitax militant kamikazied his plane into an IRS office building, killing one employee; an eighty-eight-year-old white supremacist killed a security guard at the Holocaust Memorial Museum with a .22-caliber rifle; a libertarian attempted to storm the Pentagon with two 9 mm handguns, wounding two cops; and after a bloody shootout, California highway police arrested a forty-five-year-old man carrying a high-powered hunting rifle, a pistol, and a shotgun. According to police, he had hoped to incite a revolution by shooting employees of the ACLU and the Tides Foundation, a progressive nonprofit that O'Reilly and Beck have featured in their conspiracy charts.[38]

In April 2009, white supremacist Richard Poplawski shot and killed three Pittsburgh cops with a semiautomatic AK-47, the kind of gun that had been illegal under the assault weapons ban. According to his best friend, Poplawski feared "the Obama gun ban that's on the way."[39] Poplawski's Web postings indicated that he had internalized the NRA's jackbooted thug narrative. "What happens when the [government] is the only entity with any real firepower, and they feel like trampling you?" he rhetorically asked at one discussion forum. "With what instruments will you fight the tyranny?" At another forum he commented, "A group of friends and I are considering purchasing a lot of military surplus rifles." At a third he warned, "You know what they say about the tree of liberty."[40]

David Brian Stone Sr. also hoped to feed the tree of liberty. He led a fanatical Christian militia creatively named the Hutaree.* The Hutaree had been preparing for battle against a fearsome alliance between the Antichrist and the new world order. In March 2010, the government indicted Stone and eight other Hutareeans for plotting to murder a Michigan cop and then bomb the mourners who attended the victim's funeral. That would surely have sent a clear message to the Antichrist.

"RELOAD!"

Fortunately, conservative leaders are aware of the problem of right-wing violence and have come out hard against it. For instance, after the bricks and the epithets and the spitting, House minority whip Eric Cantor (R-VA) excoriated Democratic leaders who made an issue of the threats for "dangerously fanning the flames by suggesting that these incidents be used as a political weapon."†[41] Sarah Palin tweeted, "Don't Retreat, Instead—RELOAD!"[42] In case the metaphor wasn't clear enough, she then directed her Twitter followers to her Facebook page, which showed a map that marked the locations of vulnerable Democratic congresspeople with rifle crosshairs.[43]

Rep. Steve King (R-IA) "empathized" with IRS kamikaze Joseph Andrew Stack and said of the attack, "It's sad the incident in Texas happened, but by the same token, it's an agency that is unnecessary and

---

* "Hutaree." According to Stone, *Hutaree* comes from the group's private dialect, known only to Stone and four other privileged individuals. A linguist at the University of Pennsylvania hypothesized that the group's hierarchical paramilitary ranks—Radok, Boramander, Zulif, Arkon, and Lukore—may have been derived from the Pokemon characters Arbok, Charmander, Zubat, and Rokon. (Doug Guthrie, "Hutaree dialect—rooted in religion or Pokemon?" *Detroit News,* 29 Mar. 2010, http://detnews.com/article/20100329/METRO/3290413/Hutaree-dialect-rooted-in-religion-or-Pokemon.)

† "Dangerously fanning the flames." Cantor's logic was murky. Perhaps he meant that Democrats' complaints just made the extremists madder.

when the day comes when that is over and we abolish the IRS, it's going to be a happy day for America."[44]

After the Hutaree story broke, Glenn Beck's radio stand-in, Chris Baker, called the arrests "nothing more than attack on faith and free speech."[45] And Fox News commentator Monica Crowley wrote in an opinion column:

> If you go to church, believe in protecting innocent life, own a gun or defend your country, the Democrats consider you a potential enemy of the state.[46]

In other words, the FBI's arrests of the members of a bizarre militia who plotted to murder a cop and bomb the funeral mourners was actually a Democratic assault on the free speech of churchgoers. But lest you think that Crowley was cynically manipulating public opinion by claiming Christian persecution, she assured readers that it was actually the other way round:

> It's mind-blowingly coincidental that these raids on a supposedly "Christian" militia group would come at the exact moment that Democrats were trying to change public opinion on Obamacare by claiming persecution by their opponents.

So Crowley was manipulating public opinion by claiming persecution of churchgoers at the hands of Democrats who she contends were manipulating public opinion by claiming persecution at the hands of churchgoers. How's that for Freudian projection?

During an interview of Rep. Michelle Bachmann (R-MN), Sean Hannity continued the Fox News line that criticizing violent rhetoric was an attack on conservatives' free speech. He stated, "There seems to be a coordinated effort to intimidate, silence and demonize any critic of this administration." Bachmann felt the same way. She replied:

> I think violence is when the Democrat-controlled base, whether it's President Obama, Harry Reid or Speaker Pelosi—when they feel like their

political position of power is being attacked, that's what they equate violence with . . . They want to silence the voices that are opposing them.[47]

Bachmann, of course, is one of those voices that are opposing the
Democrats. For instance, she opposed the Democrats' environmental
policy, saying:

> I want people in Minnesota armed and dangerous on this issue of the
> energy tax because we need to fight back. Thomas Jefferson told us,
> having a revolution every now and then is a good thing, and the peo-
> ple—we the people—are going to have to fight back hard if we're not
> going to lose our country. And I think this has the potential of changing
> the dynamic of freedom forever in the United States.

Not that she condones violence.

The Bachmann–Fox News defense has a certain rhetorical beauty; it
employs persecution politics to attack the critics of persecution politics.
Any attempt to criticize the outrageous language that the right has been
employing is an assault on the First Amendment rights of conservatives.
It is a common refrain on Fox News. When Bill O'Reilly complained
that critics who accused him of bigotry were libeling him and violating
his First Amendment rights, a lawyer whom he had invited into the *No
Spin Zone* tried to educate him on the difference between criticism,
libel, and First Amendment violations. But O'Reilly would have none
of it. He retorted, "I don't care about the law. My rights were violated
here because they tried to punish me for my speech. It's happening all
over the place."[48]

"Let's Roll"

But there is one right-wing leader who does truthfully seem sensitive
to the violence . . . Glenn Beck. Alluding to Gandhi and Martin Luther
King Jr., Beck admonished his audience, "If you ever hear someone
thinking about or talking about turning violent, it is your patriotic

duty to stop them. The only way to save our republic is to remain peaceful—forceful but peaceful."[49] But Beck offered a curious reason for his opposition to violence: he's concerned that it would be counterproductive to the cause. Worse, it could give the evil progressives the excuse they're looking for to crack down on the real Americans. As he explained:

> Just one lunatic, like Timothy McVeigh, could ruin everything that everyone has worked so hard for, because these people in Washington won't pass up the use of an emergency.[50]

In other words, the progressives *want* conservatives to commit violence. It's all part of their secret plan. "Why are they trying to poke you and poke you and poke you?" Beck asked his audience. "They need you to be violent. They are begging you for it. You are being set up. Do not give them what they want."[51]

See, it's the progressives who are provoking violence, not the reasonable conservatives of Fox News and talk radio, not Glenn Beck. A few weeks before killing three cops, Richard Poplawski posted a YouTube video of Beck and Representative Ron Paul discussing paranoid allegations of secret concentration camps run by the Federal Emergency Management Agency (FEMA).[52] But after the tragedy, Beck excused himself of any responsibility by comparing himself to a flight attendant:

> Blaming TV or radio hosts for the nutjob who killed three Pittsburgh police officers over the weekend is like blaming a flight attendant after a terrorist takes down a plane. In other words: Giving passengers a safety talk to prepare them for a worst-case scenario doesn't mean you are responsible should a terrorist make that worst-case scenario happen. One person is providing important information. The other is a nutjob who would've acted no matter what.[53]

Beck's analogy isn't quite right, however. He hasn't been calmly telling the passengers where to find their life jackets and thanking them for flying with Fox News. He has been hysterically shouting, "THE PILOT IS TRYING TO CRASH THE PLANE! WE'RE ALL GONNA DIE!" For example, here is a "safety talk" that Beck delivered to his Fox News passengers a few months after he invoked the flight attendant defense:

> I told you yesterday buckle up your seatbelt, America. Find the exit. There's one here, here and here. Find the exit closest to you and prepare for a crash-landing because this plane is coming down because the pilot is intentionally steering it into the trees . . . They are taking you to a place to be slaughtered.[54]

That's some safety talk. A safety talk like that might lead some passengers to do more than just buckle their seatbelts. It might even lead some "nutjob" to shout, "Let's roll!" and rush the cockpit.

I highly doubt that Glenn Beck is deliberately encouraging violence, and I believe that he was sincere when he told his audience that violence would be counterproductive to the conservative cause. In this regard, he shows more sense than some of his colleagues who have avoided telling their constituents to calm the hell down. But that's not the point.

Whether or not Beck and other right-wing leaders intend to provoke violence, their incendiary rhetoric has the effect of provoking it. When these leaders persuade people that a malicious and alien adversary is trying to destroy everything that they believe in, to appropriate their wages and property, to abolish their religion, to restrict their freedom of speech, and even to arrest or injure them, these people will become scared and angry. When the NRA and other gun rights supporters simultaneously persuade them that keeping arms is the only way to prevent such a calamity, many of these scared and angry people will take up arms. They will train and prepare for the day when they will need to defend their country from these terrible enemies.

And some of them, the most credulous and unstable among them, will conclude that the calamity is already upon them. They will internalize the appealing wondrous story that their leaders have been telling them. They will imagine that they are the heroes who will save their country, their religion, their race, and their way of life from the jack-booted thugs, Marxist revolutionaries, manipulative Jews, vicious perverts, black radicals, immigrant criminals, and minions of Satan who seek to subjugate them. And they will strike.

13

THE TENT OF FREEDOM

How Persecution Politics Bewitched the Republican Party
and Opened the Gates to Tea Party Barbarians

*The Republican Party is the Party of the Future because it is the party
that draws people together, not drives them apart. Our Party detests
the technique of pitting group against group for cheap political advantage.*

— Dwight D. Eisenhower

A S I BURROWED INTO the history of the modern conservative moment while writing this book, the Republican Party often took
me by surprise—not because of the extremism of some Republican
leaders but because of the wide diversity of opinions and ideologies
that the party once tolerated. The GOP has grown increasingly conservative over the past few decades, but to read prominent Republicans
expressing opinions that would now be considered heresy was nonetheless startling—as when the chairman of the Wisconsin Republican
Party told Paul Weyrich, "Our businesspeople would think it was
strange that we are getting involved in a religious issue."[1] Or the party's
timid, noncommittal abortion plank from 1976:

The question of abortion is one of the most difficult and controversial
of our time. It is undoubtedly a moral and personal issue but it also involves complex questions relating to medical science and criminal justice. There are those in our Party who favor complete support for the
Supreme Court decision which permits abortion on demand. There are
others who share sincere convictions that the Supreme Court's decision

must be changed by a constitutional amendment prohibiting all abortions. Others have yet to take a position, or they have assumed a stance somewhere in between polar positions.[2]

But starting in the late 1970s, such heterodox ideas began falling out of the party platform. There was no single moment of metamorphosis but rather a series of small mutations, as younger right-wing ideologues gradually displaced the liberal and moderate Republicans of a previous era. These mutations are still taking place. With the liberal Republicans long gone and the moderates nearly extinct, dogmatic Tea Party supporters are now expunging conservative legislators who are not conservative enough; they are continuing to push the party even further into the sooty, smoky fire of paranoid extremism.

Over the years, political analysts have offered various explanations for the rightward drift of the GOP. Some point to nationwide disenchantment with large public social programs, some to a backlash against the cultural shifts of the 1960s, and some to the increasing conservatism of aging baby boomers. Most of these explanations place the impetus on the mood of the American electorate, suggesting that liberal and moderate Republicans died out because they failed to adapt to the changing political climate.

I submit an alternative hypothesis: the liberal and moderate Republicans were hunted into extinction by their more aggressive conservative cousins who wielded a powerful new weapon that was highly effective at galvanizing their political base. The weapon was persecution politics.

Even as conservatives extended their dominance over the Republican Party and the country as a whole, their sense of persecution increased. They turned up their attacks on powerful liberal "elites" and invented a new victim class that fused whites, Christians, and the working class into a loose affiliation they called "conservatives," "traditionalists," or "real Americans." The formation of the new victim class precipitated the widespread fear and paranoia that exploded after Obama's election and spawned the Tea Parties; the Tea Parties then inherited the mantle of persecution politics. To see how this happened, we will need to return once more to the beginning of the story.

The New Right

Once upon a time, rare and exotic creatures lurked in the fetid swamps of the District of Columbia and urban jungles of the northeastern seaboard. The scientific name for the species was *Republicanus liberalus,* but most people called them Rockefeller Republicans after Nelson Rockefeller, a prominent Republican governor from New York who expanded his state's universities, parks, welfare programs, and housing projects. Rockefeller Republicans were pro-business capitalists who often espoused liberal principles on gun control, welfare, women's rights, affirmative action, abortion, education, and environmentalism. True believers in the "party of Lincoln," they also wanted nothing to do with the new Southern strategy initiated by Barry Goldwater and Richard Nixon. According to legend, these strange Republicans were known for civility, pragmatism, and human decency (though some cynics dismiss the possibility that such wondrous beasts ever existed).

The species was relatively plentiful in the 1960s but went into steep decline in the late 1970s and was virtually extinct by the end of the 1980s. Their disappearance coincided almost exactly with the alleged onslaught of secular humanists, gay militants, jackbooted thugs, and other early villains of persecution politics. The timing was not coincidental. The two men credited with leading the purge against liberal Republicans happened to be the same two who mobilized the right wing to battle the secular humanists at the IRS. We've previously discussed Paul Weyrich, founder of the Heritage Foundation and the architect of Jerry Falwell's Moral Majority. During the 1970s, he and Richard Viguerie, an ambitious, talented, and extremely conservative political fundraiser, initiated a grassroots movement to remake the Republican Party. It was called the New Right.*

After President Richard Nixon resigned in 1974, Vice President Gerald Ford assumed the presidency. When Ford appointed Nelson Rock-

---

* "New Right." In fact, there were a few New Rights in the twentieth century, so the movement should perhaps have been called the New New Right or even the New New New Right. But *new* is one of those perverse adjectives where the more *news* you string together, the less new your idea sounds, so most people just ignored the previous New Rights.

efeller vice president, conservative Republicans went apoplectic. Richard Viguerie wrote:

> Nelson Rockefeller—the high-flying, wild-spending leader of the Eastern Liberal Establishment. As a conservative Republican, I could hardly have been more upset if Ford had selected Teddy Kennedy.[3]

The day after Ford's announcement, Viguerie organized a meeting with some fifteen conservative friends, including Weyrich, to discuss strategies for thwarting the Rockefeller appointment. While Viguerie ultimately concluded that they couldn't stop it, the meeting spurred him to launch an initiative to challenge Republican leadership and empower the right wing.

The New Right of Weyrich and Viguerie bore much in common with today's Tea Parties. Its adherents were extremely hostile to liberals and intolerant of any dissent from conservative principles. They were suspicious of government and emphasized social issues, like abortion and school prayer. And they practiced persecution politics. Weyrich, for example, described the conflict between the Christians and the secular humanists as "the most significant battle of the age-old conflict between good and evil, between the forces of God and the forces against God, that we have seen in our country."[4] Viguerie deliberately exploited hostility toward secularists and homosexuals in his direct mail campaigns to white Christian voters. "People are motivated by anger and fear much more so than positive emotions," he explained in a 2005 interview. He defended his negative campaigns by alluding to slavery and civil rights. "It's sometimes very good to have anger," he continued, "Abraham Lincoln was very angry about slavery. Martin Luther King was very angry about how minorities and African-Americans were treated back in the 50s and 60s."[5] Viguerie would know. He had raised millions of dollars for George Wallace's race-baiting presidential campaigns.[6]

Like the Tea Parties, the New Right also sought to harness grassroots activism to challenge the Republican establishment and purge legislators that they deemed insufficiently conservative. For instance, in 1978 the New Right supported primary challenges to Clifford Case, a four-term Republican senator from New Jersey, and Edward Brooke, a two-term Republican senator from Massachusetts (and the only African American in the Senate at the time). Case lost in the primary. Brooke won, but both seats went to Democrats in the general election—two fewer Rockefeller Republicans in the Senate.*[7]

In one of his most brazen undertakings, Viguerie also targeted Rep. John B. Anderson (R-IL), the number-three-ranking Republican in the House. Anderson had begun his political career as a religious conservative, and the National Association of Evangelicals named him "Outstanding Layman of the Year" in 1964.[8] But when the GOP began implementing the Southern strategy, Anderson went in the other direction. His eloquent defense of the Civil Rights Act of 1968 was credited with turning sentiment in favor of the bill. He also supported welfare, abortion rights, desegregation busing, and environmentalism.[9] In 1976, Anderson voted against the measure to prohibit federal funds for educational programs "involving any aspect of the religion of secular humanism," which infuriated religious conservatives.

In 1978, a fundamentalist minister challenged Anderson in the Republican primary, denouncing him for "allowing secular humanism to be taught in schools" and "talking like some god of the East."[10] Richard Viguerie supported the challenge with fundraising letters that called Anderson "part of the liberal establishment clique."[11] Anderson complained of a deliberate right-wing crusade against him, telling reporters:

> I'm the test case for this whole effort to purge the Republican Party of any progressive element. Mine is an early primary, and if they can defeat the chairman of the House Republican Conference, they can put the fear of God into a lot of other Republicans.[12]

Much as today's right-wing Tea Party has captured the attention and interest of the media, the political pundits of 1978 obsessed over the

---

* Incidentally, Weyrich declined to support George Bush Jr.'s 1978 congressional campaign, explaining, "We do not regard him as a conservative."

challenge from the New Right. One popular columnist, commenting on John Anderson's opposition to the secular humanism measure, wrote:

> Trust the zany right-wingers to work themselves into a perfect lather because Anderson voted against Washington issuing an unintelligible decree [concerning secular humanism] to local schools . . . The Republican "left" has been shrinking even faster than the party itself has been. Today, the GOP is a conservative party, with less diversity than exists within Britain's Labour and Conservative parties, and more ideological uniformity than any major American party has had in this century.[13]

The journalist who wrote these words back in 1978 was George Will, the conservative Pulitzer Prize–winning columnist for the *Washington Post*. (Republican Party circa 1978 to George Will: "You ain't seen nothin' yet.")

Nonetheless, the Republican establishment stuck by Anderson. He won his primary and retained his seat. The acrimonious campaign soured him on Congress, however.[14] He resigned his seat in 1980 and ran for president. When Ronald Reagan trounced him in the Republican primary, Anderson ran as an independent, winning less than 7 percent of the vote. Thus were the liberals cast off into the political wilderness as conservatives began to take control of the GOP.

The Republican Revolution

When Rockefeller Republicans roamed the halls of the Capitol building, moderates dominated the leadership of the Republican Party. They maintained their power by mediating the competing demands of liberals and conservatives at either end of the party. As conservatives supplanted liberals in the 1980s, moderates lost the authority of the middle, and conservative legislators eventually launched a parliamentary coup against them. In 1992, the Heritage Foundation organized orientation sessions for Republican freshmen where Paul Weyrich encouraged them to rebel against House leaders. Soon after, the Republican caucus elected conservatives Dick Armey (R-TX) and Newt

Gingrich (R-GA) to leadership positions. One Democratic analyst predicted that the 1992 conservative uprising would be detrimental to the GOP, arguing, "They are silencing the more moderate elements in their party and seeking an ideological purity from the right. A marginalized, right-wing Republican Party will be less competitive with Bill Clinton in 1996 than a more inclusive and centrist Republican Party."[15]

But the analyst failed to appreciate the power of persecution politics. Capitalizing on a backlash against jackbooted ATF thugs, "reverse racism," and White House conspiracy theories, Republicans mobilized evangelical Christians in record numbers and made huge inroads in Southern states, capturing 68 percent of white voters in the 1994 midterm elections. They picked up fifty-four seats in the House and eight seats in the Senate, taking control of both houses for the first time since 1954. Analysts credited much of the GOP's success to aggressive advertising by conservative interest groups like the Christian Coalition, led by the paranoid Pat Robertson, and the NRA, led by the paranoid Wayne LaPierre.[16]

Another new paranoid conservative star also made his mark in 1994. Rush Limbaugh, who had by then attracted a radio audience of 20 million, exhorted his listeners to vote Republican in what he called Operation Restore Democracy.[17] "Rush is as responsible for what happened here as much as anyone," said Vin Weber, a former representative from Minnesota.[18] And in a 2001 congressional tribute to Limbaugh, Tom DeLay raved, "He was the standard by which we ran . . . He played a huge part in what happened in 1994 and, thereby, played a huge part in all of the successes that we have been able to do over the last 7 years."[19]

The Heritage Foundation honored Limbaugh's achievements with a keynote speech at its orientation for the 1994 Republican freshman class.[20] In the speech, Limbaugh encouraged the new congressmen (they were all men) to stay mean: "This is not the time to get moderate. This is not the time to start trying to be liked." At the end, he quipped:

> Please, whatever you do, leave some liberals alive. I think we should have at least, on every college campus, one communist professor and two liberal professors, so we never forget who these people are and what

they stand for. We can always show our children what they were and what they are—living fossils, ladies and gentlem[e]n.[21]

"The Vito Corleone of the House"

But when the Republican revolution petered out a few years later, there were still quite a few liberals holed away in the nation's ivory towers. In 1998, Newt Gingrich's resignation amid Republican losses and a swath of ethics scandals led many to conclude that the party had gone too far to the extreme. "The emerging cliche seems to be that the Republicans, having lost an unexpected five seats in the House and a couple of statehouses they thought were forever in their camp, will forge a new political message that is pragmatic and much less ideological, a shift in emphasis that will endear the party to moderate voters," wrote a *Chicago Tribune* political analyst. Some Republicans looked to emulate the "pragmatic" approach of Governor George W. Bush, who had developed a reputation for governing by consensus in Texas.[22]

We know how that turned out. Though Bush ran for president as a "unifier," his governing approach was based on "carefully tending to the Republican Party's conservative base" and "trying to vanquish political adversaries rather than split the difference with them."[23] Following advisor Karl Rove's political strategy, Bush employed "wedge issues" that "super-charged the moral minority."[24] While Bush did not directly engage in paranoia or persecution politics, his wedge issues, including a proposed constitutional amendment to ban same-sex marriage, came straight from the persecution politics agenda that Republican legislators and right-wing media stars had been actively promoting.

The strategy worked. In 2004, Bush lost the moderate vote by nine percentage points, but he won 84 percent of self-described conservatives, who made up a third of the electorate.[25] Twenty-one percent of voters said that moral values were the most important issue, and 78 percent of those voted for Bush. [26]

Not only did Bush win reelection despite growing unemployment and the increasingly unpopular war in Iraq, hard-line Republican legislators rode his coattails, resulting in the most conservative Congress in recent history. Speaker Dennis Hastert (R-IL) officially led the House Republicans, but it was the ultraconservative majority leader Tom DeLay (R-TX) who really ran the show. "DeLay is the Vito Corleone of the House," said Stephen Moore, head of the conservative political group Club for Growth. "Everyone now in leadership basically was put there by him."[27]

Tom DeLay, one of the most powerful politicians in the country, drank deep from the chalice of persecution politics. Facing indictments for ethical violations in 2005, DeLay claimed, "One thing God has brought to us is Terri Schiavo to elevate the visibility of what's going on in America." What was going on in America, according to DeLay, was persecution of conservatives. He explained:

> The other side has figured out how to win and to defeat the conservative movement, and that is to go after people personally, charge them with frivolous charges, link up with all these do-gooder organizations funded by George Soros, and then get the national media on their side. That whole syndicate that they have going on right now is for one purpose and one purpose only, and that is to destroy the conservative movement. It is to destroy conservative leaders, and not just in elected office, but leading . . . This is a huge nationwide concerted effort to destroy every-thing we believe in.[28]

In other words, God had induced a cardiac arrest in a young woman in 1990 and maintained her in a vegetative state for fifteen years in order to reveal the secret liberal plot to destroy the career of Tom DeLay and undermine the Republican Congress.

"We're Watching Their Votes"

DeLay's theme of conservative persecution was a relatively new front in the culture war. It wasn't just whites and Christians that George Soros and company despised and tormented; it was an entire political class whose representatives just happened to control the U.S. government. Another man who warned of the new bigotry against conservatives was Stephen Moore, who had likened DeLay's authority to Don Corleone. In a column for the *National Review* after the 2004 election, he sarcastically chided, "The party that preaches tolerance as the preeminent virtue just can't tolerate one thing: conservatives." Crowing over the Republican victory, Moore encouraged disgruntled liberals to move to Canada: "When you get a fanny-whupping like the Left got on Election Day—when every one of your core values (tax hikes on the rich, abortion on demand, government-run health care, reparation payments for slavery, one-world government, polygamy) has been rejected by your bigoted and narrow-minded fellow citizens—it's cowardly to stick around."[29]

Moore was the president of a political action committee innocuously named Club for Growth. The organization came out swinging in 2004 with an advertisement that pressed Democratic candidate Howard Dean to "take his tax-hiking, government-expanding, latte-drinking, sushi-eating, Volvo-driving, *New York Times*-reading, Hollywood-loving, left-wing freak show back to Vermont where it belongs."[*][30]

But the Club for Growth's primary targets are not latte-drinking Democrats. It spends most of its money attacking latte-drinking Republicans whom the organization calls RINOs—Republican in name only. The best way for a Republican politician to get on the Club for Growth's "RINO Watch" list is to cast a vote with the Democratic Party—though driving a Volvo probably helps too. The Club for Growth has spent millions backing conservative challengers in Republican primaries. It has been blamed for defeating a number of moderate Republican incumbents in the House and for contributing to Sen. Lincoln Chafee's (R-RI) election loss by drawing his resources into a primary battle.[31] The

---

* "Back to Vermont." Moore's philosophy in a nutshell: "Go north, young liberal." An Illinois native, Moore seems to view the northeast as some kind of reservation for confused socialists. In 1997, he wrote, "The Northeast is dying, victim of the same sclerosis now paralyzing Europe. Republicans may well have no choice but to write it off. With each passing day, the region's shrinking conservative voting base is retreating to the more economically robust and culturally normal places like Georgia, North Carolina, Florida and Texas." (Stephen Moore, "Is the Northeast necessary?" *American Spectator*, 30:12 [Dec. 1997]: 41)

Club for Growth also backed Pat Toomey's 2004 primary challenge to Senator Arlen Specter of Pennsylvania. Moore ominously warned, "It will put all Republicans in the House and Senate on notice that we're watching their votes."[32] Specter won the primary but later calculated that he would lose to Toomey in 2010 and defected to the Democrats. With Sen. George Voinovich (R-OH) retiring in 2011, there remain only two Republican moderates in the Senate, both from Maine (which should suit Stephen Moore's geographic sensibilities).

Club for Growth beneficiaries include some of the most paranoid right-wing members of the House, such as Michele Bachmann, who told Hannity, "A revolution every now and then is a good thing," and Paul Broun, who accused Obama of preparing a civilian security force to enforce his radical Marxist ideology.[33] It christened Steve King (R-IA), who empathized with kamikaze pilot Andrew Joseph Stack, "Defender of Economic Freedom."[34] The Club for Growth has also been heavily supporting Tea Party candidates, but we'll get to that in a moment.

By 2006, the Republicans' star had begun to sink. Americans had grown unhappy with lingering wars, a deteriorating economy, and a relentless series of political scandals. Republicans had controlled both Houses of Congress for ten of the previous twelve years and the presidency for six; the electorate was ready for change. When Democrats swept back into Congress during the midterm elections, political analysts declared that the Republicans had lost the center, and strategists encouraged them to follow the "California way" of moderate Republican Arnold Schwarzenegger.[35] Pundits touted the former mayor of New York, moderate Republican Rudi Giuliani, as a likely presidential candidate in 2008.

But conservatives would have none of it. The problem was not that the party was too conservative, they argued, it was that it wasn't conservative enough. "There's no doubt in my mind it was not a repudiation of conservatives but it was a repudiation of the Republican Party," argued Pat Toomey, who replaced Stephen Moore at the helm of the Club for Growth after losing to Specter.[36] Rush Limbaugh concurred, "Republicans lost last night but conservatism did not." Instead, he blamed "blue-blood, country club, corporate type . . . Rockefeller-type"

Republicans.[37] But the Rockefeller-type Republicans had gone extinct years before, and most of the surviving moderates had been wiped out in the 2006 election. It was Rush Limbaugh's GOP if it was anyone's.

Something about Sarah

What Limbaugh's GOP lacked, however, was a viable presidential candidate in the 2008 election. Mike Huckabee was popular among evangelicals, but small government conservatives despised him. The Club for Growth produced ads in Iowa that portrayed him as a tax-and-spend liberal, exclaiming, "He even wants to tax the Internet."[38] Gradually and somewhat reluctantly, the party began to coalesce around McCain, if only because there was no one better to coalesce around. As McCain said, "I feel like Will Smith in *I Am Legend*. You know I'm the last guy standing who is not a zombie."[39]

McCain was no moderate, but he had established a reputation as a maverick, which means that he only voted with George Bush 95 percent of the time.[40] He had also once called Jerry Falwell and Pat Robertson "agents of intolerance," condemning "the evil influence that they exercise over the Republican Party." But in 2006, McCain and Falwell made up. "I think he is genuinely a state's righter," said Falwell, "and so am I."[41]

James Dobson was not so easily mollified, however. He vowed to sit out the election if McCain were nominated. "I am convinced Sen. McCain is not a conservative," he argued. "He has at times sounded more like a member of the other party."[42] Rush Limbaugh was even more alarmed, warning of a GOP takeover by Rockefeller elitists who disdained working-class Christian conservatives. He said:

> The Rockefeller Republican wing of the Republican Party is doing everything it can to take over, to get rid of conservatism as a dominant force in the party for a whole bunch of reasons. They're embarrassed of the pro-life community. They're embarrassed when they have to go to Republican conventions and show up at cocktail parties with Billy Bob

and Ellie Mae coming up from Mississippi and so forth, 'cause their wives, the guys, Republican guys, their wives henpeck 'em and give 'em all kinds of trouble for being in the pro-life party and so forth and so on. So the nomination of McCain here is basically an attempt to rid the Republican Party of conservative influence, as you can see by McCain consistently reaching out across the aisle to independents and Democrats.[43]

Faced with the risk of massive defection by the conservative base, McCain offered Limbaugh and Dobson the treat they were hungering for: Sarah Palin. Combining charisma, religion, and deep social conservatism with a wholesome small-town image, Palin was the perfect conservative candidate. "This is a very exciting and encouraging day for conservatives and pro-family activists. I am just very, very pleased," raved Dobson. "If I had to go into the . . . voting booth today, I would pull that lever."[44] Rush Limbaugh gushed like a love-struck teenager:

Sarah Palin's family, sitting there watching—the little seven-year-old Piper moistening her fingers and patting down the hair of the baby? Heart was going crazy. Mind was going nuts . . . This lady has turned it all around. And I'm here to tell you today that John McCain, from now on, on this program, regarding this choice, will be known as John McBrilliant.[45]

In addition to her conservatively correct policy positions, Palin knew how to play persecution politics. Taking a phrase from Glenn Beck, she described Greensboro, North Carolina, as one of "these wonderful little pockets of what I call the real America."[46] Barack Obama of Honolulu and Chicago (and Kenya!) was not from such a wonderful little pocket; he was not like them. In another speech, Palin told supporters, "I am just so fearful that this is not a man who sees America the way that you and I see America."[47] Barack Obama, Sarah Palin explained, believed in "spreading the wealth." She didn't say whose wealth Obama wanted to spread and to whom he wanted to spread it, but she told her audience what "Joe the Plumber" and "Ed the Dairy Man" thought of all this spreading: "They think that it sounds more like socialism."*[48] Palin also would have liked to go after Obama's Rev. Wright associations. She told conservative columnist Bill Kristol:

> I don't know why that association isn't discussed more, because those were appalling things that that pastor had said about our great country, and to have sat in the pews for 20 years and listened to that—with, I don't know, a sense of condoning it, I guess, because he didn't get up and leave—to me, that does say something about character. But, you know, I guess that would be a John McCain call on whether he wants to bring that up.[49]

But Palin's greatest contribution to persecution politics was herself. Even as she surged out of the starting gate—before the disastrous Katie Couric interview or Tina Fey's stinging impersonations—conservative columnist Bill Kristol predicted that the liberal media would persecute Sarah Palin. He wrote:

> So what we will see in the next days and weeks—what we have already seen in the hours after her nomination—is an effort by all the powers of the old liberalism, both in the Democratic party and the mainstream media, to exorcise this spectre. They will ridicule her and patronize her. They will distort her words and caricature her biography. They will appeal, sometimes explicitly, to anti-small town and anti-religious prejudice.[50]

Conservative talk show host Laura Ingraham said, "Because this woman is strong, conservative, independent and pro-life, and politically and personally lives her life that way, she's reviled and hated."[51] One-time presidential candidate Fred Thompson claimed, "She is from a small town, with small-town values, but that's not good enough for those folks who are attacking her and her family."[52] Rep. Adam Putnam (R-

---

* "Joe the Plumber and Ed the Dairy Man." What about Dion the Drug Dealer and Juanita the Welfare Queen?

FL) asserted, "The media doesn't understand life membership in the NRA; they don't understand getting up at 3 a.m. to hunt a moose; they don't understand eating a mooseburger; they don't understand being married to a guy who likes to snowmobile for fun. I am not surprised that they don't get it. But Americans get it. A mooseburger means she is like one of us."[53]

With all due respect to Representative Putnam, a fifth-generation Floridian who has spent his entire life in the state, what the hell does he know about mooseburgers?[54] One of the absurdities of persecution politics is that what Palin and Beck call "real America" is a mishmash of cultures, creeds, professions, and lifestyles. Representative Putnam is an Episcopalian rancher's son from the sundrenched southeastern tip of the country, while Governor Palin is a Catholic-to-Pentecostal schoolteacher's daughter from the nation's icy northwestern extremity. But because they are both white Christian pro-life NRA members, they are kindred spirits united by their appreciation of the essence of moose-burgerness—in contrast with "the media" for whom the mysteries of moose meat are forever inaccessible no matter how much they might devour.

We'll return to this theme in the next chapter. The important point for the moment, succinctly illustrated in Putnam's mooseburger comment, is that Sarah Palin is not just a politician who takes conservative positions; she embodies conservatism. As a white, evangelical, gun-toting, middle-class, small-town mother of five, she is the quintessential "lesser citizen" that Charlton Heston described when he asked, "What color star will they pin on our coats?" Palin's supporters interpreted the media barrage and late-night parodies as denigrations not only of their own political beliefs but of their way of life. "You're being told by the media propagandists that Sarah Palin is not qualified to be vice president. You're being told she's dumb," said Rush Limbaugh. "These attacks on Governor Palin are attacks on you and attacks on me. They are attacking every single person outside the Beltway, outside the New York–Washington axis, outside their social circle of elitist friends that represents what's great about this country."[55]

Meanwhile, as the media propagandists were attacking Sarah Palin and every single person outside the New York–Washington axis, something unusual was happening on the campaign trail. Before Palin joined the Republican ticket, McCain rallies averaged 1,000 participants. With Palin at his side, crowds ranged from 5,000 to 10,000.[56] Journalists initially described Palin fans as "euphoric" and "energized." Soon, they began to call them "angry" and "ugly." When Palin evoked Obama's name, people would shout out "traitor," "terrorist," "treason," "liar," and on one occasion, "Kill him!"[57] When Palin criticized Katie Couric after her "less-than-successful interview with kinda mainstream media," the crowd turned on the press area, screaming obscenities. One Palin supporter shouted a racial epithet at an African American sound man for one of the networks and told him, "Sit down, boy!"[58] Around this time, the Secret Service reported a sharp increase in the number of violent threats against Barack Obama. Shaken, Michelle Obama asked a top campaign aide, "Why would they try to make people hate us?"[59] But Rush Limbaugh was delighted with the behavior of the crowds. "Fifteen years of frustration is coming out joyously in the voices of GOP supporters at these rallies," he wrote.*[60]

What was it about Sarah Palin's political rallies that invited so much joyous frustration? The frightening specter of a black liberal president was certainly a factor, but there was more than that; McCain didn't inspire such crowds until after he selected Palin as his running mate. There was something about Sarah. Through her "real America" rhetoric and her embodiment of the persecuted victim of an elitist media in love with an African American president, Palin catalyzed the race-driven fears and class-driven animosities of her constituents. With Palin's nomination, the 2008 presidential election transformed from a political contest between two men with different opinions into a pivotal battle between "us" and "them," where the embattled mooseburger-loving Sarah Palin represented "us" and the elitist, socialistic, great black hope, Barack Obama, represented "them."

---

* "Fifteen years of frustration." That would be since 1993, just before Newt Gingrich's Republican revolution took over Congress and initiated conservatives' twelve-year reign.

"The Shout Heard 'Round the World"

The joyous frustration that Palin aroused didn't cease with the election. The man that her supporters so reviled became president, and their resentment against the media elite metamorphosed almost overnight into resentment against the government. Glenn Beck became an instant sensation by deftly shepherding that resentment into his conspiracy theories about Marxist czars and angry black men. Sarah Palin made millions selling books and giving speeches to malcontent supporters. (Victimhood has its charms.) And then there were the Tea Parties.

The Tea Parties, which have become the standard-bearers of right-wing persecution politics, are neither political parties nor social gatherings. Some refer to a Tea Party movement, which is vague enough to capture the muddled pastiche of organizations and ideologies that constitute this latest right-wing insurgency.* Credit for popularizing the term *Tea Party* goes to CNBC business news editor, Rick Santelli. One month after Obama's inauguration, Santelli delivered a televised rant from the trading floor of the Chicago Mercantile Exchange lambasting the administration's mortgage refinancing plan. "How about this, President and new administration?" he yelled as commodity traders cheered and whistled. "Why don't you put up a website to have people vote on the Internet as a referendum to see if we really want to subsidize the losers' mortgages?"[61] Then he called to the traders, "How many of you people want to pay for your neighbor's mortgage that has an extra bathroom and can't pay their bills?" The traders boisterously booed to indicate that they did not want to pay the mortgages of their overbathroomed neighbors. Then Santelli, aroused by the hot-blooded

---

* "Tea Party movement." There is also a question of what to call Tea Party supporters. After one protester carried a sign that read TEA BAG THE LIBERAL DEMS BEFORE THEY TEA BAG YOU, cheeky liberals began calling them teabaggers.

Teabagging is slang for a sexual act involving oral stimulation of the scrotum, and the label gave rise to a spurt of double entendres about Tea Party members. Conservatives subsequently objected to the label, which some compared to the N-word. Journalists variously refer to them as Tea Party supporters, backers, activists, members, protesters, or simply Tea Partiers (which brings to mind a frat party without beer). (Alex Koppelman, "Your guide to teabagging," *Salon.com*, 14 Apr. 2009, http://www.salon.com/news/politics/war_room/2009/04/14/teabagging_guide.)

enthusiasm of the commodities traders, proceeded to metamorphose from cable news business editor into Revolutionary Hero of the Chicago Mercantile Exchange. "We're thinking of having a Chicago Tea Party in July!" he roared to the cheering traders, "All you capitalists that want to show up to Lake Michigan, I'm gonna start organizing!"* Soon after, the *Drudge Report* heralded Santelli's diatribe in a giant, dazzling red font, accompanied by a flashing siren logo to convey its urgent import:

TRADERS REVOLT: CNBC HOST CALLS FOR NEW "TEA PARTY"[62]

For the right wing, it was love at first sight. The 1773 Boston Tea Party, featuring the plucky Sons of Liberty versus the tyrannical King George III and the tax-loving British parliament, offered the perfect metaphor for the antigovernment resentment that exploded within weeks of Obama's inauguration. Its fertile symbolism easily incorporated various right-wing mythologies, from Christian persecution to jackbooted ATF thugs, health care "redistribution" to the glorious heritage of Anglo-Saxon America. Plus, it provided a fun excuse to dress in knickers, hose, and tricorn hats and to write clever protest signs like RUSSIA CALLED, THEY WANT THEIR SOCIALISM BACK. Or somewhat less clever protest signs like KEEP THE GUVMINT OUT OF MY MEDICARE.[63]

In little more than a week after Santelli's rant, which CNBC proudly called "The Shout Heard 'Round the World," grassroots organizers hastily convened Tea Parties in forty-eight cities, according to an organizer.[64] By tax day, April 15, there were hundreds of Tea Party protests across the country, many of which drew thousands of participants. On September 12, tens of thousands of Tea Party protesters marched on Washington, DC.†

As the protests unfolded, Fox News provided nonstop fair and balanced promotion of the events. Glenn Beck held a Tea Party fundraiser

---

* Jon Stewart's comment on Santelli's rant: "Wall Street is mad as hell! And they're not going to take it anymore! Unless by *it* you mean two trillion dollars in bailout money. *That* they will take." (Jon Stewart, "CNBC Financial Advice," *The Daily Show,* 4 Mar. 2009, http://www.thedailyshow.com/watch/wed-march-4-2009/cnbc-financial-advice.)

† As often happens when angry people march on Washington, a debate ensued over exactly how many angry people marched on Washington. Newspapers came up with 60,000 to 75,000. At the other end of the spectrum, Glenn Beck estimated 500,000, a number that

and reported live from a protest at the Alamo, where he gushed about the enthusiasm of the participants.[65] Sarah Palin keynoted the National Tea Party Convention, telling participants, "America is ready for another revolution."[66] The religious right also joined the fray, represented by Tony Perkins, the president of James Dobson's Family Research Council, and Dr. Rick Scarborough, a well-known Baptist preacher ("I'm not a Republican. I'm not a Democrat. I'm a Christocrat."[67]) Richard Viguerie even reemerged, calling the Tea Party movement "an unfettered new force of the middle class" and offering training courses for organizers.[68] Former representative Tom Tancredo represented the xenophobic wing. At one Tea Party convention, he blamed Obama's election on an alliance between elitist liberals and illegal immigrants, telling participants:

> The revolution has come. It was led by the cult of multiculturalism, aided by leftist liberals all over, who don't have the same ideas about America as we do . . . People who could not spell the word 'vote,' or say it in English, put a committed socialist ideologue in the White House. His name is Barack Hussein Obama.[69]

Without a single organization or leader running the show, and with every conservative ideologue in the country seeking to cash in on Tea Party fervor, the movement became a grab bag of right-wing doctrines and conspiracy theories. If there is a single unifying sentiment shared by all who claim allegiance to the Tea Parties, it is a profound hatred of government. And not just any government. The Tea Party supporters' unbridled hostility toward President Obama suggests that maybe, just maybe, their chief concern is not the power of government per se but the power of those who are currently running the government.

---

he called "really conservative." But Glenn Beck's idea of "really conservative" is a little different from what most people mean by "really conservative." (Joe Markman, "Crowd estimates vary wildly for Capitol march," *Los Angeles Times,* 15 Sep. 2009, http://articles.latimes.com/2009/sep/15/nation/na-crowd15; "Beck, Limbaugh run wild with estimates on size of 9/12 protests," *Media Matters,* 14 Sep. 2009, http://mediamatters.org/research/200909140047.)

After all, most of today's right-wing heroes had defended President George W. Bush's defiant expansions of executive power. America's founding fathers, so revered by today's Tea Parties, assigned specific powers to three separate branches of government with checks and balances to keep any one branch from gaining too much authority. But President Bush used executive signing statements and recess appointments to bypass the constitutional authority of Congress; and he used warrantless wiretaps, indefinite detentions, and secret military tribunals to bypass the constitutional authority of the Supreme Court. Nonetheless, in Bush's eight years in office, there were no Tea Parties, and the only people to express any fear of tyranny were liberals. But when President Obama suggested expanding the AmeriCorps volunteer program during his campaign—look out, America, here comes Hitler!

To be clear, there are legitimate political concerns mixed in with vitriol. Reasonable opposition to the health care bill, government spending, and other Democratic policies is good for the country. The problem lies in the way the right wing has been articulating its objections and motivating supporters. For the most part, Tea Party leaders have not been attacking the administration's policies on their merits; they have been demonizing Obama, the Democratic leadership, and liberal supporters with scare tactics modeled on the persecution formula. These tactics have reached a level of intensity and maliciousness that the country has not seen since the Red Scare.

Why does Obama inspire such fear? His race is certainly a factor, but the answer is more complex than simple racism. Today's Tea Parties are a far cry from George Wallace's race-driven campaigns. Indeed, one Tea Party–supported congressional nominee in North Carolina is African American, and the Tea Party–backed gubernatorial nominee in South Carolina is the daughter of Indian immigrants.

But there's also a reason that only 1 percent of Tea Party supporters are black and only 41 percent believe that Obama was born in the United States.[70] For over three decades, the right wing has been developing a powerful narrative according to which an alliance of liberal elites, racial minorities, and other marginal groups seek to persecute white, Christian conservatives. In the age of Fox News, talk radio, and conservative political dominance, that narrative is more popular than ever before. And at the very moment that this persecution mythology flooded into the mainstream, the government was taken over by Democrats and led by a man who by his skin color, his ancestry, his church, and his politics perfectly symbolizes the fearsome adversary that right-wing leaders have been warning their constituents against. Just as Sarah Palin personifies the righteous conservative victim, Barack Obama personifies the dangerous alliance between elites and minorities. That Obama's policies are no more liberal than Bill Clinton's and a good deal less liberal than Jimmy Carter's or even, in some ways, Richard Nixon's is irrelevant. The myth of Obama's secret revolutionary intentions is so entrenched that the right wing's view of the man has become completely detached from reality. No matter what he says or does, the Tea Party conservatives know him only as "the socialist ideologue in the White House."

Getting Rid of RINOs

As the Tea Parties mobilized against the enemy, the Republican Party once again sought to harness right-wing paranoia for political gain. A number of ultraconservative Republicans, like Sen. Jim DeMint (R-SC) and Representative Michelle Bachmann, have been outspoken proponents of the Tea Parties from the beginning, but the Republican leadership has also gotten involved. Republican National Committee chairman Michael Steele met with fifty Tea Party leaders in February 2010 after telling a radio host, "I'm a tea partier, I'm a town haller, I'm a grass-roots-er."[71] House minority leader John Boehner likewise insisted, "There really is no difference between what Republicans believe in and what the tea party activists believe in."[72] And in a speech to thousands of Tea Party protesters in Washington, he played the part to the hilt, declaring, "This [health care] bill is the greatest threat to freedom I have seen in the 19 years I have been here in Washington." In the crowd, someone carried a poster that read OBAMA TAKES HIS ORDERS FROM THE ROTHCHILDS [*sic*]. Others held up signs that portrayed Obama as Hitler, Mao Tse-Tung, and Little Black Sambo.[73]

In many ways, the GOP is indeed benefiting from paranoia about Obama. The Tea Parties have already helped the Republicans capture the late Ted Kennedy's Senate seat in Massachusetts, and they will aggressively mobilize their constituents to vote Republican in the November 2010 midterms. But they have exacted a price. In AD 376, the Roman emperor Flavius Julius Valens permitted the Visigoths to settle in Roman territory, seeing in them "a splendid recruiting ground for his army."[74] Two years later, the Visigoths decimated the Roman army and killed the emperor, eventually sacking Rome itself. Similarly, the Tea Partiers at the gates have launched yet another purge of insufficiently doctrinaire Republicans.

The first victim was Dede Scozzafava. The state Republican Party nominated her for a special election to fill a vacant congressional seat in upstate New York. But Scozzafava was a moderate who supported abortion rights and same-sex marriage. Even worse, conservative blogger Erick Erickson of RedState.com reported that she had been backed by (gasp!) ACORN. He wrote, "We need to make sure Scozzafava is destroyed at the polls. It would be bad news to have an ACORN backed candidate infiltrating the GOP in Congress."[75] Rush Limbaugh accused Scozzafava of "widespread bestiality . . . She has screwed every RINO in the country."[76] (Get it? R[H]INO.) Tea Party leaders and conservative Republicans, including Sarah Palin, endorsed Conservative Party candidate Doug Hoffman, and the moderate-hunting Club for Growth spent over a million dollars on his campaign.[77] Eventually, Scozzafava dropped out of the race and threw her support to the Democratic candidate, who narrowly defeated Hoffman. Hoffman conceded but then unconceded after concluding that the election was stolen by (gasp!) ACORN. He alleged on his campaign website, "Recent developments leave me to wonder who is scheming behind closed doors, twisting arms and stealing elections from the voters of NY-23 . . . We know this would not be the first time for the ACORN faithful to tamper with democracy."[78]

The next RINO to go was Governor Charlie Crist in a Florida Senate race. Crist is a pro-gun, anti-abortion, and anti–gay marriage Republican governor who had approval ratings in the high sixties as he entered the primary, and GOP leaders enthusiastically endorsed him. But Crist backed Obama's economic-stimulus plan and even went so far as to give Obama a hug—in public. For this treachery and a list of other violations of true conservatism, the right backed his challenger, Marco Rubio.[79] With Tea Party leaders endorsing Rubio and the omnipresent Club for Growth bankrolling him, Rubio surged ahead in the polls. Crist did the math and pulled out of the primary to run as an independent.

Crist is arguably a moderate Republican, at least by 2010 standards, but Sen. Bob Bennett (R-UT) is a genuine conservative by any standard. He has received top lifetime performance ratings from the NRA, National Right to Life, the Family Research Council, the American Conservative Union, Americans for Tax Reform, and the U.S. Chamber of Commerce.[80] But Bennett committed two grievous errors. One, he voted for the Troubled Asset Relief Program (TARP) to bail out teetering banks—along with thirty-three other Republican senators, not to mention President Bush who signed the bill and a crowd of economists who endorsed it. Two, Bennett cosponsored the Healthy Americans Act, a 2007 bipartisan health bill that was less comprehensive than the Democrats' 2010 health bill but still required individuals to purchase health insurance. As a result, the Tea Parties despised him, the Club for Growth attacked him, his opponents labeled him "Bailout Bob," and the Utah Republican Party denied him the nomination.[81]

Rep. Bob Inglis (R-SC) also voted for TARP. Worse, he voted to rebuke Representative Joe Wilson after he shouted, "You lie!" during Obama's State of the Union address. And worst of all, he told constituents at a rally to turn off the television when Glenn Beck came on. "You know why?" Inglis insisted. "He's trading on fear. You know what? Here's what I think. If you trade on fear, what you're doing is, you're not leading. You're just following fearful people." Inglis lost the Republican primary runoff by 71 percent to 29 percent.[82]

During the Scozzafava-Hoffman race, Rush Limbaugh predicted that in 2010 "conservatives are gonna finally get rid of RINOs. The American people have had enough."[83] But on the contrary, 2010 has already shown that the RINOs will never become extinct; they will simply be redefined. The Rockefeller Republicans that Paul Weyrich and Richard

Viguerie attacked in the 1970s were genuine liberals—pro-choice, pro–gun control, pro–affirmative action, pro-welfare liberals. But the Rockefeller Republicans are long gone, and the ranks of the once dominant moderates have been decimated; yet the right wing is still hunting RINOs and the Tea Parties are now ousting conservatives for not being conservative enough.

Sen. Jim DeMint (R-SC) disagrees with the notion that right-wing heretic hunters have shrunk the Republican "big tent." He explained, "We're seeing across the country right now that the biggest tent of all is the tent of freedom."[84] It's hard to argue with the man. After all, who doesn't love freedom? Well, except for Obama, Pelosi, ACORN, Van Jones, and all those other Marxists, of course. But there are plenty of other folks who love freedom, like Sharron Angle, the Club for Growth–backed Republican nominee in the Nevada Senate race who has spoken of refreshing the tree of liberty and "Second Amendment remedies" to government excess;[85] like Bill Randall, a Tea Party–backed Republican nominee for Congress in North Carolina who suggested that BP and the government colluded to create the oil leak in the Gulf of Mexico, suggesting, "Maybe they wanted it to leak";[86] and like Rand Paul, the Tea Party leader and Republican nominee in the Kentucky Senate race who has expressed reservations about the 1964 Civil Rights Act and concern about the ten-lane NAFTA superhighway.[87] The "tent of freedom" is big all right; it just has a wall on the left side. You might call it the big lean-to of freedom.

Some Democrats welcome the Republican heretic hunts, reassuring themselves that ultraconservatives like Rand Paul and Sharon Angle might win in the primaries, but they're too extreme to win general elections. This optimism has some basis. Doug Hoffman's candidacy in New York alienated moderates, so the Democratic candidate won in a Republican district. The same thing may happen in November 2010.

But even if Republican extremism hurts the party in the short run, history suggests that the long run is another matter. When the New Right purged Rockefeller Republican incumbents in 1978, Democrats captured Senate seats in Massachusetts and New Jersey. Nonetheless, in other parts of the country, ultraconservative ideology combined with the persecution narrative attracted voters, and by 1994 conservatives swept into power. Today's GOP now includes people like Michele Bachmann, Paul Broun, Steve King, Louie Gohmert, and Ron Paul. Even GOP "mavericks" like John McCain have turned right to insulate themselves from purges, endorsing positions that they might secretly detest and refusing to compromise with Democrats for fear of being labeled RINOs.

In short, as the Republican Party became more extreme, it became more powerful, and as it became more powerful, it became more extreme. The Democratic wins of 2006 and 2008 had much to do with unhappiness over the Iraq war, the collapsing economy, and Republican political scandals. When the wheel of American politics turns again, as it invariably does, the most conservative and paranoia-prone GOP in recent history may well come to power with a popular mandate to "take back the country."

The fact of the matter is that right-wing persecution mythology is extraordinarily compelling to many Americans, as has been repeatedly demonstrated by Paul Weyrich, Richard Viguerie, Jerry Falwell, Pat Buchanan, Rush Limbaugh, Bill O'Reilly, Glenn Beck, and Sarah Palin, to name a few. It has seduced millions into embracing right-wing ideology by convincing them that only the right appreciates them and defends their interests. It has mobilized the most fanatical voters in the country to turn out for elections in order to destroy imaginary enemies. It has obliterated the possibility of bipartisanship by pretending that compromise is treason and by punishing the "traitors." It has encouraged America's most violent to fulfill their fantasies of armed insurrection.

It has accomplished these ends by breaking the nation in half. In persecution politics, there is no America, one nation indivisible. There is Red America versus Blue America, Real America versus Berkeley and Washington, DC, Christians versus Secularists, Freedom-loving Patriots versus Despotic Marxists, Moose Burger Appreciators versus Arugula Munchers, Regular Schmos versus Liberal Elites, Black Radicals, Militant Homosexuals, and Subversive Illegals.

Once upon a time in America, there were genuine radical progressives who fomented class warfare by pitting the working class against the "robber barons." Such people are hard to find these days. Radical conservatives have supplanted them. For almost forty years, the right wing has been studiously developing a new class-consciousness. The new class is not delineated by income. It is vaguely circumscribed by a black cloud of animosity and hysteria that right-wing leaders have composed from assorted bits of race, religion, ideology, education, geography, and culture. Each year, it seeps deeper into the nation's bones. It will not be easy to excise this cancer.

14

WAKE UP, AMERICA

Breaking the Spell

You've got to slap the bully in the face.
—Maureen Dowd

IN THE SPRING OF 2010, President Obama gave an interview on the *CBS Early Show*. As he and coanchor Harry Smith casually strolled the White House grounds, Smith asked, "I've been out and about, listening to talk radio. The kindest of terms you're sometimes referred to out in America is a 'socialist.' The worst of which I've heard is called a 'Nazi.' Are you aware of the level of enmity that crosses the airwaves and that people have made part of their daily conversation about you?"

"Well, I mean, I think that when you listen to Rush Limbaugh or Glenn Beck, it's pretty apparent, and it's troublesome," Obama placidly replied with a creased brow. "But, keep in mind that there have been periods in American history where this kind of vitriol comes out. It happens often when you've got an economy that is making people more anxious, and people are feeling as if there is a lot of change that needs to take place . . . I don't get too worried when things aren't going as well because I know that over time these things turn."[1] If sincere, this opinion suggests a degree of complacency. Obama seems to regard the outbreak of right-wing paranoia as an unfortunate side effect of an economic recession that will eventually clear up on its own.

Democratic consultant James Carville went further, describing the paranoia of the Tea Parties as a political opportunity for the Democratic Party. After the tax day protests, he crowed, "Most Democrats I know are delighted by this . . . I think if anything it was harmless and damaging to Republicans."[2]

A Troublesome Movement

One of my purposes in writing this book has been to show these opinions to be false. Those wacky Tea Party candidates may hand an election or two to the Democrats, as Carville would like, but they will also send a few more paranoid Republican fearmongers to Washington, people who may one day become senior senators and representatives chairing powerful subcommittees. The thirty-five-year flowering of the paranoid right has certainly been damaging to Republicans but not in the way that Carville meant. While right-wing conservatives have subjugated the party of Lincoln, their victory has not transformed it into a fringe party doomed to perpetual minority status. Instead, the growth of persecution politics has brought the fringe ideas to the mainstream and turned far-right crackpots into electable candidates.

The long history also contradicts the administration's idea that the Tea Party hysteria is a product of the recession, a position that I challenged in my critique of the frustration-aggression theory. Glenn Beck and the Tea Parties did not suddenly emerge from the clouds like avenging angels of the financial crisis. They were carefully nurtured for years in a petri dish of fear and hostility. And as successive generations matured and spawned, the colony grew and eventually spilled out into American culture as a potent political force. Glenn Beck inherited the culture war from Bill O'Reilly who inherited from it from Rush Limbaugh who inherited it from Pat Buchanan who inherited it from George Wallace and the New Right.

I don't mean to suggest that the Tea Parties are the product of some vast right-wing conspiracy. I don't subscribe to the conspiracy theory of society, and to my knowledge, there is no secret club of omnipotent puppet masters who created Buchanan, Limbaugh, O'Reilly, Beck, and other practitioners of persecution politics. The various right-wing leaders have their own agendas and motivations, and their specific political philosophies often differ. But taken together, their ideas constitute a more or less coherent movement—what I have been calling persecution politics. As with any movement, this one incorporates substantial cross-germination of ideas and frequent alliances, but it is nonetheless a loosely interconnected movement, not an organized conspiracy.

That makes it no less "troublesome," however. The movement has proven both infectious and resilient. With each decade, the Republican Party has grown more conservative and its leaders more prone to demagoguery. Successive right-wing media stars have captured ever-larger audiences even as their messages have become more radical and more paranoid. Conservative grassroots campaigns keep getting bigger. Simply put, the growth of persecution politics is not slowing down; it is speeding up.

A New Class-Consciousness

The most disquieting aspect of the growth of persecution politics has been the formation of a new class-consciousness. In the last two chapters, I described how conservatives have sought to unify white Christian heterosexual blue-collar gun owners under the rubric of "conservatives," "traditionalists," and "real Americans." Their primary instrument for fusing what are really disparate socioeconomic classes is the persecution narrative. A Pentecostal farmer from South Carolina may not have much in common with a Mormon plumber from Colorado, but according to right-wing mythology they are united in suffering deprivation inflicted by the liberal elites, black radicals, and so on. You could call them brothers-in-oppression.

The production of class identity through persecution narratives is not a new phenomenon, and it is not always malignant. Genuine victims of social repression have often formed social identities around historical suffering. Centuries of slavery and discrimination inform African American culture and identity, American Indians share a history of persecution by European immigrants, and Jewish identity developed under two millennia of oppression in Europe. The persecution narratives that underlie the identities of oppressed communities can actually have beneficial effects by empowering individuals to unite in a battle for equality.

But when a dominant majority fabricates persecution and projects hostility onto a vulnerable minority, it's an entirely different story. In that case, the fantasies of persecution become rationalizations for discrimination or worse. Such rationalizations have contributed to some of the greatest horrors in modern history. Serbian national identity, for example, incorporates historical persecution by the Ottoman Turks two centuries ago. But the Ottomans are long gone, and Serbs dominated Yugoslavia's political class and armed forces in the twentieth century. Nonetheless, during the Balkan Wars, Serbian leaders cited Turkish aggression as an excuse for slaughtering Bosnian Muslims. At his war crimes trial, Bosnian Serb leader Radovan Karadzic called the violence "just and holy," declaring, "There were fundamentalist goals to change the destiny and appearance of the whole region . . . Their aim was 100 per cent power, as it was in the Ottoman Empire."[*3]

Similarly, in the 1930s the Nazis stoked German nationalist sentiments by claiming persecution by Jews. Josef Goebbels wrote in 1932:

> The Jew caused our problems, and lives from them. That is why we oppose the Jew as nationalists and as socialists. He has ruined our race, corrupted our morals, hollowed out our customs and broken our strength. We owe it to him that we today are the Pariah of the world.[4]

Such genocidal horrors are unimaginable in the United States, but right-wing leaders here have used identity politics to rationalize lesser forms of discrimination against minorities. George Wallace, for example, used the fantasy of Southern persecution by Washington elites to jus-

---

[*] "Serbian national identity." Pat Buchanan, who has questioned whether American involvement in World War II was "worth it," also hinted at a chilling sympathy with Serbian nationalists when he wrote, "As the Serbs are losing Kosovo, so we may have lost the Southwest." (Patrick Buchanan, "Was World War II worth it?" *WorldNetDaily*, 11 May 2005, http://www.wnd.com/news/article.asp?ARTICLE_ID=44210; Patrick J. Buchanan, *Day of Reckoning: How Hubris, Ideology, and Greed Are Tearing America Apart* (New York: Thomas Dunne Books, 2007): 10–11.

tify opposition to civil rights reforms. Likewise, conservative leaders from Anita Bryant to James Dobson have used the specter of Christian persecution to rationalize their opposition to civil rights protection for homosexuals.

The risk of discrimination is not the only problem. When a large portion of the population forms a class identity around perceived persecution by political opponents, it cuts a jagged gash in the nation's social fabric. Conservatives who are committed to the notion that liberals represent the interests of an alien class of people who hate and oppress "real Americans" tend to be averse to any kind of political compromise. Distrusting the intentions of their opponents, they assume that liberal policies are not well-intentioned proposals to help the country but merely schemes to disenfranchise and persecute white Christian conservatives: health care reform is a form of slavery reparations; same-sex marriage is an excuse to destroy families; season's greetings are an attempt to abolish Christmas. Such conservatives have also retaliated against their own political representatives who compromise with the enemy, regarding them not as moderates or mavericks but traitors to their class. If you are concerned about the partisan fervor that has turned Capitol Hill into a war zone, look to persecution politics for the culprit.

"The Jackass Quotient"

So what can we do about it? Some reformers have advocated structural solutions, arguing that the current primary system favors extremist candidates. Party primaries tend to draw the most passionate voters, who therefore gain a disproportionate voice in the selection of nominees.

One proposal for solving this problem is California Proposition 14, known as the Top Two Primaries Act. In June 2010, California passed a ballot measure that amended the state constitution to adopt an open primary system in which all registered voters can participate. The top two candidates then run against each other in the general election. Moderates like Governor Arnold Schwarzenegger championed the measure in the hope that it would give nonpartisan independents a greater say in selecting nominees for the general elections. *Newsweek*'s Jonathan Alter predicted that the initiative would reduce "the jackass quotient" among legislators.[5] (If it truly expels the jackasses from government, this initiative will count as the greatest political reform since the invention of democracy—which is not necessarily that high a bar.)

The trouble is that no one knows whether it will work as planned. The experts are divided, and as Gail Collins of the *New York Times* observed, "It's a good rule of thumb to figure that anything approved in a California referendum will make things worse."[6] Similar systems in the states of Louisiana and Washington have had inconclusive results. Washington State only implemented its system in 2008, but Louisiana, which used a runoff system for decades, has had no shortage of jackasses. For instance, David Duke, one of America's greatest living jackasses, finished a strong second in Louisiana's open primary for senator in 1990 and again in the 1991 governor's race.*

The problem with trying to address persecution politics through structural change is that the core problem is not structural but societal. Alan Abramowitz, a political science professor at Emory University, predicted that Proposition 14 "will have no effect on partisanship and polarization because the fundamental cause of these is that the electorate is deeply partisan and polarized. Tinkering with the election rules doesn't change that."[7] Moreover, as Duke's success in Louisiana demonstrated, a charismatic demagogue can win plenty of votes regardless of the electoral system if the voters are receptive to his tactics. And in an open primary, mainstream candidates may well divide the moderate vote, allowing extremist candidates with committed constituents to break through.

Another structural proposal to thwart the right wing is to create a more favorable environment for third parties. For instance, the distin-

---

* David Duke's campaign manager said that the problem with Duke's Senate candidacy was his obsessive anti-Semitism: "The Jews just aren't a big issue in Louisiana. We keep telling David, stick to attacking the blacks. There's no point in going after the Jews, you just piss them off and nobody here cares about them anyway." (Gideon Rachman, "Iran, David Duke and me," *Financial Times*, 12 Dec. 2006, http://blogs.ft.com/rachmanblog/2006/12/iran-david-dukehtml/.)

guished columnist and writer Thomas Friedman has called for "a Tea Party of the radical center" along with electoral changes that would support it.[8] To this proposal, I say: watch out what you wish for. Consider the special election in New York where the Conservative Party candidate knocked out the Republican nominee and came close to winning the election. If there were a viable third party in the 2010 election, it would almost certainly be a Tea Party—and not one that represents the radical center. Many foreign countries with strong multiparty democracies, like Austria, Switzerland, and Israel, have had significant problems with powerful xenophobic right-wing parties. Though such parties rarely win national elections, they have been able to take control of regional governments and to play kingmakers to the national governments, which gives them power to impose their demands. There is no reason to think that the United States is immune to such effects. Once again, persecution politics is a societal problem, and if we elevate third parties without having solved it, we risk further empowering the very people that we are trying to stop.

Thus, while America's electoral system is imperfect, and it's worth trying experiments like California's Proposition 14, such structural changes are no substitute for addressing the social phenomenon of persecution politics. Though the "jackass quotient" is certainly a problem, the real leaders of the social phenomenon are not the jackasses in Congress like Michele Bachmann and Steve King but the jackasses on television and talk radio like Bill O'Reilly, Glenn Beck, Pat Buchanan, and Rush Limbaugh.

"Nuances Don't Work on the Radio"

In order to combat the deleterious effects of the right-wing media, some Democratic legislators have proposed reinstating the Fairness Doctrine.[9] The Federal Communications Commission (FCC) established the doctrine in 1949 to address concerns that the three main television networks— NBC, ABC, and CBS—could abuse their near total control of broadcast television. The doctrine required broadcasters to cover controversial topics of public importance and to provide a reasonable opportunity for the presentation of opposing views. It remained in effect until the 1980s, when Ronald Reagan's FCC chief stopped enforcing it, and an FCC panel repealed it altogether in 1987.

Reagan's motives were most likely antiregulatory rather than partisan, and some conservatives even opposed the move out of concern that the media would refuse to air conservative views.[10] But the repeal of the Fairness Doctrine turned out to be a boon for conservative talk radio. Without the expense of offering competing viewpoints and the risk of losing their radio licenses for airing one-sided opinions, conservative talk radio stations thrived and almost singlehandedly revived the dying AM spectrum in the 1980s.[11] WABC in New York hired Rush Limbaugh in 1988, right after the Fairness Doctrine was repealed, and he skyrocketed into history with a horde of hate jockeys swarming in his wake.

Limbaugh's success raises a difficult question: why did conservatives take over talk radio rather than liberals? Liberals have radios with AM buttons, but conservative talk radio listeners outnumber liberals by 45 percent to 18 percent, and liberal attempts to replicate conservative talk shows have mostly failed miserably.[12] Air America, for example, declared bankruptcy in 2010 after stumbling through its six years of existence.

One reason may be demographics. Talk radio listeners are mostly middle-aged males, a big conservative constituency. But it's not clear whether the demographic of the audience is a cause or an effect of the popularity of right-wing radio.

I propose an alternative hypothesis: the provocative chunks of rage and fear that fit neatly into the talk radio format offer an ideal delivery mechanism for persecution politics, over which the right-wing reigns supreme. As Richard Viguerie explained:

> Talk radio is an emotional medium. It's something that people evaluate very quickly. You come to a conclusion about how you feel on something very quickly. It's a populist medium, and most of these gut populist issues are conservative issues, not entirely, but mostly . . . And also, lib-

erals deal with a lot of nuances. They say well on the one hand there's this, then we must consider this. And nuances don't work on the radio. Radio works for people who take strong positions and can do it in a few words—sound bytes if you would.[13]

In other words, talk radio is the ideal medium for simpleminded bull-shit, at which the paranoid right excels and pedantic liberals seem unable to master.

So all we have to do is reinstate the Fairness Doctrine, right? Conservative radio stations and Fox News will be forced to diversify or go bankrupt, and maybe Glenn Beck's head will explode when his paranoid fantasy comes true. Hooray, America is saved.

But it's not going to happen. First, the Democrats lack the votes in the face of stiff resistance to pass a bill that would require the FCC to reinstate it, and President Obama has twice indicated through spokespeople that he opposes reinstatement.[14] Second, even if the doctrine were restored, this genie is out of the bottle. A new fairness doctrine would create burdens for talk radio and cable news stations; they might cut marginal conservative programs, but headliners like Limbaugh and Beck are far too profitable to drop. Most stations would simply introduce a few liberal programs and take the hit on their lower ratings.

In addition, the rationale for reinstating the Fairness Doctrine is flawed. The original doctrine was never designed to block extreme political speech. If it had, it would have been unconstitutional on First Amendment grounds. When the doctrine was written, electronic media was a limited resource, so the FCC sought to ensure that Americans would have access to opposing views on controversial issues. But today, with hundreds of cable channels and millions of news sites, blogs, and podcasts, as well as satellite radio and Internet radio, the nation is awash in opposing views on controversial issues. Heck, we've got opposing views on noncontroversial issues. Even the Flat Earth Society has a web page and a Twitter account. (One of its tweets: "I finally have a follower. Hello, little follower. *4:45 PM Jun 4th via TwitBird iPhone.*")[15] And as broadband technologies improve, we will continue to receive more and more video and audio content over the Internet where the potential sources of information are for all intents and purposes limitless.

Thus, technology has demolished the Fairness Doctrine's raison d'être. To argue that Americans lack access to a diversity of perspectives would be disingenuous. In short, we cannot look to the government to suppress right-wing persecution paranoia because despite what Glenn Beck says, even progressives believe in the First Amendment.

Boycott Beck

But there is another way to restrain the media fearmongers. The Constitution gives the citizenry power that the government lacks. As any good conservative will agree, the government can't tell the people where to spend their money, and money, as they say, is power. We can use our freedom of choice in the marketplace to pressure the companies that offer platforms to the demagogues—media companies like Rupert Murdoch's News Corporation, which owns Fox News, and radio conglomerates like Clear Channel, whose subsidiaries host Glenn Beck, Rush Limbaugh, Sean Hannity, and Michael Savage. Regardless of the political affiliations of their owners, these companies' first allegiance is to the dollar, and effective advertising boycotts can at least push them to rein in the worst offenses of their right-wing stars.

After citizens launched a boycott against Beck's show because of his comment that President Obama hated white people, he has generally avoided inflammatory race rhetoric. Fox News chairman Roger Ailes has also reportedly talked to Beck about his "negative tone."[16] According to one of the boycott's promoters, *The Glenn Beck Program* lost over half its revenue during the first month of the boycott when sixty-two advertisers signed on. The number of boycotters soon grew to over two hundred in 2010.[17] While the program has found replacements for lost sponsors, these have been lower-tier advertisers who are likely paying less than what Fox News used to charge for the spots. And in the UK, *The Glenn Beck Program* has been running without any sponsors at all for months.[18] One sign that the boycotts are taking a toll has been the amount of airtime Glenn Beck has devoted to wallowing in conspiracy theories about the liberal plot to destroy him and begging his audience to help him through the crisis by signing up for his website's premium subscription service.[19]

To combat persecution politics, the boycott should be expanded beyond Glenn Beck. We should press companies to refuse to advertise on any program with inflammatory content, as Kraft Foods has done, or even to avoid Fox News entirely as long as it hosts such content, as Apple and Nestlé have done.[20] But let's also be clear about the objective. The goal must not be to eliminate conservative opinions or even biased journalism from the media but to curb the paranoid and intolerant rhetoric that many of the top conservative commentators have been promoting.

For the record, Fox News is not the only offender on cable. Pat Buchanan hosted CNN's *Crossfire* for years and is now a commentator on MSNBC. And in 2003, MSNBC offered a weekly show to Michael Savage—one of the nastiest bigots on the radio. MSNBC's president described Savage as "brash, passionate and smart" and promised that he would provide "compelling opinion and analysis with an edge."[21] A few months later, MSNBC fired the brash, passionate, smart Savage after he told a gay caller, "Oh, you're one of the sodomites. You should only get AIDS and die, you pig."[22]

Back at CNN, host Lou Dobbs began mixing anti-immigrant hostility with conspiracy theories about the North American Union, the Mexican Reconquista, and Obama's birth certificate. After outcries from liberals, Dobbs resigned in 2009 in order to, as he explained, "engage in constructive problem-solving, as well as to contribute positively to a better understanding of the great issues of our day."[23] CNN replaced him with Erick Erickson, a right-wing blogger who received renown for his gracious send-off to retiring Justice David Souter, delivered via Twitter: "The nation loses the only goat fucking child molester to ever serve on the Supreme Court."*[24]

---

* Erick Erickson also likes to fantasize about shooting federal employees who invade his doorstep. When Washington State banned dishwasher detergent containing phosphates, Erickson spoke of readying his gun to protect his property from "government apparatchiks coming to enforce nonsensical legislation," i.e., confiscate his dishwasher detergent. On another program, he threatened to scare off census workers with a shotgun. Perhaps he

The trouble is that inflammatory content sells. MSNBC hired Savage after circulating an internal memo warning that "our competitors are waving the flag at every opportunity."[25] Media outlets compete with one another to hire commentators who can out-flame those of their competitors, creating a vicious cycle of ever-increasing viciousness.* It's time for the American people to apply the brakes to the cycle using the power of the marketplace. Just say no to media thugs.

Freedom of Speech

Right-wing leaders object to the use of such tactics against corporations, of course (unless the corporations are denigrating the spirit of Christmas, in which case they deserve it). For example, Glenn Beck warned, "Our rights are slipping away. They are trying to squelch free speech through mockery, intimidation, intimidation of advertisers, the Internet—anyway they can."[26]

But let's talk about freedom of speech for a moment. In their zeal to present examples of conservative persecution, right-wing leaders often conflate criticism of their opinions with government censure. Recall Bill O'Reilly's complaint that media critics violated his First Amendment rights—"I don't care about the law. My rights were violated here because they tried to punish me for my speech. It's happening all over the place." O'Reilly got it backward, however. Government censorship of his opinions would violate the First Amendment; criticism of his opinions is *protected* by the First Amendment.

---

should just put up a sign in his yard: BEWARE OF BLOGGER! It might help with the Jehovah's Witnesses too. (Erick Erickson, "At What Point Do People Revolt?" 31 Mar. 2009, http://www.redstate.com/erick/2009/03/31/at-what-point-do-people-revolt/; "CNN's Erickson: I'll '[p]ull out my wife's shotgun' if they try to arrest me for not filling out the American Community Survey," *Media Matters*, 1 Apr. 2010, http://mediamatters.org/mmtv/201004010050.)

* "Vicious cycle." In theory, the cycle can also spin to the left, and liberal commentators like MSNBC's Keith Olbermann have turned up the heat since the mild days of Phil Donahue. Olbermann's rhetoric hardly compares to the savage paranoia of his right-wing opponents, but should liberal paranoia rise sometime in the future, the solution should be the same as I've advocated against conservative media shows.

Such criticism is not only protected, it is important for a healthy society. In addition to laws and moral and religious standards, fear of stigmatization keeps people from violating societal norms. Taken to an extreme, social control can result in a repressive society, but that does not mean that all social control is repressive. Indeed, it's impossible for a society to function without it. We've all grown up within a rich network of social norms that proscribe a wide range of behaviors, from promise breaking to offensive language to public nose picking. While it would be repressive and unhealthy to stigmatize political opinions, stigmatizing racism and paranoia are essential for a just society and a functioning democracy.

Right-wing leaders have been steadily chipping away at such stigmas in several ways. First, they employ subtle and ambiguous language to indirectly skirt America's political taboos. They attack health care "reparations," for example, rather than saying, "Undeserving black people will steal white people's benefits." Similarly, if Glenn Beck were to baldly present his conspiracy theories as fact, he would be dismissed by everyone as a paranoid lunatic and drummed back out to the fringe. So instead he employs indirect language. He speculates and describes worst case scenarios.

Second, right-wing leaders have been gradually pushing the limits of permissible mainstream discourse. Wayne LaPierre shocked the nation in 1995 when he called ATF agents "jack-booted government thugs." But with media stars and members of Congress now comparing Obama to Hitler, LaPierre's language seems tame and a little quaint by comparison.

Third, the right wing has increased its constituency, its media presence, and its political muscle, all of which boost the perceived credibility of its paranoia. When the House majority leader alleges a Soros-led conspiracy to oust him, and one of America's favorite media figures is Glenn Beck, you know that paranoia has hit the mainstream.

Thus, if we want to control the wild growth of persecution politics, the American community must banish the worst excesses of the right to the fringe. We must use our freedom of speech to fortify our society's faltering stigmas by declaring that the right wing's fantasies of persecution have no place in American politics or national dialogue.

Connecting with Others

The psychological nature of persecution politics actually makes that job easier. As we've seen, right-wing persecution paranoia is a form of rationalization. Those who indulge in political paranoia do so not because of any reliable evidence but because of the psychological benefits that it offers. The powerful stories that they hear on Fox News and talk radio offer them a fantasy world that turns their bigotries into virtues and transforms ordinary men and women into heroes and heroines of the republic. The stories scare the hell out of them, and it feels great. Often paranoid believers go to great lengths to preserve their convenient fantasies, filtering out contrary information and inhibiting their critical faculties. Their desire for righteousness trumps their discomfort with self-deception.

But here's the key. The desire for righteousness may lead people to suppress the psychological discomfort of self-deception, but it cannot completely eliminate it. Most of the Americans who fall for the right-wing conspiracy theories are not insane. Their grasp of reality is firm enough for them to function perfectly well in ordinary life. Their political paranoia is an exception to the way that they normally make sense of the world. On some level, they know that they're lying to themselves, and that doesn't feel so good. The fantasies produce cognitive dissonance between what they want to believe and what they know to be true.

And so, like the UFO cultists that Leon Festinger studied, the right-wing conspiracists seek affirmation from others. They turn on their televisions and radios to let the soothing scare stories of Glenn Beck and Rush Limbaugh reassure them that their dark fantasies are real. They go to the Internet to read angry bloggers telling them that what they fear is true. They attend Tea Parties to find kindred spirits who also believe that Obama is a fascist Marxist from Kenya, much as the previous generation of paranoid conservatives once met in local restaurants to warn one another of the peril of secular humanism. Glenn Beck himself described the Tea Partiers' hunger for mutual reinforcement:

This is an opportunity for people to connect with each other and to see that they're not alone and to see, "Oh, my gosh. Oh, my gosh, I didn't know you—really, you believe in this, too?" And be able to connect with each other.[27]

Of course, we cannot and should not try to interfere with whom people speak to or what they watch, read, and listen to, but we can undercut these affirmation strategies by clearly and adamantly contradicting and condemning the right wing's paranoid beliefs— through mockery, condemnation, boycotts, and other challenges. Bill O'Reilly and Glenn Beck are so sensitive to criticism because they and their listeners really do care what the rest of the country thinks. External criticism threatens to upend the carefully laid table of persecution politics just as the guests are sitting down to gorge. Criticism tugs at believers' suppressed awareness that their paranoid beliefs are only fantasy and that their heroes are feeding them lies. Thus, criticism can expose the charlatanry and prod the paranoia back into the dark corner of society where it once lurked.

"Every Good Christian"

That makes it sound easy. For those on the left, criticism is easy enough. Many liberals have already pilloried the Tea Parties, Fox News, and talk radio. But liberals aren't the ones who really matter. They're the enemy. The right wing can easily fold their attacks into their paranoid dreams by dismissing these efforts as liberal attempts to suppress their freedom of speech.

Moreover, one segment of society cannot on its own establish social stigmas that the whole community will respect. If the majority of conservatives refuse to condemn the tactics of the right wing, censure from the left will not produce any nationwide stigma.

Thus, for criticism from liberals to be effective, it must influence at least some conservatives, and accomplishing that is extremely difficult.

For starters, liberals first need to strip partisan overtones from their criticism. We must try to separate conservative political positions from the ugly tactics of persecution politics and to distinguish the worst of the demagogues from the average Republican voter. There are plenty of reasonable Republicans who oppose abortion or support fiscal discipline yet disdain the paranoia of the right wing. If we lump them all together as Christian fanatics or Republican bad guys—"Repuglicans" in the left-wing vernacular—then we alienate potential allies.

The paranoid right likes to pretend that "real Americans" are on their side—that every plumber, farmer, and small business owner between Washington, DC, and Berkeley is an indignant victim of the liberal elites. This story is as mythical as every other paranoid fantasy. Far from being "real Americans," Glenn Beck and Sarah Palin represent a politically powerful minority whose paranoid and divisive beliefs are antithetical to America's proud culture and the visions of the founding fathers. We need the real real Americans, regardless of their religious faiths and political temperaments, to repudiate the men and women who howl hateful ideas in their names. As Barry Goldwater once said in his later years, "Every good Christian ought to kick Falwell right in the ass."[28]

One liberal leader who has not exercised his influence to combat the growth of persecution politics is the man who has the most to lose from its success—President Barack Obama. In the fall of 2009, the White House made a show of announcing a new "aggressive" response strategy to combat negative media coverage, particularly from Fox News. The aggressive response strategy mostly consisted of a series of disparaging comments by White House communications director Anita Dunn about how Fox News is a "wing of the Republican Party." The news media responded to the aggressive response strategy by endlessly analyzing whether it was a prudent political move or might instead make Obama look petty—as if they'd never heard a politician criticize the media before. Fox News responded to the aggressive response strategy by trying to explain the difference between its news reporters and its opinion shows—without much success.* Glenn Beck responded to the aggressive response strategy by exposing Anita Dunn's secret reverence for Chairman Mao. A month later, Dunn resigned—for family reasons, according to the White House—and that was the end of the aggressive response strategy.[29]

With all due respect to the White House political strategists, it will require more than a few snide comments from the White House communications director to change public opinion of Fox News. Moreover, Fox News's journalistic pretenses are not the most pressing issue, and the problem of persecution politics is bigger than Fox in any case. It extends to talk radio, the Tea Parties, religious leaders, conservative political organizations, and many Republican leaders. Obama can avoid the perception of a grudge match with any particular individuals or organizations by tackling the broader national problem. He and his representatives should communicate to the nation as a whole to deliver his vision of a better America and to challenge those who seek to divide it through fear and hate. They should do so forcefully and repeatedly, using the authority of the president to spur a public discussion about America's values and political problems. (I also recommend that they leave the snarky barbs to the bloggers and comedy shows with no presidential gravitas to lose.)

A Few Good Men

Nonetheless, while Obama and other liberal leaders do have some influence, the only individuals who truly have the power to wean the right from its regular diet of persecution politics are conservatives. For liberals, criticizing right-wing paranoia is painless and pragmatic, but for those on the right, challenging the demagogues bears a heavy cost. We've seen

---

* "Opinion shows." Jon Stewart helpfully tried to clarify: "For the audience here, let me help you out—because it does get confusing. The three hours you spend in the morning with *Fox & Friends*: not news. Your 4 o'clock to 5 o'clock post–tea and crumpets Neil Cavudo break: not news. The 5 o'clock to 6 o'clock emotional whirlwind and national group therapy session that is Glenn Beck: not even close to news. O'Reilly, Hannity, van Susteren-en-en-en: not news. This is according to Fox News. Those people—the ones featured in promos about how fair and balanced Fox News is—are not news. These people—otherwise known as the only people you ever think of when you think of Fox News—are not news. They are Fox 'opinutainment.'" (Jon Stewart, "For Fox Sake!" *The Daily Show*, 29 Oct. 2009, http://www.thedailyshow.com/watch/thu-october-29-2009/for-fox-sake-.)

incumbent Republican congressmen go down for offenses ranging from voting for TARP to telling constituents to shut off Glenn Beck.

A few other conservative leaders who have dared to challenge the hegemony of the right-wing media have wilted almost immediately after furious blowback. In March 2009, Michael Steele tried to marginalize Rush Limbaugh by dismissing him as an "entertainer" and calling his rhetoric "incendiary" and "ugly." Forty-eight hours later, Steele apologized and wrote, "I respect Rush Limbaugh, he is a national conservative leader, and in no way do I want to diminish his voice."[30]

Rep. Phil Gingrey (R-GA) didn't even last twenty-four hours after belittling right-wing media stars. He too apologized and wrote, "Rush Limbaugh, Sean Hannity, Newt Gingrich, and other conservative giants are the voices of the conservative movement's conscience. Every day, millions and millions of Americans—myself included—turn on their radios and televisions to listen to what they have to say, and we are inspired by their words and by their determination."[31]

Even John McCain, the courageous war hero and proud maverick of the Republican Party, is running scared. You won't find him battling the "agents of intolerance" these days. Instead, he has endorsed Arizona's harsh anti-immigration law in order to fend off a primary challenge from the right. "I never considered myself a maverick," he told *Newsweek* in 2010. "I consider myself a person who serves the people of Arizona to the best of his abilities."[32]

Rep. Bob Inglis (R-SC), who lost his seat in the 2010 primary, explained, "We're being driven as herd by these hot microphones—which are like flame throwers—that are causing people to run with fear and panic, and Republican members of Congress are afraid of being run over by that stampeding crowd."[33]

But there are a few conservatives who have shown more guts, though perhaps not people with whom many are familiar. Writer David Frum, for example, has sterling conservative credentials. He has been an editor of conservative publications like the *National Review* and the *Wall Street Journal*'s editorial page, and he has worked for conservative think tanks like the American Enterprise Institute. He was also a speechwriter for George W. Bush and has been credited with coining the term Axis of Evil.[34] The *Wall Street Journal* lauded him as "one of the leading political commentators of his generation."[35] Once a frequent guest on *The O'Reilly Factor,* Frum has long been a staunch military hawk and a consistent advocate of small government.

But he despises the tactics of persecution politics, which he regards as disastrous for the nation and for the Republican Party. When John McCain selected Sarah Palin as his running mate, Frum called the decision "a huge mistake."[36] He later said of Palin, "Her divisiveness is not just within the country, it's divisive within the party." He also wrote a *Newsweek* article titled "Why Rush Is Wrong" and called Glenn Beck's success "a product of the collapse of conservatism as an organized political force, and the rise of conservatism as an alienated cultural sensibility."[37] After the health care bill passed, Frum chastised Republicans for obstructing when they should have been compromising. Calling the bill's passage the Republican's "Waterloo," he wrote:

> We followed the most radical voices in the party and the movement, and they led us to abject and irreversible defeat. There were leaders who knew better, who would have liked to deal. But they were trapped. Conservative talkers on Fox and talk radio had whipped the Republican voting base into such a frenzy that deal-making was rendered impossible. How do you negotiate with somebody who wants to murder your grandmother? Or—more exactly—with somebody whom your voters have been persuaded to believe wants to murder their grandmother?[38]

Most compellingly, Frum has hammered at the very foundations of persecution politics, eloquently explaining how the rise of Rush Limbaugh, Glenn Beck, and Sarah Palin has turned the conservative movement on its head. He wrote:

> Back in the 1960s and 1970s, we'd been fighting to protect the common-sense instincts of ordinary people from elite interference. Now, in the Terri Schiavo euthanasia case, with stem cell research, on gay rights issues, it was we who had become the interfering elite, against a society that was reaching its own new equilibrium. Of course, that's not how

conservatives saw it. We saw a country divided in two, red states and blue, NASCAR vs. NPR, real America against the phonies in the cities. A movement that had begun as an intellectual one now scornfully pooh-poohed the need for people in government to know anything much at all . . . Instead, we rallied to Sarah Palin and Joe the Plumber.[39]

For these opinions, Frum has become a pariah within his own party who is regularly trashed on the right-wing blogs. You won't find Frum on Fox News these days. The only media commentators who seek his opinion want to ask him about his critical views of the conservative movement. The *Wall Street Journal,* which had once lavished such praise on its former editor, editorialized, "Mr. Frum now makes his living as the media's go-to basher of fellow Republicans, which is a stock Beltway role. But he's peddling bad revisionist history that would have been even worse politics."[40] The American Enterprise Institute ended Frum's fellowship days after his widely publicized (and denigrated) Waterloo column. While its president denied that the dismissal had anything to do with Frum's article, the timing led analysts—and Frum himself—to conclude otherwise.[41]

Charles Johnson is another brave critic. He founded Little Green Footballs, one of the earliest and most popular conservative blogs, which served as an inspiration to many of the right-wing bloggers who followed him. During the Bush administration, Johnson aggressively promoted the Iraq War and Bush's antiterrorism policies. But in 2009, he began to criticize the paranoid right, including Glenn Beck, Ron Paul, and some of the popular bloggers whose careers he had once fostered.[42] Finally, in November 2009, he officially split with the right, citing the growth of racism, homophobia, conspiracy theories, hate speech, and other hallmarks of persecution politics. He wrote, "The American right wing has gone off the rails, into the bushes, and off the cliff. I won't be going over the cliff with them."[43]

Worse than RINOs, Frum and Johnson have not violated conservative principles; they have publicly challenged the right wing's paranoid fantasies. As conservatives who cannot be easily dismissed as members of the liberal elite, they represent the greatest threat to the hegemony of the right wing, for their disaffirmations of the right's fabrications feed the small flame of doubt burning quietly in the hearts of the believers. If there were more conservatives like David Frum and Charles Johnson, the tiny flame could bloom into a wildfire, and the whole brittle paper world of right-wing persecution politics would collapse into ashes.

But there are precious few like Frum and Johnson these days. If Republicans have any hope of rescuing their party and the country from the paranoia that has engulfed it, the wobbly-kneed critics need some help. When Michael Steele and other conservatives muster the courage to take on the right wing, their colleagues need to get their backs. When Rush Limbaugh retaliates, someone has to say, "Steele is right. Limbaugh's rhetoric is ugly and incendiary, and he does not lead our party." The more people who stand up, the harder it will be for the right to force Republican critics to apologize and genuflect, the harder it will be for paranoid conservatives to cling to their precious fantasies of persecution, and the harder it will be for demagogues of the right to exert their influence on the political culture and the government of the nation.

"Scorn and Derision"

To see how quickly the precarious edifice of political paranoia can crumble when determined leaders from both ends of the political spectrum start whacking at it, we need only look to our history.

In January 1962, four of the founding fathers of modern conservatism and a public relations consultant met in a hotel room in Palm Beach, Florida, to discuss Senator Barry Goldwater's plan to run for president. They included Senator Goldwater; William F. Buckley Jr., founder of the *National Review;* William Baroody, head of the American Enterprise Institute (the think tank that would eject David Frum decades later); Russell Kirk, author of *The Conservative Mind;* and Jay Hall the PR guy.[44]

One of the chief topics of discussion was the John Birch Society (JBS). The JBS had been growing rapidly and seducing conservative leaders across the country. From 1,500 members at the beginning of 1960, it had attracted between 60,000 and 100,000 members by the end of 1961.[45] The five men in Palm Beach despised the paranoia of JBS founder Robert Welch, who had accused Dwight Eisenhower of being a communist agent. They were also concerned that the JBS's support of Goldwater would discredit his candidacy. So they came up with a plan to marginalize it, dividing up the responsibilities. William F. Buckley Jr. promised to expose Welch to "scorn and derision" in the *National Review*. Russell Kirk said, "I'll just say, if anybody gets around to asking me, that the guy is loony and should be put away."[46]

In the next issue of the *National Review,* Buckley published a five-thousand-word excoriation of Welch in which he encouraged conservatives not to "acquiesce quietly" to Welch's wrongheaded ideas. Senator Goldwater then published a response in the subsequent issue, writing, "I believe the best thing Mr. Welch could do to serve the cause of anti-Communism in the United States would be to resign . . . We cannot allow the emblem of irresponsibility to attach to the conservative banner."[47]

After Goldwater had lost his presidential bid, the *National Review* continued to attack Robert Welch and the JBS. In an even more scathing 1965 article, Buckley assailed Welch's "conspiratorial mania," "paranoid and unpatriotic drivel," and "psychosis of conspiracy."[48]

In the meantime, Richard Hofstadter published "The Paranoid Style in American Politics" in *Harper's* magazine. The essay described the tactics and characteristics of paranoid political movements and singled out the JBS as the most prominent contemporary proponent of the paranoid style.

Between the efforts of Buckley, Goldwater, and Hofstadter, the JBS became associated with pernicious extremism and outlandish paranoia. For instance, the California Fact-Finding Subcommittee on Un-American Activities had praised the JBS in 1963, but two years later the same subcommittee declared that the organization had attracted "a lunatic fringe" and "emotionally unstable people."[49] The JBS's membership evaporated, and it vanished into the political fringe where it has remained ever since. Almost. In 1997, Glenn Beck invited JBS spokesman Sam Antonio onto his CNN show to discuss Antonio's views of the government conspiracy to smuggle drugs across the Mexican border. "Sam, I have to tell you," Beck professed, "When I was growing up, the John Birch Society, I thought they were a bunch of nuts, however, you guys are starting to make more and more sense to me."[50]

"No Sense of Decency"

But even at its height, the JBS never reached an audience even close to that of Glenn Beck, so it was relatively easy to marginalize. For a more commensurate comparison, we need to step back one more decade to the last great epidemic of political paranoia in the United States. In the early 1950s, the country was wrought with anxiety over communism. The Soviets had acquired nuclear weapons, Mao Tse-tung had taken over China, and the Korean War threatened to expand communism around the globe. In addition, a series of high-profile spy cases, including those of Alger Hiss and the Rosenbergs, provoked fears of subversion from within.

Sen. Joe McCarthy (R-WI) harnessed these growing anxieties to convert the anticommunist paranoia that had been simmering on the fringe into a full-blown epidemic of paranoia. Across the nation, governments, companies, schools, and other organizations imposed loyalty oaths, inquisitions, and blacklists. Conservatives attacked unions and civil rights leaders for supposedly collaborating with the Soviet Union. Careers were destroyed, books were banned, and anti-intellectualism ran rampant.

As has been happening today, Republicans encouraged the paranoia for political gain. Joe McCarthy often campaigned for his colleagues, and historians have credited his anticommunist crusade with the defeat of several prominent Democrats in the 1950 elections. Dwight Eisenhower despised McCarthy, but that didn't stop him from campaigning with him through Wisconsin in pursuit of the presidency. Once in office, Eisenhower cut his ties to McCarthy but refused to publicly condemn him, concluding that "nothing will be so effective in combating his particular kind of trouble-making as to ignore him."*⁵¹

But ignoring McCarthy didn't help. Nor did Eisenhower's attempts to co-opt McCarthy's platform by purging federal employees in a loyalty campaign. Instead, the dismissals encouraged anticommunist Republicans to boast loudly of the 1,456 "subversives" that the government had sacked.⁵² Like today's paranoid right, the anticommunists' success in intimidating and marginalizing critics affirmed their paranoia and emboldened them to spin even more outrageous conspiracy theories.

And that would finally prove their undoing. For when Joe McCarthy expanded his attacks to the U.S. Army and the nation's churches, he finally provoked the one force that could stop him: public condemnation.

At first, the army tried to appease McCarthy, which only encouraged him to humiliate a celebrated general in subcommittee hearings. And after a lunch meeting with Secretary of the Army Robert Stevens, McCarthy crowed that Stevens "could not have given in more abjectly if he had got down on his knees."⁵³

Finally, in 1954 the army fought back, accusing McCarthy of improperly pressuring military officials to give an enlisted former aide preferential treatment. The U.S. Army–McCarthy hearings were broadcast on national television, and Joe McCarthy did not come off well. After weeks of McCarthy's bullying and belligerent disruptions, the army's attorney, Joseph Welch, issued his famous rhetorical masterstroke as McCarthy sought to vilify one of his colleagues: "Let us not assassinate this lad further, Senator. You've done enough. Have you no sense of decency, sir, at long last? Have you left no sense of decency?"⁵⁴

---

* "Ignore him." There was one brave exception to the Republican wall of silence. In 1950, Margaret Chase Smith, a freshman senator from Maine, showed a good deal more courage than her political heirs, Olympia Snowe and Susan Collins. In a fifteen-minute address titled "A Declaration of Conscience," she protested that the Senate had been "debased to the level of a forum of hate and character assassination."

(Senator Margaret Chase Smith, "A Declaration of Conscience," *United States Senate,* 1 Jun. 1950, http://www.senate.gov/artandhistory/history/minute/A_Declaration_of_Conscience.htm.)

While the hearings proceeded, the famous war correspondent Edward R. Murrow assailed McCarthy from another direction. Liberal journalists had criticized McCarthy's tactics since 1950, but none commanded the audience and widespread respect that Murrow did. In March 1954, Murrow hosted a program titled "A Report on Senator Joseph R. McCarthy" that exposed McCarthy's ugliest tactics and hypocrisies. At the end of the program, he concluded:

This is no time for men who oppose Senator McCarthy's methods to keep silent . . . The actions of the junior Senator from Wisconsin have caused alarm and dismay amongst our allies abroad, and given considerable comfort to our enemies. And whose fault is that? Not really his. He didn't create this situation of fear; he merely exploited it—and rather successfully. Cassius was right. "The fault, dear Brutus, is not in our stars, but in ourselves."[55]

The words of Joseph Welch and Edward Murrow pulled the curtain from the Great and Terrible Wizard of Wisconsin, exposing a cruel, deceitful, manipulative little man. As if awakened from a daze, Americans across the political spectrum finally began to speak up. Though McCarthy was tremendously popular among Catholics, Chicago bishop Bernard Shell condemned him, calling on Americans to "cry out against the phony anti-Communism that mocks our way of life, flouts our traditions and democratic procedures and our sense of fair play, feeds on the meat of suspicion and grows great on the dissension among Americans."[56] Sen. Ralph Flanders (R-VT) proposed to strip McCarthy of his committee chairmanships. A small-town Republican newspaper editor from Wisconsin launched a Joe Must Go campaign. The Republican governor of Indiana urged Eisenhower to "discipline the recalcitrants." A Republican congressional nominee from Ohio warned the White House that "'McCarthyism' has become a synonym for witch-hunting, star-chamber methods and the denial of . . . civil liberties."[57]

On December 2, 1954, the Senate voted to censure McCarthy. The vote was 67-22, with twenty-two Republicans voting for censure. The wave of paranoia that had swept the nation collapsed almost immediately. The

Red Scare was over, and McCarthy's name would forever be remembered
in infamy.

Almost. In her book *Treason: Liberal Treachery from the Cold War
to the War on Terrorism,* Ann Coulter wrote:

> The myth of "McCarthyism" is the greatest Orwellian fraud of our times.
> Liberals are fanatical liars, then as now. The portrayal of Sen. Joe
> McCarthy as a wild-eyed demagogue destroying innocent lives is sheer
> liberal hobgoblinism. Liberals weren't hiding under the bed during the
> McCarthy era. They were systematically undermining the nation's abil-
> ity to defend itself, while waging a bellicose campaign of lies to blacken
> McCarthy's name. Liberals denounced McCarthy because they were
> afraid of getting caught, so they fought back like animals to hide their
> own collaboration with a regime as evil as the Nazis.[58]

(Perhaps Coulter is right. Let us not assassinate this man further, liberals. We have done enough. Have we no sense of decency, at long last?)

But in the magical land of persecution politics, there are no decent
liberals, just as there are no wicked conservatives. McCarthy was a conservative, so he must have been a virtuous American patriot ruthlessly
persecuted by the sadistic liberal elite. Any evidence that contradicts
the core storyline is a lie, an intrigue, a trick. When you live in a fantasy, you cannot permit any flaws to mar the perfect surface of your
beautiful, frightening little world. Because if you should find a crack,
if you should start to question, if you should indulge those tiny nag-
ging doubts—it could shatter all to pieces, and you could find yourself
on the floor surrounded by shards of broken glass and fake plastic
snowflakes in a cold, confusing world with no good guys or bad guys
or happily-ever-afters.

There will always be a small core of true believers who will never
relinquish their fantasies. But most people who have fallen prey to persecution politics have simply been swept up in the wave of social hysteria. They rely on a constant flow of affirmation from their leaders and
peers to keep their fantasy worlds intact. If that stream should run dry
or go sour, the spell will inevitably break.

So if we wish to break the spell, we will have to find a way to dam that stream. We will need to find the Joseph Welchs and Edward R. Murrows of the modern day with voices too loud to be ignored. We will need to persuade the millions of Americans who aren't using their voices to speak up and condemn the paranoia. We will need to join together and say as one nation that the men and women who have produced these fantasies are not heroes; they do not represent the vision of our founding fathers; they do not speak for us. We are the real Americans.

To paraphrase my good friend Glenn Beck: Wake up, America. It's time to take our country back.

NOTES

Preface

1. Noel Sheppard, "Pat Buchanan and Rachel Maddow Debate Sonia Sotomayor," *NewsBusters,* 17 Jul. 2009, http://newsbusters.org/blogs/noel-sheppard/2009/07/17/pat-buchanan-rachel-maddow-debate-sonia-sotomayor.

2. Rush Limbaugh, "America's Piñata Strikes Back: We Won't Shut Up on Sotomayor, May 29, 2009," *The Rush Limbaugh Show,* 29 May 2009, http://www.rushlimbaugh.com/home/daily/site_052909/content/01125106.guest.html; "'Countdown with Keith Olbermann for Wednesday, July 29," 29 Jul. 2009, http://www.msnbc.msn.com/id/32218739/ns/msnbc_tv-countdown_with_keith_olbermann/.

3. David Limbaugh, *Persecution: How Liberals Are Waging War Against Christians* (Washington, DC: Regnery Publishing, Inc., 2003): 235, 330.

4. Mike Allen, "GOP Congressman Calls Democrats Anti-Christian," *Washington Post,* 21 Jun. 2005, http://www.washingtonpost.com/wp-dyn/content/article/2005/06/20/AR2005062001194.html.

5. Rachel Maddow, "Sherrod story demonstrates 'scare white people' tactic," *MSNBC,* 21 Jul. 2010, http://www.msnbc.msn.com/id/21134540/vp/38353636.

Chapter 1. How Bill O'Reilly Saved Christmas

1. Bill O'Reilly, "Walter Cronkite, Barack Obama, and the American Media," *The O'Reilly Factor,* 21 July 2009, transcript, http://www.foxnews.com/story/0,2933,534213,00.html.

2. "Bill O'Reilly Calls Himself 'T-Warrior,'" *ABC News,* 20 Sept. 2006, http://abcnews.go.com/2020/story?id=2465303.

3. Bill O'Reilly, *Culture Warrior* (New York: Broadway Books, 2006): 5.

4. Bill O'Reilly, "Christmas Under Siege: The Big Picture," *The O'Reilly Factor,* 24 Dec. 2004, transcript, http://www.foxnews.com/story/0,2933,140742,00.html.

5. Bill O'Reilly, "Take Your Christmas and Stuff It," *The O'Reilly Factor,* 9 Dec. 2004, transcript, http://www.billoreilly.com/column?pid=18833.

6. "FOX hypes stories to claim 'Christmas Under Siege,'" *Media Matters,* 10 Dec. 2004, http://mediamatters.org/research/200412100006.

7. "O'Reilly: 'There's a very secret plan . . . to diminish Christian philosophy in the U.S.A.,' *Media Matters,* 30 Nov. 2005, http://mediamatters.org/mmtv/200511300007.

8. "Thoroughly debunked, O'Reilly dreams up new, apparently sinister Soros-Media Matters link," *Media Matters,* 4 May 2007, http://mediamatters.org/research/200705040008.

9. "O'Reilly on ACLU: 'I think they're a terrorist group . . . I think they're terrorists,'" *Media Matters,* 3 Mar. 2005, http://mediamatters.org/research/200503030007.

10. Bill O'Reilly, "Christmas Under Siege: The Big Picture," *The O'Reilly Factor,* 14 Dec. 2004, transcript, http://www.foxnews.com/story/0,2933,140742,00.html.

11. "O'Reilly promised to 'bring horror' to alleged 'anti-Christian forces' who oppose Christmas," *Media Matters,* 7 Dec. 2005, http://mediamatters.org/research/200512070010.

12. Pat Buchanan, "Christianophobia," *World Net Daily* 12 Dec. 2004, http://www.wnd.com/news/article.asp?ARTICLE_ID=41900.

13. Rev. Jerry Falwell, "The impending death of Christmas?: Part 2," *World Net Daily,* 13 Dec. 2004, http://www.wnd.com/news/article.asp?ARTICLE_ID=41904.

14. "Christmas Under Siege . . ." *Hannity & Colmes,* 16 Dec. 2004, transcript, http://www.foxnews.com/story/0,2933,141774,00.html.

15. Judi McLeod, "Guardian angel of the downtrodden under attack by politically correct," *CanadianFreePress.com,* 16 Dec. 2004, http://www.canadafreepress.com/2004/cover121604.htm. Dana Flavelle, "Cheap-chic retailer Target coming to Canada," *Toronto Star,* 22 Jan. 2010, http://www.thestar.com/business/article/754191---cheap-chic-retailer-target-coming-to-canada.

16. Charles Krauthammer, "Just Leave Christmas Alone," *Washington Post,* 17 Dec. 2004: A33.

17. Paul Weyrich, "Make a Difference with 'Merry Christmas,'" *Renew America,* 17 Dec. 2004, http://www.renewamerica.com/columns/weyrich/041217.

18. Bill O'Reilly, "Take Your Christmas and Stuff It," *The O'Reilly Factor,* 9 Dec. 2004, transcript, http://www.billoreilly.com/column?pid=18833.

19. Bill O'Reilly, "Pressing the Point," *The O'Reilly Factor,* 22 Dec. 2005, transcript, http://www.billoreilly.com/column?pid=19444.

20. Anthony Browne, "We are committing cultural suicide," *Times,* 21 Dec. 2004: 16.

21. Oliver North, "Oliver North: Merry Christmas," *Military.com,* 22 Dec. 2004, http://www.military.com/Opinions/0,,FreedomAlliance_122204,00.html.

22. William F. Buckley Jr., "Fighting the Secularist Fight," *New York Sun,* 22 Dec. 2004: 9.

23. "O'Reilly: 'If I had not done the campaign, then the forces of darkness would have won' the 'war' on Christmas," *Media Matters,* 5 Dec. 2007, http://mediamatters.org/research/200712050006.

24. "Despite his repeated efforts to provoke one, O'Reilly conceded 'there is no attack on Easter,'" *Media Matters,* 17 Apr. 2006, http://mediamatters.org/research/200604170006.

25. Patrick J. Buchanan, *Day of Reckoning: How Hubris, Ideology, and Greed Are Tearing America Apart* (New York: Thomas Dunne Books, 2007): 11.

26. Rush Limbaugh, "America's Piñata Strikes Back: We Won't Shut Up on Sotomayor, May 29, 2009," *The Rush Limbaugh Show,* 29 May 2009, transcript, http://www.rushlimbaugh.com/home/daily/site_052909/content/01125106.guest.html.

27. Bill O'Reilly, "Evil White Men," *The O'Reilly Factor,* 16 July 2009, transcript, http://www.foxnews.com/story/0,2933,533040,00.html.

28. Rush Limbaugh, "America's Piñata Strikes Back: We Won't Shut Up on Sotomayor, May 29, 2009," *The Rush Limbaugh Show,* 29 May 2009, transcript, http://www.rushlimbaugh.com/home/daily/site_052909/content/01125106.guest.html. "Countdown with Keith Olberman," *MSNBC,* 29 July 2009, transcript, http://www.msnbc.msn.com/id/32218739/ns/msnbc_tv-countdown_with_keith_olbermann/.

29. Glenn Beck, "What's Driving President Obama's Agenda?" *The Glenn Beck Program,* 23 July 2009, transcript, http://www.foxnews.com/story/0,2933,534643,00.html.

30. Greg Lewis, "Fill-In Steyn Claims Gov't Will Treat Illegal Immigrants Instead of Elderly," *Media Matters* 18 Aug. 2009, http://mediamatters.org/research/200908180033.

31. Suzy Khimm, "The Attack on Obamacare: Gay Conspiracy Edition," *New Republic,* 13 Aug. 2009, http://www.tnr.com/blog/the-treatment/the-attack-obamacare-gay-conspiracy-edition.

32. "Quinn: Tanning tax is a 'race-based tax' from 'the most racist administration . . . since Woodrow Wilson,'" *Media Matters,* 6 Jul. 2010, http://mediamatters.org/mmtv/201007060006.

33. "'Death Book' Debate on 'Fox News Sunday,'" *Fox News,* 23 Aug. 2009, transcript, http://www.foxnews.com/story/0,2933,541820,00.html.

34. Glenn Beck, "The Horror of Eugenics Happened; What Can We Learn from That Mistake?" *The Glenn Beck Program,* 12 Aug. 2009, transcript, http://www.foxnews.com/story/0,2933,539000,00.html.

35. "As Beck slices watermelon, AFP's Kerpen declares cap-and-trade bill 'green on the outside, and inside it's deep, communist red,'" *Media Matters,* 26 June 2009, http://mediamatters.org/mmtv/200906260032.

36. "Beck imitates Obama pouring gasoline on 'average American'; says: 'President Obama, why don't you just set us on fire? . . . We didn't vote to lose the Republic,'" *Media Matters,* 9 Apr. 2009, http://mediamatters.org/mmtv/200904090036.

37. Glenn Beck, "Time for a Czar Czar?" *The Glenn Beck Program,* 9 June 2009, transcript, http://www.foxnews.com/story/0,2933,525594,00.html.

38. "Glenn Beck: Czars Czars and More Czars!" *The Glenn Beck Program,* 3 Aug. 2009, transcript, http://www.glennbeck.com/content/articles/article/198/28817/.

39. "Limbaugh on Attacks on Freedom of Speech," *Fox News,* 26 Aug. 2009, transcript, http://www.foxnews.com/story/0,2933,543682,00.html.

40. Glenn Beck, "Glenn Beck: A Call to Action," *The Glenn Beck Program,* 28 Aug. 2009, transcript, http://www.glennbeck.com/content/articles/article/198/29868/.

41. Joe Tacopino, "Oprah, Glenn Beck are America's favorite TV personalities," *NYDailyNews.com,* 25 Jan. 2010, http://www.nydailynews.com/entertainment/tv/2010/01/25/2010 01-25 _oprah_glenn_beck_are_americas_favorite_tv _personalities_poll_.html.

42. *Time,* 174:12 (28 Sep. 2009): front cover.

43. Sarah Palin, "Sarah Palin: An Invitation," *Facebook,* 26 Aug. 2009, http://www.facebook.com/note.php?note_id=123152423434.

44. "Limbaugh on Attacks on Freedom of Speech," *Fox News,* 26 Aug. 2009, transcript, http://www.foxnews.com/story/0,2933,543682,00.html.

45. "Jon Stewart in the No Spin Zone," *The O'Reilly Factor,* 4 Feb. 2010, http://www.foxnews.com/story/0,2933,584805,00.html.

46. Stan Greenberg, James Carville, and Karl Agne, "The Very Separate World of Conservative Republicans," *Democracy Corps,* 16 Oct. 2009, http://gqrr.com/index.php?ID=2398.

47. Ali Frick, "Bachmann: 'I Want People . . . Armed and Dangerous on This Issue' of Cap and Trade," *Think Progress,* 23 Mar. 2009, http://thinkprogress.org/2009/03/23/bachmann-armed-and-dangerous/.

48. Jon Ralston, "Ad rings true of Sharron Angle on Social Security," *Las Vegas Sun,* 16 Jun. 2010, http://www.lasvegassun.com/news/2010/jun/16/ad-rings-true-angle-social-security/. Greg Sargent, "Sharron Angle floated possibility of armed insurrection," *Washington Post,* 15 Jun. 2010,http://voices.washingtonpost.com/plum-line/2010/06/sharron_angle_floated_possibil.html.

49. Emily Kotecki, "N.C. GOP congressional candidate on oil spill: 'Maybe they wanted it to leak,'" *Washington Post,* 16 Jun. 2010, http://voices.washingtonpost.com/44/2010/06/nc-gop-congressional-candidate.html.

50. "Rand Paul on 'Maddow' fallout begins," *The Maddow Blog,* 20 May 2010, http://maddowblog.msnbc.msn.com/_news/2010/05/20/4313688-rand-paul-on-maddow-fallout-begins. Justin Elliott, "Rand Paul in '08: Beware the NAFTA Superhighway!" *Talking Points Memo,* 21 May 2010, http://tpmmuckraker.talkingpointsmemo.com/2010/05/rand_paul_beware_the_nafta_superhighway_video.php.

51. "Glenn talks with Congresswoman Bachmann," *The Glenn Beck Program,* 27 Mar. 2009, http://www.glennbeck.com/content/articles/article/196/23295/.

52. "Congressman: Obama wants Gestapo-like force," *MSNBC,* 11 Nov. 2008, http://www.msnbc.msn.com/id/27655039/.

53. Charles Babington, "Iowa Republican lawmaker says Obama favors blacks," *Associated Press,* 15 May 2010, http://www.google.com/hostednews/ap/article/ALeqM5gi2UTOrnQ_0aQCJe2ATPijRAVgHgD9GBQPDO0.

54. "As Senate Prepares to Take Up Hate Crimes Bill, Far Right's Inflammatory Claims Should Not Be Taken Seriously," *People for the American Way,* 2 Feb. 2010, retrieved, http://www.pfaw.org/rww-in-focus/senate-prepares-to-take-hate-crimes-bill-far-right-s-inflammatory-claims-should-not-be-.

Chapter 2. Weep for Your Children

1. Misfit4Peace, "Obama to make unprecedented address to all public school students," *DailyPaul.com,* 27 Aug. 2009, http://74.125.93.132/search?q=cache:JxRuxJelgzYJ:www.dailypaul.com/node/104812+%22%22Obama+to+make+unprecedented+address+to+all+public+school+students%22&cd=1&hl=en&ct=clnk&gl=us.

2. Jim Greer, "Greer Condemns Obama's Attempt to Indoctrinate Students," *RPOF.org,* 1 Sep. 2009, http://www.rpof.org/article.php?id=754.

3. "Malkin: The Left Has Always Used Kids as Guinea Pigs and as Junior Lobbyists for Their Social Liberal Agenda," *Crooks and Liars,* 3 Sep. 2009, http://videocafe.crooksandliars.com/cspanjunkie/malkin-left-has-always-used-kids-guinea-pigs.

4. "Colmes Mocks Ingraham and Crowley: Next You're Going to Accuse Them of Implant Chips in These Kids' Brains," *Crooks and Liars,* 3 Sep. 2009, http://videocafe.crooksandliars.com/heather/colmes-mocks-ingraham-and-crowley-next-you.

5. "Beck calls Obama's stay-in-school speech to students 'indoctrination,'" *Media Matters,* 2 Sep. 2009, http://mediamatters.org/mmtv/200909020011.

6. "Beck endorses Twitter campaign to skip school on day of Obama student address," *Media Matters,* 2 Sep. 2009, http://mediamatters.org/mmtv/200909020013.

7. Ewen MacAskill, "Schools boycott Obama speech as critics abruptly change tone," *Guardian,* 8 Sep. 2009, http://www.guardian.co.uk/world/2009/sep/08/obama-school-speech-boycott-protest.

8. "Mr. President, Stay Away from Our Kids," *novatownhall blog,* 7 Sep. 2009, http://novatownhall.com/2009/09/07/mr-president-stay-away-from-our-kids/.

9. "Prepared Remarks of President Barack Obama: Back to School Event," *whitehouse.gov,* 8 Sep. 2009, http://www.whitehouse.gov/mediaresources/PreparedSchoolRemarks/.

10. "September 8, 2009: National Keep Your Child at Home Day," *American Elephant,* 1 Sep. 2009, http://americanelephant.com/blog/commentary/september-8-2009-national-keep-your-child-at-home-day/.

11. "President Obama's Address to Students across America, September 8, 2009," *Docstoc,* 30 Aug. 2009, http://www.docstoc.com/docs/10582301/President-Obama%27s-Address-to-Students-Across-America-September-8-2009.

12. "The History of the Globe Theater," *William Shakespeare info,* http://www.william-shakespeare.info/william-shakespeare-globe-theatre.htm.

13. Robert Beddard, *A Kingdom without a King: the Journal of the Provisional Government in the Revolution of 1688* (Oxford: Phaidon Press, 1988): 127.

14. Bruce Shapiro, "Rad-Baiting Comes to Brookline," *Nation,* 250:20 (21 May 1990): 689.

15. Fredric Wertham, *Seduction of the Innocent* (New York: Rinehart, 1954): 34.

16. Max Blumenthal, "Agent of Intolerance," *Nation,* 16 May 2007, http://www.the nation.com/article/agent-intolerance.

17. Joseph Crespino, *In Search of Another Country: Mississippi and the Conservative Counterrevolution* (Princeton: Princeton University Press, 2007): 228.

18. *"Green v. Kennedy,"* Loislaw, 12 Jan. 1970, http://www.loislaw.com/advsrny/doclink. htp?alias=FDCR&cite=309+F.+Supp.+1127.

19. William Martin, *With God on Our Side: The Rise of the Religious Right in America* (New York: Broadway Books, 1996): 70.

20. Richard A. Shaffer, "Enrollment in Private Schools Continues to Climb," *Wall Street Journal,* 17 Dec. 1973: p. 17, col. 3.

21. Dan Gilgoff, *The Jesus Machine: How James Dobson, Focus on the Family, and Evangelical America Are Winning the Culture War* (New York: St. Martin's Press, 2007): 74–75.

22. Interview with Paul Weyrich, *C-SPAN,* 27 Mar. 2005, http://www.q-and-a.org/ Transcript/?ProgramID=1016.

23. Aif Tomas Tonnessen, *How Two Political Entrepreneurs Help Create the American Conservative Movement, 1973–1981: The Ideas of Richard Viguerie and Paul Weyrich* (Lewiston, NY: Edwin Mellen Press, 2009): 176.

24. Dan Gilgoff, *The Jesus Machine: How James Dobson, Focus on the Family, and Evangelical America Are Winning the Culture War* (New York: St. Martin's Press, 2007): 77.

25. Randall Balmer, *Thy Kingdom Come: How the Religious Right Distorts the Faith and Threatens America: An Evangelical's Lament* (New York: Basic Books, 2006): 12–13.

26. Ibid.

27. Ibid., 16.

28. Dan Gilgoff, *The Jesus Machine: How James Dobson, Focus on the Family, and Evangelical America Are Winning the Culture War* (New York: St. Martin's Press, 2007): 77.

29. William Martin, *With God on Our Side: The Rise of the Religious Right in America* (New York: Broadway Books, 1996): 173.

30. Thomas Byrne Edsall, Mary D. Edsall, *Chain Reaction: The Impact of Race, Rights, and Taxes on American Politics* (New York: W. W. Norton & Company, 1992): 132.

31. William Safire, "On Language; Secs Appeal," *New York Times,* 26 Jan. 1986: sec. 6, p. 6, col. 3.

32. Kurt Andersen, "To the Right, March!: Jesse Helms," *Time,* 14 Sep. 1981.

33. William George Peck, *The Social Implications of the Oxford Movement* (New York: Charles Scribner's Sons, 1933): 110.

34. "Free Church Ministers in Anglican Pulpits," *Manchester Guardian,* 26 May 1943: 6.

35. George Dugan, "'Illiterate' Trend in Religion Underscored; Episcopal Bishops, in Pastoral as Convention Ends, Flay 'Secular Humanism,'" *New York Times,* 8 Oct. 1949: 14

36. Pope Paul VI, "Address during the last general meeting of the Second Vatican Council," *EWTN Global Catholic Network,* 7 Dec. 1965, http://www.ewtn.com/library/papal doc/p6tolast.htm.

37. Max Rafferty, "Suffer, Little Children," *Phi Delta Kappan,* 1 Dec. 1956: 92.

38. Christopher P. Toumey, "Evolution and Secular Humanism," *Journal of the American Academy of Religion,* 61:2 (Summer, 1993): 279.

39. Dorothy Nelkin, "From Dayton to Little Rock: Creationism Evolves," *Science, Technology, & Human Values,* 1 Jul. 1982.

40. Dale Singer, "Parents Fight Against Secularism," *Spokane Daily Chronicle,* 25 May 1977: 26.

41. Christopher P. Toumey, "Evolution and Secular Humanism," *Journal of the American Academy of Religion,* 61:2 (Summer, 1993): 279–280.

42. David E. Anderson, "Smithsonian Sued for Evolution Exhibit," *Milwaukee Journal,* 22 Apr. 1978: 5.

43. "Christian School Administrators Vow to Fight Judge's Decision," *Wilmington Morning Star,* 6 Sep. 1978: 2-A.

44. Megan Rosenfeld, "Fundamentalists Challenge State Licensing of Their Schools," *Washington Post,* 24 Jul. 1978: first sec., A2.

45. Patrick J. Buchanan, "Federal Paw on Religious Education," *Lundington Daily News,* 6 Oct. 1978: 4.

46. Godfrey Hodgson, *The World Turned Right Side Up: A History of the Conservative Ascendancy in America* (Boston: Houghton Mifflin, 1996): 177.

47. Jesse Helms, *When Free Men Shall Stand* (Grand Rapids, MI: Zondervan, 1976): 27.

48. R. J. Rooney quoted in Homer Duncan, *Secular Humanism: The Most Dangerous Religion in America* (Lubbock, TX: MC International Publications, 1979): 85.

49. Ibid.

50. Homer Duncan, *Secular Humanism: The Most Dangerous Religion in America* (Lubbock, TX: MC International Publications, 1979): 2.

51. Tim LaHaye, *The Battle for the Mind* (Old Tappan, NJ: Fleming H. Revell Company, 1979): 9.

52. William A. Link, *Righteous Warrior: Jesse Helms and the Rise of Modern Conservatism* (New York: St. Martin's Press, 2008): 179.

53. Alice Feinstein, "Dallas Coach Landry Fears 'Secular Humanism,'" *Spokane Chronicle,* 17 Apr. 1982: 6.

54. Advertisement, *Wilmington Morning Star,* 18 May 1981: 3A.

55. Advertisement, *Ocala Star-Banner,* 19 Jul. 1981: 12B.

56. Dena Kleiman, "Parents Groups Purging Schools of 'Humanist' Books and Classes," *New York Times,* 17 May 1981: sec. 1, p. 11.

57. Ibid.

58. Christopher P. Toumey, "Evolution and Secular Humanism," *Journal of the American Academy of Religion,* 61:2 (Summer, 1993): 283.

59. Dena Kleiman, "Parents Groups Purging Schools of 'Humanist' Books and Classes," *New York Times,* 17 May 1981: sec. 1, p. 11.

60. Ibid.

61. Christopher P. Toumey, "Evolution and Secular Humanism," *Journal of the American Academy of Religion,* 61:2 (Summer, 1993): 281.

62. Stuart Taylor Jr., "Judge Who Banned Textbooks: Hero of the Right," *New York Times,* 7 Mar. 1987, http://www.nytimes.com/1987/03/07/us/judge-who-banned-textbooks-hero-of-the-right.html.

63. Bernard Schwartz, *A Book of Legal Lists: The Best and Worst in American Law* (Oxford: Oxford University Press, USA, 1999) 177–178.

64. Stuart Taylor Jr., "Judge Who Banned Textbooks: Hero of the Right," *New York*

Times, 7 Mar. 1987, http://www.nytimes.com/1987/03/07/us/judge-who-banned-text-books-hero-of-the-right.html .

65. Glenn Beck, "The One Thing: Battle for the Soul of the Democratic Party," *Fox News,* 19 Jan. 2010, http://www.foxnews.com/search-results/m/28433839/the-one-thing-1-19.htm.

66. Glenn Beck, "Marxists Everywhere!" *The Glenn Beck Program,* 31 Aug. 2009, http://www.glennbeck.com/content/articles/article/198/29920/.

3. More or Less Normal People

1. Andrew Dickson White, "'Demoniacal Possession' and Insanity," *Popular Science Monthly,* Feb. 1889: 440–441.

2. William S. Haubrich, *Medical Meanings: A Glossary of Word Origins* (Philadelphia: American College of Physicians, 2003): 195.

3. Sigmund Freud, *The Schreber Case,* trans. Andrew Webber, Penguin Classics ed., 2003 (New York: Penguin Books, 1943): 53.

4. Richard Hofstadter, "The Paranoid Style in American Politics," *Harper's Magazine,* Nov. 1964: 77.

5. Ibid., 81.

6. Rob Boston, "Left Behind," *Americans United for Separation of Church and State,* 1 Feb. 2002, http://www.au.org/media/church-and-state/archives/2002/02/if-best-selling.html.

7. Max Blumenthal, "Agent of Intolerance," *Nation,* 16 May 2007, http://www.thenation.com/article/agent-intolerance. "The Nation's Best Bible College Gets Low Grades on Racial Diversity," *Journal of Blacks in Higher Education* 1 Mar. 2001: 43.

8. "45,000 Challenged at Charismatic Conference," *Daily News,* 15 Jul. 1977: 8.

9. Richard Hofstadter, "The Paranoid Style in American Politics," *Harper's Magazine,* Nov. 1964: 85.

10. Frederick Clarkson, "Christian Reconstructionism: Theocratic Dominionism Gains Influence," 1 Jul. 1999: 78, http://www.publiceye.org/magazine/v08n1/chrisre1.html.

11. "John Birch Society," *PublicEye.org,* 28 Jan. 2010, retrieved, http://www.publiceye.org/tooclose/jbs.html.

12. "The Politics of Frustration," *Harper's Magazine,* Jan. 1968: 64.

13. James Taranto, "Nobody's Watching Charlie Rose," *Wall Street Journal,* 16 Jan. 2010, http://online.wsj.com/article/SB10001424052748703436504574641192528461858.html.

4. Attack of the Gay Fascists

1. "Dobson: Same-sex marriage would lead to 'marriage between daddies and little girls . . . between a man and his donkey'," *Media Matters,* 7 Oct. 2005, http://mediamatters.org/mmtv/200510070004.

2. "The wisdom of Bill O'Reilly," *Media Matters,* 31 Mar. 2005, http://mediamatters.org/research/200503310004.

3. "Bill O'Reilly's continuing obsession with inter-species marriages," *Media Matters,* 16 Sep. 2005, http://mediamatters.org/mmtv/200509160009.

4. "Excerpt from Santorum interview," *USAToday.com,* 23 Apr. 2003, http://www.usatoday.com/news/washington/2003-04-23-santorum-excerpt_x.htm.

5. Lois Romano and Sen. John Cornyn (R-Tex.), "Quotables," *Washington Post,* 12 Jul. 2004, http://www.washingtonpost.com/wp-dyn/articles/A43048-2004Jul11.html.

6. Maggie Gallagher, "The Stakes: Why We Need Marriage," *National Review Online,* 14 Jul. 2003, http://www.nationalreview.com/comment/comment-gallagher071403.asp.

7. James Dobson, "Eleven Arguments Against Same-Sex Marriage," *Focus on the Family,* 14 Mar. 2004, http://web.archive.org/web/20040619130737/http://www.family.org/cforum/extras/a0032427.cfm. Matt Corley, "Pat Robertson: Gay marriage is 'the beginning in a long downward slide' to legalized child molestation," *Think Progress,* 7 May 2009, http://thinkprogress.org/2009/05/07/robertson-child-molestation/. "FRC Urges Citizen Action Following Votes in Vermont, DC," *Family Research Council,* 7 Apr. 2009, http://news.prnewswire.com/DisplayReleaseContent.aspx?ACCT=104&STORY=/www/story/04-07-2009/0005002510&EDATE=.

8. "Majority Continues to Support Civil Unions," *The Pew Forum on Religion & Public Life,* 9 Oct. 2009, http://pewforum.org/docs/?DocID=481.

9. Jason Clayworth and Thomas Beaumont, "Iowa Poll: Iowans evenly divided on gay marriage ban," *Des Moines Register,* 21 Sep. 2009. http://www.desmoinesregister.com/article/20090921/NEWS10/909210321/1001/NEWS.

10. *The American Reports: Containing All Decisions of General Interest Decided in the Courts of Last Resort of the Several States with Notes and References by Irving Browne Vol. XXXII,* ed. Irving Browne (San Francisco: Bancroft-Whitney Company, 1880): 551.

11. George Chauncey, *Why Marriage? The History Shaping Today's Debate over Gay Equality* (New York: Basic Books, 2004): 158.

12. Wayne R. Besen, *Anything But Straight: Unmasking the Scandals and Lies Behind the Ex-Gay Myth* (Binghamton, NY: Harrington Park Press, 2003): 113.

13. "Letter Six, December 1994," *Wes & Tom's Cool Site,* 31 Jan. 2010, http://www.officerwes.com/coolsite/pris_06a.htm.

14. Wayne R. Besen, *Anything But Straight: Unmasking the Scandals and Lies Behind the Ex-Gay Myth* (Binghamton, NY: Harrington Park Press, 2003): 113.

15. "Dr. Stanley Monteith on Alex Jones TV: 'Eugenics Wars,'" *Prison Planet,* 6 Sep. 2008, http://www.prisonplanet.com/drstanley-monteith-on-alex-jones-tveugenics-wars.html.

16. "Same-sex marriage will impact all families and children, video shows," *Catholic News Agency,* 27 Oct. 2008, http://www.catholicnewsagency.com/news/samesex_marriage_will_impact_all_families_and_children_video_shows/.

17. Ronnie W. Floyd, *The Gay Agenda: It's Dividing the Family, the Church, and a Nation* (Green Forest, AR: New Leaf Press, 2004): 15.

18. Alan Sears, Craig Osten, *The Homosexual Agenda: Exposing the Principal Threat to Religious Freedom Today* (Nashville, TN: Broadman & Holman Publishers, 2003): 37.

19. Cynthia Krueger, "How the Gay Agenda Will Affect Our Future," *Tea Party Nation,* 14 Jan. 2010, http://www.teapartypatriots.org/BlogPostView.aspx?id=049ac8e5-92a3-4cd4-b2a2-bdddc5dd9d95.

20. Justice A. Scalia, "Scotus: Lawrence v. Texas," *LII/Supreme Court Collection,* 26 Jun. 2003, http://www.law.cornell.edu/supct/html/02-102.ZD.html.

21. James Dobson, "Marriage Under Fire," *Focus on the Family,* 6 Oct. 2005, http://web.archive.org/web/20051006010344/http://www.family.org/docstudy/bookshelf/a0032438.cfm.

22. James Dobson, "Marriage on the Ropes," *Dr. Dobson's Study, September 2003 Newsletter,* 1 Sep. 2003, http://www2.focusonthefamily.com/docstudy/newsletters/A000000771.cfm.

23. Michael O'Brien, "Congressman: Same sex marriage part of push for socialism,"

Hill, 23 Sep. 2009, http://thehill.com/blogs/blog-briefing-room/news/60007-congressman-same-sex-marriage-part-of-push-for-socialism.

24. Morton Lukoff, "Bias Law on Gays Draws Opposition of Anita Bryant," *Miami News,* 17 Jan. 1977: 8A.

25. Dudley Clendinen, Adam Nagourney, *Out for Good: The Struggle to Build a Gay Rights Movement in America* (New York: Touchstone Books, 1999): 299.

26. Anita Bryant, *The Anita Bryant Story: The Survival of Our Nation's Families and the Threat of Militant Homosexuality* (Old Tappan, New Jersey: Fleming H. Revell Company, 1977): 42.

27. David Eisenbach, *Gay Power: An American Revolution* (New York: Carroll & Graf, 2006): 279.

28. Tom Mathews, Tony Fuller, and Holly Camp, "Battle over Gay Rights," *Newsweek* 6 Jun. 1977: 25.

29. Stonewall Library and Archives Exhibition, "Days Without Sunshine: Anita Bryant's Anti-Gay Crusade," *Exhibition,* retrieved 6 Jun. 2007: Panel 13, http://www.stonewall-library.org/anita/.

30. "A Gay Activist Campaign," *Washington Post,* 8 Apr. 1977: B10.

31. "Anita Bryant 'Blacklisted,'" *Boca Raton News,* 24 Feb. 1977: 5.

32. Larry Hall, "Anita Bryant's Rise and Fall Was Captured During Visits," *Richmond Times-Dispatch,* 1 Aug. 2007: B4.

33. Tim LaHaye, *The Unhappy Gays: What Everyone Should Know About Homosexuality* (Wheaton, IL: Tyndale House, 1978): 204.

34. Ibid., 197.

35. Hans Johnson and William Eskridge, "The Legacy of Falwell's Bully Pulpit," *Washington Post,* 19 May 2007, http://www.washingtonpost.com/wp-dyn/content/article/2007/05/18/AR2007051801392.html.

36. Judith Michaelson, "Felt Ones Living Large After Fuss," *Los Angeles Times,* 17 Apr. 1999, http://articles.latimes.com/1999/apr/17/entertainment/ca-28136.

37. David D. Kirkpatrick, "Conservatives Taking Aim at Soft Target," *New York Times,* 20 Jan. 2005: A16.

38. Carolyn Plocher, "American Library Association's Not-So-Hidden Gay Agenda," *NewsBusters,* 5 Jan. 2010, http://newsbusters.org/blogs/carolyn-plocher/2010/01/05/american-library-association-s-not-so-hidden-gay-agenda. Don Behm, "West Bend Couple Circulate petitions to Remove Library Books They Consider Obscene," *Milwaukee Journal Sentinel,* 31 Mar. 2009, http://www.jsonline.com/news/ozwash/42239872.html.

39. "Hillsdale College Student on Radical Leftist Marriage Book," *The Rush Limbaugh Show,* 11 Dec. 2009, http://www.rushlimbaugh.com/home/daily/site_121109/content/01125112.guest.html.

40. "Sally Lloyd-Jones," *Amazon.com,* 27 Jul. 2010, retrieved. http://www.amazon.com/Sally-Lloyd-Jones/e/B001H6J3XQ.

41. "Anti-Gay Politics and the Religious Right," *People for the American Way,* retrieved 10 Jan. 2010, http://www.pfaw.org/media-center/publications/anti-gay-politics-and-the-religious-right.

42. Ibid.

43. "Gingrich: '"[T]here is a gay and secular fascism in this country that wants to impose its will on the rest of us,'" *Media Matters,* 17 Nov. 2008, http://mediamatters.org/mmtv/200811170014.

44. Richard Plant, *The Pink Triangle: The Nazi War Against Homosexuals* (New York: Henry Holt & Co, 1988): 149, 154.

45. Scott Lively and Kevin Abrams, *The Pink Swastika: Homosexuality in the Nazi Party* (Keizer, OR: Founders Publishing, 1997): 58.

46. David W. Dunlap, "Gay Advertising Campaign on TV Draws Wrath of Conservatives," *New York Times,* 12 Nov. 1995, http://www.nytimes.com/1995/11/12/us/gay-advertising-campaign-on-tv-draws-wrath-of-conservatives.html.

47. Zachary Roth, "Top Social Conservative: Hitler Used Gay Soldiers Because They Had 'No Limits,'" *Talking Points Memo,* 26 May 2010, http://tpmmuckraker.talkingpoints memo.com/2010/05/top_social_conservative.php.

48. Alfred N. Delahaye, "The Case of Matthew Shepard," in Lloyd Chiasson, ed., *Illusive Shadows: Justice, Media, and Socially Significant American Trials* (Westport, CT: Praeger Publishers, 2003), 183–188.

49. Levendosky, "Wyoming Snow Quiets Sorrow at Matthew Shepard's Funeral," *Seattle Post-Intelligencer,* 21 Oct. 1998: A12.

50. Wendy Cloyd, "Dr. Dobson Asks the Nation to Oppose Hate-Crimes Bill," *citizenlink.com,* 5 Jan. 2007, http://www.citizenlink.org/content/A000004525.cfm.

51. Ibid.

52. "As Senate Prepares to Take Up Hate Crimes Bill, Far Right's Inflammatory Claims Should Not Be Taken Seriously," *People for the American Way,* retrieved 2 Feb. 2010, http://www.pfaw.org/rww-in-focus/senate-prepares-to-take-hate-crimes-bill-far-right-s-inflammatory-claims-should-not-be-.

53. "Hate Crimes Legislation Attached to the Defense Appropriation Bill," *C-SPAN Video Library,* 6 Oct. 2009, http://www.c-spanvideo.org/videoLibrary/clip.php?appid= 595111387.

54. "Pro-Homosexual/Drag Queen 'Hate Crimes' Bill Introduced," *The Traditional Values Coalition,* 22 Mar. 2007, http://www.traditionalvalues.org/read/3052/prohomosexualdrag-queen-lsquohate-crimesrsquo-bill-introduced/.

5. Mad as Hell?

1. Ryan Grim, "Virginia Foxx: Story of Matthew Shepard's Murder a 'Hoax,'" *Huffington Post,* 29 Apr. 2009, http://www.huffingtonpost.com/2009/04/29/virginia-foxx-story-of-ma_n_192971.html.

2. Donald Wildmon, *Speechless: Silencing the Christians: How Liberals and Homosexual Activists Are Outlawing Christianity (and Judaism) to Force Their Sexual Agenda on America* (Minneapolis, MN: Richard Vigilante Books, 2009): front flap.

3. Ibid., xviiii.

4. Kate Zernike and Megan Thee-Brenan, "Poll Finds Tea Party Backers Wealthier and More Educated," *New York Times,* 14 Apr. 2010, http://www.nytimes.com/2010/04/15/us/politics/15poll.html.

5. *Newsweek,* 153:13 (30 Mar. 2010): front cover.

6. *Time,* 174:12 (28 Sep. 2009): front cover.

7. Robert Reich, "Is Obama Responsible for Wall Street's Meltdown?" *Salon.com,* 5 Mar. 2009, http://www.salon.com/opinion/feature/2009/03/05/populist_rage/index.html.

8. Thomas Frank, *What's the Matter with Kansas?: How Conservatives Won the Heart of America,* paperback ed., 2005 (New York: Henry Holt and Company, 2004): 123.

9. Glenn Beck, "The One Thing: Battle for the Soul of the Democratic Party," *Fox News,* 19 Jan. 2010, http://www.foxnews.com/search-results/m/28433839/the-one-thing-1-19.htm.

10. "Beck 'Explains' His Meltdown," *News Hounds,* 15 Jul. 2009, http://www.news hounds.us/2009/07/21/beck_explains_his_meltdown.php.

11. Kate Zernike and Megan Thee-Brenan, "Poll Finds Tea Party Backers Wealthier and More Educated," *New York Times,* 14 Apr. 2010, http://www.nytimes.com/2010/04/15/us/politics/15poll.html.

12. "The Outrage Factor," *Newsweek,* 21 Mar. 2009, http://www.newsweek.com/2009/03/20/the-outrage-factor.html.

13. David Von Drehle, "Mad Man: Is Glenn Beck Bad for America?" *Time,* 17 Sep. 2009, http://www.time.com/time/politics/article/0,8599,1924348,00.html.

14. Robert Reich, "Is Obama Responsible for Wall Street's Meltdown?" *Salon.com,* 5 Mar. 2009, http://www.salon.com/opinion/feature/2009/03/05/populist_rage/index.html.

15. Stephanie Condon, "Obama: 'I Can Go to My Right, but I Prefer My Left,'" *CBS News,* 1 Apr. 2010, http://www.cbsnews.com/8301-503544_162-20001596-503544.html.

16. "Axelrod suggests 'Tea Party' movement is 'unhealthy,'" *CNN,* 19 Apr. 2009, http://politicalticker.blogs.cnn.com/2009/04/19/axelrod-suggests-tea-party-movement-is-unhealthy/?fbid=OfqtMHEN2Km.

17. Rupert Brown, "Intergroup Relations," in *Introduction to Social Psychology: A European Perspective,* ed. Miles Hewstone and Wolfgang Stroebe (Malden, MA: Wiley-Blackwell, 2001): 485.

18. Stewart Emory Tolnay, E. M. Beck, *A Festival of Violence: An Analysis of Southern Lynchings, 1882–1930* (Urbana: University of Illinois Press, 1995): 121.

19. Rupert Brown, "Intergroup Relations," *Introduction to Social Psychology: a European Perspective,* ed. Miles Hewstone and Wolfgang Stroebe (Malden, MA: Wiley-Blackwell, 2001): 485. Stewart Emory Tolnay and E. M. Beck, *A Festival of Violence: An Analysis of Southern Lynchings, 1882–1930* (Urbana: University of Illinois Press, 1995): 121.

20. Kate Zernike and Megan Thee-Brenan, "Poll Finds Tea Party Backers Wealthier and More Educated," *New York Times,* 14 Apr. 2010, http://www.nytimes.com/2010/04/15/us/politics/15poll.html.

21. Markus Brückner and Hans Peter Grüner, "Economic Growth and the Rise of Political Extremism: Theory and Evidence," *Center for Economic Policy Research,* Discussion Paper No. 7723 (March 2010): 14–15.

22. Donald Wildmon, *Speechless: Silencing the Christians: How Liberals and Homosexual Activists Are Outlawing Christianity (and Judaism) to Force Their Sexual Agenda on America* (Minneapolis, MN: Richard Vigilante Books, 2009): back cover.

23. Charles G. Lord, Lee Ross, and Mark R. Lepper, "Biased Assimilation and Attitude Polarization: the Effects of Prior Theories on Subsequently Considered Evidence," *Journal of Personality and Social Psychology,* 37:11 (Nov. 1970): 2105.

6. Obama's America

1. "Brutal Beating," *Fox News,* 15 Sep. 2009, http://www.foxnews.com/search-results/m/26423836/brutal-beating.htm.

2. "Kelly's Court: Brutal Bus Beating," *Fox News,* 16 Sep. 2009, http://www.foxnews.com/search-results/m/26435619/brutal-bus-beating.htm.

3. "Limbaugh: '[I]n Obama's America, The White Kids Now Get Beat Up with the Black Kids Cheering,'" *Media Matters,* 15 Sep. 2009, http://mediamatters.org/research/2009 09150023.

4. "Intro: Violence against White Children," *The Daily Show,* 15 Sep. 2009, http://www.thedailyshow.com/watch/tue-september-15-2009/intro—violence-against-white-children.

5. Nicholas J.C. Pistor, Elizabethe Holland, and David Hunn, "Bus attack called bullying, not racial," *St. Louis Post-Dispatch,* 16 Sep. 2009: A1.

6. Blythe Bernhard and Terry Hillig, "Dual rallies held over bus attack," *St. Louis Post-Dispatch,* 27 Sep. 2009: A3.

7. "Your request is being processed . . . Interracial Couple Denied Marriage License by Louisiana Justice of the Peace," *Huffington Post,* http://www.huffingtonpost.com/2009/10/15/interracial-couple-denied_n_322784.html.

8. David Duke, "On the O'Reilly Factor," *DavidDuke.com,* 25 Feb. 2005, http://www.davidduke.com/general/david-duke-responds-to-the-oreilly-factor_262.html.

9. "Illinois: Nigger, Go Home," *Time,* 7 Jul. 1961, http://www.time.com/time/magazine/article/0,9171,872523,00.html.

10. Amy Ansell, "The Color of America's Culture Wars," ed. Amy Ansell, *Unraveling the Right: The New Conservatism in American Thought and Politics* (Boulder, CO: Westview Press, 2001): 174–175.

11. *George Wallace: Settin' the Woods on Fire,* dir. Daniel McCabe and Paul Stekler (2000; PBS), http://www.pbs.org/wgbh/amex/wallace/filmmore/transcript/index.html.

12. Ibid.

13. Ibid.

14. Ralph McGill, "George Wallace Tradition of Demagoguery," *Los Angeles Times,* 17 Dec. 1967: 18.

15. *George Wallace: Settin' the Woods on Fire,* dir. Daniel McCabe and Paul Stekler (2000; PBS), http://www.pbs.org/wgbh/amex/wallace/filmmore/transcript/index.html.

16. Ibid.

17. "Wallace Symbolized Segregation, Reconciliation," *CNN,* http://www.cnn.com/ALLPOLITICS/stories/1998/09/14/wallace.obit/wallace.bio.html.

18. "The Presidency: Nixon's Paradox," *Time,* 3 Oct. 1969, http://www.time.com/time/magazine/article/0,9171,901502,00.html.

19. Robert B. Semple Jr., "Nixon Scores U.S. Method of Enforcing Integration," *New York Times,* 13 Sep. 1968: 1. Thomas Byrne Edsall and Mary D. Edsall, *Chain Reaction: The Impact of Race, Rights, and Taxes on American Politics* (New York: W. W. Norton & Company, 1991): 89.

20. Max Johnson, "Agnew Insults Leaders," *Baltimore Afro-American,* 13 Apr. 1968: 15. Matthew D. Lassiter, *The Silent Majority: Suburban Politics in the Sunbelt South* (Princeton: Princeton University Press, 2006): 233.

21. "The 'Code Word' Innuendo," *Chicago Tribune,* 18 Aug. 1968: 24.

22. Pete Hamill, "The Revolt of the White Lower Middle Class," *New York Magazine,* 14 Apr. 1969, http://nymag.com/news/features/46801/.

23. Scott Spitzer, "Nixon's Northern Strategy: Welfare Reform and Race after the Great Society," *The American Political Science Association,* 3 Sep. 2009: 13–14.

24. Ibid., 32.

25. "TV Monitor," *The Hotline,* 16 Jan. 1992, http://www.nationaljournal.com/hotline/h_19920116_1.php..

26. Patrick Buchanan, "Discrimination in Reverse," *Chicago Tribune,* 26 Oct. 1975: A6.

27. Herman D. Bloch, "Discrimination against the Negro in Employment in New York, 1920–1963," *American Journal of Economics and Sociology,* 24.4 (Oct., 1965): 369.

28. "Bias in Reverse?" *Wall Street Journal,* 12 Aug. 1963: 1.

29. Paul Frymer, "Acting When Elected Officials Won't: Federal Courts and Civil Rights Enforcement in U.S. Labor Unions, 1935–85," *American Political Science Review,* 97:3 (Aug. 2003): 489. Douglass Smith, "Black-White Population Ratio Almost Same Here over Decade," *Pittsburgh Post-Gazette,* 2 Jan. 1972: A-4.

30. Patrick Buchanan, "The Supreme Court Punts," *Hendersonville Times-News,* 5 Aug. 1978: 2.

31. "If He Is Elected: Reagan Will Consider Blacks for the Supreme Court and His Cabinet," *Jet,* 58:23 (21 Aug. 1980): 6; Laurence I. Barrett, *Gambling with History: Ronald Reagan in the White House* (Garden City, NY: Doubleday Books, 1983): 426.

32. "California: Proposition 14," *Time,* 25 Sep. 1964, http://www.time.com/time/magazine/article/0,9171,876158,00.html.

33. Home page, *CaliforniaRepublicanAssembly.com* (4 Mar. 2010, retrieved), http://www.californiarepublicanassembly.com/.

34. Michael Lind, "The Southern Coup," *New Republic,* 19 Jun. 1995, http://www.tnr.com/article/politics/the-southern-coup.

35. "'Welfare Queen' Becomes Issue in Reagan Campaign," *New York Times,* 15 Feb. 1976: 51.

36. Jon Nordheimer, "Reagan Is Picking His Florida Spots," *New York Times,* 5 Feb. 1976: 24.

37. Lou Cannon, "Reagan: Two-Part Effort to Defuse $90 Billion Issue," *Washington Post,* 28 Jan. 1976: A2.

38. "'Welfare Queen' Becomes Issue in Reagan Campaign," *New York Times,* 15 Feb. 1976: 51.

39. James Mellon, ed., *Bullwhip Days: The Slaves Remember* (New York: Grove Press, 2002): 291.

40. John Herbers, "The Klan: Its Growing Influence; Membership Placed at 10,000 in South," *New York Times,* 20 Apr. 1965: 24.

41. "The Basic Speech: Ronald Reagan," *New York Times* 29 Feb. 1980: B4.

42. *Sex Discrimination in the Workplace, 1981: Hearings Before the Committee on Labor and Human Resources* (USGPO, 1981): 504.

43. "U.S. Supreme Court: *Bob Jones Univ. v. Simon,* 416 U.S. 725 (1974)," *Chan Robles Virtual Law Library,* 15 May 1974, http://www.chanrobles.com/usa/us_supremecourt/416/725/case.php.

44. Lynn Emmerman, "Bob Jones blasts Reagan, 'devil' Bush," *Chicago Tribune,* 1 Mar. 1982: 3.

45. Julie Johnson, "Reagan Vetoes Bill That Would Widen Federal Rights Law," *New York Times,* 17 Mar. 1988, http://www.nytimes.com/1988/03/17/us/reagan-vetoes-bill-that-would-widen-federal-rights-law.html.

46. Thomas Byrne Edsall, Mary D. Edsall, *Chain Reaction: The Impact of Race, Rights, and Taxes on American Politics* (New York: W. W. Norton & Company, 1991): 182.

47. "Survey: Young Whites Now More Anti-Black," *St. Petersburg Times,* 12 Jun. 1993: 4A.

48. Martin Gilens, *Why Americans Hate Welfare: Race, Media, and the Politics of Anti-poverty Policy* (Chicago: University of Chicago Press, 1999): 140.

49. "Bush Vetoes Civil Rights Bill," *Washington Post,* 23 Oct. 1990: A1.

50. "For the Civil Rights Act of 1991," *Chicago Tribune,* 30 Apr. 1991: 16.

51. "Civil Rights Act Signed into Law," *Chicago Tribune,* 22 Nov. 1991: 10.

52. Lally Weymouth, "Buchanan: Throwing a Hard Right at Bush," *Washington Post,* 22 Dec. 1991: C1.

53. Michael Duffy and Nancy Traver, "Republicans: How Bush Will Battle Buchanan," *Time,* 2 Mar. 1992, http://www.time.com/time/magazine/article/0,9171,974987-2,00.html.

54. Ron Gomez, *My Name Is Ron, and I'm a Recovering Legislator: Memoirs of a Louisiana State Representative* (Lafayette, LA: Zemog Publishing, 2000): 158. Tyler Bridges, *The Rise of David Duke* (Jackson: University Press of Mississippi, 1994): 229.

55. Peter Applebome, "The 1992 Campaign: The South; Duke Plays to Empty Houses as Spotlight Trails Buchanan," *New York Times,* 6 Mar. 1992, http://www.nytimes.com/1992/03/06/us/1992-campaign-south-duke-plays-empty-houses-spotlight-trails-buchanan.html?.

56. "In Buchanan's Words," *Washington Post,* 29 Feb. 1992: A2.

57. "Patrick Buchanan's Speech to 1992 GOP Convention," *Wikisource,* 17 Aug. 1992, http://en.wikisource.org/wiki/Patrick_Buchanan%27s_Speech_to_1992_GOP_Convention.

58. Amy Wallace, "Buchanan Twisted L.A. Riot Story," *Los Angeles Times,* 19 Aug. 1992, http://articles.latimes.com/1992-08-19/news/mn-5619_1_angry-mob.

59. Ronald Brownstein, "Buchanan Links L.A. Riot to Immigration Problems," *Los Angeles Times,* 14 May 1992: 4.

60. "America's Immigrant Challenge," *Time,* 2 Dec. 1993, http://www.time.com/time/magazine/article/0,9171,979725,00.html.

61. Patrick Buchanan, "What Kind of U.S. in 2084?" *Times-News, Hendersonville, NC,* 6 Jun. 1984: 4.

62. Patrick Buchanan, "United States Is Turning into a Third World Nation," *Day,* 26 Jun. 1990: A11.

63. Julie Rovner, "New Congress: Women, Blacks, Lots of Gray Hair, Many Smiths," *Toledo Blade,* 19 Nov. 1988: C3.

64. Patrick J. Buchanan, *Day of Reckoning: How Hubris, Ideology, and Greed Are Tearing America Apart* (New York: Thomas Dunne Books, 2007): 8.

65. Ibid.

66. "GE, Microsoft Bring Bigotry to Life," *FAIR,* 12 Feb. 2003, http://www.fair.org/index.php?page=1632.

67. Patrick J. Buchanan, *Day of Reckoning: How Hubris, Ideology, and Greed Are Tearing America Apart* (New York: Thomas Dunne Books, 2007): 8.

68. Ibid., 184.

69. "Mexico's Affluent Middle Class on a Buying Spree in U.S. Sun Belt," *Telegraph,* 25 Jan. 1982: 15.

70. Patrick J. McDonnell, "Brash Evangelist," *Los Angeles Times,* 15 Jul. 2001: 1. Max Blumenthal, "Vigilante injustice," *Salon.com,* 22 May 2003, http://www.salon.com/news/feature/2003/05/22/vigilante/index3.html.

71. Patrick Joseph Buchanan, *State of Emergency: The Third World Invasion and Conquest of America* (New York: Thomas Dunne Books, 2006): 126–128.

72. "NBC still hosting Buchanan on immigration; Malkin told O'Reilly that reconquista is 'mainstream' among immigrants," *Media Matters,* 24 Aug. 2006, http://mediamatters.org/research/200608240011.

73. "Ignoring his own attack on liberals, O'Reilly accused liberal columnists of 'labeling people' with whom they may disagree as 'bigots,'" *Media Matters,* 9 Aug. 2006, http://mediamatters.org/research/200608090007.

74. Patrick Buchanan, "Whose country is this?" *World Net Daily,* 26 Apr. 2010, http://www.wnd.com/index.php?pageId=146341.

75. "House of Representatives HB 2281," *Arizona State Legislature,* 18 Mar. 2010. http://www.azleg.gov/FormatDocument.asp?inDoc=/legtext/49leg/2r/summary/h.hb2281_03-18-10_houseengrossed.doc.htm.

76. Tamar Lewin, "Citing Individualism, Arizona Tries to Rein in Ethnic Studies in School," *New York Times,* 13 May 2010, http://www.nytimes.com/2010/05/14/education/14arizona.html.

77. Patrick Buchanan, "Whose War?" *American Conservative,* 24 Mar. 2003, http://www.amconmag.com/article/2003/mar/24/00007/.

78. Michael D Shear, Dan Balz, "In Debate, Romney and Giuliani Clash on Immigration Issues," *Washington Post,* 29 Nov. 2007: A1.

79. "Beck, O'Reilly Afraid to Speak Their Minds Around African-Americans," *Media Matters,* 6 Feb. 2007, http://mediamatters.org/research/200702060012.

80. "Latching on to L.A. Times op-ed, Limbaugh sings 'Barack, The Magic Negro,'" *Media Matters,* 20 Mar. 2007, http://mediamatters.org/mmtv/200703200012.

81. "A Little Less Than 'Magic,'" *Washington Post,* 31 Dec. 2008, http://www.washingtonpost.com/wp-dyn/content/article/2008/12/30/AR2008123002633.html.

82. "Limbaugh on Dem primary: If 'feminazis' had remembered to oppose 'affirmative action for black guys . . . they wouldn't face the situation they face today,'" *Media Matters,* 21 May 2008, http://mediamatters.org/mmtv/200805210009.

83. "Limbaugh on Obama: His 'only chance of winning is that he's black,'" *Media Matters,* 2 Jun. 2008, http://mediamatters.org/mmtv/200806020006.

84. "Beck said 'to be consistent,' Clinton should give Obama '5 percentage points' because of affirmative action," *Media Matters,* 28 Jan. 2008, http://mediamatters.org/research/200801280005.

85. "Coulter: Obama's 'first big accomplishment' was 'being born half-black . . . He wouldn't be running for president if he weren't half-black,'" *Media Matters,* 8 Feb. 2008, http://mediamatters.org/research/200802080017.

86. "Limbaugh called 'Barack Hussein Obama' a 'half-minority,'" *Media Matters,* 17 Jan. 2007, http://mediamatters.org/research/200701170010. "Limbaugh on Obama: 'Halfrican American,'" *Media Matters* 24 Jan. 2007, http://mediamatters.org/research/200701240010.

87. "Monica Crowley forwarded smear that Obama has lied about his ethnicity," *Media Matters,* 26 Jun. 2008, http://mediamatters.org/research/200806260002.

88. "Hannity guest on Obama's church: Its 'scary doctrine' is 'something that you'd see in more like a cult,'" *Media Matters,* 1 Mar. 2007, http://mediamatters.org/research/200703010012.

89. "On Hannity & Colmes, Rev. Peterson compared Obama's church to KKK," *Media Matters,* 23 Jan. 2008, http://mediamatters.org/research/200801230010.

90. "Ignoring Obama's statement on Trumpet award, Hannity suggested that Obama 'associated' himself with Farrakhan," *Media Matters,* 18 Jan. 2008, http://mediamatters.org/research/200801180006.

91. "After asking, 'Do the Obamas have a race problem of their own?' Hannity contin-

ued to smear Barack and Michelle Obama," *Media Matters*, 5 Mar. 2008, http://media matters.org/research/200803050004.

92. "New Details Emerge on Polygamy Raid; McCain Makeover?" *CNN*, 10 Apr. 2008, transcript, http://transcripts.cnn.com/TRANSCRIPTS/0804/10/ec.01.html.

93. Geoffrey Dickens, "Chris Matthews Hails Obama Speech as 'Worthy of Abraham Lincoln,'" *NewsBusters*, 18 Mar. 2008, http://newsbusters.org/blogs/geoffrey-dickens/2008/03/18/chris-matthews-hails-obama-speech-worthy-abraham-lincoln.

94. "Limbaugh: "Obama has disowned his white half . . . he's decided he's got to go all in on the black side," *Media Matters*, 21 Mar. 2008, http://mediamatters.org/research/200803210012.

95. Mike Allen, "McCain, advisers divided over Wright," *Politico*, 15 Oct. 0008, http://www.politico.com/news/stories/1008/14587.html.

96. Patrick Buchanan, "An Unnecessary Defeat?" *Townhall.com*, 7 Nov. 2008, http://townhall.com/columnists/PatBuchanan/2008/11/07/an_unnecessary_defeat.

97. "McCain: Buchanan has already abandoned GOP," *CNN*, 22 Sep. 1999. http://www.cnn.com/ALLPOLITICS/stories/1999/09/22/president.2000/mccain.buchanan/.

98. Sam Stein, "J. D. Hayworth: Gay Marriage Law Could Produce Man-Horse Nuptials," *Huffington Post*, http://www.huffingtonpost.com/2010/03/15/jd-hayworth-gay-marriage_n_498973.html.

99. Melissa Harris-Lacewell, "Rush and Reparations," *Nation*, 12 May 2009, http://www.thenation.com/blog/rush-and-reparations.

100. Glenn Beck, "What's Driving President Obama's Agenda?" *The Glenn Beck Program*, 23 July 2009, transcript, http://www.foxnews.com/story/0,2933,534643,00.html.

101. "Buchanan claims that 'it appears' that Sotomayor 'believe[s] in reverse discrimination against white males,'" *Media Matters*, 27 May 2009, http://mediamatters.org/mmtv/200905270001. "Outrageous comments about Sotomayor," *Media Matters*, 13 Jul. 2009, http://mediamatters.org/research/200907130047. "Buchanan claims that 'it appears' that Sotomayor 'believe[s] in reverse discrimination against white males,'" *Media Matters*, 27 May 2009, http://mediamatters.org/mmtv/200905270001.

102. "Hour 1: Limbaugh Reacts to Sotomayor Nomination: 'Horrible,' 'Hack,' 'Disaster' Nominee Who Should 'Fail,'" *Media Matters*, 26 May 2009, http://mediamatters.org/limbaughwire/2009/05/26. "Limbaugh compares Sotomayor nomination to nominating David Duke," *Media Matters*, 29 May 2009, http://mediamatters.org/mmtv/200905290018.

103. "Beck calls Sotomayor a 'racist,' who 'is not that bright' and 'divisive,'" *Media Matters*, 28 May 2009, http://mediamatters.org/mmtv/200905280008.

104. Ali Frick, "Tancredo: Sotomayor Is a Member of the 'Latino KKK without the Hoods or the Nooses," *Think Progress*, 28 May 2009, http://thinkprogress.org/2009/05/28/tancredo-latino-kkk/.

105. Andy Barr, "Newt Gingrich: Sonia Sotomayor a 'racist,'" *Politico*, 27 May 2009, http://www.politico.com/news/stories/0509/23024.html

106. "Senators Offer Competing Views of Sotomayor," *NPR*, 28 May 2009, transcript, http://www.npr.org/templates/transcript/transcript.php?storyId=104683393.

107. "Meet the Press," *MSNBC*, 31 May 2009, transcript, http://www.msnbc.msn.com/id/31015497/.

108. Greg Sargent, "Steele: GOP Needs to Stop 'Slammin' and Rammin'' on Sotomayor," *Who Runs Gov*, 29 May 2009, http://theplumline.whorunsgov.com/republican-national-committee/steele-gop-needs-to-stop-slammin-and-rammin-on-sotomayor/.

109. Rush Limbaugh, "America's Piñata Strikes Back: We Won't Shut Up on Sotomayor, May 29, 2009," *The Rush Limbaugh Show,* 29 May 2009, http://www.rushlimbaugh.com/home/daily/site_052909/content/01125106.guest.html.

110. "Exclusive: Rush Unleashed, Parts 1 and 2," *Fox News,* 25 Jul. 2009, http://www.foxnews.com/story/0,2933,534701,00.html.

111. Countdown with Keith Olberman, "'Countdown with Keith Olbermann' for Wednesday, July 29," 29 Jul. 2009, http://www.msnbc.msn.com/id/32218739/ns/msnbc_tv-countdown_with_keith_olbermann/.

112. "Ad Boycott Costs Glenn Beck Over 50% of Ad Dollars: 62 Companies Refusing to Advertise with Beck Cost Fox Nearly $600k Per Week," *Color of Change,* 14 Sep. 2009, http://colorofchange.org/beck/more/release-9-14-09.html.

113. "Hour 1: Limbaugh Reacts to Sotomayor Nomination: 'Horrible,' 'Hack,' 'Disaster' Nominee Who Should 'Fail,'" *Media Matters,* 26 May 2009. http://mediamatters.org/limbaughwire/2009/05/26.

114. Jennifer Bendery, "King Downplays Protesters' Racial Slurs Against Congressmen," *Roll Call,* 21 Mar. 2010, http://www.rollcall.com/news/44466-1.html?CMP=OTC-RSS. Andrea Nill, "GOP Rep. Nunes Excuses Racist, Homophobic Tea Partier Slurs as a Response to 'Totalitarian Tactics,'" *Think Progress,* 21 Mar. 2010, http://thinkprogress.org/2010/03/21/nunes-tea-part/.

115. "A Message to the President: Freedom Knows No Race, Sir," *The Rush Limbaugh Show,* 26 Apr. 2010, http://www.rushlimbaugh.com/home/daily/site_042610/content/01125108.guest.html.

7. The Sweetest of Drugs

1. Leon Festinger, Henry W. Riecken, Stanley Schachter, *When Prophecy Fails,* Kindle ed. (London: Pinter & Martin Ltd, 1956): 136.

2. Ibid., 2781.

3. Ibid., 583.

4. Richard J. Herrnstein, Charles A. Murray, *The Bell Curve: Intelligence and Class Structure in American Life,* Free Press ed. (New York: Simon & Schuster, 1994): 508, 548.

5. Ibid., 525–526.

6. Po Bronson and Ashley Merryman, "See Baby Discriminate," *Newsweek,* 5 Sep. 2009, http://www.newsweek.com/2009/09/04/see-baby-discriminate.html.

7. Jake Tapper, "Obama Talks More about 'Typical White Person' Grandmother," *ABC News,* 20 Mar. 2008, http://blogs.abcnews.com/politicalpunch/2008/03/obama-talks-mor.html.

8. Charles Murray, "The Inequality Taboo," *Commentary Magazine,* September 2005, http://www.commentarymagazine.com/viewarticle.cfm/the-inequality-taboo-9934.

9. "The Impact on Georgia," *TooManyAborted.com,* retrieved 5 Feb. 2010, http://www.toomanyaborted.com/?page_id=642.

10. John Rogers, "'Toxic Spiritual Nature' . . . and Those Desks Pinch," *Kung Fu Monkey,* 2 Jun. 2005, http://kfmonkey.blogspot.com/2005/06/toxic-spiritual-nature-and-those-desks.html.

11. Ulrich Bonnell Phillips, "The Central Theme of Southern History," *American Historical Review,* 34 (Oct. 1928): 31.

12. C. Vann Woodward, "The Search for Southern Identity," C. Vann Woodward, *The Burden of Southern History,* third ed. (Baton Rouge: Louisiana State University Press, 1968): 11.

13. *George Wallace: Settin' the Woods on Fire,* dir. Daniel McCabe and Paul Stekler (2000; PBS), http://www.pbs.org/wgbh/amex/wallace/filmmore/transcript/index.html.

14. Thomas Frank, *What's the Matter with Kansas?: How Conservatives Won the Heart of America,* paperback ed., 2005 (New York: Henry Holt and Company, 2004): 133–134.

15. *George Wallace: Settin' the Woods on Fire,* dir. Daniel McCabe and Paul Stekler (2000; PBS), http://www.pbs.org/wgbh/amex/wallace/filmmore/transcript/index.html.

16. Richard Nixon, "Radio Address on the Philosophy of Government," *The American Presidency Project,* 21 Oct. 1972, http://www.presidency.ucsb.edu/ws/index.php?pid=3637.

17. "Hannity falsely claimed 'Obama can't point to a single instance in which . . . Sean Hannity or talk radio' has 'made an issue of Obama's race,'" *Media Matters,* 7 Aug. 2008, http://mediamatters.org/research/200808070009.

18. Alex Seitz-Wald, "Bigoted Tea Party Leader Mark Williams: 'It's Impossible for There to Be a Racist Element in The Tea Party,'" *Think Progress,* 16 Jul. 2010, http://thinkprogress.org/2010/07/16/williams-impossible-racism/. "Tea Party leader says he's done talking about race controversy," *CNN,* 19 Jul. 2010, http://www.cnn.com/2010/POLITICS/07/18/tea.party.imbroglio/index.html.

19. Thomas Byrne Edsall, Mary D. Edsall, *Chain Reaction: The Impact of Race, Rights, and Taxes on American Politics* (New York: W. W. Norton & Company, 1991): 78.

20. Patrick Buchanan, "Discrimination in Reverse," *Chicago Tribune* 26 Oct. 1975: A6.

21. Morton Lukoff, "Bias Law on Gays Draws Opposition of Anita Bryant," *Miami News,* 17 Jan. 1977: 8A.

22. Rush Limbaugh, "America's Piñata Strikes Back: We Won't Shut Up on Sotomayor May 29, 2009," *The Rush Limbaugh Show,* 29 May 2009, http://www.rushlimbaugh.com/home/daily/site_052909/content/01125106.guest.html.

23. Ali Frick, "Tancredo: Sotomayor Is a Member of the 'Latino KKK without the Hoods or the Nooses,'" *Think Progress,* 28 May 2009, http://thinkprogress.org/2009/05/28/tancredo-latino-kkk/.

24. Zachary Roth, "Tea Party Leader on Obama: 'Our Half White, Racist President,'" *Talking Points Memo,* 23 Feb. 2010, http://tpmmuckraker.talkingpointsmemo.com/2010/02/tea_party_leader_on_obama_our_half_white_racist_pr.php. "Business Leaders vs. Pres. Obama; Your Health at Risk; BP's Cap on the Gulf Well," *CNN,* 17 Jul. 2010, http://transcripts.cnn.com/TRANSCRIPTS/1007/17/sitroom.01.html.

25. "Ignoring his own attack on liberals, O'Reilly accused liberal columnists of 'labeling people' with whom they may disagree as 'bigots,'" *Media Matters,* 9 Aug. 2006, http://mediamatters.org/research/200608090007.

26. Molly Ivins, "Faith alive, well in public discourse," *Fort Worth Star-Telegram,* 14 Sep. 1993: 21.

8. Return of the International Jew

1. Michael T. Kaufman, *Soros: The Life and Times of a Messianic Billionaire* (New York: Random House, 2002): 29.

2. Raphael Patai, *The Jews of Hungary: History, Culture, Psychology* (Detroit: Wayne State University Press, 1996): 545–546.

3. Lucy S. Dawidowicz, *The War Against the Jews, 1933–1945,* tenth anniversary ed. (New York: Bantam Books, 1975): 403.

4. Karl R. Popper, *The Open Society and Its Enemies,* fifth ed., reprint (London: Routledge Classics, 1945): 104.

5. Ibid., 144.

6. Anne Newman, "George Soros Slates $100 Million Gift to Support Science," *Wall Street Journal,* 9 Dec. 1992: A17.

7. Ibid.

8. F. William Engdahl, "The Secret Financial Network Behind 'Wizard' George Soros," *Executive Intelligence Review,* 1 Nov. 1996, http://www.questionsquestions.net/docs04/engdahl-soros.html.

9. "Rothschild Rockefeller Fear Competition : Why Michael Jackson Was Murdered!" *Political Vel Craft,* 15 May 2010, http://politicalvelcraft.org/2010/05/15/rothschild-rockefeller-fear-competition-why-michael-jackson-was-murdered-michael-jackson-was-murdered/.

10. Henry Ford, *The International Jew: The World's Foremost Problem, Volume 2* (Weedy, WV: Liberty Bell Publications, 1921): 43-44.

11. Ibid., 173.

12. Ibid.

13. Ibid., 164–169.

14. Michael Dobbs, "Ford and GM Scrutinized for Alleged Nazi Collaboration," *Washington Post,* 30 Nov. 1998: A1, http://www.washingtonpost.com/wp-srv/national/daily/nov98/nazicars30.htm.

15. Neil Baldwin, *Henry Ford and the Jews: The Mass Production of Hate* (New York: Public Affairs, 2001): 297.

16. "America and the Holocaust," *PBS,* retrieved 29 Mar. 2010, http://www.pbs.org/wgbh/amex/holocaust/peopleevents/pandeAMEX96.html.

17. F. William Engdahl, "The Secret Financial Network behind 'Wizard' George Soros," *Executive Intelligence Review,* 1 Nov. 1996, http://www.questionsquestions.net/docs04/engdahl-soros.html.

18. Ibid.

19. Michael T. Kaufman, *Soros: The Life and Times of a Messianic Billionaire* (New York: Random House, 2002): 37.

20. Ibid.

21. F. William Engdahl, "The Secret Financial Network behind 'Wizard' George Soros," *Executive Intelligence Review,* 1 Nov. 1996, http://www.questionsquestions.net/docs04/engdahl-soros.html.

22. Jeffrey Steinberg, "George Soros: Drug Pusher for the Queen," *Executive Intelligence Review,* 24:35 (29 Aug. 1997). Scott Thompson, "'Inside-Outside' Job for the Oligarchy," *Executive Intelligence Review,* 28:32 (24 Aug. 2001).

23. Michele Steinberg and Scott Thompson, "Dope Czar Soros Bids to Buy Up Democratic Party," *Executive Intelligence Review,* 31:2 (16 Jan. 2004).

24. Amir Mizroch, "Malaysian officials hand out copies of 'International Jew,'" *Jerusalem Post,* 22 Jun. 2003: 3.

25. Ibid.

26. John Cassity, "The Ringleader," *New Yorker,* 81:22 (1 Aug. 2005): 42.

27. Laura Blumenfeld, "Soros's Deep Pockets vs. Bush," *Washington Post,* 11 Nov. 2003: A3.

28. "George Soros Contributions to 527 Organizations, 2004 cycle," *OpenSecrets.org,* retrieved 31 Mar. 2010, http://www.opensecrets.org/527s/527indivsdetail.php?id=U0000000364&cycle=2004.

29. Robert G. Kaiser and Ira Chinoy, "Scaife: Funding Father of the Right," *Washington*

Post, 2 May 1999, http://www.washingtonpost.com/wp-srv/politics/special/clinton/stories/scaifemain050299.htm.

30. Brooks Jackson, "Who Is Richard Mellon Scaife?" *CNN,* 27 Apr. 1998, http://www.cnn.com/ALLPOLITICS/1998/04/27/scaife.profile/.

31. Jon Friedman, "Chris Ruddy: Conservatives' great online ally," *MarketWatch,* 13 Mar. 2009, http://www.marketwatch.com/story/rush-limbaugh-matt-drudge-trail-news-max.

32. Dirk Smillie, "A Great Right Hope," *Forbes.com,* 6 Mar. 2009, http://www.forbes.com/2009/03/06/newsmax-christopher-ruddy-business-media-ruddy.html.

33. David A. Patten, "Sarah Palin Says Newsmax 'Very Valuable,'" *NewsMax,* 17 Nov. 2009, http://www.newsmax.com/InsideCover/palin-newsmax-kudos/2009/11/17/id/336290.

34. Richard Poe, "George Soros' Coup," *NewsMax,* May 2004 (1 May 2004): 23–24, http://w3.newsmax.com/a/soros/.

35. Ibid.

36. "NewsMax's Poe on O'Reilly Factor: George Soros is a 'madman'; O'Reilly on Radio Factor: George Soros is 'a real sleazoid,'" *Media Matters,* 19 May 2004, http://mediamatters.org/research/200405190007.

37. Leslie Wayne, "And for His Next Feat, a Billionaire Sets Sights on Bush," *New York Times,* 31 May 2004, http://www.nytimes.com/2004/05/31/politics/campaign/31soros.html. "NewsMax's Poe on O'Reilly Factor: George Soros is a 'madman'; O'Reilly on Radio Factor: George Soros is 'a real sleazoid,'" *Media Matters,* 19 May 2004, http://mediamatters.org/research/200405190007. "O'Reilly smeared Soros . . . again," *Media Matters,* 1 Jun. 2004, http://mediamatters.org/research/200406010004. Eric Alterman, "The Soros Slander Campaign Continues," *Nation,* 17 Jun. 2004, http://www.thenation.com/doc/20040705/alterman. "O'Reilly says Soros is 'like the guy that James Bond goes after,'" *Media Matters,* 7 Apr. 2009, http://mediamatters.org/mmtv/200904070040. "O'Reilly: 'They ought to hang this Soros guy,'" *Media Matters,* 3 Jan. 2006, http://mediamatters.org/mmtv/200601030007. "One week after comparing Soros to Mussolini, O'Reilly declared Soros 'believes' 'we're Nazis' because of U.S. policies," *Media Matters,* 12 Oct. 2006, http://mediamatters.org/research/200610120013. "O'Reilly on Soros: An 'incredible imbecile, with all due respect'; 'a guy who doesn't understand evil,' despite having 'fled the Holocaust,'" *Media Matters,* 17 Aug. 2006, http://mediamatters.org/mmtv/200608170007.

38. "O'Reilly denies 'go[ing] after' Soros—doesn't explain prior comment that '[t]hey ought to hang' him," *Media Matters,* 13 Oct. 2006, http://mediamatters.org/research/200409170003.

39. Michael T. Kaufman, *Soros: The Life and Times of a Messianic Billionaire* (New York: Random House, 2002): 242.

40. "O'Reilly says Soros is 'like the guy that James Bond goes after,'" *Media Matters,* 7 Apr. 2009, http://mediamatters.org/mmtv/200904070040.

41. Bill O'Reilly, *Culture Warrior* (New York: Broadway Books, 2006): 65–66.

42. Bill O'Reilly, "Buying Political Power," *Fox News,* 24 Apr. 2007, http://www.foxnews.com/story/0,2933,268043,00.html.

43. "O'Reilly: ACLU is America's 'most dangerous organization . . . second next to Al Qaeda,'" *Media Matters,* 8 Jun. 2004, http://mediamatters.org/research/200406080005.

44. "O'Reilly: 'It is not a stretch to say MoveOn is the new Klan,'" *Media Matters,* 24 Jul. 2008, http://mediamatters.org/research/200807240007.

45. "O'Reilly on 'assassins who work for Media Matters and Move On,'" *Media Matters,* http://mediamatters.org/mmtv/200709060006.

46. "About Us," *Media Matters,* 2 Apr. 2010, retrieved, http://mediamatters.org/p/about_us/.

47. Laura Kipnis, "Brock Attack," *Slate,* 18 May 2004, http://www.slate.com/id/2100712/.

48. "O'Reilly falsely accused Media Matters of lying about Soros funding," *Media Matters,* 27 Apr. 2007, http://mediamatters.org/research/200704270006.

49. "O'Reilly purported to chart an intricate web leading to 'vile propaganda outfit' Media Matters," *Media Matters,* 24 Apr. 2007, http://mediamatters.org/research/200704240003. "O'Reilly falsely accused Media Matters of lying about Soros funding," *Media Matters,* 27 Apr. 2007, http://mediamatters.org/research/200704270006.

50. "O'Reilly called Media Matters 'paid assassins,' told caller they 'will never set foot, not only in my program, but at Fox News Channel,'" *Media Matters,* 17 Oct. 2005, http://mediamatters.org/research/200510170010.

51. *Compete.com,* 18 July 2010, retrieved, http://compete.com.

52. "O'Reilly purported to chart an intricate web leading to 'vile propaganda outfit' Media Matters," *Media Matters,* 24 Apr. 2007, http://mediamatters.org/research/200704240003.

53. Bill O'Reilly, *Culture Warrior* (New York: Broadway Books, 2006): 15.

54. "O'Reilly purported to chart an intricate web leading to 'vile propaganda outfit' Media Matters," *Media Matters,* 24 Apr. 2007, http://mediamatters.org/research/200704240003.

55. "MoveOn.org: Top Contributors, 2004 Cycle," *OpenSecrets.org,* 4 Apr. 2010, retrieved, http://www.opensecrets.org/527s/527cmtedetail_contribs.php?cycle=2004&ein=200234065. Paul Farhi, "Deluge Shuts Down Post Blog," *Washington Post,* 21 Jan. 2006, http://www.washingtonpost.com/wp-dyn/content/article/2006/01/20/AR2006012001909.html.

56. Carol J. Loomis, "Sex. Reefer? and Auto Insurance! Peter Lewis Has Built Progressive Corp. into a Smashingly Successful Insurance Company and a Stock Market Star," *CNN,* 7 Aug. 1995, http://money.cnn.com/magazines/fortune/fortune_archive/1995/08/07/205140/index.htm. "Setting the Story Straight on Marijuana," *Washington Post,* 11 Jan. 2005: A14.

57. Jacob Berkman, "At least 139 of the Forbes 400 are Jewish," *JTA* 5 Oct. 2009, http://blogs.jta.org/philanthropy/article/2009/10/05/1008323/at-least-139-of-the-forbes-400-are-jewish.

58. Amotz Asa-El, "The Sorrows of George Soros," *Jerusalem Post,* 21 Nov. 2003: 20.

59. Henry Ford Sr., *The International Jew: The World's Foremost Problem, Volume 3* (Weedy, W. Virginia: Liberty Bell Publications, 1921): 30–31.

60. "Gingrich: George Soros 'wants to spend $75 million defeating George W. Bush because Soros wants to legalize heroin,'" *Media Matters,* 31 Aug. 2004, http://mediamatters.org/research/200408310010.

61. Jack Shafer, "Dennis Hastert on Dope," *Slate,* 1 Sep. 2004, http://www.slate.com/id/2106077/.

62. "On FOX, Tony Blankley called Soros 'a Jew who figured out a way to survive the Holocaust,'" *Media Matters,* 4 Jun. 2004, http://mediamatters.org/research/200406040004.

63. "Coulter smeared Soros: He 'blam[es] anti-Semitism on the Jews,'" *Media Matters,* 16 Jun. 2004, http://mediamatters.org/research/200406160003.

64. Eric Alterman, "The Soros Slander Campaign Continues," *Nation,* 17 Jun. 2004, http://www.thenation.com/article/soros-slander-campaign-continues.

65. "Coulter goes LaRouchie: NFL players would rather play for Rush Limbaugh than

George Soros, a 'Nazi collaborator,'" *Crooks and Liars,* 16 Oct. 2009, http://www.thenation.com/article/soros-slander-campaign-continues..

66. Jill Zuckman, "Embattled DeLay says he's sorry; Comment on Schiavo judges called 'inartful,'" *Chicago Tribune,* 14 Apr. 2005: 1.

67. "Transcript of interview with Tom DeLay," *Washington Times,* 13 Apr. 2005, http://www.washingtontimes.com/news/2005/apr/13/20050413-111439-5048r/.

68. "Media repeat anti-Soros propaganda by DeLay defenders," *Media Matters,* 19 Apr. 2005, http://mediamatters.org/research/200504190004.

69. Richard Poe, "Soros Shadow Party Stalks DeLay," *FrontPageMagazine.com,* 12 Apr. 2005, http://frontpagemagazine.com/readArticle.aspx?ARTID=8955.

70. "LaRouche Denounces 'Obama's Godfather' George Soros behind Attempt to Start World War III in the Caucasus," *Executive Intelligence Review,* 10 Aug. 2008, http://www.larouchepub.com/pr_lar/2008/lar_pac/080809soros_behind_war.html/.

71. Rush Limbaugh, "Who's Really Running Obama?" *The Rush Limbaugh Show,* 27 Apr. 2009, http://www.rushlimbaugh.com/home/daily/site_042709/content/01125111.guest.html.

72. Rowan Scarborough, "George Soros' Liberal Agenda Will Carry Weight in Obama Presidency," *Human Events,* 5 Nov. 2008, http://www.humanevents.com/article.php?id=29359.

9. A Goat for Azazel

1. Tom Douglas, *Scapegoats: Transferring Blame* (London: Routledge, 1995): 7.

2. Mark Schaller and Steven L. Neuberg, "Intergroup Prejudices and Intergroup Conflicts," ed. Charles B. Crawford and Dennis Krebs, *Foundations of Evolutionary Psychology* (New York: Lawrence Erlbaum Associates, 2008): 405.

3. Ibid., 403.

4. Norman Rufus Colin Cohn, *Warrant for Genocide: The Myth of the Jewish World—Conspiracy and the Protocols of the Elders of Zion* (New York: Harper & Row, 1967): 254.

5. "Glenn Beck: Know Your Czars!" *The Glenn Beck Program,* 7 Aug. 2009, http://www.glennbeck.com/content/articles/article/198/29083/.

6. "Conservative media unleash anti-gay rhetoric in attacks on Jennings," *Media Matters,* 1 Oct. 2009, http://mediamatters.org/research/200910010008.

10. The Progressive Hunter

1. Adrian McCoy, "Glenn Beck Set to Skewer the Holidays," *Pittsburgh Post-Gazette,* 7 Dec. 2004: E1.

2. "Glenn Beck Joins CNN Headline News," *CNN,* 17 Jan. 2006, http://www.cnn.com/2006/SHOWBIZ/TV/01/17/glenn.beck/index.html.

3. "Is Foiled Terror Plot Part of Something Bigger?; Is Iran Working Towards the Apocalypse?" *CNN,* 10 Aug. 2006, http://archives.cnn.com/TRANSCRIPTS/0608/10/gb.01.html.

4. "Beck, Carlson noted that apocalyptic August 22 predictions were wrong; Beck still foresees a 'world war of biblical proportions,'" *Media Matters,* 23 Aug. 2006, http://mediamatters.org/research/200608230009.

5. John Amato, "Frum: Republicans work for Fox News Now," *Crooks and Liars,* 23 Mar. 2010, http://crooksandliars.com/john-amato/frum-republicans-work-fox-news-now.

6. W. Cleon Skousen, *The Naked Capitalist,* 1974 printing (Salt Lake City, UT: W. C. Skousen, 1970): 24–25.

7. Ibid., 6.

8. Howard Witt, "Slipping into the Mainstream," *Orlando Sentinel,* 11 Jun. 1995, http://articles.orlandosentinel.com/1995-06-11/news/9506120302_1_united-nations-state-legislatures-conference-of-state.

9. Glenn Beck, "Political talk with Glenn," *The Glenn Beck Program,* 18 Sep. 2006.

10. Simon Maloy, "Stop me when this starts sounding familiar," *Media Matters,* 20 Oct. 2009, http://mediamatters.org/blog/200910200010.

11. Lou Dobbs, "Top Democrats and Leading Republican Join Forces to Challenge President's Conduct of Iraq War; White House to Allow Federal Court to Oversee Warrantless Wiretap Program; Members of Congress Lashed Out at President Bush Over Inaction in Border Patrol Agent," *CNN,* 17 Jan. 2007, http://transcripts.cnn.com/TRANSCRIPTS/0701/17/ldt.01.html. Justin Elliott, "Rand Paul in '08: Beware the NAFTA Superhighway!" *Talking Points Memo,* 21 May 2010, http://tpmmuckraker.talkingpointsmemo.com/2010/05/rand_paul_beware_the_nafta_superhighway_video.php.

12. Gretel C. Kovach, "Highway to Hell?" *Newsweek,* 10 Dec. 2007, http://www.newsweek.com/id/73372.

13. Michael Dobbs, "A 'Superhighway' to Nowhere," *washingtonpost.com,* 3 Dec. 2007, http://voices.washingtonpost.com/fact-checker/2007/12/a_superhighway_to_nowhere.html.

14. "The NAFTA Superhighway," *Ron Paul's Texas Straight Talk,* 30 Oct. 2006, http://www.house.gov/paul/tst/tst2006/tst103006.htm.

15. Gretel C. Kovach, "Highway To Hell?" *Newsweek,* 10 Dec. 2007, http://www.newsweek.com/id/73372.

16. "Liberty in Peril: What You Need to Know," *CNN,* 24 Oct. 2007, http://transcripts.cnn.com/TRANSCRIPTS/0710/24/gb.01.html.

17. "Beck said Gore using 'same tactic' in fight against global warming as Hitler did against Jews," *Media Matters,* 1 May 2007, http://mediamatters.org/research/200705010003.

18. Brian Stelter and Bill Carter, "Fox News's Mad, Apocalyptic, Tearful Rising Star," *New York Times,* 29 Mar. 2009. Bill Carter and Brian Stelter, "Fox News Hires Glenn Beck Away from CNN," *New York Times,* 16 Oct. 2008, http://www.nytimes.com/2008/10/17/business/media/17fox.html.

19. Brian Stelter and Bill Carter, "Fox News's Mad, Apocalyptic, Tearful Rising Star," *New York Times,* 29 Mar. 2009, http://www.nytimes.com/2009/03/30/business/media/30beck.html.

20. "Obama's Many Policy 'Czars' Draw Ire from Conservatives," *Washington Post,* 16 Sep. 2009, http://www.washingtonpost.com/wp-dyn/content/article/2009/09/15/AR2009091501424.html. Amanda Schaffer, "The Family Un-Planner," *Slate,* 21 Nov. 2006, http://www.slate.com/id/2154249/.

21. "List of Obama's Czars," *The Glenn Beck Program,* 21 Aug. 2009, http://www.glennbeck.com/content/articles/article/198/29391/.

22. "Obama's Many Policy 'Czars' Draw Ire from Conservatives," *Washington Post,* 16 Sep. 2009, http://www.washingtonpost.com/wp-dyn/content/article/2009/09/15/AR2009091501424.html. Jess Henig, "Czar Search," *FactCheck.org,* 25 Sep. 2009, http://www.factcheck.org/2009/09/czar-search/. Kay Bailey Hutchison, "Czarist Washington," *Washington Post,* 13 Sep. 2009, http://www.washingtonpost.com/wp-dyn/content/article/2009/09/11/AR2009091103504.html.

23. Brian Wilson, "Obama's Czars Spark Concerns among Some Lawmakers," *Fox News,* 17 Apr. 2009, http://www.foxnews.com/politics/2009/04/17/obamas-czars-spark-concerns-lawmakers/.

24. Glenn Beck, "Time for a Czar Czar?" *Fox News,* 9 Jun. 2009, http://www.foxnews.com/story/0,2933,525594,00.html.

25. Glenn Beck, "Glenn Beck: All the President's Men," *The Glenn Beck Program,* 26 Aug. 2009. http://www.glennbeck.com/content/articles/article/198/29702/.

26. Michael Elliott, "Heroes of the Environment 2008," *Time,* 24 Sep. 2008, http://www.time.com/time/specials/packages/article/0,28804,1841778_1841781_1841811,00.html.

27. "The 12 Most Creative Minds of 2008," *Fast Company,* 23 Dec. 2008, http://www.fastcompany.com/multimedia/slideshows/content/creative-minds-2008.html?page=4.

28. "Glenn Beck: Van Jones unhinged," *The Glenn Beck Program,* 1 Sep. 2009, http://www.glennbeck.com/content/articles/article/198/29967/. "Glenn Beck on Importance of Van Jones' Resignation," *Fox News,* 8 Sep. 2009, http://mediamatters.org/mmtv/2009 09080046. "Glenn Beck's Health Care Special," *Fox News,* 12 Aug. 2009, http://www.foxnews.com/story/0,2933,539162,00.html. "Glenn Beck: Know Your Czars!" *The Glenn Beck Program,* 7 Aug. 2009. http://www.glennbeck.com/content/articles/article/198/29083/.

29. Eliza Strickland, "The New Face of Environmentalism," *East Bay Express,* 2 Nov. 2005, http://www.eastbayexpress.com/gyrobase/the-new-face-of-environmentalism/Content?oid=1079539. Eva Paterson, "Glenn Beck's Attack on Van Jones: Fantasies & Falsehoods," *Equal Justice Society,* 28 Aug. 2009, http://www.equaljusticesociety.org/2009/08/glenn_beck_van_jones/.

30. "Glenn Beck: Your Science Czar Is a Commie," *The Glenn Beck Program,* 23 Jul. 2009, http://www.glennbeck.com/content/articles/article/198/28315/.

31. "Glenn Beck: Van Jones Unhinged," *The Glenn Beck Program,* 1 Sep. 2009, http://www.glennbeck.com/content/articles/article/198/29967/.

32. Glenn Beck, "Is Obama Taking Pointers from Hugo Chavez?" *Fox News,* 11 Jan. 2010, http://www.foxnews.com/story/0,2933,582806,00.html. "Just a Happy Warrior: Glenn Beck Interview," *NewsMax,* 29 Sep. 2009. http://w3.newsmax.com/a/oct09/beck/interview.cfm. Glenn Beck, "Glenn Beck: Speak without Fear," *The Glenn Beck Program,* 27 Aug. 2009, http://www.glennbeck.com/content/articles/article/198/29753/.

33. Mark Lloyd, "Comments of FCC Chief Diversity Officer Mark Lloyd at Social Media, Net Neutrality, and Future of Journalism event," *Media Access, Project* 14 Dec. 2009, http://www.mediaaccess.org/articles/comments-of-keynote-speaker-mark-lloyd-at-social-media-net-neutrality-and-future-of-journalism-event.

34. Alexi Mostrous, "Coalition Organizes in Support of Mark Lloyd," *Washington Post,* 16 Sep. 2009, http://voices.washingtonpost.com/44/2009/09/16/coalition_organizes_in_support.html.

35. "Congressman: Obama wants Gestapo-like force," *MSNBC,* 11 Nov. 2008, http://www.msnbc.msn.com/id/27655039/.

36. "Glenn Beck: Obama TOLD us this was coming . . ." *The Glenn Beck Program,* 28 Jul. 2009, http://www.glennbeck.com/content/articles/article/198/28533/. "Glenn Beck: No One Took Obama at His Word," *The Glenn Beck Program,* 28 Jul. 2009, http://www.glennbeck.com/content/articles/article/198/28547/. "Glenn's Interview with Michelle Malkin," *The Glenn Beck Program,* 28 Jul. 2009, http://www.glennbeck.com/content/articles/article/196/28528/. "Glenn Beck: Town Hall meetings intensify," *The Glenn Beck Program,* 7 Aug. 2009, http://www.glennbeck.com/content/articles/article/198/29077/?ck=1. "Glenn Beck: Barack Obama's Civilian Army," *The Glenn Beck Program,* 28 Aug. 2009,

http://www.glennbeck.com/content/articles/article/198/29815/. "Glenn Beck: More Van Jones Lunacy," *The Glenn Beck Program,* 2 Sep. 2009, http://www.glennbeck.com/content/articles/article/198/30037/. "Glenn Beck talks with Ann Coulter," *The Glenn Beck Program,* 30 Oct. 2008, http://www.glennbeck.com/content/articles/article/196/17513/.

37. "Glenn Beck: A politician who gets it?" *The Glenn Beck Program,* 8 Sep. 2009, http://www.glennbeck.com/content/articles/article/198/30208/.

38. "Glenn Beck: Barack Obama's Civilian Army," *The Glenn Beck Program,* 28 Aug. 2009, http://www.glennbeck.com/content/articles/article/198/29815/.

39. Brooks Jackson, "Is Obama planning a Gestapo-like 'civilian national security force'?" *FactCheck.org,* 11 Nov. 2008, http://www.factcheck.org/askfactcheck/is_obama_planning_a_gestapo-like_civilian_national.html.

40. "Glenn Beck Exclusive: Warns of 'Reichstag Event'," *NewsMax,* 29 Sep. 2009, http://newsmax.com/InsideCover/beck-obama-reichstag-fox/2009/12/12/id/341897.

41. "Beck: 'Key is being turned . . . I fear a Reichstag moment, a—God forbid—another 9-11, something that will turn this machine on,'" *Media Matters,* 7 Oct. 2009, http://mediamatters.org/mmtv/200910070007.

42. Glenn Beck, "Glenn Beck: Speak without Fear," *The Glenn Beck Program,* 27 Aug. 2009, http://www.glennbeck.com/content/articles/article/198/29753/. "Limbaugh on Attacks on Freedom of Speech," *Fox News,* 26 Aug. 2009, http://www.foxnews.com/story/0,2933,543682,00.html.

43. "Naming Names," *Fox News,* 2 Nov. 2009, http://www.foxnews.com/search-results/m/27221712/naming-names.htm.

44. "Glenn's Interview with Michelle Malkin," *The Glenn Beck Program,* 28 Jul. 2009, http://www.glennbeck.com/content/articles/article/196/28528/.

45. "Is Foiled Terror Plot Part of Something Bigger?; Is Iran Working Towards the Apocalypse?" *CNN,* 10 Aug. 2006, http://archives.cnn.com/TRANSCRIPTS/0608/10/gb.01.html.

46. "Obama, in His Own Words," *Fox News,* 21 Sep. 2009, http://www.foxnews.com/search-results/m/26515079/obama-in-his-own-words.htm.

47. Thomas Harry Williams, Richard Nelson Current, Frank Burt Freidel, *A History of the United States,* third ed. (New York: Knopf, 1959): 281.

48. "Beck attacks social justice," *Media Matters,* 12 Mar. 2010, http://mediamatters.org/research/201003120055.

49. "Glenn Beck on Progressivism in America," *Fox News,* 1 Mar. 2010, http://www.foxnews.com/story/0,2933,587671,00.html.

50. "The One Thing: We love you too, Van Jones," *Fox News,* 1 Mar. 2010, http://www.foxnews.com/search-results/m/29252598/the-one-thing-3-1.htm.

51. "Beck claims 'this game is for keeps' with 'the left', asks listeners to 'pray for protection,'" *Media Matters,* 8 Sep. 2009, http://mediamatters.org/mmtv/200909080010.

52. "Glenn Beck: Politics of Fear," *The Glenn Beck Program,* 25 Mar. 2010, http://www.glennbeck.com/content/articles/article/198/38467/.

53. "Glenn dines with George Soros on earth day," *The Glenn Beck Program,* 23 Apr. 2009, http://www.glennbeck.com/content/articles/article/198/24436/.

54. Glenn Beck, "Beck likens himself to 'Israeli Nazi hunters': 'to the day I die, I am going to be a progressive hunter,'" *Media Matters,* 20 Jan. 2010, http://mediamatters.org/mmtv/201001200016.

55. James Taranto, "Nobody's Watching Charlie Rose," *Wall Street Journal,* 16 Jan. 2010, http://online.wsj.com/article/SB10001424052748703436504574641192528461858.html.

56. "Van Jones out, Glenn reacts," *The Glenn Beck Program,* 8 Sep. 2009, http://www.glennbeck.com/content/articles/article/198/30212/.

57. "Glenn Beck: Expanding Obama's Coalition," *Fox News,* 25 Mar. 2010, http://www.foxnews.com/story/0,2933,589982,00.html.

58. "Beck's latest conspiracy theory surrounds Andy Stern stepping down: 'Something's not right,'" *Media Matters,* 13 Apr. 2010, http://mediamatters.org/mmtv/201004130024.

59. "Controversial Obama Adviser Jones Resigns," *CBS News,* 6 Sep. 2006, http://www.cbsnews.com/stories/2009/09/06/politics/main5290652.shtml. Scott Shane, "Conservatives Draw Blood from Acorn," *New York Times,* 15 Sep. 2009, http://www.nytimes.com/2009/09/16/us/politics/16acorn.html.

60. "Glenn responds to *The View* debacle," *The Glenn Beck Program,* 21 May 2009, http://www.glennbeck.com/content/articles/article/201/25653/.

61. Lacey Rose, "Glenn Beck Inc," *Forbes,* 8 Apr. 2010, http://www.forbes.com/forbes/2010/0426/entertainment-fox-news-simon-schuster-glenn-beck-inc.html.

62. "The Resurrection of Van Jones," *Fox News,* 24 Feb. 2010, http://www.foxnews.com/search-results/m/29198471/the-resurrection-of-van-jones.htm.

63. Glenn Beck, "The Fight to Mainstream Socialism," *Fox News,* 22 Apr. 2010, http://www.foxnews.com/story/0,2933,591383,00.html.

64. "Glenn Beck: SEIU's Outrageous Intimidation Tactics," *The Glenn Beck Program,* 21 May 2010, http://www.glennbeck.com/content/articles/article/198/40926/.

65. "Panic Time at Fox News as Glenn Beck loses 50% of his Viewers," *The Glenn Beck Program,* 17 May 0201, http://www.politicususa.com/en/glenn-beck-ratings-drop.

66. "Meltdown: The intricate conspiracy to 'destroy' Glenn Beck, his family, God, and the founders," *Media Matters,* 25 May 2010, http://mediamatters.org/research/201005250049.

67. Jillian Rayfield, "I'm Sayin' He Is a Gold Digger: Weiner Takes On Beck's Goldline Ties," *Talking Points Memo,* 20 May 2010, http://tpmlivewire.talkingpointsmemo.com/2010/05/-weiner-takes-on-becks-goldline-ties.php.

68. "American Nightly Scoreboard for May 24, 2010," *CBS MoneyWatch.com,* 24 May 2010, http://findarticles.com/p/news-articles/finance-wire/mi_8120/is_20100524/american-nightly-scoreboard-24-2010/ai_n53779281.

69. "Meltdown: The intricate conspiracy to 'destroy' Glenn Beck, his family, God, and the founders," *Media Matters,* 25 May 2010, http://mediamatters.org/research/201005250049.

11. An Appealing Wondrous Story

1. Brian Stelter and Bill Carter, "Fox News's Mad, Apocalyptic, Tearful Rising Star," *New York Times,* 29 Mar. 2009, http://www.nytimes.com/2009/03/30/business/media/30beck.html.

2. Glenn Beck, "Political talk with Glenn," *The Glenn Beck Program,* 18 Sep. 2006.

3. Erving Goffman, *Frame Analysis: An Essay on the Organization of Experience,* First Northeastern University Press edition, 1986 (Lebanon, NH: Northeastern University Press, 1974): 10–11.

4. Buck Wolf, "Hungry for Miracles? Try Jesus on a Fish Stick," *ABC News,* 30 Nov. 2004, http://abcnews.go.com/Entertainment/WolfFiles/story?id=307227&page=1.

5. Jed Lewison, "Beck conspiracy theory: 'Cash for clunkers' site lets Feds control your

PC," *Daily Kos,* 1 Aug. 2009, http://www.dailykos.com/storyonly/2009/8/1/760538/-Beck-conspiracy-theory:-Cash-for-clunkers-site-lets-Feds-control-your-PC.

6. Glenn Beck, "Things That Make You Go 'Hmm,'" *Fox News,* 30 Jun. 2010, http://www.foxnews.com/story/0,2933,595707,00.html.

7. "Beck, conservative media fearmonger that cap-and-trade would grant president Chavez-like powers," *Media Matters,* 12 Nov. 2009, http://mediamatters.org/research/200911120036.

8. "Cap n Trade bill," *The Glenn Beck Program,* 26 Jun. 2009, http://www.glennbeck.com/content/articles/article/198/27284/.

9. Jerome Bruner, *Actual Minds, Possible Worlds,* Kindle ed. (Cambridge, MA: Harvard Univ. Press, 1986). *Narrative Psychology: The Storied Nature of Human Conduct,* ed. Theodore R. Sarbin (Westport, CT: Praeger Publishers, 1986).

10. Elissa Lee and Laura Leets, "Persuasive Storytelling by Hate Groups Online: Examining Its Effects on Adolescents," *American Behavioral Scientist,* 45:6 (Feb. 2002): 928, 951.

11. Theodore R. Sarbin, *Narrative Psychology: The Storied Nature of Human Conduct* (Westport, CT: Praeger Publishers, 1986): 17.

12. Michael Bader, "We Need to Have Empathy for Tea Partiers," *Psychology Today,* 5 Mar. 2010, http://www.psychologytoday.com/blog/what-is-he-thinking/201003/we-need-have-empathy-tea-partiers.

13. "Glenn Beck on Progressivism in America," *Fox News* 1 Mar. 2010, http://www.foxnews.com/story/0,2933,587671,00.html.

14. George E. Marcus, "The Paranoid Style Now," *Paranoia within Reason: A Casebook on Conspiracy as Explanation,* George E. Marcus, ed. (Chicago: University of Chicago Press, 1999): 5.

12. Second Amendment Remedies

1. Tom Harkin, "Why I Am a Progressive Populist," *Progressive Populist,* 1:1 (November 1995), http://www.populist.com/11-95.Harkin.html.

2. Adam Lowenstein, "Kubby won't run again for City Council," *Cedar Rapids Gazette,* 26 May 1999: A1.

3. Osha Gray Davidson, *Under Fire: The NRA and the Battle for Gun Control,* expanded ed. (Iowa City,: University of Iowa Press, 1993): 46.

4. Ibid., 45.

5. Fox Butterfield, "Terror in Oklahoma: Echoes of the N.R.A.," *New York Times,* 8 May 1995, http://www.nytimes.com/1995/05/08/us/terror-oklahoma-echoes-nra-rifle-association-has-long-practice-railing-against.html.

6. Kim Masters, "Recoil from the NRA's Two Top Guns," *Washington Post,* 29 Apr. 1995: D1.

7. "Use of Force: ATF Policy, Training and Review Process Are Comparable to DEA's and FBI's," *United States General Accounting Office,* 29 Mar. 1996: 64.

8. Fox Butterfield, "Terror in Oklahoma: Echoes of the N.R.A.," *New York Times,* 8 May 1995, http://www.nytimes.com/1995/05/08/us/terror-oklahoma-echoes-nra-rifle-association-has-long-practice-railing-against.html.

9. Ibid.

10. "Use of Force: ATF Policy, Training and Review Process Are Comparable to DEA's and FBI's," *United States General Accounting Office,* 29 Mar. 1996: 64.

11. Ben Smith, "NRA: Obama most anti-gun candidate ever, will ban guns," *Politico*, 6 Aug. 2008, http://www.politico.com/blogs/bensmith/0808/NRA_Obama_most_antigun_candidate_ever_will_ban_guns.html.

12. Jim Abrams, "Democrats show little appetite for gun control," *San Francisco Chronicle*, 3 Mar. 2009, http://www.sfgate.com/cgi-bin/article.cgi?f=/n/a/2009/03/03/national/w113127S88.DTL.

13. Fox Butterfield, "Terror in Oklahoma: Echoes of the N.R.A.," *New York Times*, 8 May 1995, http://www.nytimes.com/1995/05/08/us/terror-oklahoma-echoes-nra-rifle-association-has-long-practice-railing-against.html.

14. Patrik Jonsson, "NRA: The new face of the American right?" *Christian Science Monitor*, 18 May 2009, http://www.csmonitor.com/USA/Society/2009/0518/p02s04-ussc.html.

15. Julie Rose, "Anti-Government Sentiment Fuels NRA Push," *N.P.R.*, 18 May 2010, http://www.npr.org/templates/story/story.php?storyId=126907128.

16. Patrik Jonsson, "NRA: The new face of the American right?" *Christian Science Monitor*, 18 May 2009, http://www.csmonitor.com/USA/Society/2009/0518/p02s04-ussc.html.

17. Will Sullivan, "Armed and in the Middle," *U.S. News & World Report*, 13 May 2007, http://www.usnews.com/usnews/news/articles/070513/21qa.htm.

18. Jim Spellman, "Ammo hard to find as gun owners stock up," *CNN*, 4 May 2009, http://www.cnn.com/2009/US/05/04/ammo.shortage/index.html.

19. Andrew Purcell, "Fear over Obama's gun laws sparks massive rush to pack a pistol," *Sunday Herald*, 5 Jul. 2009, http://www.heraldscotland.com/fear-over-obama-s-gun-laws-sparks-massive-rush-to-pack-a-pistol-1.829092.

20. Timothy B. Tyson, *Radio Free Dixie: Robert F. Williams and the Roots of Black Power* (Chapel Hill: University of North Carolina Press, 1999): 87, 149, 153, 198, 242, 277.

21. Osha Gray Davidson, *Under Fire: The NRA and the Battle for Gun Control*, Expanded ed. (Iowa City: University of Iowa Press, 1993): 20.

22. Nicholas M. Horrock and Tom Hundley, "NRA's romantic view fading into sunset," *Chicago Tribune*, 22 Mar. 1989: 1.

23. Ben Smith, "NRA: Obama most anti-gun candidate ever, will ban guns," *Politico*, 6 Aug. 2008, http://www.politico.com/blogs/bensmith/0808/NRA_Obama_most_antigun_candidate_ever_will_ban_guns.html.

24. Mary C. Curtis, "Sarah Palin Tells NRA Convention Obama Would Ban Guns if He Could," *Politics Daily*, 15 May 2010, http://www.politicsdaily.com/2010/05/14/sarah-palin-tells-nra-convention-obama-would-ban-guns-if-he-coul/.

25. Mary C. Curtis, "Glenn Beck Tells NRA Members: Fight the 'Marxists' at the Polls," *Politics Daily*, http://www.politicsdaily.com/2010/05/16/glenn-beck-tells-nra-members-fight-the-marxists-at-the-polls/.

26. Emilie Raymond, *From My Cold, Dead Hands: Charlton Heston and American Politics* (Lexington: University Press of Kentucky, 2006): 6. "Documents Regarding Charlton Heston's Support for Gun Control Following the 1968 Assassinations of Robert Kennedy and Martin Luther King, Jr.," *Violence Policy Center*, 26 May 2010, retrieved, http://www.vpc.org/nrainfo/docs.htm.

27. Emilie Raymond, *From My Cold, Dead Hands: Charlton Heston and American Politics* (Lexington: University Press of Kentucky, 2006): 211.

28. "Speech by National Rifle Association First Vice President Charlton Heston Delivered at the Free Congress Foundation's 20th Anniversary Gala," *Violence Policy Center*, 7 Dec. 1997, http://www.vpc.org/nrainfo/speech.html.

29. Chip Berlet, "Christian Identity, Survivalism & the Posse Comitatus," *PublicEye.org,* 5 May 2010, retrieved, http://www.publiceye.org/rightist/idennlns.html.

30. "Terror From the Right," *Southern Poverty Law Center,* 27 Jul. 2010, retrieved. http://www.splcenter.org/get-informed/publications/terror-from-the-right. "Kahl's Remains Identified; Fugitive Tax Protester Killed in Gun Battle at Arkansas Farm," *Boston Globe,* 6 Jun. 1983: 1.

31. "The Patriot Movement," *Southern Poverty Law Center—Intelligence Report,* Spring 1998, http://www.splcenter.org/get-informed/intelligence-report/browse-all-issues/1998/spring/the-patriot-movement. Mark Potok, "Rage on the Right," *Intelligence Report,* Spring 2010, http://www.splcenter.org/get-informed/intelligence-report/browse-all-issues/2010/spring/rage-on-the-right..

32. "More threats against Obama since election," *MSNBC,* 14 Nov. 2008, http://www.msnbc.msn.com/id/27724965/.

33. Joan Walsh, "Who was that gun-toting anti-Obama protester?" *Salon.com,* 12 Aug. 2009, http://www.salon.com/news/opinion/joan_walsh/politics/2009/08/12/william_kostric.

34. Rachel Slajda, "Man with Assault Rifle Outside Obama Event: 'We Will Forcefully Resist,'" *Talking Points Memo,* 18 Aug. 2009, http://tpmlivewire.talkingpointsmemo.com/2009/08/watch-man-carries-an-assault-rifle-outside-obama-event.php.

35. Justin Elliott, "Pastor of Gun-Toter at Obama Event Prayed for Obama to Die," *Talking Points Memo,* 27 Aug. 2009, http://tpmmuckraker.talkingpointsmemo.com/2009/08/pastor_of_gun-toter_at_obama_event_day_before_even.php.

36. Philip Rucker, "Lawmakers concerned as health-care overhaul foes resort to violence," *Washington Post,* 25 Mar. 2010, http://www.washingtonpost.com/wp-dyn/content/article/2010/03/24/AR2010032402122.html.

37. Paul Kane, "'Tea party' protesters accused of spitting on lawmaker, using slurs," *Washington Post,* 20 Mar. 2010, http://www.washingtonpost.com/wp-dyn/content/article/2010/03/20/AR2010032002556.html.

38. Henry K. Lee, "Alleged gunman says he wanted 'a revolution,'" *San Francisco Chronicle,* 21 Jul. 2010, http://www.sfgate.com/cgi-bin/article.cgi?f=/c/a/2010/07/21/MNMN1EHB37.DTL.

39. "Gunman Kills 3 Pittsburgh Police Officers," *CBS News,* 4 Apr. 2009, http://www.cbsnews.com/stories/2009/04/04/national/main4919337.shtml.

40. "Richard Poplawski: The Making of a Lone Wolf," *Anti-Defamation League,* 8 Apr. 2009, http://www.adl.org/learn/extremism_in_the_news/White_Supremacy/poplawski+report.htm.

41. Mike Madden, "Cantor: Blame the victims for violence against lawmakers," *Salon.com,* 25 Mar. 2010, http://www.salon.com/news/politics/war_room/2010/03/25/cantor_threats.

42. Sarah Palin, "Don't Retreat, Instead—RELOAD!" *Twitter,* 23 Mar. 2010, http://twitter.com/SarahPalinUSA/status/10935548053.

43. Sarah Palin, "Don't Get Demoralized! Get Organized! Take Back the 20!" *Facebook,* 23 Mar. 2010, http://www.facebook.com/notes/sarah-palin/dont-get-demoralized-get-organized-take-back-the-20/373854973434.

44. Zachary Roth, "Steve King to Conservatives: 'Implode' IRS Offices," *Talking Points Memo,* 22 Feb. 2010, http://tpmlivewire.talkingpointsmemo.com/2010/02/steve-king-to-conservatives-implode-irs-offices.php. Lee Fang, "Rep. King Justifies Suicide Attack on IRS: Sympathizes with Hatred of IRS, Hopes for Its Destruction," *Think Progress,* 22 Feb. 2010, http://thinkprogress.org/2010/02/22/king-justifies-irs-terrorism/.

45. Eric Boehlert, "Post-Hutaree: How Glenn Beck and Fox News spread the militia message," *Media Matters,* 6 Apr. 2010, http://mediamatters.org/columns/201004060005.

46. Monica Crowley, "Enemies of the state," *Washington Times,* 31 Mar. 2010, http://www.washingtontimes.com/news/2010/mar/31/enemies-of-the-state/.

47. "Interview with Rep. Michele Bachmann," *RealClearPolitics,* 19 Apr. 2010, http://www.realclearpolitics.com/articles/2010/04/19/interview_with_rep_michele_bachmann_105246.html.

48. "How Left-Wing Zealots Are Violating Our Civil Rights," *Fox News,* 31 May 2009, http://www.foxnews.com/story/0,2933,523617,00.html.

49. Glenn Beck, "Beck implores viewers to not turn violent: 'Just one lunatic like Timothy McVeigh could ruin everything.'" *Media Matters,* 24 Mar. 2010, http://mediamatters.org/mmtv/200908030052.

50. Ibid.

51. Glenn Beck, "Radicals Have Reversed the Roles," *Fox News,* 24 Mar. 2010, http://www.foxnews.com/story/0,2933,589943,00.html.

52. "Richard Poplawski: The Making of a Lone Wolf," *Anti-Defamation League,* 8 Apr. 2009, http://www.adl.org/learn/extremism_in_the_news/White_Supremacy/poplawski+report.htm.

53. Jason Linkins, "Glenn Beck: 'Nutjob' in Pittsburgh Not My Fault, I'm Just a 'Flight Attendant,'" *Huffington Post,* 4 Jul. 2009, http://www.huffingtonpost.com/2009/04/07/glenn-beck-nutjob-in-phil_n_184205.html.

54. "Beck: White House and progressives are 'taking you to a place to be slaughtered,'" *Media Matters,* 3 Nov. 2009, http://mediamatters.org/mmtv/200911030042.

13. The Tent of Freedom

1. Dan Gilgoff, *The Jesus Machine: How James Dobson, Focus on the Family, and Evangelical America Are Winning the Culture War* (New York: St. Martin's Press, 2007): 74–75.

2. "Republican Party Platform of 1976," *The American Presidency Project,* 18 Aug. 1976, http://www.presidency.ucsb.edu/ws/index.php?pid=25843.

3. Richard Viguerie, "Ends and Means," Robert W. Whitaker, *The New Right Papers* (New York: St. Martin's Press, 1982): 51.

4. Jean Hardisty, "Constructing Homophobia," Chip Berlet, *Eyes Right!: Challenging the Right Wing Backlash* (Boston: South End Press, 1995): 100.

5. "Fresh Air: From Direct Mail to 'America's Right Turn,'" *NPR,* 15 Dec. 2004, http://www.npr.org/templates/story/story.php?storyId=4229442.

6. Mark Zingarelli, "House of God?" *Mother Jones,* 1 Nov. 1995, http://motherjones.com/politics/1995/11/house-god.

7. Aif Tomas Tonnessen, *How Two Political Entrepreneurs Help Create the American Conservative Movement, 1973–1981: The Ideas of Richard Viguerie and Paul Weyrich* (Lewiston, NY: Edwin Mellen Press, 2009): 142–153.

8. George Will, "Illinois Republican Looking for Way Out," *Wilmington Morning Star,* 28 Oct. 1978: 4-A.

9. "David E. Rosenbaum, "Anderson's Shift from Orthodox Conservatism," *New York Times,* 28 Apr. 1980: D10.

10. George Will, "Illinois Republican Looking for Way Out," *Wilmington Morning Star,* 28 Oct. 1978: 4-A. Walter Shapiro, "John Anderson: The Nice Guy Syndrome," *Atlantic,* 80:2 (February 1980), http://www.theatlantic.com/past/docs/issues/80feb/anderson.htm.

11. Adam Clymer, "Right Wing Seeks to Unseat Rep. Anderson," *New York Times,* 16 Feb. 1978: A18.

12. Walter Shapiro, "John Anderson: The Nice Guy Syndrome," *Atlantic,* 80:2 (February 1980), http://www.theatlantic.com/past/docs/issues/80feb/anderson.htm.

13. George Will, "Illinois Republican Looking for Way Out," *Wilmington Morning Star,* 28 Oct. 1978: 4-A.

14. Walter Shapiro, "John Anderson: The Nice Guy Syndrome," *Atlantic,* 80:2 (February 1980), http://www.theatlantic.com/past/docs/issues/80feb/anderson.htm.

15. Kenneth J. Cooper, "With More Conservative Cast, House GOP Vows 'Militant' Approach," *Washington Post,* 14 Dec. 1992: A9.

16. William M. Welch, "Southern lights are now shining on Republicans," *U.S.A. Today* 10 Nov. 1994: 7A. Andrew Glass, "Congress runs into 'Republican Revolution' Nov. 8, 1994," *Politico,* 8 Nov. 2007, http://www.politico.com/news/stories/1107/6757.html. Richard Morin, Barbara Vobejda, "94 May Be the Year of The Man," *Washington Post,* 10 Nov. 1994: A27.

17. Bill Lambrecht, "Radio Activity—in a Big Rush, Voters Take Their Anger from Airwaves to Ballot Box, Boosting GOP Fortunes," *St. Louis Post-Dispatch,* 13 Nov. 1994: 1B.

18. Katharine Q. Seelye, "Republicans Get a Pep Talk from Rush Limbaugh," *New York Times,* 12 Dec. 1994, http://www.nytimes.com/1994/12/12/us/republicans-get-a-pep-talk-from-rush-limbaugh.html.

19. "Tribute to Rush Limbaugh," *Congressional Record 107th Congress (2001–2002),* 16 Oct. 2001, http://thomas.loc.gov.

20. Robin Toner, "The 1994 Campaign: Broadcaster; Election Jitters in Limbaughland," *New York Times,* 3 Nov. 1994, http://www.nytimes.com/1994/11/03/us/the-1994-campaign-broadcaster-election-jitters-in-limbaughland.html?pagewanted=1.

21. Rush Limbaugh, "Address to Incoming House GOP Freshmen," *American Rhetoric,* 10 Dec. 1994, http://www.americanrhetoric.com/speeches/rushlimbaughhousegop.htm.

22. Charles M. Madigan, "GOP Wonders Which Way to Go," *Chicago Tribune,* 15 Nov. 1998: 1.

23. John F. Harris, "For Bush and GOP, a Validation," *Washington Post,* 3 Nov. 2004, http://www.washingtonpost.com/wp-dyn/articles/A20547-2004Nov3.html.

24. Dan Froomkin, "How Did He Do It?" *Washington Post,* 3 Nov. 2004, http://www.washingtonpost.com/wp-dyn/articles/A22221-2004Nov3.html.

25. "U.S. President/National/Exit Poll," *CNN,* 3 Nov. 2004, http://www.cnn.com/ELECTION/2004/pages/results/states/US/P/00/epolls.0.html.

26. Dan Froomkin, "How Did He Do It?" *Washington Post,* 3 Nov. 2004, http://www.washingtonpost.com/wp-dyn/articles/A22221-2004Nov3.html.

27. Janet Hook, "Conservatives Make Gains in GOP Congress," *Los Angeles Times,* 14 Nov. 2002: A20.

28. Karen Tumulty, "Tom DeLay: 'It Is More Than Just Terri Schiavo,'" *Time,* 23 Mar. 2005, http://www.time.com/time/nation/article/0,8599,1040968,00.html.

29. Stephen Moore, "Export a Liberal!" *National Review Online,* 17 Nov. 2004, http://old.nationalreview.com/moore/moore200411170839.asp.

30. "Judy Woodruff's Inside Politics," *CNN,* 6 Jan. 2004, http://transcripts.cnn.com/TRANSCRIPTS/0401/06/ip.00.html.

31. Peter Overby, "Examining Club for Growth's Impact on GOP," *NPR,* 29 Apr. 2009, http://www.npr.org/templates/story/story.php?storyId=103619010.

32. Douglas Waller, "On the Trail Of RINOs," *Time,* 22 Sep. 2003, http://www.time.com/time/magazine/article/0,9171,1005745,00.html.

33. "Michele Bachmann," *OpenSecrets.org,* 24 May 2010, retrieved, http://www.open secrets.org/politicians/summary.php?cycle=Career&cid=N00027493. "Paul Broun Jr.," *OpenSecrets.org,* 24 May 2010, retrieved, http://www.opensecrets.org/politicians/summary.php?cid=N00028986&cycle=Career.

34. Tim Rohwer, "Club names King 'Defender of Economic Freedom' award winner," *Southwest Iowa News,* 16 Mar. 2007, http://www.zwire.com/site/news.cfm?newsid= 18089448.

35. John Pomfret, "Schwarzenegger Implores GOP to Follow Script of His Sequel," *Washington Post,* 11 Nov. 2006, http://www.washingtonpost.com/wp-dyn/content/article/2006/11/10/AR2006111001538.html. Ed Stoddard, "U.S. Republicans in dilemma over 'Religious Right,'" *Reuters,* 9 Nov. 2006, http://uk.reuters.com/article/idUKL0992986220061109.

36. Tom Hamburger and Peter Wallsten, "Election 2006: Parties Take Stock," *Los Angeles Times,* 9 Nov. 2006: A20.

37. "Republicans Lost, But Conservatism Did Not," *The Rush Limbaugh Show,* 8 Nov. 2006, http://www.rushlimbaugh.com/home/estack_12_13_06/Republicans_Lost_But_Conservatism_Did_Not.guest.html.

38. Domenico Montanaro, "Club for Growth hits Huckabee hard," *MSNBC,* 2 Aug. 2007, http://firstread.msnbc.msn.com/archive/2007/08/02/301617.aspx.

39. Josh Rogers, "McCain Depending on New Hampshire," *NPR,* 31 Dec. 2007, http://m.npr.org/news/front/17716266.

40. Emi Kolawole, "Is it true John McCain voted with George Bush 95 percent of the time?" *FactCheck.org,* 13 Jun. 2008, http://www.factcheck.org/askfactcheck/is_it_true_john_mccain_voted_with.html.

41. Byron York, "John McCain: Can He Be a Falwell Republican?" *Washington Post,* 7 May 2006, http://www.washingtonpost.com/wp-dyn/content/article/2006/05/05/AR2006 050501745.html. Teddy Davis, "McCain Woos the Right, Makes Peace with Falwell," *ABC News,* 28 Mar. 2006, http://abcnews.go.com/Politics/story?id=1779141.

42. "Dobson won't vote if McCain wins GOP," *World Net Daily,* 5 Feb. 2008, http://www.wnd.com/?pageId=55665.

43. "Rockefeller GOP Aims to Eliminate the Conservative Wing of the Party," *The Rush Limbaugh Show,* 23 Jun. 2008, http://www.rushlimbaugh.com/home/daily/site_062308/content/01125106.guest.html.

44. Dennis Prager, "Dobson: "I Would Pull that Lever" for McCain-Palin," *Townhall.com,* 29 Aug. 2008, http://townhall.com/columnists/DennisPrager/2008/08/29/dobson_%E2%80%9Ci_would_pull_that_lever%E2%80%9D_for_mccain-palin.

45. "Your Guiding Light," *The Rush Limbaugh Show,* 4 Sep. 2008, http://www.rush limbaugh.com/home/daily/site_090408/content/01125100.guest.html.

46. Juliet Eilperin, "Palin's 'Pro-America Areas' Remark: Extended Version," *Washington Post,* 17 Oct. 2008, http://voices.washingtonpost.com/44/2008/10/17/palin_clarifies_her_pro-americ.html.

47. Ed Henry and Ed Hornick, "Rage rising on the McCain campaign trail," *CNN,* 11 Oct. 2008, http://www.cnn.com/2008/POLITICS/10/10/mccain.crowd/.

48. Scott Conroy, "Palin: Obama's Plan Is 'Experiment with Socialism,'" *CBS News,* 19 Oct. 2008, http://www.cbsnews.com/8301-502443_162-4531388-502443.html.

49. William Kristol, "The Wright Stuff," *New York Times,* 5 Oct. 2008, http://www.nytimes.com/2008/10/06/opinion/06kristol.html.

50. William Kristol, "Let Palin Be Palin," *Weekly Standard,* 13:48 (8 Sep. 2008): 7, http://www.weeklystandard.com/Content/Public/Articles/000/000/015/500wrhjq.asp.

51. Brad Wilmouth, "Estrich and Ingraham Slam Media's 'Vicious Attacks' on Sarah Palin," *NewsBusters,* 3 Sep. 2008, http://newsbusters.org/blogs/brad-wilmouth/2008/09/03/estrich-ingraham-decry-media-s-vicious-attacks-sarah-palin.

53. Jonathan Martin, "McCain lashes out at press over Palin," *Politco,* 2 Sep. 2008, http://www.politico.com/news/stories/0908/13107.html.

54. "About Adam," *United States House of Representatives website,* 25 May, 2010, retrieved, http://adamputnam.house.gov/bio.shtml.

55. Thomas Frank, "Blessed Are the Persecuted," *Wall Street Journal,* 29 Oct. 2008. http://online.wsj.com/article/SB122523858126178227.html.

56. Bret Hovell, "McCain Campaign Crowds Grow Exponentially," *ABC News,,* 9 Sep. 2008, http://abcnews.go.com/Politics/Vote2008/story?id=5755471.

57. "At Palin rally, reporter hears threat to Obama: 'Kill him!,'" *New York Daily News* 16 Oct. 2008, http://www.nydailynews.com/news/politics/2008/10/16/2008-10-16_at_palin_rally_reporter_hears_threat_to_.html.

58. Dana Milbank, "Unleashed, Palin Makes a Pit Bull Look Tame," *Washington Post,* 7 Oct. 2008, http://www.washingtonpost.com/wp-dyn/content/article/2008/10/06/AR2008100602935.html.

59. Greg Sargent, "Report: Threats to Obama Rose as Palin's Crowds Grew More Frenzied," *Talking Points Memo,* 5 Nov. 2008, http://tpmelectioncentral.talkingpointsmemo.com/2008/11/report_threats_to_obama_ruse_a.php.

60. Jonathan Martin, "Panic attacks: Voters unload at GOP rallies," *Politico,* 10 Oct. 2008, http://www.politico.com/news/stories/1008/14445.html.

61. "Santelli's Tea Party," *CNBC,* 19 Feb. 2009, http://www.cnbc.com/id/15840232?video=1039849853.

62. "Traders Revolt: CNBC Host Calls for New 'Tea Party'; Chicago Floor Mocks Obama Plan," *DrudgeReportArchives.com,* 19 Feb. 2009, http://www.drudgereportarchives.com/data/2009/02/19/20090219_164153.htm.

63. "The Most Outrageous March 16 Tea Party Protest Signs," *Huffington Post,* http://www.huffingtonpost.com/2010/03/16/the-most-outrageous-march_n_500842.html. Eric Kleefeld, "Tea Party Sign: 'Keep the Guvmint Out of My Medicare,'" *Talking Points Memo,* 10 Aug. 2009, http://tpmdc.talkingpointsmemo.com/2009/08/tea-party-sign-keep-the-guvmint-out-of-my-medicare.php.

64. Judson Berger, "Modern-Day Tea Parties Give Taxpayers Chance to Scream for Better Representation," *Fox News,* 9 Apr. 2009, http://www.foxnews.com/politics/2009/04/09/modern-day-tea-parties-taxpayers-chance-scream-better-representation.

65. "Glenn Beck 'On the Record' at the Alamo," *Fox News,* 16 Apr. 2009, http://www.foxnews.com/story/0,2933,516620,00.html. "Glenn Beck backs out as San Antonio Tea Party keynote speaker," *WOIA,* 9 Apr. 2009, http://www.woai.com/content/blogs/headlines/story/Discuss-Glenn-Beck-backs-out-as-San-Antonio-Tea/yCHUBz36kUW7I-4SVzB0cA.cspx.

66. "Sarah Palin's Keynote Speech at National Tea Party Convention," *Moderate Voice,* 7 Feb. 2010, http://themoderatevoice.com/62060/sarah-palins-keynote-speech-at-national-tea-party-convention/.

67. "New Report Says Iraq's Leaders Are Unable to Govern; Interview with Barack Obama," *CNN,* 23 Aug. 2007, http://transcripts.cnn.com/TRANSCRIPTS/0708/23/sitroom.02.html.

68. "Richard Viguerie: Tea Party Represents Revolt of the Middle Class, Unfettered New Force," *ConservativeHQ.com,* 15 Apr. 2010, http://conservativehq.com/blog_post/show/426.

69. Jonathan Raban, "At the Tea Party," *New York Review of Books,* 25 Mar. 2010, http://www.nybooks.com/articles/archives/2010/mar/25/at-the-tea-party/.

70. Kate Zernike and Megan Thee-Brenan, "Poll Finds Tea Party Backers Wealthier and More Educated," *New York Times,* 14 Apr. 2010, http://www.nytimes.com/2010/04/15/us/politics/15poll.html.

71. Chris Stirewalt, "Shock jock Steele does his best to get fired," *Washington Examiner,* 11 Jan. 2010, http://www.washingtonexaminer.com/politics/Shock-jock-Steele-does-his-best-to-get-fired-8746370-81096172.html.

72. Michael O'Brien, "Boehner: No difference in beliefs between GOP and tea partiers," *Hill,* 4 Feb. 2010, http://thehill.com/blogs/blog-briefing-room/news/79725-boehner-no-difference-in-beliefs-between-gop-and-tea-partiers. Philip Rucker, "Tea party leaders will meet with Steele and other Republican operatives," *Washington Post* 16 Feb. 2010, http://www.washingtonpost.com/wp-dyn/content/article/2010/02/15/AR2010021502211.html.

73. Domenico Montanaro, "Scenes from the 'Super Bowl,'" *MSNBC,* 5 Apr. 2009. http://firstread.msnbc.msn.com/_news/2009/11/05/4430445-scenes-from-the-super-bowl. Gene Lyons, "What were the Republicans smoking?" *Salon.com,* 11 Nov. 2009, http://www.salon.com/news/opinion/feature/2009/11/11/republican_crazies/index.html?source=rss&aim=/opinion/feature.

74. J. F. C. Fuller, *Armament and History: The Influence of Armament on History from the Dawn of Classical Warfare to the End of the Second World War* (New York: Da Capo Press, 1998, c1945): 55.

75. Erick Erickson, "New York Republicans Put Up ACORN Backed Candidate in NY-23," *RedState.com,* 24 Sep. 2009, http://www.redstate.com/erick/2009/09/24/new-york-republicans-put-up-acorn-backed-candidate-in-ny-23/.

76. "Limbaugh: We can say Scozzafava is 'guilty of widespread bestiality; she has screwed every RINO in the country,'" *Media Matters,* 2 Nov. 2009, http://mediamatters.org/mmtv/200911020022.

77. Chris Good, "NY-23: Who Spent What?" *Atlantic,* http://www.theatlantic.com/politics/archive/2009/11/ny-23-who-spent-what/29550/.

78. "Doug Hoffman Calls Glenn Beck His Mentor," *Huffington Post,* 11 Mar. 2009, http://www.huffingtonpost.com/2009/11/03/doug-hoffman-calls-glenn_n_343676.html.

79. Tim Padgett, "Can Crist Survive a Right-Wing Uprising in Florida?" *Time,* 29 Dec. 2009, http://www.time.com/time/politics/article/0,8599,1950222,00.html.

80. Andrew Romano, "Bennett Lost in Utah. Should Other Conservatives Be Scared?" *Newsweek,* 9 May 2010, http://www.newsweek.com/blogs/the-gaggle/2010/05/09/bennett-lost-in-utah-should-other-conservatives-be-scared.html.

81. Carl Hulse and David M. Herszenhorn, "Bank Bailout Is Potent Issue for Both Parties in Fall Races," *New York Times,* 10 Jul. 2010, http://www.nytimes.com/2010/07/11/us/politics/11tarp.html. Andrew Romano, "Bennett Lost in Utah. Should Other Conservatives Be Scared?" *Newsweek,* 9 May 2010, http://www.newsweek.com/blogs/the-gaggle/2010/05/09/bennett-lost-in-utah-should-other-conservatives-be-scared.html.

82. David Weigel, "GOP Congressman: Glenn Beck Is 'Trading on Fear,'" *Washington Independent,* 7 Aug. 2009, http://washingtonindependent.com/54327/gop-congressman-glenn-beck-is-trading-on-fear. Eric Kleefeld, "Bob Inglis's Defeat Sends Warning Signal to GOP: Don't Badmouth Glenn Beck," *Talking Points Memo,* 23 Jun. 2010, http://tpmdc.talkingpointsmemo.com/2010/06/bob-ingliss-defeat-sends-signal-for-gop-dont-badmouth-glenn-beck.php.

83. "Limbaugh: We can say Scozzafava is 'guilty of widespread bestiality; she has screwed every RINO in the country,'" *Media Matters,* 2 Nov. 2009, http://mediamatters.org/mmtv/200911020022.

84. Glenn Thrush, "Jim DeMint's big 'tent of freedom,'" *Politico,* 28 Apr. 2009, http://www.politico.com/blogs/glennthrush/0409/Jim_DeMints_big_tent_of_freedom.html.

85. Greg Sargent, "Sharron Angle floated possibility of armed insurrection," *Washington Post,* 15 Jun. 2010, http://voices.washingtonpost.com/plum-line/2010/06/sharron_angle_floated_possibil.html.

86. Emily Kotecki, "N.C. GOP congressional candidate on oil spill: 'Maybe they wanted it to leak,'" *Washington Post,* 16 Jun. 2010, http://voices.washingtonpost.com/44/2010/06/nc-gop-congressional-candidate.html.

87. "Rand Paul on 'Maddow' fallout begins," *The Maddow Blog,* 20 May 2010, http://maddowblog.msnbc.msn.com/_news/2010/05/20/4313688-rand-paul-on-maddow-fallout-begins. Justin Elliott, "Rand Paul in '08: Beware the NAFTA Superhighway!" *Talking Points Memo,* 21 May 2010, http://tpmmuckraker.talkingpointsmemo.com/2010/05/rand_paul_beware_the_nafta_superhighway_video.php.

14. Wake Up, America

1. Stephanie Condon, "Obama: 'I Can Go to My Right, but I Prefer My Left,'" *CBS News,* 1 Apr. 2010, http://www.cbsnews.com/8301-503544_162-20001596-503544.html.

2. "Axelrod suggests 'Tea Party' movement is 'unhealthy,'" *CNN,* 19 Apr. 2009, http://politicalticker.blogs.cnn.com/2009/04/19/axelrod-suggests-tea-party-movement-is-unhealthy/?fbid=OfqtMHEN2Km.

3. David Charter, "Radovan Karadzic defends 'just and holy' war against Muslims," *Times,* 2 Mar. 2010, http://www.timesonline.co.uk/tol/news/world/europe/article7045059.ece.

4. Joseph Goebbels, "Those Damned Nazis," *German Propaganda Archive,* 1 Jan. 1932, http://www.calvin.edu/academic/cas/gpa/haken32.htm.

5. Jonathan Alter, "The Jackass-Reduction Plan," *Newsweek,* 19 Sep. 2009. http://www.newsweek.com/2009/09/18/the-jackass-reduction-plan.html.

6. Gail Collins, "S.C. Strikes Again," *New York Times,* 11 Jun. 2010. http://www.nytimes.com/2010/06/12/opinion/12collins.html.

7. "Calif. Prop 14 Promises Voters Change, but Likely Will Result in More of the Same," *Emory University,* 10 Jun. 2010. http://shared.web.emory.edu/emory/news/releases/2010/06/calif-prop-14-promises-voters-change-but-likely-will-result-in-more-of-the-same.html.

8. Thomas L. Friedman, "A Tea Party Without Nuts," *New York Times,* 23 Mar. 2010, http://www.nytimes.com/2010/03/24/opinion/24friedman.html.

9. Michael Calderone, "Sen. Harkin: 'We need the Fairness Doctrine back,'" *Politico,* 11 Feb. 2009, http://www.politico.com/blogs/michaelcalderone/0209/Sen_Harkin_We_need_the_Fairness_Doctrine_back_.html?showall.

10. Matthew Lasar, "Fairness Doctrine Panic hits FCC, spreads through blogosphere," *Ars Technica,* 17 Aug. 2008. http://arstechnica.com/old/content/2008/08/fairness-doctrine-panic-hits-fcc-spreads-through-blogosphere.ars.

11. Donna L. Halper, *Icons of Talk: the Media Mouths That Changed America* (Westport, CT: Greenwood Press, 2008): 61. Michael C. Keith, *Talking Radio: An Oral History of American Radio in the Television Age* (Armonk, NY: M.E. Sharpe, Inc., 2000): 78.

12. "News Audiences Increasingly Politicized," *Pew Research Center,* 8 Jun. 2004, http://people-press.org/report/?pageid=834.

13. "Fresh Air: From Direct Mail to 'America's Right Turn,'" *NPR,* 15 Dec. 2004, http://www.npr.org/templates/story/story.php?storyId=4229442.

14. "White House: Obama Opposes 'Fairness Doctrine' Revival," *Fox News,* 18 Feb. 2009, http://www.foxnews.com/politics/2009/02/18/white-house-obama-opposes-fairness-doctrine-revival/.

15. Daniel Shenton, *Twitter,* 4 June 2010, linked from http://theflatearthsociety.org, http://twitter.com/danielshenton/.

16. Howard Kurtz, "The Beck Factor at Fox: Staffers say comments taint their work," *Washington Post,* 15 Mar. 2010, http://www.washingtonpost.com/wp-dyn/content/article/2010/03/14/AR2010031402312.html.

17. "Ad Boycott Costs Glenn Beck Over 50% of Ad Dollars 62 Companies Refusing to Advertise with Beck Cost Fox Nearly $600k Per Week," *Color of Change,* 14 Sep. 2009, http://colorofchange.org/beck/more/release-9-14-09.html. Howard Kurtz, "The Beck Factor at Fox: Staffers say comments taint their work," *Washington Post,* 15 Mar. 2010, http://www.washingtonpost.com/wp-dyn/content/article/2010/03/14/AR2010031402312.html.

18. "4 Months of Zero Advertisers for Glenn Beck in U.K.," *stopbeck.com,* 9 Jun. 2010, http://stopbeck.com/2010/06/09/4-months-of-zero-advertisers-for-glenn-beck-in-u-k/.

19. "Meltdown: The intricate conspiracy to 'destroy' Glenn Beck, his family, God, and the founders," *Media Matters,* 25 May 2010, http://mediamatters.org/research/2010 05250049.

20. "Kraft Pulls Ads from Glenn Beck's Show," *stopbeck.com,* 20 Aug. 2009, http://stopbeck.com/2009/08/20/kraft-pulls-ads-from-glenn-becks-show/. "Confirmed: No More Nestle Ads on Glenn Beck or Any Fox News Show," *stopbeck.com,* 23 Nov. 2009, http://stopbeck.com/2009/11/23/confirmed-no-more-nestle-ads-on-glenn-beck-or-any-fox-news-show/. Howard Kurtz, "The Beck Factor at Fox: Staffers say comments taint their work," *Washington Post,* 15 Mar. 2010, http://www.washingtonpost.com/wp-dyn/content/article/2010/03/14/AR2010031402312.html.

21. "GE, Microsoft Bring Bigotry to Life," *FAIR,* 12 Feb. 2003, http://www.fair.org/index.php?page=1632.

22. "MSNBC Fires Shock Host Michael Savage after He Tells Caller, 'Get AIDS and Die, You Pig,'" *Democracy NOW!,* 8 Jul. 2003, http://www.democracynow.org/2003/7/8/msnbc_fires_shock_host_michael_savage.

23. Andrew Malcolm, "Lou Dobbs abruptly quits CNN on the air," *Los Angeles Times,* 11 Nov. 2009, http://latimesblogs.latimes.com/washington/2009/11/lou-dobbs-cnn.html.

24. Erick Erickson, *Twitter,* 30 Apr. 2009, http://twitter.com/ewerickson/status/1665525087.

25. "MSNBC Fires Shock Host Michael Savage after He Tells Caller, 'Get AIDS and Die, You Pig,'" *Democracy NOW!,* 8 Jul. 2003, http://www.democracynow.org/2003/7/8/msnbc_fires_shock_host_michael_savage.

26. Glenn Beck, "Your Rights Are Slipping Away," *Fox News,* 5 Apr. 2010, http://www.foxnews.com/story/0,2933,590464,00.html.

27. "Glenn Beck on Town Halls, the Tea Party Express and ACORN," *FOX News,* 15 Sep. 2009, http://www.foxnews.com/story/0,2933,550241,00.html.

28. Ed Magnuson, Evan Thomas, Joseph J. Kane, Phoenix, "The Brethren's First Sister: Sandra Day O'Connor," *Time,* 20 Jul. 1981, http://www.time.com/time/magazine/article/0,9171,954833-2,00.html.

29. Michael Scherer, "Calling 'Em Out: The White House Takes on the Press," *Time,* 8 Oct. 2009, http://www.time.com/time/politics/article/0,8599,1929058,00.html. Sam Stein, "Anita Dunn: Fox News an Outlet for GOP Propaganda," *Huffington Post,* 10 Nov. 2009, http://www.huffingtonpost.com/2009/10/11/anita-dunn-fox-news-an-ou_n_316691.html. "White House Escalates War of Words with Fox News," *Fox News,* 12 Oct. 2009, http://www.foxnews.com/politics/2009/10/12/white-house-escalates-war-words-fox-news/. Jim Vandehei & Mike Allen, "Obama strategy: Marginalize most powerful critics," *Politico,* 21 Oct. 2009, http://www.politico.com/news/stories/1009/28532.html. "The Radical Truth about Anita Dunn," *Fox News,* 18 Oct. 2009, http://www.foxnews.com/story/0,2933,567701,00.html. Josh Gerstein and Carol E. Lee, "Dunn's deputy to take over," *Politico* 11 Nov. 2009, http://www.politico.com/politico44/perm/1109/pfeiffer_moves_up_2cfe419d-8135-4d2e-b6c9-72abc93122a7.html.

30. Josh Marshall, "Hang Time," *Talking Points Memo,* 2 Mar. 2009, http://www.talkingpointsmemo.com/archives/2009/03/keeping_score.php. "GOP chairman Steele backs off Limbaugh criticism," *CNN,* 3 Mar. 2009, http://edition.cnn.com/2009/POLITICS/03/02/gop.steele.limbaugh/.

31. Jonathan Martin, "Gingrey apologizes over Limbaugh," *Politico,* 28 Jan. 2009, http://www.politico.com/news/stories/0109/18067.html.

32. "The McCain Mutiny," *Newsweek,* 3 Apr. 2010, http://www.newsweek.com/2010/04/02/the-mccain-mutiny.html.

33. David Corn, "Confessions of a Tea Party Casualty," *Mother Jones,* 3 Aug. 2010, http://motherjones.com/politics/2010/08/bob-inglis-tea-party-casualty.

34. Timothy Noah, "David Frum's 'Axis of Evil'" *Slate,* 5 Feb. 2002, http://www.slate.com/id/2061695.

35. "David Frum," *FrumForum,* 22 Jun. 2010, retrieved, http://www.frumforum.com/davidfrum.

36. Kyle Drennen, "CBS 'Early Show' Uses Republican to Call Palin a 'Huge Mistake,'" *NewsBusters,* 13 Oct. 2008, http://newsbusters.org/blogs/kyle-drennen/2008/10/13/cbs-early-show-uses-republican-call-palin-huge-mistake.

37. David Frum, "Why Rush Is Wrong," *Newsweek,* 7 Mar. 2009, http://www.newsweek.com/2009/03/06/why-rush-is-wrong.html. Brian Stelter and Bill Carter, "Fox News's Mad, Apocalyptic, Tearful Rising Star," *New York Times,* 29 Mar. 2009, http://www.nytimes.com/2009/03/30/business/media/30beck.html.

38. David Frum, "Waterloo," *FrumForum,* 21 Mar. 2010, http://www.frumforum.com/waterloo.

39. David Frum, "Welcome FF Party Crashers!" *FrumForum,* 26 Mar. 2010, http://www.frumforum.com/welcome-to-ff-party-crashers.

40. "Republicans and ObamaCare," *Wall Street Journal,* 23 Mar. 2010, http://online.wsj.com/article/SB10001424052748704117304575138071192342664.html.

41. Mike Allen, "Frum thinks critique of GOP led to boot," *Politico,* 26 Mar. 2010, http://www.politico.com/playbook/0310/playbook998.html.

42. David Weigel, "Civil War Raging in Right-Wing Blogosphere," *Washington Independent,* 21 Apr. 2009, http://washingtonindependent.com/39629/civil-war-raging-in-right-wing-blogosphere.

43. Charles Johnson, "Why I Parted Ways with the Right," *Little Green Footballs,* 30 Nov. 2009, http://littlegreenfootballs.com/article/35243_Why_I_Parted_Ways_With_The_Right.

44. William F. Buckley Jr., "Goldwater, the John Birch Society, and Me," *Commentary*

Magazine, March 2008, http://www.commentarymagazine.com/viewarticle.cfm/goldwater-the-john-birch-society-and-me-11248.

45. "John Birch Society," *PublicEye.org,* 28 Jan. 2009, http://www.publiceye.org/tooclose/jbs.html.

46. William F. Buckley Jr., "Goldwater, the John Birch Society, and Me," *Commentary Magazine,* March 2008, http://www.commentarymagazine.com/viewarticle.cfm/goldwater-the-john-birch-society-and-me-11248.

47. Ibid.

48. "The John Birch Society and the Conservative Movement," *National Review Online,* 19 Oct. 1965, http://www.nationalreview.com/nroriginals/?q=YzM0ODg0YTEyNzhkM2Rj NGQzOTY5ODI5MWVkZjk3NWI=&w=MA==.

49. Lisa McGirr, *Suburban Warriors: The Origins of the New American Right* (Princeton: Princeton University Press, 2001): 219.

50. "What Is the Government Hiding in Imprisoned Border Patrol Case?" *CNN,* 25 Jul. 2007, http://transcripts.cnn.com/TRANSCRIPTS/0707/25/gb.01.html.

51. Richard M. Fried, *Nightmare in Red: The McCarthy Era in Perspective,* Kindle ed. (New York: Oxford University Press, 1990): 1717, 1752.

52. Ibid., 1736.

53. Richard Halworth Rovere, *Senator Joe McCarthy,* paperback ed., 1996 (Berkeley: University of California Press, 1959), 30–31.

54. "McCarthy-Welch Exchange," *American Rhetoric,* 9 Jun. 1954, http://www.americanrhetoric.com/speeches/welch-mccarthy.html.,

55. Edward R. Murrow, "A Report on Senator Joseph R. McCarthy," *CBS-TV* 9 Mar. 1954, http://www.lib.berkeley.edu/MRC/murrowmccarthy.html.

56. "National Affairs: For Joe:Phooey!" *Time,* 19 Apr. 1954, http://www.time.com/time/magazine/article/0,9171,860528,00.html.

57. Richard M. Fried, *Nightmare in Red: The McCarthy Era in Perspective,* Kindle ed. (New York: Oxford University Press, 1990): 1811.

58. Ann H. Coulter, *Treason: Liberal Treachery from the Cold War to the War on Terrorism* (New York: Crown Forum, 2003): 10.

SELECTED BIBLIOGRAPHY

Altemeyer, Bob. The Authoritarians. Self-published, 2006. http://home.cc.umanitoba.ca/~altemey/.

Anderson, Terry H. *The Pursuit of Fairness: A History of Affirmative Action.* Oxford: Oxford University Press, 2004.

Ansell, Amy. "The Color of America's Culture Wars." Ed. Amy Ansell. *Unraveling the Right: The New Conservatism in American Thought and Politics.* Boulder, CO: Westview Press, 2001: 173–191.

Avlon, John. *Wingnuts: How the Lunatic Fringe Is Hijacking America.* Kindle ed. New York: Beast Books, 2010.

Baldwin, Neil. *Henry Ford and the Jews: The Mass Production of Hate.* New York: Public Affairs, 2001.

Balmer, Randall. *Thy Kingdom Come: How the Religious Right Distorts the Faith and Threatens America: An Evangelical's Lament.* New York: Basic Books, 2006.

Barkun, Michael. *A Culture of Conspiracy: Apocalyptic Visions in Contemporary America.* Berkeley, CA: University of California Press, 2003.

Barsamian, David. "Media Power: The Right-Wing Attack on Public Broadcasting." Ed. Chip Berlet. *Eyes Right!: Challenging the Right Wing Backlash.* Boston: South End Press, 1995: 159–190.

Berlet, Chip, and Martha Quigley. "Theocracy & White Supremacy." Ed. Chip Berlet. *Eyes Right!: Challenging the Right Wing Backlash.* Boston: South End Press, 1995: 15–43.

Berlet, Chip, and Matthew Nemiroff Lyons. *Right-Wing Populism in America: Too Close for Comfort.* New York: The Guilford Press, 2000.

Blumenthal, Max. "Who Started the War on Christmas?" *The Daily Beast* 9 Dec. 2008. http://www.thedailybeast.com/blogs-and-stories/2008-12-09/who-started-the-war-on-christmas/.

Blumenthal, Max. *Republican Gomorrah: Inside the Movement that Shattered the Party.* New York: Nation Books, 2009.

Boyer, Paul. "The Evangelical Resurgence in the 1970s: American Protestantism." Ed. Bruce J. Schulman, Julian E. Zelizer. *Rightward Bound: Making America Conservative in the 1970s.* Cambridge, MA: Harvard University Press, 2008: 29–51.

Brock, David. *The Republican Noise Machine: Right-Wing Media and How It Corrupts Democracy.* Kindle ed. New York: Crown Publishers, 2004.

Brückner, Markus, and Hans Peter Grüner. "Economic Growth and the Rise of Political Extremism: Theory and Evidence." *Center for Economic Policy Research* Discussion Paper No. 7723 (March 2010).

Brugge, Doug. "Pulling Up the Ladder: The Anti-Immigrant Backlash." Ed. Chip Berlet. *Eyes Right!: Challenging the Right Wing Backlash.* Boston: South End Press, 1995: 191–209.

Bruner, Jerome. *Actual Minds, Possible Worlds*. Kindle ed. Cambridge, MA: Harvard University Press, 1986.

Buchanan, Patrick J. *The Death of the West: How Dying Populations and Immigrant Invasions Imperil Our Country and Civilization*. New York: Thomas Dunne Books, 2002.

Buchanan, Patrick J. *Day of Reckoning: How Hubris, Ideology, and Greed Are Tearing America Apart*. New York: Thomas Dunne Books, 2007.

Buchanan, Patrick Joseph. *State of Emergency: The Third World Invasion and Conquest of America*. New York: Thomas Dunne Books, 2006.

Castelli, Elizabeth A. "Persecution Complexes." *differences* 18:3 (2007): 152–180.

Clarkson, Frederick. "Christian Reconstructionism: Theocratic Dominionism Gains Influence." Ed. Chip Berlet. *Eyes Right!: Challenging the Right Wing Backlash*. Boston: South End Press, 1995: 59–80.

Continetti, Matthew. *The Persecution of Sarah Palin: How the Elite Media Tried to Bring Down a Rising Star*. Kindle ed. New York: Sentinel, 2010.

Crespino, Joseph. "Civil Rights and the Religious Right." Ed. Bruce J. Schulman, Julian E. Zelizer. *Rightward Bound: Making America Conservative in the 1970s*. Cambridge, MA: Harvard University Press, 2008: 90–105.

Crespino, Joseph. *In Search of Another Country: Mississippi and the Conservative Counterrevolution*. Princeton, NJ: Princeton University Press, 2007.

Davidson, Osha Gray. *Under Fire: The NRA and the Battle for Gun Control*. Expanded ed. Iowa City, IA: University Of Iowa Press, 1993.

Delahaye, Alfred N. "The Case of Matthew Shepard." Ed. Lloyd Chiasson. *Illusive Shadows: Justice, Media, and Socially Significant American Trials*. Westport, CT: Praeger Publishers, 2003: 183–200.

Diamond, Sara. *Roads to Dominion: Right-Wing Movements and Political Power in the United States*. New York: Guilford Press, 1995.

Diamond, Sara. "The Personal Is Political: The Role of Cultural Projects in the Mobilization of the Christian Right." Ed. Amy Ansell. *Unraveling the Right: The New Conservatism in American Thought and Politics*. Boulder, CO: Westview Press, 2001: 41–55.

Douglas, Tom. *Scapegoats: Transferring Blame*. London: Routledge, 1995.

Duncan, Homer. *Secular Humanism: the Most Dangerous Religion in America*. (Revised) Tenth Printing, 1984. Lubbock, TX: MC International Publications, 1979.

Edsall, Thomas Byrne, and Mary D. Edsall. *Chain Reaction: The Impact of Race, Rights, and Taxes on American Politics*. New York: W. W. Norton & Company, 1991.

Engdahl, F. William. "The Secret Financial Network Behind 'Wizard' George Soros." *Executive Intelligence Review* 1 Nov. 1996.

Festinger, Leon, Henry W. Riecken, and Stanley Schachter. *When Prophecy Fails*. Kindle ed. London: Pinter & Martin Ltd, 1956.

Frank, Thomas. *What's the Matter with Kansas?: How Conservatives Won the Heart of America*. Holt Paperbacks ed., 2005. New York: Henry Holt and Company, 2004.

Freeman, Jason, and Daniel Freeman. *Paranoia: The Twenty-First Century Fear*. Oxford: Oxford University Press, 2008.

Freud, Sigmund. *The Schreber Case*. Trans. Andrew Webber. Penguin Classics ed., 2003. New York: Penguin Books, 1943.

Fried, Richard M. *Nightmare in Red: The McCarthy Era in Perspective*. Kindle ed. New York: Oxford University Press, 1990.

Fromm, Erich. *Escape from Freedom*. Holt Paperback edition, 1994. New York: Henry Holt and Company, 1941.

"George Wallace: Settin' the Woods on Fire." Dir. Daniel McCabe and Paul Stekler. *PBS* 1 Jan. 2000. http://www.pbs.org/wgbh/amex/wallace/filmmore/transcript/index.html

Gibson, John. *The War on Christmas: How the Liberal Plot to Ban the Sacred Christian Holiday Is Worse Than You Thought.* New York: Sentinel, 2005.

Gilgoff, Dan. *The Jesus Machine: How James Dobson, Focus on the Family, and Evangelical America Are Winning the Culture War.* New York: St. Martins Press, 2007.

Goffman, Erving. *Frame Analysis: An Essay on the Organization of Experience.* Northeastern University Press ed., 1986. Lebanon, NH: Northeastern University Press, 1974.

Goldberg, Jonah. *Liberal Fascism: The Secret History of the American Left, from Mussolini to the Politics of Change.* New York: Doubleday, 2007.

Goldberg, Michelle. *Kingdom Coming: The Rise of Christian Nationalism.* New York: W.W. Norton, 2007.

Green, Philip. "Cultural Rage and the Right-Wing Intellectuals." Ed. Michael J. Thompson. *Confronting the New Conservatism: The Rise of the Right in America.* New York: New York University Press, 2007: 31–55.

Greenberg, Stan, James Carville, and Karl Agne. "The Very Separate World of Conservative Republicans." *Democracy Corps* 16 Oct. 2009. http://gqrr.com/index.php?ID=2398.

Hardisty, Jean. "Constructing Homophobia." Ed. Chip Berlet. *Eyes Right!: Challenging the Right Wing Backlash.* Boston: South End Press, 1995: 86–108.

Hofstadter, Richard. "The Paranoid Style in American Politics." *Harper's Magazine* Nov. 1964: 77–86.

Jacobs, Ronald N. "The Narrative Integration of Personal and Collective Identity in Social Movements." Ed. Timothy C. Brock and Melanie C. Green. *Narrative Impact: Social and Cognitive Foundations.* 2nd ed. Thousand Oaks, CA: Sage Publications, Inc, 2005: 205–228.

Judd, Diana M. "Tearing Down the Wall: Conservative Use and Abuse of Religion in PolICTS." Ed. Michael J. Thompson. *Confronting the New Conservatism: The Rise of the Right in America.* New York: New York University Press, 2007: 125–143.

Kaufman, Michael T. *Soros: the Life and Times of a Messianic Billionaire.* New York: Random House, 2002.

Kruse, Kevin M. *White Flight: Atlanta and the Making of Modern Conservatism.* Princeton, NJ: Princeton University Press, 2005.

LaHaye, Tim. *The Battle for the Mind.* Old Tappan, NJ: Fleming H. Revell Company, 1979.

LaHaye, Tim. *The Unhappy Gays: What Everyone Should Know About Homosexuality.* Paperback. Wheaton, IL: Tyndale House, 1978.

Lakoff, George. *Don't Think of an Elephant: Know Your Values and Frame the Debate—The Essential Guide for Progressives.* White River Junction, VT: Chelsea Green, 2004.

Lassiter, Matthew D. *The Silent Majority: Suburban Politics in the Sunbelt South.* Princeton, NJ: Princeton University Press, 2006.

Lichtman, Allan J. *White Protestant Nation: The Rise of the American Conservative Movement.* New York: Atlantic Monthly Press, 2008.

Lively, Scott, and Kevin Abrams. *The Pink Swastika: Homosexuality in the Nazi Party.* Keizer, OR: Founders Publishing, 1997.

Maloy, Simon. "Glenn Beck and the Paranoid Style." *Media Matters* 18 Dec. 2009. http://mediamatters.org/columns/200912180003.

Marcus, George E. "The Paranoid Style Now." Ed. George E. Marcus. *Paranoia within Reason: A Casebook on Conspiracy as Explanation.* Chicago: University Of Chicago Press, 1999: 1–12.

Martin, William. *With God On Our Side: The Rise of the Religious Right in America*. New York: Broadway Books, 1996.

McGirr, Lisa. *Suburban Warriors: the Origins of the New American Right*. Princeton, NJ: Princeton University Press, 2001.

Neiwert, David. *The Eliminationists: How Hate Talk Radicalized the American Right*. Sausalito, CA: PoliPoint Press, 2009.

O'Reilly, Bill. *Culture Warrior*. New York: Broadway Books, 2006.

Pipes, Daniel. *Conspiracy: How the Paranoid Style Flourishes and Where It Comes From*. Kindle ed. New York: Simon & Schuster, 1997.

Poe, Richard. "George Soros' Coup." *NewsMax* May 2004. http://w3.newsmax.com/a/ soros/.

Popper, Karl R. *The Open Society and Its Enemies*. 5th ed., reprint. London: Routledge Classics, 1945.

Press, Bill. *How the Republicans Stole Christmas*. New York: Doubleday, 2005.

Reich, Wilhelm, and trans. Theodore P. Wolfe. *The Mass Psychology of Fascism*. 3rd ed. New York: Orgone Institute Press, 1946.

Robertson, Pat. *The New World Order*. Dallas, TX: Word Publishing, 1991.

Robins, Robert S., and Jerrold M. Post. *Political Paranoia: The Psychopolitics of Hatred*. New Haven, CT: Yale University Press, 1997.

Sarbin, Theodore R. *Narrative Psychology: The Storied Nature of Human Conduct*. Westport, CT: Praeger Publishers, 1986.

Scatamburlo, Valerie L. *Soldiers of Misfortune: The New Right's Culture War and the Politics of Political Correctness*. New York: Peter Lang, 1998.

Schaeffer, Francis A. *How Should We Then Live? The Rise and Decline of Western Thought and Culture*. Old Tappan, New Jersey: Fleming H. Revell Company, 1976.

Schaeffer, Frank. *Crazy for God: How I Grew Up as One of the Elect, Helped Found the Religious Right, and Lived to Take All (or Almost All) of It Back*. Kindle ed., 2008. Cambridge, MA: Da Capo Press, 2007.

Schaller, Mark, and Steven L. Neuberg. "Intergroup Prejudices and Intergroup Conflicts." Ed. Charles B. Crawford and Dennis Krebs. *Foundations of Evolutionary Psychology*. New York: Lawrence Erlbaum Associates, 2008: 401–414.

Teles, Steven Michael. *The Rise of the Conservative Legal Movement: The Battle for Control of the Law*. Princeton, NJ: Princeton University Press, 2008.

Tonnessen, Aif Tomas. *How Two Political Entrepreneurs Help Create the American Conservative Movement, 1973-1981: The Ideas of Richard Viguerie and Paul Weyrich*. Lewiston, NY: Edwin Mellen Press, 2009.

Zaitchik, Alexander. "Meet the man who changed Glenn Beck's life." *Salon.com* 16 Sep. 2009. http://www.salon.com/news/feature/2009/09/16/beck_skousen/print.html.

Zernike, Kate, and Megan Thee-Brenan. "Poll Finds Tea Party Backers Wealthier and More Educated." *The New York Times* 14 Apr. 2010. http://www.nytimes.com/2010/04/15/ us/politics/15poll.html.

ACKNOWLEDGMENTS

Thank you to the many people whose warmth and wisdom carried me through this marvelous terrifying adventure. To Tanya for your love, your faith . . . and your patience. To Jerry for shrewd and generous advice that made me a better writer. To Mom, Dad, Shnave, and Laura, for your love, enthusiasm, and terrific help. To my co-bloggers at *dagblog.com* for your fellowship, brilliance, and endlessly entertaining snark. To Josh Marshall for inspiring me to write and the good folks of Talking Points Memo Café for cracking me up and encouraging me to write more. To Carole Fetter and Nate McVaugh for your generous research assistance. To Jane Dystel and Bob Pigeon for putting your trust in me and guiding my way as I labored to turn a bare idea into words and pages and chapters. To Christine Marra, her team, and the Da Capo staff for sleepless efforts to press those words and pages and chapters into a handsome book. To my other friends and acquaintances whose ideas and enthusiasm contributed to this work and my courage to write it. Thank you all.

INDEX